Why Humans

Malešević offers a novel sociological answer to the age-old question: 'Why do humans fight?' Instead of focusing on the motivations of solitary individuals, he emphasises the centrality of the social and historical contexts that make fighting possible. He argues that fighting is not an individual attribute, but a social phenomenon shaped by one's relationships with other people. Drawing on recent scholarship across a variety of academic disciplines as well as his own interviews with the former combatants, Malešević shows that one's willingness to fight is a contextual phenomenon shaped by specific ideological and organisational logic. This book explores the role biology, psychology, economics, ideology, and coercion play in one's experience of fighting, emphasising the cultural and historical variability of combativeness. By drawing from numerous historical and contemporary examples from all over the world, Malešević demonstrates how social pugnacity is a relational and contextual phenomenon that possesses autonomous features.

SINIŠA MALEŠEVIĆ is Professor of Sociology at the University College, Dublin, and Senior Fellow at CNAM, Paris. His recent books include *Contemporary Sociological Theory* (with S. Loyal, 2021), *Grounded Nationalisms* (2019), *The Rise of Organised Brutality* (2017) and *Nation-States and Nationalisms* (2013). His work has been translated into 13 languages.

Why Humans Fight

The Social Dynamics of Close-Range Violence

Siniša Malešević

CAMBRIDGE
UNIVERSITY PRESS

CAMBRIDGE
UNIVERSITY PRESS

University Printing House, Cambridge CB2 8BS, United Kingdom

One Liberty Plaza, 20th Floor, New York, NY 10006, USA

477 Williamstown Road, Port Melbourne, VIC 3207, Australia

314–321, 3rd Floor, Plot 3, Splendor Forum, Jasola District Centre,
New Delhi – 110025, India

103 Penang Road, #05–06/07, Visioncrest Commercial, Singapore 238467

Cambridge University Press is part of the University of Cambridge.

It furthers the University's mission by disseminating knowledge in the pursuit of
education, learning, and research at the highest international levels of excellence.

www.cambridge.org
Information on this title: www.cambridge.org/9781009162791
DOI: 10.1017/9781009162807

© Siniša Malešević 2022

First published 2022

A catalogue record for this publication is available from the British Library.

ISBN 978-1-009-16279-1 Hardback
ISBN 978-1-009-16281-4 Paperback

For all family members and friends who were displaced by the 1990s wars of Yugoslav succession and are now scattered all over the world.

Contents

Acknowledgements

I wanted to write a book on this topic for many years. As somebody who has experienced the violent collapse of Yugoslavia in the 1990s, I have dedicated much of my academic career to understanding war, violence, ethnic conflicts, and nationalisms. However, my previous work on violence has largely focused on the macro-historical level with an aim of explaining the long-term trajectories of organised violence. In contrast, this book explores the micro and meso sociological processes that make fighting possible. This shift in my focus follows in part the research questions that could not have been answered without looking more closely at the interactional and intra-social levels of violence. On a more personal level the book is also an attempt to understand how and why many of my peaceful, mostly pleasant, and polite neighbours suddenly transformed into avid supporters of, and in some cases enthusiastic participants in, the bloodshed and carnage of 1990s ex-Yugoslavia. I also wanted to understand why others who found themselves in the same social conditions reacted very differently and refused to fight.

While writing this book I have benefited enormously from support, comments, reflections, criticisms, and suggestions from many friends and colleagues. I would like to thank Elin Bjarnegard, Daniel Bultmann, Miguel Centeno, Randall Collins, Sophie De Schaepdrijve, Peter Halden, John A. Hall, Katy Hayward, Jonathan Heaney, Stathis Kalyvas, Ville Kivimäki, Krishan Kumar, Jonathan Leader Maynard, Sean L'Estrange, Steve Loyal, Michael Mann, Aogan Mulcahy, Niall Ó Dochartaigh, Larry Ray, Peter Romijn, Kevin Ryan, Stacey Scriver, Avi Sharma, Ori Swed, Ismee Temes, Jennifer Todd, Uğur Ümit Üngör, Sylvia Walby, and Tim Wilson. The final version of the book was completed while I was a research fellow at the Netherlands Institute for Advanced Study in the Humanities and Social Sciences (NIAS/NIOD) in Amsterdam. I have benefited greatly from this experience and would like to thank all participants at the NIAS/NIOD seminars for commenting on my presentations from this project. I am particularly grateful to

Lea David, Ilmari Käihkö, and Christian Olsson who read the full manuscript and provided invaluable comments and suggestions.

Several chapters in the book draw to some extent from articles that have been published before. Chapter 7 analyses data previously reported in S. Malešević and N. Ó Dochartaigh (2018), Why Combatants Fight: The Irish Republican Army and the Bosnian Serb Army Compared. *Theory and Society* 47(3): 293–326. Chapter 8 draws in parts from S. Malešević (2018), The Structural Origins of Social Cohesion: The Dynamics of Micro-Solidarity in 1991–1995 Wars of Yugoslav Succession. *Small Wars & Insurgencies* 29(4): 735–53. Chapter 9 is an expanded, revised, and updated version of S. Malešević (2021), Emotions and Warfare: The Social Dynamics of Close-Range Fighting. In W. Thompson (ed.), *The Oxford Research Encyclopaedia of Politics*. Oxford: Oxford University Press. Chapter 10 draws in parts on S. Malešević (2021), The Act of Killing: Understanding the Emotional Dynamics of Violence on the Battlefield. *Critical Military Studies* 7(3): 313–34 and S. Malešević (2021), Is It Easy to Kill in War? Emotions and Violence in the Combat Zones of Croatia and Bosnia and Herzegovina (1991–1995). *European Journal of Sociology* 61(2): 301–31. I am grateful to the various publishers for allowing me to draw on these publications.

Much of this book was written during the Covid 19 pandemic crisis which impacted negatively on so many aspects of our everyday life. Yet, the pandemic has also provided unique opportunity for my family to spend much time together and to enjoy each other's company. I am really thankful for this invaluable time, and I am grateful for having unlimited amounts of support and love from Alex, Luka and Vesna. Dobro je!

Introduction
The Social Anatomy of Fighting

Human history is often narrated as a story of fighting. The earliest written records including engravings in clay tokens, limestone tablets, ancient monuments, and antique documents contain extensive descriptions of human belligerence. For example, one of the early etchings found in the ruins of ancient Near East settlements and attributed to Ashurnasirpal II, king of Assyria from 884 to 859 BCE, is completely centred on the experience of fighting and killing. The inscription depicts Ashurnasirpal's first military campaign that involved quashing an armed rebellion in the city of Suru in 883 BCE. This record provides a detailed depiction of close-range human-on-human violence:

I flayed all the chiefs who had revolted, and I covered the pillar with their skins. Some I impaled upon the pillar on stakes and others I bound to stakes round the pillar. I cut the limbs off the officers who had rebelled. Many captives I burned with fire and many I took as living captives. From some I cut off their noses, their ears, and their fingers, of many I put out their eyes. I made one pillar of the living and another of heads and I bound their heads to tree trunks round about the city. Their young men and maidens I consumed with fire. The rest of their warriors I consumed with thirst in the desert of the Euphrates. (Finegan 2015: 170–1)

Other ancient and early modern written accounts also contain numerous descriptions of close-range fighting including wars, rebellions, uprisings, insurgencies, assassinations, acts of rioting and massacres of civilians (Bestock 2018; Classen 2004; D'Huys 1987). Similarly, the history textbooks published over the last three centuries are full of extensive depictions of violent conflicts where soldiers, police officers, revolutionaries, rebels, insurgents, terrorists, protesters, paramilitaries, and ordinary individuals fight and kill other human beings (Bentrovato et al. 2016; Ferro 2004). The military scholarship from Thucydides, Machiavelli, and Clausewitz to the contemporary neo-realism of Waltz and Mearsheimer has identified fighting as a crucial element of social and political order. As Clausewitz (2008 [1832]: 227) emphasises: 'Fighting is the central military act; all other activities merely support it. Its nature consequently needs close examination. Engagements mean fighting. The object of fighting is the destruction or defeat of the enemy.'

This focus on fighting is not only discernible in the writings of political, military, and cultural elites but is also present among ordinary populations. For example, the numerous memoirs of former soldiers often contain graphic descriptions of combat. A typical example is the following description from Myron Napier Bartlett, a former combatant who fought in the American Civil War (1861–5). He narrates his battlefield experience in *A Soldier's Story of War*:

The enemy had ... the advantage in position ... Every shot they fired tore through our ranks, killing and wounding the men, and smashing the pieces ... In the progress of the battle twenty-three of our horses were killed, and nine men killed and twelve wounded ... Lieutenant Brewer sent word to his friends at home that he had tried to live like a Christian and die like a soldier. He was buried at night in St James church yard, with the bodies of other of our own men, who died on the same battlefield. (Bartlett 1874: 111–12)

Religious scriptures including the Bible, Qur'an, and Tanakh also make extensive reference to human-on-human fighting and killing. In some cases, violence is proscribed as a sinful act while in other instances fighting and killing are justified with direct reference to one's religious duty. Thus, the book of Joshua in the Old Testament (6:21) depicts divinely sanctioned violence where God instructs his obedient believers to annihilate all the inhabitants of Canaan: 'At the edge of the sword they utterly destroyed everything in the city – man and woman, young and old, oxen, sheep, and donkeys' (The Holy Bible 2008: 695). The sword verse of Qur'an also refers to human-on-human violence in the context of religious belief: 'And slay them wherever you find them and drive them out of the places whence they drove you out, for persecution is worse than slaughter ... and fight them until fitnah is no more, and religion is for Allah' (The Qur'an 2008: 2:191). Similarly, in the Torah (2010), Book of Deuteronomy (13:1–11), fighting and killing human beings is justified on religious grounds. The worshipping of other gods is a mortal sin: 'you must not yield to or heed any such persons. Show them no pity or compassion and do not shield them. But you shall surely kill them; your own hand shall be first against them to execute them, and afterwards the hand of all the people. Stone them to death for trying to turn you away from the Lord your God, who brought you out of the land of Egypt, out of the house of slavery.'

Close-range acts of violence are also depicted extensively in contemporary mass media (Bushman 2017; Grimes et al. 2008). Although current sensibilities entail issuing warnings before images of violence are shown to the public, there is no shortage of such images in popular media. The editors of most news programmes are still guided by a sensationalist impulse and acts of human violence receive prominent and widespread media coverage (often following the infamous journalistic motto 'if it bleeds, it leads'). In a similar vein, much of the entertainment industry focuses on fighting and close-range violence: from crime novels, violent films, and TV programmes to computer games, martial arts shows, and re-enactments of battles, among others (Wittekind 2012).

Nevertheless, this imagistic obsession with fighting and killing has less to do with the historical and contemporary reality of violence and much more with the social concerns of groups that generate and use such images. Rather than simply reflecting reality the proliferation of violent imagery often serves specific organisational or ideological goals. In this sense the traditional narratives of fighting and killing cannot be taken at face value. Conventional depictions of historical violence often exaggerate and, in some instances, completely fabricate the events and experiences of combat (Bestock 2018; Malešević 2017).

The earliest accounts of mass killings that are attributed to ancient rulers such as Ashurnasirpal II cannot be read as records of actual events. These descriptions were not intended to impart factual information but were deliberately written in a hyperbolic language of gruesome violence to send a message to anybody who would threaten the rule of the emperor. As Bestock (2018: 5) rightly points out in the context of ancient Egypt, 'committing violence and making pictures of it are fundamentally different tactics of power, regardless of the "realism" of the image'. The ancient and many pre-modern inscriptions of violence often served as a tactical political manoeuvre and a didactic tool for one's own population as well as for potential enemies. The primary function of such texts was to depict the ruler as omnipotent and beyond reproach and in this context the focus was on conveying a sense of fear, awe, and reverence. The same logic can be applied to the religious scriptures where hyperbole and symbols were deployed to strike fear and ensure obedience among the believers. Such traditional narratives of violence cannot tell us much about the social dynamics of fighting and killing. Rather than providing realistic accounts of the combat experience such texts tell us much more about the symbolic value of violence in the official representations. Such texts use violent images as a means of communication and representation within and between societies. As such, their focus is not on depicting the reality of violence at all.

Contemporary representations of violence are more realistic and often grounded in facts about experiences from wars, revolutions, genocides, uprisings, everyday policing, gangsterism, or terrorist acts. Nevertheless, the media portrayals of fighting remain centred on providing dramatic, sensational, and coherent narrative plots where violent excesses receive more attention than the non-excessive but much more common acts of violence (Goldstein, 1998). Furthermore, in such narratives fighting often tends to be completely decontextualised or mischaracterised by being framed into already established representations of a specific conflict (Galtung and Ruge 1965). In this sense a particular violent episode can be used for ideological or more narrowly propagandistic purposes. In times of war, a violent act can be utilised to denounce or delegitimise the actions of the enemy or to justify the behaviour of one's own side (i.e., monstrous acts of the cowardly enemy vs. noble and brave fighting of 'our boys'). In more peaceful contexts, episodes of violent behaviour (gang fights, pub brawls, football fan hooliganism, etc.) can be used to advance a specific ideological doctrine (e.g., calls for tougher prison sentences, more police, or alternatively for addressing rising inequalities or rampant unemployment). Thus, descriptions of violence can never be taken at face value but require contextual and historical decoding.

Nevertheless, this abundance of violent narrative representations stands in stark contract with the actual experience of face-to-face fighting and killing which is remarkably rare (Collins 2008, 2011). Despite the numerous visual and textual representations of close-range violence throughout history, face-to-face fighting has been and remains an atypical social phenomenon. Even the professional purveyors of coercive power such as soldiers, police officers, military contractors, members of paramilitary organisations, gangsters and many others rarely experience hand-to-hand fighting. The technological and organisational developments of the last three centuries have made close contact unnecessary for the successful conduct of many military and policing operations. Since the early nineteenth century, fighting at a distance has become the dominant way in which militaries operate. Most soldiers die from long-distance weaponry: drones, missiles, cannon fire, tank projectiles and shells, airplane bombs, grenades, mines, and bullets. In many wars soldiers rarely if ever see their opponents as much of the fighting takes place at a substantial distance. Military scholars have demonstrated convincingly that in modern warfare very few soldiers find themselves in a situation of fighting face to face (Bourke 2000; Grossman 1996; Holmes 1985; Keegan 1994). For example, during the Second World War, more than 95 per cent of British military casualties were inflicted at distance with 85 per cent of fatalities being caused by aerial bombing, artillery shells, mortars and grenades, anti-tank shells and bullets (Holmes 1985: 210). Although face-to-face fighting was more common before modern times, it was still rarely practised as a form of combat. Many pre-modern military organisations utilised alternative modes of fighting in order to avoid direct contact. The Greek and Roman phalanx armies waged wars as pushing matches with a clear focus on breaking the front line of the enemy phalanx whereas the medieval European armies avoided direct confrontation by laying sieges around the towns and major castles in an attempt to exhaust the enemy (Collins 2008; Keegan 1994; Malešević 2010). Many other armies throughout history used ambushes, periodic raids, force concentration, surprise attacks, encirclement of the enemy forces, or unexpected attacks at night all of which minimised the possibility of close-range fighting. For example, the famous battle of the Second Punic War (218–201 BCE) fought around the Trebia river in 218 BCE between the Roman army led by Sempronius Longus and the Carthaginian forces under Hannibal was a successful ambush. Hannibal's concealed forces surprised the Roman army by attacking them from the rear. This strategic advantage allowed the Carthaginians to defeat the large Roman forces and in this melée half of the Roman army of 40,000 soldiers were killed (Erdkamp 2015). However, most of them died while retreating and very few soldiers were involved in face-to-face confrontation.

The conventional images of war with vast battlefields where huge militaries face each other in direct and protracted combat, as often portrayed in popular culture, are far from being an accurate representation of the overwhelming majority of violent conflicts throughout history (Collins 2008; Holmes 1985; Keegan 1994, Malešević 2010). Most fighting is nothing like that. Instead, violent conflicts are often messy, chaotic, unpredictable, and significantly over-reliant on complex technology and organisation. In many cases they are also fought at substantial distance.

The same applies to the popular representations of violence in revolutions, uprisings, insurgencies, paramilitarism, policing, genocide, or terrorism (Lawson 2019; Üngör 2020; Wilson 2020). In most conventional narratives of violent conflict, fighting is depicted as an almost automatic response of combatants, something that does not require much explanation. However, fighting is a complex social phenomenon that is context dependent and highly variable.

The key paradox here is that despite such profusion of popular representations of violence we still do not know enough about the specific social mechanisms that make fighting and killing possible. The conventional depictions of close-range fighting often tend to reproduce stereotypical, formulaic, and almost identical narratives centred on providing morality tales instead of attempting to understand the social dynamics of fighting. In other words, although images of fighting have received a colossal amount of attention throughout history and are even more widely represented today, there is little engagement with the sociological processes that underpin social fights. The social dynamics of face-to-face violent confrontation is still largely under-analysed, under-theorised, and not well understood. There is a plethora of descriptive narratives that zoom in on the experience of combatants in different conflicts. Nevertheless, such narratives are rarely analysed and contextualised using the conceptual and explanatory tools of sociology. At the same time, conventional sociology remains largely uninterested in the study of close-range violence. Although fighting and killing are quintessentially social experiences these phenomena have, for the most part, been neglected by mainstream sociological theory and research. One of the principal aims of this book is to deploy sociological tools to understand the social processes that make close-range fighting possible.

I.1   Understanding Social Pugnacity

In this book I explore why and under which social conditions human beings are likely to fight, injure, or kill other human beings in combat situations. In this context I analyse the role of biology, economic motivations, ideological commitments, coercive pressure, and the emotional bonds of micro-solidarity. Drawing on a variety of primary and secondary research I also study the structural contexts that make fighting possible as well as how and when individuals avoid involvement with close-range violence. The book offers a sociological analysis of the combat zone and the role organisational power plays in the development of group cohesion. I explore the role that emotions play in people's willingness to fight and especially how shared emotional dynamics shape the experience of killing in violent conflicts.

The focal point of this study is the experience of fighting in a variety of group contexts. The conventional definitions interpret fighting as a form of purposeful violent social conflict aimed at establishing dominance over one's opponent (Kellett 2013). In this sense, fighting is often perceived to be a means to an end – a tool of political, economic, ideological, or military power. While the structural contexts influence and shape the trajectories of violence, social fighting is rarely, or ever, just an instrument of external forces. Instead, social fights possess a sui generis quality, they develop their own logic and their own social dynamics that influences the actions and thoughts of individuals who take part in combat. A social fight represents an autonomous human experience that generates its own sociological consequences. Individuals involved in violent fighting are profoundly moulded by this experience and in turn they also shape the experiences of other people – the combatants and the non-combatants.

In the conventional understanding, fighting is perceived to be a tool of power or an instrument of self-preservation. Human beings are seen as creatures who fight for domination over others or for their own survival (Gat 2006; Martin 2018; Pinker 2011). However, such reductionist views misunderstand the structural complexity and the sociability of fighting. Just as human sexuality cannot be reduced to procreation but involves complex emotional and cognitive interactions, the same applies to social fighting. The experience of fighting generates strong emotional responses, and it impacts on knowledge and understanding of one's social environment and the groups involved in combat. The individuals who share protracted fighting experience often form unique emotional bonds which impact on their joint social action. In contrast to dominant biological, psychological, and economistic views of combatants as individual self-preservers, it is essential to analyse fighting first and foremost as a social phenomenon. As Simmel (1971 [1908]: 70) pointed out long ago, conflict is a form of sociation. It is a social act aimed at resolving divergent dualism in order to attain unity, even if this involves the physical destruction of one's opponent. In this sense fighting as a form of violent conflict involves deep social interaction between the two hostile sides. Close-range fighting is premised on the existence of physical and mental contact between the combatants. The individuals involved in a fight develop emotional and cognitive reactions and as such establish interaction with their opponents. Thus, fighting entails active sociation. As a rule, the combatants are not indifferent towards their enemy. Instead, they are socially engaged with their fighting opponents. Thus, the experience of combat is a form of positive sociation. In Simmel's (1971 [1908]: 71) view, this differentiates conflict from disinterest: 'whether it implies the rejection or the termination of sociation, indifference is purely negative. In contrast to such pure negativity, conflict contains something positive. Its positive and negative aspects, however, are integrated: they can be separated conceptually, but not empirically.'

Obviously fighting is not necessarily an act involving opponents of equal strength. On the contrary many social fights are highly asymmetrical (Collins 2008). Even in situations of symmetry some combatants might show unwillingness or inability to fight, or they might change their attitudes while fighting and decide to switch sides or stop their involvement. The key issue here is that the experience of fighting is dynamic, situational, and variable.

To better understand the social dynamics of close-range fighting, it is necessary to focus one's attention on the phenomenon of social pugnacity. Although the conventional use of the term pugnacity often implies inherent aggressiveness, the intimidating or confrontational character of an individual, the original Latin term is more neutral.[1] The terms pugna, pugno, and pugnatum, mean fighting, fight, battle, struggle, or dispute (Simpson 2000). In this context I use the concept of social pugnacity to capture the relational, changeable, and collective character of close-range fighting. Social pugnacity is not an individual attribute, it is not a product of one's biology or psychology, but a phenomenon generated by the contextual interplay between structure and agency. In other words, social pugnacity is a collectively engendered phenomenon that results from the cumulative action of social organisations, ideological diffusion, and micro-interactional dynamics. The trajectory of fighting is shaped by what Go and Lawson (2017: 3) call 'entities in motion' – 'the contextually bound, historically situated configurations of events and experiences that constitute social fields'. In this relational understanding, social pugnacity is not an inherent quality of an individual or a group but a relational response produced by the confluence of different structures, actors, and events. Simply put, human relations are not defined by fixed biological, psychological, or other characteristics but are created through the interactions of specific social organisations, ideological frames, and micro-interactional processes. This means that fighting and killing are not uniform, transhistorical and transcultural practices with fixed and recognisable patterns but are diverse, variable, and context-dependent phenomena. However, this is not to say that there is nothing common in the practices and perceptions of fighting across time and space. On the contrary, and this will become visible throughout the book, many combatants describe their own experiences of close-range fighting in similar terms. The point is that there is no single and typical response to violence that one could associate with all conflicts, all combat situations, and all combatants. Instead, the close-range violent action transpires in variety of forms and some of these

---

[1] One of the earliest uses of the term pugnacity in social sciences was by William McDougall in *An Introduction to Social Psychology* (1908). However, he deployed this term in a biological determinist and racist way where pugnacity was just a synonym for innate violent tendencies. Hence, he regularly refers to 'the instinct of pugnacity'. For example, he states that 'The races of men certainly differ greatly in respect to the innate strength of this instinct [of pugnacity]; but there is no reason to think that it has grown weaker among ourselves under centuries of civilisation; rather, it is probable, as we shall see presently, that it is stronger in the European peoples than it was in primitive man' (McDougall 2015 [1908]: 285).

forms might share similarities with other conflicts and other combat experiences. At the same time, other experiences of close-range fighting might have no adequate equivalents elsewhere.

The same applies to the role of biology, psychology, and economics in violence. While all human beings possess some universal physiological, anatomical, and other biological predispositions it is the specific social and historical contexts that make fighting possible in some cases and unlikely in others. However, the sheer variety of combat realities and diverse historical experiences does not imply that every situation of close-range violence is inimitable and incomparable. Obviously, in some trivial sense all human experiences are unique and unrepeatable. Nevertheless, social science aims to make sense of these unique experiences in order to provide generalisable findings about human behaviour. Hence relational analyses of social phenomena aim to identify common configurations without reducing them to a number of fixed variables or static categories of analysis.

The concept of social pugnacity aims to encapsulate this social, cultural, and historical flexibility of the combat experience. It aims to situate fighting in its distinct social environment by exploring its contextual dynamics through sociological lenses. In this understanding social pugnacity is not a property of an individual combatant or of a specific collectivity but a social process that is shaped by a variety of agents and structural forces. In my analysis I explore the impact of different structural powers on the dynamics of fighting including economic, political, cultural, and military factors. In particular I focus on the rise and fall of organisational capacity and the extent of ideological penetration within a group. I also analyse the influence of shared biological prerequisites, psychological variables, and micro-interactional processes. In this context my analysis zooms in especially on the role of emotions in fighting and killing.

I argue that since the phenomenon of close-range fighting emerges in variable social and historical contexts it cannot be explained through the prism of individual motivations. The conventional explanations of fighting usually focus on the motivations of individual combatants ranging from economic self-interest, personality traits, ideological indoctrination, and interpersonal bonds, to individual political commitment. Despite offering very different understandings of motivation all of these individualist perspectives associate fighting with the choices made by individual agents. However, as Clausewitz (2008 [1832]: 78) noted almost two centuries ago, fighting is never an isolated experience that can be reduced to narrow military utility: 'war is never an isolated act' and the will of the opponent is regularly 'dependent on externals'. In other words, the outbreak and the trajectory of fighting is always moulded by the social environment. Moreover, the character, intensity, timing, and duration of fighting is recurrently determined by specific structural forces such as the organisational capacity of coercive entities that initiate conflict, the extent of ideological penetration within the units involved in fighting, or the ability of coercive organisations to tap into existing micro-level solidarities. Hence the combatants cannot be analysed as social atoms divorced from their social environments and the coercive organisations that spearhead and govern their actions in combat situations.

Furthermore, the collective participation in fighting endangers its own social dynamics. The individuals who are recruited into the specific coercive organisations are almost never the same once they acquire fighting experience. The very act of fighting transforms individuals and generates new social constellations. In this sense social pugnacity is an autonomous phenomenon that can generate new forms of social action. The protracted and shared experience of fighting often creates new social realities that can also impact on the organisational and ideological processes that underpin a specific conflict. This sui generis quality of collective fighting is most visible in the changing dynamics of group solidarity in the combat zone. In this context social pugnacity is a distinctly social phenomenon. As I aim to show throughout this book, rather than being a mechanism of domination or self-preservation social pugnacity is in most cases premised on the idea of fighting for (significant) others. Human beings are social creatures that thrive on deep interactions with other humans. As Simmel (1971 [1908]) made clear, these interactions are not necessarily positive and fighting with other human beings is a form of sociation. Nevertheless, a hostile interaction with another human is still an interaction. Wishing to destroy an enemy soldier or a member of a competing gang still involves a whole gamut of cognitive and emotional responses. In contrast an inanimate object such as a rock usually does not receive any reaction or even an acknowledgement. The experience of close-range fighting predisposes a degree of social involvement. It cannot be based on indifference. Even when human beings are completely dehumanised and systematically killed, as in genocides, they are never treated as rocks. There is always social reflection that accompanies the violent action. The Schutzstaffel (SS) troops and the Interahamwe militia justified their killings in reference to specific ideological creeds. The Jews and Tutsis were not killed out of disinterest and indifference. Instead, the genocidal acts were premised on deep involvement and social interaction.

Much of classical sociology from Weber, Marx, and Hintze, to Gumplowicz and Ratzenhofer conceptualised social relations through the prism of conflict (Loyal and Malešević 2021). Human beings are understood to be conflict-oriented creatures who struggle over power, status, and material resources. In this understanding history is also interpreted through the prism of social conflicts in terms of class (Marx), status (Weber), or cultural difference (Gumplowicz). More recently, contemporary sociological theorists such as Collins (2008), Mann (1993, 2022), and Bourdieu (1990, 2014) have extended this line of argument further by specifying under which social and historical conditions social conflicts can attain violent form. For Mann, this transformation is linked to the changing socio-spatial networks of power; for Bourdieu it involves interplay between habitus, field, social capital, and symbolic violence; while Collins focuses his attention on the interaction of ritual chains. In all of these approaches, conflict looms large and human beings are understood to be conflict-oriented creatures. However, as these scholars rightly emphasise, most conflicts remain distinctly non-violent: although human beings are constantly involved in social conflicts, competition, and status or class struggle these rarely involve physical attacks, injuries, and acts of killing. Hence what is interesting to analyse is when, why, and how violent acts unfold. Rather than taking violence for granted it is crucial to track its social mechanisms. What differentiates violent fighting from social conflict is the intensity and physicality of the former. Social pugnacity is a sociological process where conflicts are amplified to the extent that human beings attack, injure, or kill other human beings. This book aims to explore how social pugnacity operates across time and space. More specifically I aim to answer the following questions: Why and when do humans engage in physical fights with other humans? Under which conditions is fighting more likely to happen? Is the use of violence related to an individual's sense of attachment to small groups? Under which circumstances are humans willing to sacrifice themselves for others? How is the micro-level dynamics of violence related to the macro-structural context? Is fighting for others a universal phenomenon or something specific to some historical and geographic contexts?

The book combines theoretical analysis with the empirical research material that I have collected in fieldwork over the last ten years. In theoretical terms this study builds on my previous work that attempted to articulate a *longue durée* analysis of violence by emphasising the workings of three interconnected historical processes: the cumulative bureaucratisation of coercion, centrifugal ideologisation, and the envelopment of micro-solidarity (Malešević 2010, 2013, 2017, 2019). However, unlike the previous work which was mostly focused on historical and macro-structural realities this book zooms in more on the micro and meso sociology of close-range fighting.

I.2   The Structure of the Book

Human beings are warm-blooded, hairy creatures with complex brains that give birth to offspring like the rest of the mammalian world. In this sense it is necessary to explore how human biology and physiology impact on social behaviour and particularly how are they related to fighting. Hence in Chapter 1, I analyse the recent scholarship on interpersonal violence in biology, neuroscience, palaeontology, anthropology, and cognitive evolutionary psychology. The focus here is on identifying how human violence differs from the aggressive behaviour of other species. I argue that the conventional biologically determinist explanations of violence cannot adequately explain the social logic of close-range fighting. Instead, the recent experimental studies indicate that social fights are variable and often significantly moulded by the social environment. While human anatomy, physiology, and psychology are all important for understanding the social behaviour involved in fighting for others, they are not decisive in shaping the dynamics of social pugnacity.

Chapter 2 explores the economics of micro-level violence. I analyse arguments developed by the rationalist and utilitarian perspectives on close-range fighting in criminology and civil war studies. Although the relevance of economic motivations is acknowledged, I argue that the self-interest alone is insufficient for accounting for the variability and contextual diversity of social pugnacity.

In Chapter 3 I analyse the role of belief systems, values, and cultural orientations in interpersonal violence. The focus here is on so-called ideological fighters and the impact that secular and religious doctrines have on people's participation in interpersonal violence. The chapter challenges the conventional views of ideological power and argues that beliefs and cultural norms by themselves rarely motivate violent action. Instead, social pugnacity is often shaped by a constellation of different structural and agential factors where ideologisation helps justify the use of violence.

Individuals are often coerced into fighting and forced to injure and kill other human beings. Hence Chapter 4 zooms in on the role of coercive power in social pugnacity. I look at the role of state and non-state authorities in forcing individuals to use violence, the policing of fighting and non-fighting, the compulsory recruitment into violent gangs, and other coercive practices. I also analyse the social dynamics of conformity and the impact of organisational authority in making fighting possible.

I argue that coercion has been and remains a crucial social mechanism for compelling individuals to fight but that force alone is not enough to explain the sheer historical and social diversity in the human disposition to fighting.

Chapter 5 shifts the focus towards the social interactions with other individuals. More specifically I analyse when and why humans are prepared to fight for other people. In contrast to biological, psychological, and economic perspectives which emphasise the self-interested nature of fighting I argue that most combatants fight for others rather than themselves. The patterns of social pugnacity are often moulded by specific organisational and ideological processes. However, these processes can operate successfully only when fully embedded in the micro-level solidarities. Through in-depth analysis of letters written by combatants who fought in very different conflicts I aim to show how micro-level attachments shape the dynamics of fighting in the combat zone.

In Chapter 6 I turn to the opposite side of violence – the experience of non-fighting. This chapter provides a brief historical and cross-cultural analysis of non-fighting practices. In contrast to popular views which see fighting as the anthropological norm and non-fighting as an exception I argue that the opposite view is much closer to the historical truth. My argument is that social pugnacity is a historically developed phenomenon rooted in the rise of organisational and ideological powers. Hence social fighting increases with the rise of the organisational capacity and ideological penetration of the state and non-state forces. I also show that both fighting and non-fighting are defined by similar sociological processes. Neither comes naturally to human beings.

While the first part of the book focuses on the key theoretical issues the second part explores how these general principles work in practice. Hence Chapter 7 analyses the key social processes that make fighting possible in the combat zone. By comparing and contrasting the experiences of the Provisional Irish Republican Army (PIRA) and the Bosnian Serb Army (VRS) I analyse how the formal organisation structures and the official ideological discourses differ from the experiences of ordinary combatants. I argue that the traditional emphasis on individual motivation of soldiers cannot explain the variability of fighting experience. Instead, social pugnacity is often governed by the situational complexity and shared collective action that develops autonomously in the combat zone.

Military sociology has devoted a great deal of attention to the question of social cohesion on the frontline. While some scholars argue that successful fighting is determined by interpersonal affinities of combatants, others emphasise shared performance as the key variable in enhancing social cohesion. In Chapter 8, I challenge both of these perspectives and argue that frontline social cohesion is often the product of social development linked with organisational structure. This general argument is applied to the case studies of two armed forces involved in the 1991–5 Wars of Yugoslav Succession – the Croatian Army (HV) and the Bosnian Serb Army (VRS). Drawing on in-depth interviews with former combatants I show how HV social cohesion played an important role in winning the war and how these networks of micro-level solidarity were shaped by long-term organisational development.

The focal point of Chapter 9 is the relationship between emotions and close-range fighting. Emotions play a central role in warfare. Nearly all soldiers who encounter combat zones experience intense emotional reactions. Some of these emotions are negative, such as fear, panic, anger, rage, or shame, while others are more positive, including pride, elation, joy, or exhilaration. Some scholars argue that there is inherent uniformity of emotional reactions on the battlefield. However, recent studies indicate that the emotional dynamics in the combat zone are more complex and flexible. Following this research, I argue that there are pronounced historical and cultural differences in the emotional responses of fighters in combat zones. Facing the same realities of close-range fighting, soldiers tend to display different emotional reactions and these reactions are more variable as the cultural and historical contexts change.

The killing of human beings is one of the defining features of war. Yet there has not been much research on understanding its emotional dynamics. In Chapter 10, I look at social pugnacity through the prism of close-range killing. Killing in war is often interpreted through two contrasting perspectives: the neo-Darwinian approach which sees killing as an optimal tactic of genetic survival and the micro-sociological perspective which centres on the tension and fear that arise from the inability to forge effective interaction ritual chains. While the former approach insists that taking lives in war is relatively easy, the latter perspective describes it as an extremely difficult and traumatic event. This chapter argues that neither of these approaches can explain the variability, contingency, and context dependence of killing. Rather than assuming, as the dominant perspectives do, that violence simply triggers biologically ingrained and uniform emotional responses I argue that emotional dynamics are created through the acts of violence. Drawing on primary research with ex-combatants from wars in Croatia and Bosnia and Herzegovina (1991–5) I show how the shared experience of close-range violence generates highly diverse forms of emotional dynamics.

The final chapter reflects on the future of social pugnacity. It looks at the mainstream depictions of close-range violence in post-apocalyptic narratives. Many such narratives depict a very similar future: with the collapse of governance structures, human beings automatically turn to violence. The central assumption that underpins these depictions of the future is that the disintegration of law and order would inevitably lead to vicious and bloody struggle for survival. In many respects these fictional narratives draw upon and reproduce the ideas that have dominated political and military thought for centuries. From Machiavelli and Hobbes to the contemporary neo-realists and cognitive evolutionary psychologists, violence and war are perceived to be the natural state of individuals, societies, and states. In this chapter I challenge these Hobbesian visions of violent futures and argue that the dynamics of micro-level violence is context dependent and highly variable. By focusing on the organisational, ideological, and micro-interactional processes that make violence possible, I envisage different possibilities and trajectories of social pugnacity in the future.

1 The Body and the Mind
Biology and Close-Range Violence

1.1 Introduction

To understand the motivation for fighting it is necessary to provide some analysis of the physiological and biological make-up of human beings as a species. This chapter will utilise up-to-date research on interpersonal violence across different disciplines including anthropology, biology, cognitive evolutionary psychology, neuroscience, physiology, anatomy, and palaeontology. The focus is on the biological underpinnings of violent action and especially how human violence differs from the aggressive behaviour of other species. This chapter scrutinises and critiques the dominant essentialist interpretations which attempt to explain human behaviour in terms of biological or psychological givens. I argue that the recent experimental studies across different disciplines indicate that interpersonal violence is complex and shaped by changing structural contexts. Unlike most carnivorous mammals, human beings lack bodily entailments for aggressive behaviour and hence their increased capacity for violence has distinctly non-biological origins. To compensate for their individual physical incompetence in belligerence, human beings had to devise effective social and organisational mechanisms for violent action. Hence biology plays some role in the human capacity for aggressive behaviour, but it largely does not determine or even shape much of human violent action. Psychology is also relevant in this context but neither biology nor psychology can adequately explain the enormous contextual and historical variation that characterises human relationships with close-range violence. Instead, violent action entails the interlocking presence of organisational capacity, ideological penetration, and micro-interactional social tuning.

1.2 The Physicality of Violence

The conventional representations of violence tend to overemphasise its physicality. Hence violent acts are almost exclusively depicted through images of violation and destruction of bodies and matter. These representations portray actions such as injuring or killing of humans and animals, as well as the demolition and damage of physical objects. As Ray (2016: 335) frames it: 'Violence is about the body. It is enacted by bodies; it has instrumental and ritual manifestations, it creates boundaries and destroys them, as well as violating, polluting, and destroying bodies.' Although physicality plays a crucial role in the enactment of violence, many instances of violence are not necessarily corporeal. From psychological torture, bullying, deprivation, threats, intimidation, humiliation, and maldevelopment, to isolation and neglect, violence transpires in a variety of non-corporeal ways. Moreover, with the development of organisational and ideological capacities, modernity has witnessed the proliferation of structural forms of violence that rely much more on the legitimate mechanisms of coercion and less on the injury or destruction of human bodies (Malešević 2017: 15–20; 2021). In addition, with the development of sophisticated technologies such as artificial intelligence, robotics, cybertechnology, and nanotechnology among others one can expect the development of novel types of violent action that are even more independent from the human bodily form (Coker 2013; Singer 2008). Nevertheless, precisely because most people associate violence almost solely with physicality it is important to explore the biological underpinnings of violence.

The physicality of violence relates to several different aspects of human biology. In this chapter I will zoom in on the four principal biological facets of violence: the evolutionary processes, the impact of human anatomy on aggression, neuroscience and violence, and the physiology of fighting.

1.3   Evolutionary Theory and Violence

Human beings are part and parcel of the animal world. Just like other mammals we cannot survive without air, food, and water, we need to sleep and require shelter to avoid external dangers, we are susceptible to disease, cannot withstand extremely cold and hot temperatures, and our limbs do not grow back if removed. Like other animals our very existence as a species is determined by our ability to procreate and preserve our offspring. These shared biological attributes together with our common evolutionary origins have led many scholars to the conclusion that human beings are not markedly different from the rest of the animal world and that this has direct implications for our experiences of violence.

While recognising the relative autonomy of the social and cultural sphere in human life, the evolutionary theorists insist on 'the biological basis of all social life' (Wilson 1975: 4). More specifically in this understanding, all life operates according to the same evolutionary logic where the emphasis is on survival and reproduction. For evolutionary theorists, the gene is the elementary unit of heredity. Embedded in chromosomes, and composed of DNA material, the gene possesses a replicatory capacity that is passed on from a parent to its progeny. In Dawkins's (1989: 2) words, 'we, and all other animals, are machines created by our genes'. In this interpretation, individual survival and reproduction are enhanced through collective action. In this context the reference is often made to the concept of inclusive fitness which stands for 'the sum of an individual's own fitness plus all its influence on fitness of its relatives other than direct descendants: hence the total effect of kin selection with reference to an individual' (Wilson 1975: 586). The universal principle of inclusive fitness allows genes and thus individuals to survive and procreate. As sociobiologists argue, while genes cannot reproduce directly, they are programmed to do this indirectly: an organism favours kin over non-kin and close kin over distant kin. Thus, in-group favouritism is understood to be a universal and biologically founded phenomenon. For the evolutionary theorists, individual competition and group conflict have deep biological roots as they reflect the struggle for survival between genes. For Dawkins (1989: 11) 'the fundamental unit of selection, and therefore of self-interest, is not the species, nor the group, nor even strictly the individual. It is the gene, the unit of heredity.'

In this interpretation, violence has a genetic and functional basis as it can be used to increase one's reproductive capacity. As Gat (2017: 61) argues:

Conflict and fighting in the human state of nature, as in the state of nature in general, was fundamentally caused by competition. While violence is evoked, and suppressed, by powerful emotional stimuli, it is not a primary 'irresistible' drive. Rather it is a highly tuned, both innate and optional, evolution-shaped tactic, turned on and off in response to changes in the calculus of survival and reproduction.

Other sociobiologists allow for less free will and insist that violence is inherent in animal and hence human relations. For example, one of the early sociobiologists, Konrad Lorenz (1966: 270), was adamant that 'human aggression is instinctual. Humans have not evolved any ritualised aggression-inhibiting mechanisms to ensure the survival of the species. For this reason, man is considered a very dangerous animal.' More recently Pinker (2011: 483) has tried to show that aggressive behaviour is an intrinsic quality of 'human nature' and stated explicitly that 'most of us ... are wired for violence'. Martin (2018: 1) goes even further and insists that fighting is innate to all human beings: 'Humans fight to achieve status and belonging. They do so because, in evolutionary terms, these are the surest routes to survival and increased reproduction.' In this context he understands organised violence as an immutable and static phenomenon with a fixed core: 'if follows then that this essence stems from individual human psychology' (Martin 2018: 4).

Many of these sociobiological accounts draw on the anthropological, archaeological, palaeontological, and primatological research which points out that early humans were highly aggressive creatures. While the primatologists provide evidence on the behaviour of apes, and especially chimpanzees, the archaeological and palaeontological findings are used to date the origins of human-on-human violence. Anthropological studies on contemporary hunter-gatherers are also deployed as a proxy for determining the behaviour of ancient foragers. Hence Pinker, Gat, Martin, and other sociobiologists tend to rely on data provided by scholars who are highly sympathetic to the idea that interpersonal violent conflicts and wars are as old as the human species. Moreover, this tradition of empirical analysis tends towards the conclusion that violence has a deep biological basis. Typical representatives of this position are Chagnon (1988), Keeley (1996), and LeBlanc (2007) who find hunter-gatherer communities to be much more violent than those living in established state structures. For example, Keeley (1996) argues that up to 95 per cent of all known societies have experience of warfare and that the conflicts between hunter-gatherers resulted in extreme casualty rates of up to 60 per cent dead while in modern wars the fatalities rarely go beyond 1 per cent of soldiers. His book also documents violent conflicts of various foraging groups throughout the world and indicates that 87 per cent of the indigenous populations of the Americas tended to be involved in wars with their neighbours every year. Focusing on a specific case of contemporary hunter-gatherers – the Yanomami of Amazonia – Chagnon (1988) argues that these 'fierce people' were in a constant state of war with their neighbours and that those who were involved in regular killings in war ('unokai') tended to have more children than the non-killers. These findings were seen to be fully in tune with the idea of Darwinian natural selection – success at violence is interpreted as a mechanism of natural selection. In a similar way, LeBlanc and Register (2013) have collected data from archaeological digs and ethnographic reports of hunter-gatherer populations to show that the levels of mortality in intergroup conflicts tend to be high. They argue that the archaeological and palaeontological research shows that interpersonal violence was ubiquitous throughout pre-history and come to the conclusion that one can find instances of 'warfare everywhere [and] at every time' (LeBlanc and Register 2013).

In addition to archaeological and anthropological research, primatology has also been deployed to make a case for the human species' inherent propensity to violence. Studies of ape behaviour and especially of chimpanzees (Pan troglodytes) have been regularly utilised to show that our closest biological relatives have a strong predilection for violence. Since Raymond Dart's early studies on chimpanzees many scholars have embraced the idea that apes are inherently aggressive creatures. Dart (1953) developed the original 'killer ape hypothesis' which he tested on the fossils of Australopithecines, a hominid species that inhabited Africa two million years ago. He was convinced that early hominids were predatory cannibals who were brutal and callous: 'carnivorous creatures, that seized living quarries by violence, battered them to death, tore apart their broken bodies, dismembered them limb from limb, slaking their ravenous thirst with the hot blood of victims and greedily devouring livid writhing flesh' (Dart 1953: 209). Once other archaeologists found that most of the injury marks on these hominid skeletons were inflicted by predatory animals and not by other hominids, Dart's thesis was largely discredited (Hart and Sussman 2009). Nevertheless, the scholarship invoking the idea that our hominid predecessors have always been aggressive has since focused more on the study of contemporary chimpanzees. Jane Goodall's (1986) research in Gombe Stream National Park in Tanzania contributed to new understanding of chimpanzees as a domineering, aggressive, hierarchical, territorial, and promiscuous species that regularly engage in protracted violence with other chimpanzees and also hunt and kill other primates for food (colobus monkeys). This line of argument was further developed by Wrangham and Peterson (1996) in their influential book *Demonic Males: Apes and the Origins of Human Violence*. By studying the behaviour of chimpanzees in Uganda, Wrangham and Peterson concluded that they engage in lethal raiding of other groups. The focus here is on what they call 'coalitionary killing' which is seen to be evolutionarily beneficial for those involved in the raiding. In this interpretation, killing a male from another chimpanzee troop is a way to decrease the reproductive potential of the neighbouring group while also increasing one's own chances of survival with greater access to mates, food, and territory. Recent studies written in this vein have attempted to identify the exact number of chimpanzees being killed by other chimpanzees in Africa in order to prove that aggression is innate to this species. Thus, Wilson et al. (2014: 414) identified 152 deaths throughout all study sites in Africa and have argued that killing practices are not dependent on social environment but are natural chimpanzee behaviour. In this study males were found to be most frequent attackers (92 per cent) and victims (72 per cent), and most killings came as a result of intercommunity attacks (66 per cent).

There is no doubt that the studies from primatology, archaeology, palaeontology, and anthropology contribute substantially to understanding the dynamics of interpersonal violence. However, Pinker, Gat, Martin, and other evolutionary theorists tend to over-rely on a few studies generated by the same scholars, that support their arguments while largely ignoring the evidence from a much wider range of scholarship that disputes these findings. In addition, they never address the serious methodological problems that underpin this type of research including the highly contested tradition of using the practices of contemporary hunter-gatherers and the behaviour of apes as a reliable proxy for understanding the conduct of ancient foraging groups. Finally, the sociobiological approach has been characterised as too determinist, too essentialist, and too narrow to accommodate the complexity of violent experiences among human populations.

Despite the consistent warnings by anthropologists that their ethnographic studies should not be used to make generalisations about the ancient hunter-gatherers, many sociobiologists continue to do this. When dissecting the evidence provided on violent behaviour of foragers one regularly encounters mixing of data where archaeological records are combined with research on contemporary hunter-gatherers to show that most humans have always been violent. However, this flawed strategy tends on the one hand to wrongly portray contemporary hunter-gatherers as remnants of a previous world and on the other hand to simultaneously discount the role of historical and social environment in the life of present-day foragers. This practice is oblivious to the fact that all societies change, and that contemporary hunter-gatherers are not some static entity that has not experienced social transformation for thousands of years, while the ancient foragers are also misdescribed as uniform, fixed, and undifferentiated units (Farb 1991; Hart and Sussman 2009). As Ferguson (1995, 2013), and Fry (2007, 2013) demonstrate convincingly, the most influential studies used by sociobiologists including the work of Chagnon, Keeley, and LeBlanc and Register are methodologically flawed as they inflate the data and mix very different populations. For example, both Ferguson (2013) and Fry (2007) have criticised Keeley's and LeBlanc's mixing of data whereby the cases of violent killings are not differentiated from deaths caused by disease and starvation and no distinction is made between data on of the contemporary and ancient hunter-gatherers. Chagnon's work on the Yanomami has largely been discredited and many subsequent anthropological studies have demonstrated that Yanomami lifestyle was influenced by changing political economy and increased access to metal. However, even in these conditions the Yanomami's everyday life was not particularly violent: 'Violence is only sporadic; it never dominates social life for any length of time' (Lizot 1985: 16). A similar criticism has been levelled against Bowles and Keeley's depiction of indigenous populations of North America. Where they emphasise the inherent bellicosity of the Great Plains tribes, other scholars show that these tribes did not even exist before the European colonisation of the continent and have emerged as a consequence of settler colonialism that forced the natives who survived European ethnic cleansing to forge new and more militarised tribal alliances (Farb 1991).

The use of primatological studies is also problematic for two main reasons. Firstly, there is no agreement between primatologists on how aggressive apes are in general. It seems that gorillas and orangutans are much less aggressive than chimpanzees and some troops of chimpanzees are less aggressive than others. Wilson et al.'s (2014) study of 152 dead chimpanzees has been criticised for combining very different sites and distinct death patterns some of which might have not been caused by other chimps (they amalgamated 58 actually observed deaths with 53 suspected cases and another 41 inferred from mutilated bodies). Ferguson and Sussman have questioned this approach and have also shown that the two sites alone count for 60 per cent of all deaths, indicating that if this environmentally induced outlier is removed the overall death rate would drop to 0.3 chimpanzees per year which is a very low number of violent casualties. Many other primatologists dispute the view that chimps are exceptionally aggressive creatures and suggest that the increased patterns of violence among the chimp populations are linked to changed social environments. For example, Sussman and Marschak (2010) have documented that the natural habitat for many chimps has been severely affected by human settlements and clearing of land for farms which has forced troops of chimps to live closer to each other and compete for limited resources. In some cases, humans have incited violence by bringing food (e.g., bananas) for some troops and not for others.

Secondly, the focus on one type of chimps has overshadowed the variety of ape behaviour. For example, unlike the ordinary chimps, considered to be more aggressive than other apes, the bonobo (pygmy) chimps are the epitome of non-violent behaviour. In the bonobo social order, females have a higher social status and aggression is discouraged. The bonobos are less territorial, less hierarchical, tend to avoid conflicts, and rely on sex to build social alliances (Goldstein 2001). The key issue here is that despite biological similarities apes show a variety of social behaviour, suggesting that biology does not determine violent actions. Sussman (1999: 455) nicely debunks the biological determinists who cling to some version of the man the hunter thesis: 'it could as easily have been our propensity for dancing rather than our desire to hunt that explains much of human behaviour. After all, men and women love to dance; it is a behaviour found in all cultures but has even less obvious function today than hunting.' Hence the portrayals of our predecessors as innate hunters and fighters is a highly biased speculation that is on an equal footing with the speculation of our ancestors as innate dancers.

This point leads to a more general problem with sociobiological approaches – their tendency to overgeneralise on the basis of slim or non-existent evidence. This is mostly done through metaphors, extensions, and projections made about humans using the available data from non-human research. In this process many neo-Darwinians paradoxically anthropomorphise genes while simultaneously reifying human behaviour. As Symons (1979: 11) noticed a long time ago of Dawkins and other sociobiologists: they rely on metaphors to reverse the order of things: 'genes are endowed with properties only sentient beings can possess, such as selfishness, while sentient beings are stripped of these properties and called machines'. When approaching close-range violence this extremely determinist approach leaves no room for contingencies, social influences, historical change, or variation of any kind. For Martin, Gat, and Pinker, violence is an immutable phenomenon that stems from biologically given 'human nature' and as such it is a genetic propensity that remains outside of time and space. This approach cannot help us explain the enormous variation in human relationships to violence in general and the dynamics of social pugnacity in particular.

1.4   Neuroscience and Close-Range Violence

Whereas sociobiology offers a general paradigm for understanding violent behaviour, neuroscience, biomechanics, and evolutionary morphology focus on the specifics of this relationship. Some evolutionary scholars explore how human anatomy and physiognomy have been shaped by the long-term experiences of violence. For example, David Carrier, Christian Cunningham, and Jeremy Morris have analysed how biomechanics influences the evolution of vertebrates and especially the role aggressive behaviour has played in the evolution and development of musculoskeletal systems of apes and early humans. In this context they study the physical characteristics of the human body and its relationship with violence. More specifically they argue that hominid bodies, including *Homo sapiens*, are specialised for aggressive behaviour. In a recent publication Morris et al. (2019: 731) aim to show that the emergence of sexual dimorphism in primates is linked with aggression in the sense that 'males, as compared to females, are more specialized for physical competition in their postcranial anatomy'. A similar argument has been made by Carrier and Cunningham (2017: 269) in relation to the foot posture in apes and humans which in both cases is seen to be an adaptation to increase the fighting ability: 'We found that plantigrade posture substantially increased the capacity to apply free moments to the ground and to perform a variety of behaviours that are likely to be important to fighting performance in great apes.' Carrier is also associated with the argument that aggression has played a crucial role in the evolution of human hands, face, and the ability to walk upright. For instance, in a recent paper Morgan and Carrier (2013: 236) argue that fist-fighting is a product of evolutionary development: 'the proportions of the human hand provide a performance advantage when striking with a fist. We propose that the derived proportions of hominin hands reflect, in part, sexual selection to improve fighting performance.' In their view, the development of stronger fists is also linked with the more robust facial characteristics of men as they have simultaneously evolved to withstand punching.

In a very similar vein, Aaron Sell, Liana Hone, and Nicholas Pound (2012) have attempted to show that the experience of fighting has contributed to the evolution of physical and psychological sex differences. They have compiled an extensive list of sex differences ranging from men's larger sweat capacity to greater upper body strength to show that the fighting ability of human males has played a central role in the evolution of sex differences. Their data indicates that 'better fighters feel entitled to better outcomes, set lower thresholds for anger/aggression, have self-favoring political attitudes, and believe more in the utility of warfare' (Sell et al. 2012: 30).

Some scholars working within this tradition have directly linked fighting ability and physical strength with aggressive behaviour. Hence Ainsworth and Maner (2012) and Muñoz-Reyes et al. (2012) argue that aggressiveness is predominantly a male characteristic associated with 'men's more violent nature' in the context of competition over available mates. Thus, these studies aim to show that 'mating-induced male violence is motivated by desire to assert one's dominance over other men' (Ainsworth and Maner 2012: 819) and that male late adolescents were particularly prone to aggressive behaviour with a strong link between 'fighting ability and anger' (Muñoz-Reyes et al. 2012: 611).

Nevertheless, the most influential recent research that links violence with human anatomy has centred on the brain. This brain research starts from the assumption that 'we are our brains' and to understand the dynamics of violence it is crucial to locate its workings in the neural pathways. In this context the ever-expanding field of neuroscience has focused on the study of the neural foundations of aggressive behaviour. With the recent technological advancements in brain imaging and monitoring of brainwaves the researchers are now able to isolate specific neurons and explore how their stimulation impacts on aggression. For example, in a new study Falkner et al. (2016) have conducted experiments on mice and have demonstrated that violent attacks of stronger mice on weaker mice are accompanied by activation of specific neurons in the hypothalamus: 'we found that the ventrolateral part of the ventromedial hypothalamus (VMHvl), an area with a known role in attack, was essential for aggression-seeking. Using both single-unit electrophysiology and population optical recording, we found that VMHvl neurons became active during aggression-seeking and that their activity tracked changes in task learning and extinction' (Falkner et al. 2016: 596).

Neuroscience has made substantive progress in the study of the human brain and its relationship with aggression. One strand of this research has utilised functional magnetic resonance imaging (fMRI) scans on individuals exhibiting psychopathological behaviour to show that violence is a form of 'dysfunction within corticolimbic and corticostriatal circuitry involved in affective arousal, emotion regulation, and value-based decision-making' (Poldrack et al. 2018: 116). The studies on psychopathy have indicated that the brains of these individuals differ from others in a sense that they have decreased 'amygdala and ventromedial prefrontal cortex (vmPFC) grey matter volume, as well as lower vmPFC cortical thickness' (Poldrack et al. 2018: 116). Other studies have identified a strong link between reduced prefrontal cortex and aggressive behaviour (Brower and Price 2001). Although a number of experimental studies have confirmed these findings, they have all been undertaken only on individuals exhibiting psychopathy and it is not clear yet what is the role of the amygdala in aggression per se.

Another strand of neuroscience trying to locate the neural pathways to violence has focused on ordinary individuals. Hence Fumaglli and Priori (2012: 2006) have explored the relationship between violence, moral reasoning, and the brain. In their 'neurology of abnormal behaviour' they identify strong links between dysfunctionality of prefrontal cortex, 'abnormal morality', and impulsive aggression. Moreover, they argue that 'because abnormal moral behaviour can arise from both functional and structural brain abnormalities that should be diagnosed and treated, the neurology of moral behaviour has potential implications for clinical practice'. To remedy these 'brain malfunctions', Fumaglli and Priori have developed several neuromodulation therapeutic techniques including 'deep brain simulation' and 'transcranial magnetic stimulation'.

While many cotemporary neuroscientists see violent behaviour as a product of brain activity alone, others have developed more complex understandings that emphasise the malleability of nervous systems. Hence whereas some scholars write about 'violent brains' aiming to pinpoint the brain regions responsible for aggression, others articulate more flexible approaches that recognise the interplay of biology and environmental processes. For example, essentialist scholars such as Fields (2016: 1) argue that violence is 'controlled by the brain. From the everyday road rage to domestic violence, to a suicide bombing, the biology of anger and aggression is the root cause of most violent behaviour.' Similarly, Rosenberg et al. (2006) and Dobkin (2003) find the brain as the source of violence with the amygdala as the trigger for aggressive behaviour and violence being regulated by the prefrontal cortex. Some researchers such as Richard Redding (2006) working within this tradition go as far as to claim that the neuroscience 'provides compelling explanatory evidence that frontal lobe dysfunction plays a causal role in most types of violent crime' (Pustilnik 2009: 207). In contrast, more recent scholarship in neuroscience has questioned these deterministic views and has emphasised the flexibility of neural activity. For example, research in epigenetics has demonstrated that the actions of an organism can change as a consequence of modification of gene expression. The epigenetic studies indicate that both organisms and genes are much more malleable and also influenced by environmental factors. As Palumbo et al. (2018) show, traumatic life events and persistent stress can impact on one's brain and genetic activity. In this context biological properties of an organism are substantively shaped by social conditions: 'experiencing adversities during periods of maximal sensitivity to the environment, such as prenatal life, infancy and early adolescence, may introduce lasting epigenetic marks in genes that affect maturational processes in brain, thus favouring the emergence of dysfunctional behaviours, including exaggerate aggression in adulthood' (Palumbo et al. 2018). Other researchers have developed the notion of neuroplasticity aiming to emphasise the dynamic properties of brain cells. They argue that although genes structure brain development the process of learning contributes to strengthening or weakening of synaptic links within the neural systems. Malabou (2011: 35) frames it in stark terms : 'people make their own brain, but they do not know it'. Rather than treating brains as fixed and stable biological entities this new scholarship insists on plasticity of neural structures which is visible in the ability of brains to develop, modulate, and repair themselves through interaction with the wider social and natural environment. As Ray (2016) and Fulwiler (2003) show, these external factors influence brain activity: 'Certain brain regions appear to be continually modified by experience as new cells are generated in the hippocampus and olfactory bulb' (Ray 2016: 340).

Some neuroscientists have also questioned the traditional social science explanations of violent behaviour. These approaches have argued that social and environmental variables have to be combined with the biological variables to provide a full explanation of violence. For example, DeLisi (2015) indicates that instances of human aggressiveness that are linked to one's inability for self-control are not necessarily caused by cultural factors but are often the product of neural deficits. The title of his paper is highly indicative of this approach: 'Low Self-Control Is a Brain-Based Disorder'. Other neuroscientists aim to demonstrate how disruptions of neurotransmitters that regulate hormones such as high testosterone levels and low serotonin and cortisol levels are often associated with aggressive outbursts (Mehta and Beer 2010; Ray 2016, 2018). This focus on the link between hormonal differences and aggressive behaviour features prominently in the study of Monoamine oxidase A enzyme, often referred to as the MAOA gene. The scholars have identified this enzyme as playing a crucial role in breaking down the neurotransmitters in the brain and lowering the levels of serotonin and dopamine thus contributing to aggressive behaviour. According to Taylor et al. (2015), children with high levels of MAOA are less likely to become violent adults and vice versa.

There is no doubt that neuroscience and biomechanics contribute to better understanding of aggressive behaviour. By using new advanced technological devices and high-quality experimental procedures neuroscientists and evolutionary morphologists are able to analyse the complex mechanics of human bodies and especially the inner dynamics of the brain. The recent research on the plasticity of the human neural system and epigenetics in particular help us explain the existing interrelationships between the biological and social processes that shape violent action. Nevertheless, many strands of neuroscience and biomechanics are still characterised by biological determinism and pervasive confirmation biases. For instance, the evolutionary morphologists such as Carrier, Cunningham, and Morris tend to see almost any part of human anatomy as being an evolutionary product of fighting. This approach tends to overpredict violence and leaves no room for the non-violent sources of biological and social development. However, if aggressive behaviour has been so dominant throughout human evolution it is not clear why our species has not evolved much more robust anatomical features than the ones we currently possess. Rather than having strong jaws, sturdy horns, sharp claws, piercing teeth, enlarged and pointy tusks, very thick skin, or deadly venom, human bodies are rather feeble. Unlike other carnivorous animals and the large-scale herbivorous species both of which have evolved forceful anatomical features, human beings are characterised by pronounced physical fragility (Emlen 2014). Almost uniquely among the mammals, human offspring are completely dependent on other humans for their survival for many years. Moreover, humans do not possess a strong sense of smell, sharp eyesight, ability to fly or run extremely fast, or many other biological qualities that other species possess. Thus, identifying metacarpus and fingers of human hands as being primarily designed for fighting seems truly bizarre as they are completely ineffective as a tool of attack or defence against any large non-human species. It is hard to imagine that any sane individual would try to outpunch a grizzly bear, tiger, or an elephant; instead, humans would rely on much more effective means of attack or defence. To argue that fists or foot posture evolved for fighting with other humans is even more dubious as for much of prehistory humans were nomadic foragers who would rarely encounter other groups of humans and were primarily focused on escaping carnivorous predators (Fry 2007). Furthermore, as Orr (2016) argues convincingly, even if the human fist has developed for the organism's defence or attack this in itself is not a proof that hands evolved specifically for this purpose. The consequences of anatomical developments are not the evolutionary causes of these developments. One could argue that in this context fist-fighting is not different from beautification rituals – just as the fists can be used for fighting so the human ears can hold jewellery, but it would be absurd to argue that ears have evolved specifically for the purpose of displaying earrings. Even if fist shape, foot posture, and facial features have also evolved for fighting this in itself cannot explain the variety of fighting practices that have developed among human societies. As Wiessner and Pupu (2012) show, most hunter-gatherers do not use fists to fight at all but deploy different types of fighting practices such as wrestling or kicking. Nevertheless, in most cases the use of weaponry is preferred to physical fights.

Both the evolutionary morphologists and neuroscientists emphasise sharp sex differences as playing a crucial role in the evolution of violent behaviour. In these essentialist accounts masculinity and femininity are treated as fixed biological categories that experience no change and develop in opposition to each other where men are seen to have an inherently 'violent nature' and women are largely reduced to their sexual and reproductive roles. The biomechanics focuses on the physical differences between the sexes to show that men's stronger physique predisposes them for fighting while some neuroscientists insist on different brain use between the sexes. However, much of the recent scholarship on gender and violence has questioned these essentialist assumptions by demonstrating the malleability of gender roles and the capacity of both men and women to fight on equal footing. Physical strength and body size do not determine one's propensity for fighting and when given the opportunity women are just as effective fighters as men (Goldstein 2001; Malešević 2010: 279–83). The hormonal differences between men and women also play a minimal role in the fighting context as neither the levels of testosterone nor oestrogen determine one's fighting ability (Fuentes 2012: 143). Instead, the hormones that are more relevant for fighting such as adrenalin or cortisol are not gender specific but universal. Although some research claims that men rely more on the left side of their brain while women use both sides equally, there are no significant cognitive differences between the two sexes (Angier 1995; Goldstein 2001). Most importantly the hard essentialist distinctions between sexes have recently been questioned by many empirical studies emphasising the plasticity and changing dynamics of gender through time and space. This intrinsic malleability of gender roles is also reflected in violent behaviour.

Despite their useful and novel explorations of brain activity many neurological studies overgeneralise on the basis of a very small sample size and tend to over-rely on non-human experiments to extrapolate about human aggression. Furthermore, some neuroscientists make empirically unfounded universalist claims about the individual and social behaviour solely on the basis of their research on psychopathological patients. The over-reliance on neuroimaging technology can also limit the scope of the analysis and such technology is prone to resolution limitations (Bufkin and Lutterell 2005; Canli and Amin 2002; Ray 2016). However, the most problematic issue is neuroscience's general tendency to reduce social phenomena to individual pathology. By over-emphasising the brain regions and brainwaves of 'violent offenders' this approach de-contextualises and de-historicises violence. Hence the wider social and historical processes that generate violent outcomes are often completely ignored. In this way neuroscientists and evolutionary morphologists cannot explain the changing dynamics of violence and the cultural variability of violent action. Perhaps some damaged brains do foster pathological behaviour that may lead to aggressive outbursts, but this line of reasoning could not possibly explain why millions of people fight and kill each other in times of war, revolutions, genocides, or violent uprisings. To fully understand the trajectories of organised violence it is paramount to explore the social, political, economic, cultural, and wider historical processes that make close-range violence possible. The same argument applies to the neurological studies of 'abnormal morality'. Since morality is a cultural and social phenomenon it cannot be physically located in the specific brain regions (i.e., frontal, temporal, and cingulate cortices), as claimed by Fumaglli and Priori. Instead, the concepts of morality are historically variable, situational, and often culturally specific. Abend (2011) is right in his criticism of neuroscience that tends to operate with very thin concepts of morality which are unable to explain complex ethical notions such as dignity, cruelty, integrity, exploitation, or fanaticism. The idea of 'abnormal morality' pathologises and individualises complex social relationships.

1.5   The Psychology and Physiology of Close-Range Violence

The intense emotions that soldiers experience on the battlefield are often defined by specific biological reactions. In most instances these emotional responses go hand in hand with distinct and sudden physiological changes. Hence the widespread sense of fear and dread is regularly accompanied by profuse sweating, shaking, increased heart rate, palpitations, crying, and numbness among many other reactions. In intense combat situations individuals' heart rate can dramatically increase to the point when their motor skills become very poor or completely break down. When the heart rate increases to above 175 beats per minute that individual is likely to experience sudden deterioration in cognitive, visual, and audio processing abilities. Such individuals might not be able to move at all or might start fleeing the battlefield (Grossman 2004: 31).

The anxiety, fear, and panic experienced on the battlefields has often led to soldiers losing control of their bowels and bladder. For example, during the Second World War every fourth US soldier admitted losing control of their bladders and more than 15 per cent confessed that they defecated in their clothes (Stouffer 1949). In Grossman's view (2004: 10) this number is larger when counting only those who had direct and prolonged battlefield experience: 'approximately 50 per cent of those who did see intense combat admitted they had wet their pants'. This experience has been very common throughout the history of war and has been recorded in the ancient Greek and Roman world, pre-modern China and Japan, medieval warfare, and the Spanish wars of colonisation among many others (Collins 2008; Holmes 1985; Miller 2000).

Close-range violence is also regularly accompanied by heavy breathing, stress-related body paralysis, dilation of the pupils, hearing loss, and hormonal changes. The sudden changes in breathing rhythm such as hyperventilation can be highly detrimental to one's ability to act as one can experience light-headedness, trembling and tingling in the fingers, and even loss of consciousness. Regular breathing patterns involve a balance between oxygen that comes in and carbon dioxide that goes out of one's body and hyperventilation interrupts this pattern as it suddenly lowers the supply of carbon dioxide in one's body. This imbalance leads to lower blood supply to the brain as the narrowing of the blood vessels prevents regular blood flow. To prevent this from happening many coercive organisations, including the military, police, terrorist groups, and firefighters, have devised special techniques to control breathing. Lande (2007) reports that the US military devotes a great deal of attention to teaching young recruits how to 'breathe like a soldier'. Lande shows how important this practice is for effective military tasks and describes the institutional practices focused on creating a relatively uniform breathing pattern among recruits during shooting and running. By learning specific tactical breathing skills, new soldiers become better embedded into the military structures, but they also learn how to manage stress and emotional reactions on the battlefield. In the words of one US officer responsible for teaching breathing techniques, the inexperienced cadets regularly have problems with heavy breathing: 'I was running with a cadet and she was hurting, and I was telling her to breathe, to fill herself up like a bottle and hold it, breathe in through your nose for four seconds breathe out through your mouth for two, and I kept telling her to do it, but she just keep breathing at her own pace. I kept telling her, if you want the pain to stop you have to listen and hold your breath in' (Lande 2007: 101).

In some instances, stress might lead to a situation where one's blood flow slows down leading to vasoconstriction, narrowing of blood vessels. This biological reaction can help protect parts of one's body affected by sudden injuries as it reduces the blood flow to the extremities. For example, a bullet might hit a soldier's leg without any immediate heavy blood loss as the body experiences vasoconstriction and reduces blood flow until the situation of direct threat has decreased. In a situation where the blood flow is substantially reduced a combatant often has a 'pale face' and may lose motor control to the point of not being able to shoot or even walk. Once out of danger the body experiences vasodilatation – the wide opening of veins with heavy blood flow (Grossman 2004: 45–6).

The experience of close-range violence also affects one's vision. Police officers, soldiers on the battlefield, and gang members involved in violent encounters all report that they experienced tunnel vison during the violent episodes (Collins 2008). The presence of a threat contributes to dilating of one's pupils which improves one's ability to recognise small differences in light and shapes. In other words, during close-range violence many individuals lose peripheral vision and retain only central vision as the mind becomes focused on the direct external threat. Tunnel vision is often accompanied by the perception that time slows down during the violent episode. This is a phenomenon often referred to as tachypsychia where events unfold in 'slow motion' mode. During the violent encounter the brain is overloaded with information from all senses and the processing of this information requires faster activity. Nevertheless, as researchers show, this slow-motion vision does not involve actual warping of time but is a perception experienced through 'a trick played by one's memory' (Choi 2007). Tunnel vision blocks all peripheral images and zooms in on the potential danger with heightened visual clarity. However, tunnel vision can also prevent soldiers from noticing dangers coming from peripheral zones. Hence military manuals regularly warn against this: 'The Marine must search and asses [sic] to help break tunnel vision and identify other targets. This response to a threat is one reason why flanking maneuvers can be so effective on an enemy force. The individuals focus on the threat to their front so intently that the real threat from the side is unnoticed until it is too late' (CM 2003: 6).

Close combat situations affect one's hearing too. While some individuals experience intensified sounds, an overwhelming majority of combatants report that they could not hear anything. Even the sounds of guns, artillery, or bombs tend not to be heard or are heard in a muted way. As police officer Clagett (2003) describes his own experience of gunfight: 'The rifle fires. But I don't hear it. That's not quite true; I hear it, but it sounds very far away.' In the situation of a direct threat, the human brain prioritises information processing of sounds that are relevant to the perceived threat while all other sounds are excluded. For example, in a survey of 141 police officers who took part in a gun fight, Artwohl and Christensen (1997) found that 85 per cent experienced auditory exclusion, that is, substantially diminished hearing. Although this auditory exclusion might have some initial benefits for combatants as it focuses their attention on the potential threat it can also prove to be a major obstacle as individuals are often unable to hear commands and warnings from their colleagues and friends.

In addition to these perceptual distortions, close-range combat is regularly associated with hormonal changes which also impact on one's emotional state. The military manuals describe this change as 'chemical cocktail' – 'in a high stress environment the brain, endocrine, and pituitary systems will release a combination of powerful hormones and chemicals' (CM, 2003: 4). Although fighting is usually associated with increased testosterone levels, in fact it is the surge of adrenalin, noradrenalin, and cortisol that defines close-range fighting experience. Adrenalin and noradrenalin are related hormones and neurotransmitters which act as chemical mediators that help the body prepare for quick reaction in times of danger. The sudden increase in these hormones makes individuals more alert and aware of their environment and boosts strength and performance. It also numbs pain so that an individual can fight or run despite having a serious injury. Another important hormone associated with combat is cortisol. This is a steroid hormone that alters metabolism by raising plasma glucose and in this way can help blood clot more quickly when individuals are injured. However, unlike adrenalin which has a short-term and intense effect, cortisol is designed to manage long-term stress and its increased levels can last much longer.

The intensity of emotional reactions is often associated with specific physical expressions of individuals. Some scholars argue that emotions have physical fingerprints and that one can detect specific emotional reactions in facial expressions, skeletal and autonomic responses of human bodies, and in forms of vocalisation that accompany some emotional reactions. The leading representatives of this approach, Tomkins (1991) and Ekman (1992), insist that emotions are defined by biological patterns. Tomkins (1962, 1991) uses the notion of affect to refer to the 'biological portion of emotion' which he sees as 'hard-wired, pre-programmed, genetically transmitted mechanisms that exist in each of us and are responsible for the earliest form of emotional life' (Nathanson 1998: 58). Similarly, in his experimental studies Ekman (1992) found that the key emotions are encoded in facial muscles and hence that the emotional expressions have biological fingerprints. Using the Pictures of Facial Affect (POFA) tests in different parts of the world Ekman found out that facial expressions of emotions are not culturally specific but universal and thus in his view innate. In this context Tomkins (1962) identified specific physiological expressions with corresponding emotions with fear being associated with a pale face, coldness, sweat, and erect hair; shame with blushing, lowered eyes, lowered head, and distress; and anguish with crying, rhythmic sobbing, lowered mouth, and arched eyebrows. Tomkins also identified anger and rage with a red face, a clenched jaw, and frowning expression and enjoyment and joy with smiling and lips wide and pushed out. Other scholars working in this tradition have added further physiological reactions as being strongly linked with particular emotional responses including fear being associated with dry mouth, trembling, freezing, crying, and squealing; joy with laughing and shouting; and shame and guilt with covered face, avoiding eye contact, silence and stillness, and nervous behaviour among others (Steimer 2002).

This emphasis on the physicality of emotions and their hardwired character has led Tomkins, Ekman, and others to the conclusion that emotions are universal, stable, biologically uniform, transhistorical, and transcultural phenomena. Military psychologists and some micro-sociologists have embraced this view arguing that the emotional dynamics on the battlefield indicates that most combatants across time and space experience almost identical emotions and express very similar emotional reactions (Collins 2008; Grossman 1996, 2004). Furthermore, this highly influential view is premised on the idea that one can detect inner emotional states through the observation and analysis of soldiers' facial, skeletal, and vocalisational behaviours in the combat zone. In this understanding, human psychology largely reflects human physiognomy as emotions are understood to be hardwired in our anatomy.

However, much recent research in critical neuroscience, history, anthropology, and historical sociology of emotions has questioned this interpretation (Barrett 2017; Choudhury and Slaby 2016; Plamper 2015; Reddy 2001; Rosenwein 2010, 2016). These studies clearly demonstrate that rather than being innate and fixed reflections of our bodies, emotions are variable and context dependent. Moreover, as elaborated extensively in Chapter 10, emotions do not have unambiguous physiological fingerprints. It is not possible to simply read the emotional reactions from human facial expressions and the physiological reactions of human bodies. Instead, psychology and physiognomy are not always in sync; there is a great deal of disparity in how individuals and small groups respond in different social situations and in diverse cultural and historical contexts.

These criticisms are not meant to deny that human emotional reactions are often accompanied by substantive psychological and physiological changes. There is no doubt that the experience of close-range violence regularly has profound psychological and even physiological consequences. In violent situations humans are prone to experience stress, fear, shame, dread, and many other emotions that often go with visible physical reactions such as hearing loss, impaired or enhanced vision, body paralysis, urination, or crying. The point is that not all human beings automatically experience the same emotions and have the same physiological reactions. The emotional reactions are not simple products of biology and psychology but are regularly shaped and mediated by cultural, social, and historical realities. As anthropologists have demonstrated on numerous occasions, emotional reactions are often culturally specific. All humans have capacity for fear, shame, anger, rage, and so on but different cultural contexts influence the individual and collective experience and display of these emotions. For example, as Lim (2016), Tsai (2007), and Lu and Gilmour (2004) show, the level of emotional arousal differs substantially across different cultural contexts: in individualist societies where 'high arousal emotions are valued and promoted' people tend to 'experience high arousal emotions more than low arousal emotions' (Lim 2016: 105). Studying the emotional responses of Americans and East Asians, Tsai (2007) found that the US respondents had strong preference for high arousal emotional states such as enthusiasm and excitement whereas respondents in several East Asian societies regarded low arousal emotions as showing indifference and lack of enthusiasm as ideal. Even happiness was experienced very differently with Americans associating happiness with being upbeat and Chinese respondents viewing happiness as something linked to solemn and reserved behaviour (Lu and Gilmour 2004). The key point here is that different cultural values impact substantially on diverse psychological and physical expressions of emotions.

The same logic is present in the context of close-range violence. A number of anthropologists have researched small-scale societies where aggression is a taboo and where children are socialised to avoid conflict. For example, Utku Inuits of Canada developed strong norms that leave no room for anger. Their socialisation of children was centred on attaining *ihuma* (reason) which is expressed through the control of one's emotions. These cultural norms play a central role in what it means to be an Utku and as such are deeply reflected in their psychological and physiological responses to violence. The Utkus do not understand aggression as something that resides in the will of individuals but as a force that has its own autonomy: 'troublesome thoughts (*ihumaquqtuuq*)' were seen as capable of making people ill or forcing them to injure or kill others. Hence Utkus have develop an aversion towards violence (Briggs 1970). The impact of cultural values on physiology is even more pronounced in the case of the Tahitian population where anger was conceptualised as a disease of the body that requires instant intervention. As Robert Levy (1975: 285) who undertook ethnographic work in Tahiti notes: 'The Tahitians say that an angry man is like a bottle. When he gets filled up, he will begin to spill over.' In this interpretation suppressed rage and anger makes people sick and turns their hair grey. The Tahitians also exhibited differences in the physical expression of other emotions (e.g., laughter accompanying grief) and would locate fear, desire, and anger not in one's head or heart but in the bowels (Levy 1975: 271). In direct contrast, other societies have developed extremely belligerent cultural values that normalise violence and killings as integral to one's understanding of their social reality. For example, Michelle Rosaldo (1980) conducted fieldwork in the late 1960s and early 1970s among Ilongots of Northern Philippines who still practised headhunting. However, their headhunting raids had nothing to do with existing conflicts with other groups or the struggle for material possessions. Instead, the headhunting was practised as a form of psychological relief to get rid of 'heavy' feelings: 'the raider does not care about the personal identities of his victims or limit violence to opponents of his age or sex. Grieving for lost kin, envious of past beheadings, angry at an insult, and bent upon revenge, he and his fellows are concerned primarily, to realise their liget ... in taking heads they could aspire to "cast off" an "anger" that "weighted down" and oppressed their saddened "hearths"' (Rosaldo 1980: 55, 19). All these examples indicate that the psychology and physiology of close-range violence are markedly shaped by cultural and historical contexts.

1.6   Beyond Biological Essentialism

There is no uniform biological or psychological explanation of close-range violence. Instead, there are many approaches that invoke biological and psychological variables as having a crucial explanatory role in accounting for the dynamics of interpersonal violence. However, what is common to most of these approaches is the view that violent action has universal properties that are defined by the psychological and physiological uniformity of the human species. Moreover, many of these approaches emphasise the continuity in violent behaviour across the world of vertebrates and particularly the mammals where humans are understood not to be particularly different creatures. In this view violence is conceptualised as an evolutionary strategy developed primarily as a tool for the survival of species. In this context human psychology and physiology are perceived to reflect this long-term evolutionary legacy: our violent past is mirrored in our bodies and minds. As cognitive evolutionary psychologist Steven Pinker (2003: 316) puts it bluntly: 'When we look at human bodies and brains, we find more direct signs of design for aggression. The larger size, strength, and upper body mass of men is a zoological giveaway of an evolutionary history of violent male-male competition.'

However, while human biological and psychological characteristics clearly have impact on the patterns of aggression and non-aggression, they are far from being the key determinant of close-range violence. Whereas human physiognomy and psychology provide material ingredients for potential violent action, in themselves they are neither sufficient nor essential for violence. Human bodies and minds are often integral to violent encounters and can shape the dynamics of agonistic behaviour. Nevertheless, much of human-on-human violence differs profoundly from animal-on-animal aggression in a sense that human violence is mostly mediated through organisations, technologies, and ideological projects. Unlike wolves or tigers who have to face their prey and kill to eat, humans rely on coercive organisations, technological superiority, and normative justification to inflict violence. In this context, as organisational, technological, and ideological capacities continue to expand, much of human violent action entails less and less direct involvement of our physiognomy and psychology. As Coker (2013) observes, in wars of the near future robots will be fighting robots and violence is likely to be even more disconnected from human bodies and minds.

This is not to say that evolution is irrelevant. On the contrary, it is precisely through evolutionary processes that human reliance on violence has changed and evolved through time so that it now surpasses anything that any other species have ever been able to generate. Which other vertebrate animal is capable of killing 75 million members of its own species in six years? Hence the Pinkerian line of reasoning is both logically and empirically flawed. Humans share a great deal with other mammals and especially apes, but they also differ significantly from other animals. In Jonathan Marks's (2015) apt phrase humans are 'biocultural ex-apes', a species that has evolved enormously and changed substantially from the rest of the animal world. While *Homo sapiens* are genetically similar to chimpanzees, their physique and their behaviour are profoundly different. Moreover, humans continue to evolve as they radically transform the environments they inhabit. The conventional neo-Darwinian accounts show little interest in understanding this tangible evolutionary difference and focus most of their attention on exploring the similarities between humans and other animals. This over-emphasis on similarities is in part driven by the ambition to show that human violence resembles the aggressive action of our biological predecessors. However, if humans have been responsible for hundreds of millions of deaths of other humans and billions of deaths of other species then what is striking is not the alleged similarity but in fact the staggering difference with other species. In this context violence is not an evolutionary adaptation but a product of organisational development. The analogies with the animal world do not advance the arguments about humans' alleged inherent propensity for violence, they do the opposite as no other animal has been responsible for so much destruction as *Homo sapiens*. Hence what is required is to turn the neo-Darwinian argument on its head and show that human violence is a distinctly unique evolutionary development that no other species can possibly match. To understand how humans have reached this evolutionary point it is crucial to zoom in on the differences, not just on the biological similarities with the other species.

The comparisons with other primates indicate that our species is very different in several respects. As with most other primates, human minds and bodies have not specifically evolved for aggression. Even the physiognomy and psychology of apes shows no 'design for aggression'. As Fuentes (2012) and Turner (2007) emphasise, primates are not particularly social beings and they spend most of their time in highly individualised activities such as searching for food, eating, resting, and sleeping. 'Even the most socially active of primates (macaque and baboon monkeys and chimpanzees) rarely spend more than 20 percent of their time in social interactions. Across the primate order the average total time spent in social interactions ranges from 5 to 10 percent of total active time' (Fuentes 2012: 124). In this context aggressive behaviour is the exception rather than the rule. Sussman and Garber (2007) have analysed reports on over sixty species of primates and have found that agonistic behaviour accounts for less than 1 per cent of all social interactions. The instances of aggression that cause the death of another primate are extremely rare. If humans simply resembled other primates the scale of violence that we have produced over the centuries would have been negligible and certainly would not count in the hundreds of millions of human casualties and billions of deaths among other species. The causes of this unprecedented scale of human destruction are not to be found in our biological similarity with the other primates but rather in its opposite – in the immense difference of human behaviour. Rather than searching for common genetic roots it is much more fruitful to focus on what differentiates humans from the rest of the animal world such as ideological norms, cultural practices, organisational capacities, and their links with micro-level solidarities (Malešević 2010, 2017).

In contrast to other primates, human beings are socially highly active creatures. Our sociability has developed gradually, and the variety of evolutionary changes have contributed to abilities that we have acquired over the years including the capacity to walk upright, speak, develop, and use complex languages, have power of introspection and ability to solve difficult problems, and to reflect on the world around us, among many others. The development of these relatively unique abilities has allowed human species to create institutions, technology, social organisations, belief systems, rituals, and many other social devices that no other species possesses. These novel social mechanisms have played a crucial role in the proliferation of violence over the course of human history. It is no accident that the emergence of warfare and other forms of organised violence was paralleled with the advent of sedentary lifestyle and the development of the first civilisations. The continuous rise of violence over the last five thousand years is directly linked with the growth and expansion of state power and other coercive social organisations (Malešević 2017; Mann 1986, 1993; Olsson and Malešević 2017). By focusing predominantly on the shared genetic or physiognomic similarities with the other primates one cannot explain this staggering historical transformation in the human relationship to violence.

In their overemphasis on the biological similarities between humans and the rest of the animal world the conventional neo-Darwinian perspectives do not differentiate clearly between violence and aggression. This is also the case with many neuroscientists and psychologists. For example, Fields (2016: 1) offers a rather typical view that combines neuroscience with the neo-Darwinian perspective and argues that:

we have neural circuits of rage and violence because we need them. As a species we needed deadly violence to obtain food, to protect ourselves, our family, our group, and unfortunately, we still need them today. Order in society is maintained through violence, meted out methodically by police and nations according to laws that benefit society at large, but this organized violence is founded on the same neurocircuitry of aggression wired into the human brain of every individual.

This statement represents a form of very crude biological determinism which locates complex emotions (i.e., rage) and complex social processes (i.e., violence) in specific parts of the brain and then extends this to moral claims about the necessity of 'deadly violence' to fulfil biological and social needs. Furthermore, this rampant biological determinism is then extended to the level of coercive state power (i.e., police) and historically novel form of polity (nation) to make an astounding claim that organised violence is 'founded on the same neurocircuitry of aggression wired into the human brain of every individual'. What is also noticeable here is the casual slip from violence to aggression as if the two are the same phenomenon.

Although both aggression and violence are forms of agonistic behaviour, they are in fact two very different phenomena. While aggression is a bodily response directly linked to one's physiognomy and psychology, violence is first and foremost a form of social relationship. While aggression often involves involuntary response to stimuli (e.g., fight or flight response/hyperarousal), violence is a scalar and situational phenomenon shaped by specific social dynamics. For example, experiments on mice and other rodents have demonstrated that when under threat these animals display involuntary action such as hair-fluffing/piloerection (with hair standing on end), tail-rattling (muscle contraction of the tail), sudden twitching or making unconscious loud noises (Scott 1966). Many other animals exhibit similar involuntary responses: cats fearing an attack have accelerated heartbeat, pupil dilation, and piloerection; antelopes being chased by lions have enhanced muscular ability that is supported by all the body's systems so that they can run away; chameleons instantly change their body colour to hide from predators; and many other species freeze automatically or play dead to deceive their attackers. Other animals involuntarily fight for survival: from goats and deer to rhinos and elephants many herbivores stand their ground and fight their carnivorous attackers. In all of these cases the fight or flight response kicks in instantly and the animal responses are automatic and mostly involuntary. When engaging in aggressive behaviour both the attacking and the defending animal experience similar physiological reactions including higher secretion of the ACTH hormone, increased blood pressure, higher blood sugar, and increased cortisol and epinephrine levels, among others. In a situation of direct threat humans also experience many of these responses and they can act aggressively or run away. This all points to the conclusion that aggressive behaviour is based in biological propensities that affect all vertebrates and shape their response in threatening situations.[1]

However, aggression is not the same as violence. Violence is not an innate biological response but a complex, contingent, and contextual form of individual and social action. Violence is an integral part of human historical experience that is often the product of protracted organisational and ideological activity. I define violence as 'a scalar social process in which individuals, groups or social organisations find themselves steeped in situations whereby their intentional or unintentional actions generate some substantial coercively imposed behavioural changes or produce physical, mental or emotional damage, injury or death' (Malešević, 2017: 15). Furthermore, much human violence has historically been inflicted not by individuals but by large-scale social organisations such as states, religious and political institutions, social movements, and so on. Hence to fully understand micro-level violence

---

[1] Nevertheless, human aggression still differs from the aggression of many other animals: 'In animals there is usually a clear separation in the brain behavior pathway between anger-induced and fear-induced aggression, with actual physical aggression being more restrained in anger-based behavior than in fear-based behavior. However, in humans (relative to other animals) there appears to be a wider range of ways in which aggression can be expressed and the distinction between anger-induced and fear-induced aggression is not always so clear cut' (Fuentes 2012: 122).

it is paramount to historically contextualise its emergence, development, and expansion. Thus, the social pugnacity of humans in war or revolution does not resemble in any way wolves fighting over a dead sheep. While the former is a product of organisational development (war between states) the latter is an example of animal aggression generated by biological stimuli and response. Unlike aggression which is tied firmly to the physiognomic, psychological, and neurological givens, violence is a social relation shaped by contextual dynamics, choices, contingent action, and historical conditions. In this context Fields's (2016) claim that organised violence is 'founded on the same neurocircuitry of aggression wired into the human brain of every individual' is utterly false. This wrong assumption does not only conflate aggression with violence, but it also makes no differentiation between the complex and contradictory activities of social organisations that generate organised violence and the agonistic behaviour of individuals. It is social organisations that fight wars, start revolutions and uprisings, commit genocides, and engage in planned terrorist actions and these organisations do not possess brains. While political, military, and religious leaders deploy their brainwaves to make decisions about wars, genocides, revolutions, or terrorism no single individual or even group of influential individuals can determine the course of organised violence. As Clausewitz (2008 [1832]) noticed many years ago, once unleashed organised violence has its own dynamics. States, religious organisations, or political parties are composed of millions of individuals with brains, but no social organisation could possibly possess a 'neurocircuitry of aggression' that is wired in its brain or the brains of all of its members. Organised violence is mediated, indirect, context dependent, unpredictable, and highly situational, not a product of unchanged physiology or fixed brainwaves. States do not have brains and even if they did, they cannot direct the trajectories of organised violence. Furthermore, whereas aggression represents a form of uncontrolled agonism the basic precondition of successful organised violence is discipline.[2] Unlike animal aggression which stems from biological needs (to eat or not to be eaten) human violence entails self-control, coordination of action, delegation of responsibility, long-term planning, the assessment of unintended consequences of violent action, the ability to understand the thinking of the opponent, and so many other processes

---

[2] However, it is important to emphasise that despite this automatism in fight vs. flight behaviour there is no genetic predisposition for violence: 'There is no gene or system in the body that can be identified as "for aggression." While it appears clear that genetic variation in neurotransmitters and hormones can be involved in the ways in which we express aggressive behavior, there is no direct or causal link. Our genes cannot make us aggressive' (Fuentes 2012: 144).

that simply could never be a part of an involuntary aggressive response. In the sociological sense, organised violence is the exact opposite of aggression: successful military organisations or terrorist groups have no interest in recruiting aggressive individuals who cannot control their temperament; instead the best recruits are self-disciplined and obedient individuals. Hence to fully understand the dynamics of close-range violence one has to go beyond the simple analogies with the animal world and zoom in on the micro- and macro-sociological processes that make organised violence possible and durable over the course of human history.

This criticism of the conventional neo-Darwinian views and the de-contextualised essentialism of neuroscience, biomechanics, and physiognomy does not mean that there is no room for biology in the explanation of close-range violence. On the contrary, human beings are material creatures defined by their bodies and minds and as such one has to account for these biological realities. The point is that to fully appreciate the significance of biology it is necessary to go beyond the conventional determinist interpretations. A number of evolutionary scholars including biological anthropologists and neuroscientists have moved beyond the essentialist views and have developed several promising perspectives such as critical neuroscience and new biocultural anthropology. For example, critical neuroscientists such as Jan Slaby (2010) and Suparna Choudhury (2009) have questioned the conventional neuroscience by focusing on the wider social, political, and cultural processes of experimental studies. They analyse how specific social contexts and historical trajectories inevitably shape the production and reception of knowledge generated by neuroscientists. These studies dissect some commonly held assumptions within neuroscience and demonstrate that experimental research is always embedded in and framed by its social and cultural contexts. Similarly, new biocultural anthropology has been critical of conventional evolutionary perspectives that tend to explore evolutionary change through genetic inheritance alone. For example, Jablonka and Lamb (2005) argue that evolution operates not in one but in four distinct dimensions: in addition to genetic inheritance there are also epigenetic, behavioural, and symbolic inheritance systems. While all organisms have genetic and epigenetic inheritance, most organisms have behavioural inheritance and only humans have symbolic inheritance. Hence to properly understand the evolutionary processes one has to go beyond genes and look at the hereditary variation in different areas which helps researchers to identify how evolutionary change transpires from both selection and instruction. Biocultural anthropologists such as Fuentes (2012), Kuzawa and Sweet (2009), and Sapolsky (2004) have demonstrated convincingly how biological and social factors are often interwoven in influencing a variety of physiological changes. For example by studying US black/white disparity in cardiovascular disease Kuzawa and Sweet found that the environmental context plays a crucial role in the health disparity: 'We conclude that environmentally responsive phenotypic plasticity, in combination with the better-studied acute and chronic effects of social-environmental exposures, provides a more parsimonious explanation than genetics for the persistence of CVD disparities between members of socially imposed racial categories' (Kuzawa and Sweet 2009: 2). Similarly, Sapolsky's (2004) research on stress indicates that both biological and cultural factors contribute to the levels of stress in humans and other primates. Stress-related disease seems to be higher is hierarchical social orders and among groups characterised by deep social inequalities. Other scholars (Schleim 2014; Whiteley 2012) have also questioned the over-reliance on modern technology (i.e., limitations of fMRI, face recognition programs, DNA databases as research tools) in evolutionary and neurological studies. For example, the overemphasis on brain and body scans tends to essentialise social categories of mind and body and contribute to biological determinist thinking. All these new perspectives are helping to develop a more reflexive biological model of evolutionary change. As such they are also useful in accounting for the evolutionary, neurological, biomechanical, and physiological processes involved in close-range violence. These and many other recent studies point out that social pugnacity is a highly complex phenomenon that cannot be explained through the traditional biological mechanisms alone. Instead to understand why humans fight it is also necessary to explore economic, ideological, political, and other non-biological factors.

1.7 Conclusion

Human beings are part and parcel of the natural world that has emerged and continues to develop through evolutionary processes. In this sense *Homo sapiens* shares much of its genetic, physiological, and psychological make-up with the rest of the animal world. Hence to understand the dynamics of close-range violence it is necessary to take into account our biological similarities with other vertebrates and especially the mammals. Just like many other mammalian species humans have evolved to rely on the fight or flight response to preserve their life and those of their close kin and also to occasionally deploy aggression to secure the means of survival. However, these genetic and other similarities do not define the human relationship to violence. Humans share much with other animals, but they also differ profoundly from the rest of the animal world. The cognitive evolutionary theory, neuroscience, biomechanics, and physiology all contribute to better understanding of agonistic behaviour in all species. However, these approaches tend to overemphasise similarities and behavioural uniformity over difference and variability that characterises human social action. Biology simply is not enough to account for the immense historical, cultural, and social variation that can be observed in human behaviour. The changing dynamics of violence cannot be explained through the use of biological determinist models and simple analogies with the behaviour of great apes. Since the scale of violence generated by human beings dwarfs anything else that exists in nature it is crucial to focus our attention on the long-term organisational, ideological, and micro-interactional processes that make close-range violence possible.

2 Profiting from Fighting
The Economics of Micro-Level Violence

2.1 Introduction

In this chapter I explore the economic motivations for interpersonal violence. The spotlight is on the leading rationalist and instrumentalist approaches that attempt to explain willingness to fight through the prism of individual self-interest. The chapter analyses different strands of the economics-centred paradigm: (a) approaches that have been developed in the study of civil wars and other violent conflicts; and (b) criminological theories of homicide and other violent crimes. The chapter identifies strengths and weaknesses of the agency-centred strategic and instrumentalist approaches to close-range violence as well as the more structural approaches that focus on the collective motivations and social inequalities that foster violent responses. I argue that social inequalities and economic self-interest can tilt conflict towards violent episodes, but material reasons alone cannot adequately explain human motivation to fight or the social dynamics of close-range violence. The chapter concludes with a brief critical analysis of two empirical cases that show the limits of economic models of violence.

2.2 The Rationality of Violence in Conflict Situations

One of the adjectives that is regularly deployed to describe violent behaviour is senseless. Violence is also often deemed to be irrational, illogical, and meaningless. The individuals who commit close-range violent acts are often depicted as barbaric, sadistic, or psychologically unstable. Even when violence is committed under the auspices of specific social organisations (military, police, insurgencies, etc.) those who are seen to be at ease when killing or injuring other human beings are often perceived as pathological and irrational. However, social scientists and historians show clearly that most forms of violent behaviour are grounded in rational motivations and often operate according to well understood logic. While situational contingencies and random events play an important part in all violent acts, most forms of belligerence involve a degree of rational reasoning. In this sense violence does not represent a breach in normal (peaceful) social conduct but is often a radicalised continuation of existing social behaviour. If human beings cannot implement their will through non-violent means they might turn to violence. This general understanding underpins all rationalist theories of close-range violence. These approaches conceptualise violence through the prism of the intrinsic rationality of individual or collective action. In most instances these perspectives also interpret the use of violence as a means of attaining specific economic or symbolic benefits.

The rationalist understanding of violence has deep historical roots, but it has become particularly influential in the last two centuries. From Aristotle, Machiavelli, and Clausewitz to the contemporary realist approaches in international relations, neo-Marxism, political economy perspectives, and theories of rational choice among many others, violence has been interpreted as a rational means of attaining economic, political, or symbolic advantages. Aristotle was among the first to develop an economic understanding of organised violence. In his view, wars between states are rational in the sense that they are aimed at gaining resources that are required for economic development: 'the art of war is a natural art of acquisition, for the art of acquisition includes hunting, an art which we ought to practise against wild beasts, and against men who, though intended by nature to be governed, will not submit; for war of such a kind is naturally just' (Aristotle 1988 [350 BCE]: 11). While Machiavelli and Clausewitz develop more elaborate theories of organised violence that focus on its political rather than its economic dimensions, they too conceptualise violent behaviour in instrumentalist terms. Hence for Machiavelli (1985 [1532]: 68) human beings are self-interested creatures that should not be trusted. Consequently, in *The Prince* he advises rulers that they should always prefer fear over love of their subjects:

it is much safer to be feared than loved when of the two either must be dispensed with. Because this is to be asserted in general of men, that they are ungrateful, fickle, false, cowardly, covetous ... men have less scruple in offending one who is beloved than one who is feared, for love is preserved by the link of obligation, which, owing to the baseness of men, is broken at every opportunity for their advantage; but fear preserves you by a dread of punishment which never fails. (Machiavelli 1985 [1532]: 68)

In a slightly different context, Clausewitz also emphasises the instrumental character of social relations. By zooming in on the role of violence in war he argues that without violence one cannot fulfil the goal of winning the conflict. Hence he defines war in deeply instrumentalist terms as 'a continuation of politics by other means' (Clausewitz 2008 [1832]: 44). In this context he emphasises the necessity of deploying violent means to achieve ultimate ends: 'Kind-hearted people might think that there was some ingenious way to disarm or defeat an enemy without too much bloodshed and might imagine that this is the true goal of the art of war. Pleasant as it sounds, this is a fallacy that must be exposed' (Clausewitz 2008 [1832]: 75). All of these classical accounts, and many others, posit the use of violence as a rational course of action that is centred on generating economic or political benefits.

Many contemporary social science perspectives draw on these classical accounts by emphasising the centrality of rational and strategic motivations for violence. Among the plethora of approaches that dominate current debates on the economics of violence one can identify two general perspectives: (1) the macro-economic and macro-historical analyses that explore organised violence through the prism of large-scale structural forces; and (2) the micro-level approaches that zoom in on the individual motivations for participation in violent action.

The macro-level approaches focus on the self-interested deployment of violence by states, private corporations, and other organisations. In these accounts belligerence is a product of structural developments. For example, both classical realism and neo-realism in international relations analyse the use of violence through the prism of self-interest: for classical realists such as Morgenthau (1978) international politics is shaped by the egotistic impulses of political leaders and their ambitions to maximise their advantages while neo-rationalism identifies the anarchical state system as the key catalyst of competition for geo-political control. Some neo-realists such as Waltz (1979) see states as 'security maximisers' in a sense that they have to navigate within intrinsically hostile global environments aiming to preserve themselves or expand their influence, while others such as Mearsheimer (2001) posit war as an inevitable consequence of states' struggle for power. Other structuralist accounts deploy similar rationalist and strategic logic to the actions of private corporations and other organisations centred on creation of profit. Hence neo-Marxists, theorists of globalisation, world-system and political economy approaches tend to see violence as a by-product of competing socio-economic interests. In these interpretations, organised violence is linked directly to the economic foundations of social order – wars, revolutions, terrorism, and insurgencies are understood to be caused by the competition for limited resources and markets. For example, world-system scholars such as Wallerstein (1995) and Chase-Dunn and Podobnik (1995) argue that large-scale wars are the product of changing hegemonic rivalries between the capital-intensive core states that dominate and exploit populations living in the periphery and semi-periphery of the global economy. In this view military conflicts are more likely to happen when one hegemon is in decline and is challenged by a new rising hegemonic power. In similar vein the political economy, globalisation theorists and neo-Marxist perspectives emphasise the periodic economic crises that arise within capitalism leading to the proliferation of wars. For example, Kaldor (2001) and Bauman (2002) see twenty-first-century civil wars as a direct consequence of neo-liberal globalisation. In this interpretation globalisation undermines local economies and weakens the power of already fragile states to the point of collapse as in the case of DR Congo, Somalia, Libya, or Yemen. Once the structures of the state collapse, private corporations reap profits through establishing new networks of trade with the local warlords (e.g., western weapons in exchange for access to oil and precious metals and minerals). Despite some differences between all these perspectives there is a common thread in their argument: violence is a rational tool of economic gain.

These structuralist perspectives are useful in pinpointing links between economic processes and organised violence but for the most part they have very little or nothing to say about the dynamics of close-range violence. While capitalism, globalisation, the world-system, and processes of production and trade all have an impact on the trajectories of wars, revolutions, insurgencies, and many other forms of violence they are too general and too abstract to account for the variation in violent behaviour among individuals and small groups.

In contrast to the structuralist accounts which are generally weak on tracing the social mechanisms of violence in face-to-face contexts, the micro-level approaches excel in this type of research. The scholarship on civil wars has in particular influenced wider discussions on the dynamics of violence in micro-level contexts. Collier and Hoeffler (2002, 2004) have initiated an ongoing analytical dispute that is often referred to as the greed vs. grievance debate. They attempted to show that the dominant theories of conflict including relative deprivation models, economic inequality approaches, political repression and exclusion models, and identity centred perspectives all focus on social grievances which in their view are a consequence rather than a cause of conflict.

Focusing on the use of violence in several civil wars in Africa, Asia, and Latin America they argue that the key cause of these wars is economic in the sense that the political and military leaders just as ordinary combatants involved in these conflicts are motivated by personal gain. Their research indicates that the abundance of natural resources (e.g., oil, precious metals, minerals, drugs) is highly correlated with the onset and duration of violent conflicts. The presence of resources fosters predatory behaviour from different groups interested in acquiring this wealth, but these resources also help rebel groups to finance protracted wars. For example, in Colombia and Afghanistan drugs such as coca or poppy finance civil wars while in Angola and Sierra Leone diamonds are the primary commodity resources that fuel the conflicts.

For Collier and Hoeffler (2002), low GDP per capita and high dependency on primary commodities are also linked strongly with the probability of civil war. In addition, they single out the size of diaspora networks that are willing to finance violent conflicts. For example, the Tamil diaspora has played a crucial role in financing the Liberation Tigers of Tamil Eelam (LTTE). The likelihood of war is also linked to a high number of unemployed young men who can be recruited to fight with the promise of loot in the form of primary commodities. In this interpretation, violence in civil wars is generated by greed – the ambition to enrich oneself through the direct control of economic resources. In their own words: 'Our model suggests that what is actually happening is that opportunities for primary commodity predation cause conflict, and that the grievances which this generates induce diasporas to finance further conflict. The policy intervention points here are reducing the absolute and relative attraction of commodity predation, and reducing the ability of diasporas to fund rebel movements' (Collier and Hoeffler 2002: 27).

This approach has been criticised by many scholars who question its reductionist, single factor, premise that offers a simplistic explanation of highly complex social realities (Bodea and Elbadawi 2008; Keen 2012). For example, Keen (2012) argues that greed and grievance are not mutually exclusive motivations; looting and pillaging of resources can generate profound social grievances followed by rebellion which in turn can help justify continuation of looting and pillaging. Unlike Collier and Hoeffler who understand civil wars in terms of winners and losers, Keen emphasises that many individuals involved in protracted violent conflicts have no incentive for their resolution as war conditions allow them to control access to economic resources and political power. Other critics point out that this perspective does not advance our understanding of the micro-dynamics of violence. Instead of interviewing combatants and civilians affected by civil wars or observing their behaviour, the greed perspective generalises on the basis of proxy data generated from the documentary evidence provided by international organisations. As Demmers (2006) argues, these proxy measurements can be deployed with equal vigour to show that grievances and not greed cause violence. Although this debate is useful in identifying the variety of factors that contribute to the onset of civil wars, the greed perspective has very little to say about the structural and historical mechanisms and processes that make social pugnacity possible.

The rational choice theories of violence offer a more focused analysis of the micro-processes involved in civil wars. Fearon and Laitin (2003) and Kalyvas (2006) among others have developed comprehensive theories of motivation for fighting in civil wars. This perspective aims to explain how collective action transpires and operates in the context of protracted violence. The rational choice theory interprets behaviour through the prism of instrumental rationality where human beings are understood to be advantage maximisers. However, as the use of violence is risky, costly, and unpredictable the focus is on the question of motivation for fighting: Why would rational and self-interested individuals take part in extremely dangerous acts such as violence in civil wars when they can escape or act as free riders and later benefit from the actions of other fighters? The rational choice approach explains this collective action problem through the coordination of self-interested behaviour. Hence some scholars argue that participation in civil wars is often determined by individuals' assessments of gains and losses. For example, Laitin (2007: 22) insists that civil wars have materialist foundations: 'if there is an economic motive for civil war... it is in the expectation of collecting the revenues that ownership of the state avails'. However, this motivation alone does not explain the onset of civil war or the micro-dynamics of violence. Both Laitin and Fearon have identified other factors the combination of which is likely to lead to civil wars: a severely weakened state apparatus, rampant poverty and inequalities, large populations, the availability of a stable revenue stream, and the existence of rough and inaccessible terrain (mountains, swamps, deserts, etc.) that allows the rebels to hide (Fearon and Laitin, 2003; Laitin 2007). Fearon (1994) has also singled out the question of trust and the lack of credible information which is a necessary precondition for making individual choices about participation in civil wars. Kalyvas (2006) has also explored the individual and collective motivations behind the changing patterns of violence in warfare. More specifically he analyses the strategic uses of selective and indiscriminate violence in different civil war contexts and shows how ordinary people often use civil war to pursue their own interests. In his interpretation the use of violence in civil wars is regularly shaped by rational and self-interested motivation: while political and military elites strategically deploy indiscriminate or selective violence against civilians to establish or maintain control over specific territory or population, ordinary individuals tend to map their pre-war personal animosities onto the war narratives to gain some benefits. For example, a disliked neighbour is denounced to the authorities as a traitor so that his land or other possessions can then be appropriated by those who denounce him. In both of these situations (elite and non-elite) violence is deployed in a calculated sense: either as a tool of population control or as an instrument of self-benefit. However, Kalyvas recognises that in many civil wars it is difficult to differentiate between soldiers and civilians which can create situations where violence is used indiscriminately against all (Kalyvas and Kocher 2007).

Other scholars such as Wood (2003) and Zukerman Daly (2012) have extended the conventional rational choice accounts by demonstrating empirically how rational agents can be motivated by non-material goals. Wood (2003) shows how in El Salvador's civil war the motivation for participation in fighting was driven less by the perceived material benefits and more by the 'pleasure of agency', i.e., an increased sense of self-worth through shared action with others. Zukerman Daly (2012) challenges Laitin and Fearon and shows that in many violent conflicts the presence of poverty, inequality, rough terrain, or natural resources are not the key determinants of civil war. Instead, her analysis of 274,428 municipality-month observations in Colombia indicates that organisational legacies of previous conflicts are crucial: 'the data indicate that regions affected by past mobilization are six times more likely to experience rebellion than those without a tradition of armed organized action' (Zukerman Daly 2012: 473). Other empirical studies identify strong links between different types of economic benefits and the presence of civil war. For example, Ross (2006) found a strong positive correlation between crude oil exports and civil wars while Homer-Dixon (1999) has identified mechanisms that link scarcity of natural resources such as fresh water and cropland with the onset of civil wars, insurgencies, terrorism, and genocides.

There is no doubt that these micro-economic perspectives contribute substantially towards understanding the changing dynamics of violence in civil wars and other conflicts. They rightly challenge the stereotypical perception of violence as something senseless and irrational and show convincingly that human beings are highly capable of deploying belligerent action to achieve specific goals and ambitions. Moreover, these perspectives also help us demystify and de-naturalise violence by identifying the social processes behind rational decisions made about the strategic use of violence. Instead of treating violence as inherent to our species, the rationalist perspectives demonstrate that violent acts are for the most part a matter of decisions made by specific actors. Nevertheless, the micro-economic explanations of violence are also characterised by several pronounced weaknesses. Firstly, these perspectives represent a form of economic determinism where the complexity and richness of social action tends to be reduced to self-interest alone. Indeed, there are many situations where violence is not generated by intentional and strategic reasoning but transpires as an unintended consequence of several processes. For example, the outbreak of the First World War is a typical example of a large-scale violent historical episode that was a result of unintended consequences involving the miscommunication and misunderstanding of political and military elites as well as the misreading of opponents' plans and goals (Clark 2013). Even the event that triggered the war, the assassination of Austro-Hungarian heir to the crown Archduke Franz Ferdinand in Sarajevo, was a product of contingency as the assassins initially missed their target and only later encountered Ferdinand's convoy by chance (Glenny 2017). Although the outbreak of the First World War involved rational actors responsible for specific choices it is the confluence of specific structural contexts that led to an extremely destructive war which presented no economic benefit for any of the warring parties involved.

Secondly, the micro-economic perspectives are prone to tautological reasoning which relies on ex post facto explanations. Since they start from the assumption that violent behaviour is rational per se, their empirical analyses tend to reinforce an already accepted view. Hence instead of dissecting the motivations behind violent acts the focus is on trying to prove that even seemingly irrational behaviour is ultimately motivated by self-interest. This is a form of circular logic. This tautological approach also lacks analytical tools for understanding the complexity of the emotional processes that accompany experience of violence. Instead of studying emotions on their own terms, rationalists such as Kalyvas or Laitin are prone to dismissing non-rational motivations as irrelevant or a product of alleged 'ideological irrationality'.

Thirdly, the micro-rationalist perspectives overemphasise the uniformity in individual and collective behaviour and as such cannot explain the enormous variability of violent action in time and space. As these perspectives minimise the significance of historical change and transformative ideological norms they cannot account for different attitudes and practices towards violence in different social and historical contexts. For example, all human beings fear death and pursuing one's own survival is the ultimate form of self-interest. Nevertheless, in some social and historical contexts soldiers will prefer to kill themselves rather than allow themselves to be captured by the enemy, while others will surrender in the same situation. As Barkawi (2017) shows, while many Indian soldiers who fought in the British army during the Second World War would surrender to the Japanese forces, the Japanese soldiers would regularly fight to the death or would commit suicide to avoid been taken prisoner. This contextual difference matters and it can dramatically affect human behaviour.

Finally, despite being focused nominally on the micro-dynamics of individual and collective mobilisation for violence the rationalist perspectives do not tell us much about the actual processes that shape human perceptions and practices of pugnacity. In other words, instead of dissecting the social mechanisms that make close-range fighting possible, rationalists take self-interest for granted. In this sense everything becomes a question of narrowly based instrumental behaviour – whatever soldiers or gang members do in the violent situations their actions are automatically rendered as driven by rational self-interest. Hence the decision to kill or not to kill one's adversary, just as the experience of participating or not participating in a collective violent encounter, is explained using the same interpretative frame of instrumental rationality without actually probing and understanding individuals and situations on their own terms. Thus, to fully explain the dynamics of close-range violence one has to go beyond the micro- (and macro-) economic perspectives.

2.3   The Economics of Close-Range Violence in Peace

Close-range violence is integral to the experience of warfare. Once soldiers are mobilised for war the expectation is that many of them will encounter front line combat with excessive injuries and death. Although modern technologies have made face-to-face combat rare, many soldiers are still likely to witness unprecedented carnage. In direct contrast most contemporary individuals living outside of war zones are unlikely to see people being severely injured, tortured or killed on purpose. While some individuals will experience domestic abuse, bullying at work or in school, traumatic street mugging or some other violent crime, an overwhelming majority of people living in the twenty-first-century global North are not likely to be victims or perpetrators in acts of close-range violence. Homicide in particular is an extremely rare phenomenon in much of the developed world. For example, according to the UN Office on Drugs and Crime most countries in the global North have a very low number of homicides per 100,000 inhabitants. In Europe, this ranges from 0.30 in Luxembourg, 0.50 in Switzerland and 0.90 in Ireland and Iceland to 1.20 in England and Wales, 1.30 in France, 1.70 in Belgium and 2.30 in Albania. Even the outliers such as Ukraine (6.20) and Russia (9.20) are rather low compared to some countries in Latin America where El Salvador (61.80), Venezuela (56.33) and Honduras (41.70) top the list while many other countries remain in the range of 4–30: from Chile (4.30), Argentina (5.10), Peru (7.70) and Panama (9.70), to Mexico (24.80) and Brazil (30.50).The two largest states from North America have homicide rates that resemble most European states with Canada at the lower end (1.80) and USA at the higher end (5.30) while the main outlieer here is Jamaica (57).

Most Asian societies also have a very low homicide rates: Japan and Singapore (0.20), China (0.60), India (3.20) and Pakistan (4.20). The Asian outliers are much lower than those in Latin America and are very similar to Europe: Afghanistan (7.10), Philippines (8.40), and Iraq (9.85).[1] African countries have a rather uneven number of homicides that range from as low as 1.10 in Benin and Guinea-Bissau, 1.30 in Burkina Faso, 2.10 in Morocco, and 2.51 in Egypt to as high as 35.90 in South Africa and 41.25 in Lesotho (DATAUNODC 2020).

The combined data for all continents indicates that the average homicide rate in 2017 for the whole of the world was 6.20 (DATAUNODC 2020). Although this aggregated data papers over enormous variation within each of the countries analysed, even this rather crude measure shows that homicides happen very rarely. Even in societies that are comparatively characterised by very high rates such as El Salvador or Jamaica most ordinary citizens do not necessarily witness deaths of their compatriots and many are likely to never see a violent crime in their lifetime. What the figure of 61.80 shows is that out of 100,000 citizens of El Salvador 99,938.2 will not experience homicidal violence and although some people will be affected by various forms of violent crime their overall number will remain very small. The homicides account for 0.7 per cent of all global deaths and as such are truly extremely rare events (Rosser and Ritchie 2019).

Although homicides receive disproportionate attention in the mass media and popular culture, they are also quite rare within the statistics of all violent crimes in each country. For example, in England and Wales homicides account for 0.1 per cent of violent crimes and 0.01 per cent of all crime (Ray 2018: 136). The overwhelming majority of perpetrators and victims of homicide are men. The recent UN homicide report that aggregates data from 2010 to 2017 indicates that 78.7 per cent of all homicide victims in the world have been men and also that 96 per cent of perpetrators are also men. The pattern is very similar for most states in the world and the only exceptions are Switzerland and British Virgin Islands where the gender ratio is around 50:50 for victims and several

---

[1] The homicide rates for Afghanistan and Iraq do not include deaths resulting from warfare.

countries with very low homicide rates where more women have been victims than men[2] (i.e., Japan, New Zealand, Iceland, South Korea) (DATAUNODC 2020).

Sex is not the only social category that defines homicide rates. Age and social class also play an important role as an overwhelming majority of perpetrators and victims of homicide are younger individuals from the lower social strata. For example, in the UK the group most involved in violent crime are unemployed single men between the age of 16 and 24 (Home Office 2020). The data indicate that in the US and Canada the situation is very similar: individuals between the age of 15 and 29 constitute around 20 per cent of the population and are responsible for 54.8 per cent of homicides in Canada and 49.8 per cent of all arrests for violent crimes in the US (Santos et al. 2019). In both of these countries class and 'race' are also significant predictors of homicide and other violent crimes with the minority groups from impoverished backgrounds being significantly overrepresented as victims and perpetrators (Ray 2018: 82–6). The data on the occupational backgrounds of individuals who commit homicides in Australia shows that less than 5 per cent of them 'come from occupations at the professional, managerial, or semi-professional levels' (Polk 1994: 2). The global picture is similar with the majority of deaths associated with younger populations with underprivileged backgrounds (Rosser and Ritchie 2019).

The statistical picture that emerges from the abundance of data on homicide and other violent crimes indicates that a typical victim and perpetrator is a young male from a lower socio-economic background and in most societies also likely to be a member of an ethnic minority group. This well-established socio-demographic profile has prompted many criminologists to focus on the socio-economic sources of violent crime.[3] Hence the leading criminological theories of homicide and violence identify either structural or instrumental causes as playing a central role in the development of 'violent careers' of individuals.

The structuralist explanations of violent crime and homicide centre predominantly on economic factors such as inequality and poverty. The starting position of these perspectives is the accumulated cross-national evidence showing that states with high levels of income inequality also have high rates of homicide and other violent crimes. In a recent large-

[2] Some of these countries have an extremely low number of homicides such as Tonga where there was only one victim for this whole period.

[3] There are other influential criminological theories of homicide and violent crime including cultural and sociobiological approaches. I discuss the sociobiological theories in Chapter 1 and cultural approaches in Chapter 3.

scale study on 191 countries Coccia (2017) has tested the hypothesis that the levels of intentional homicide can be explained by income inequality and thermal climate and has found that only socio-economic inequality is a predictor of violent crime: 'the findings here seem in general to support the hypothesis that differences between countries in intentional homicides (per 100,000 people) can be explained by the level of income inequality alone' (Coccia 2017: 190). Similarly, Pratt and Lowenkamp (2002: 61) found strong inverse correlation between homicide rates and economic conditions. In their time series analysis of total homicides, felony murders, and acquaintance homicides they identified strong links between adverse social and economic conditions with all types of homicide: 'although changes in economic conditions significantly predicted levels of both total and acquaintance homicides, the effect was strongest in the model predicting instrumental homicides (felony murders)'.

These and similar findings have given impetus to radical and conflict theories of violent crime. In conflict theory and radical criminology, violent forms of deviant behaviour are interpreted through the prism of deep social inequalities. Drawing on Marxist foundations, the conflict approach sees all forms of crime as a direct consequence of capitalist economic and social relations. Theorists argue that as capitalism is based on the principle of profit maximisation and exploitation of labour it inevitably generates sharp inequalities that may lead some impoverished individuals towards violent crime. Furthermore, the conflict approach identifies existing legal systems as serving the interests of the ruling class, and in doing so, they facilitate the proliferation of inequalities. The established criminal justice systems are focused on punishment and allocation of individual blame while violent crimes are generated structurally – through the reproduction of capitalism. In this view the existing laws are often deployed to criminalise disadvantaged and marginalised populations to preserve the status quo which favours big corporations and others who own the means of production. For example, legal systems severely penalise street crime while ignoring white collar crime (Box 1987). Hence violence is often a direct consequence of material inequalities that underpin the capitalist order (Chambliss 2001; Lea 2002; Taylor 1999).

Utilitarian theories of violence also emphasise economic causes of homicide and other forms of violent crime. However, instead of focusing on the structural variables such as the capitalist system they zoom in on individual motivations. In this interpretation violence is a matter of rational decision making. Criminal acts are understood to be a result of cost-benefit assessments made by individuals. As all human beings are regarded as utility maximisers the expectation is that an individual will engage in a violent criminal act only if he or she can avoid punishment and attain specific benefits. In this view criminal behaviour is based on a perception that the anticipated rewards (e.g., monetary gain, in-group respect, or the thrill of transgressing the law while avoiding punishment) will offset the potential costs of the violent crime (e.g., imprisonment, stigmatisation as a criminal, or potential threat of being injured or killed) (Cornish and Clarke 1986). The most influential utilitarian approach to the study of homicide is the deterrence theory. This approach is centred on the idea that severity and certainty of the punishment is likely to deter individuals from committing a crime. Hence the strict legal provisions for homicide such as near certain life imprisonment or capital punishment would be introduced to discourage individuals from contemplating involvement in violence. This approach identifies two types of deterrence: (a) individual deterrence is centred on the actual offender where severity of the punishment aims to dissuade the offender from committing further crimes; and (b) general deterrence where the focus is on the public knowledge which is communicated as a warning to all that particular behaviours will result in severe punishment thus potentially preventing future violent crimes (Wright 2010).

These economic theories shed some light on the wider causes of homicide and other violent crimes. There is no doubt that deeply asymmetrical access to resources, rampant poverty, and systematic inequalities contribute to the proliferation of social conflicts some of which end in violent behaviour and homicides. As many empirical studies clearly indicate, high levels of socio-economic inequality often go hand in hand with a rise in violent criminality. The deterrence approach also has some merit in the sense that it can identify motivations of some perpetrators of violent crimes and as such this theory possesses a degree of predictive capacity. However, both of these economic approaches to violence also display significant weaknesses. Firstly, these perspectives are grounded in economic determinism which leaves little room for the non-material structural causes and the non-economic motivations of social action. While deep social inequalities generated by capitalism can contribute to violent behaviour most individuals living under capitalist economic relations will not engage in violence. This is evident from all available statistics which show that violent crimes in general and homicide in particular are rare across much of the capitalist world. Furthermore, radical criminology cannot explain properly why some capitalist social orders have very low homicide rates (e.g., Japan and Singapore at 0.60 and much of western Europe around 1.0) while non-capitalist states such as North Korea (4.44), Cuba (4.99), or Laos (7.01) have higher rates of homicide. Similarly, the focus on economy alone cannot explain very high rates in El Salvador (61.80) and Venezuela (56.33), two countries that promote very different economic policies. The same criticism applies to the deterrence and other rational choice models of crime. The states that possess the most severe legal systems with draconian punishments for violent crime do not automatically have the lowest homicide rates. On the contrary some of these states such as Saudi Arabia (1.30), Vietnam (1.52), or Malaysia (2.11) have similar or slightly higher homicide rate compared with countries with the least punitive criminal systems such as Norway (0.50), Sweden (1.10), or Finland (1.20) (DATAUNODC 2020). For example, Norway has one of the most liberal criminal justice systems that focuses on restorative justice and the rehabilitation of prisoners rather than on severity of punishment. Consequently, the country has one of the lowest recidivism rates, lowest number of prisoners, and lowest crime rates in the world (Papendorf 2006). Other countries with the most severe systems of punishment have much higher homicide rates – Central African Republic (19.76), Philippines (8.40), and Eritrea (8.04) (DATAUNODC 2020). Obviously, the economy is not the only cause of these different homicide patterns.

Secondly, economic theories of violence cannot account properly for the historical changes and ongoing fluctuations in the scale of homicide and other violent crimes. Not only do these crimes predate capitalism and continue to exist in non-capitalist social orders, but historical criminologists have documented that in Europe the rise of capitalism did not result in increased homicide rates. On the contrary as Eisner (2003) shows, most forms of interpersonal violence decreased substantially across Europe from the mid-sixteenth to the early twentieth century. For example, the homicide rate in fifteenth-century Italy was around 73 while in the period 1925–49 it was 2.6; fifteenth-century Netherlands and Belgium had a homicide rate of 45 and by the beginning of the twentieth century the rate was only 1.7 (Eisner 2003: 99). This is not to say that capitalism itself was a cause of this decrease but only that the decrease occurred at the same time as capitalism was expanding and becoming fully institutionalised within the economies of many European states. The historical analyses indicate also that the deterrence theory cannot explain these long-term patterns as all European societies have experienced the same trend regardless of the pronounced differences in their criminal justice systems. Moreover, economic approaches cannot account for the periodic fluctuations across time and different regions including the significant rise in violent crime that occurred throughout western Europe from the 1970s to the 1990s (Eisner 2003: 99).

Thirdly, the economic theories of violence tend to overpredict social behaviour and as such do not help us understand complexities and nuances that generate homicides and other forms of violent crime. Since these approaches focus primarily on the economic factors of social change, they tend to overemphasise economics and ignore other sources of social action. In this context they often start from the strong economistic premises, attribute too much explanatory power to economic factors, and often end up with the tautological conclusions that just confirm their original premises. For example, assuming that human beings always act as self-interested individuals or that capitalism causes every social problem in the contemporary world the researcher tends to focus not on discovering the direct causes of violent behaviour but on the question: How I can prove that this violent act is a product of the rational action of self-interested individuals or of the structural disparities generated by the capitalist economic system? This type of analysis inevitably leads to a circular and post hoc form of reasoning. While rational choice analysts 'conceive of their task as demonstrating the fact that social practices which are prima facie irrational are actually rational after all' (Baert 1998: 166) conflict theory and radical criminology are prone to reifying capitalism by conceptualising this historically changing phenomenon as a static and uniform entity.

Finally, and most importantly for this study, economic theories are too wide and too abstract to account for the social dynamics of close-range violence. These are theories of criminal behaviour in general and not of violent action as such. While radical criminology and conflict theory offer structuralist interpretations of violent crime and rational choice and deterrence theories are agency-centred models, neither of these approaches zoom in on the social mechanisms involved in close-range violence. Moreover, they cannot explain enormous variability in the organisational dynamics and the behavioural patterns of violent acts. The economic theories can be useful in identifying relationships between structural inequalities, poverty, scarce resources, and violent criminality but they have no adequate answers for the following questions: Why do the same socio-economic conditions generate different patterns of close-range violence? Why are some individuals willing to fight and die for people that they have never met while others are reluctant to use violence under any conditions? Why is killing very difficult for some human beings and not for others? Why can the same individual mercilessly torture and butcher individuals from the enemy group in one context and then protect the representatives of the same group in other contexts? Why do some smaller groups violently dominate larger groups? To deal with these and other questions about violence it is necessary to go beyond the economic perspectives.

2.4   Beyond *Homines Economici*

Economic perspectives have dominated the study of violence for centuries and have particularly gained influence in the last few decades. Although there are many different and mutually exclusive economic theories of violence, they all interpret violence through the prism of materiality. Whether violence appears in the form of homicide, gang rape, civil war, revolution, or terrorism the economic approaches prioritise economic causes that range from greed and individual self-interest to social grievances generated by unequal structural conditions that underpin capitalist social orders. It is true that some instances of violent behaviour are directly caused by the prospect of economic gain. When a professional assassin kills an influential politician or a business leader, he or she does it for the money. Similarly, many destitute young men have often voluntarily joined armed forces, paramilitary organisations, or gangs and have embarked on violent careers for the specific material benefits they bring – from regular salary, pensions, or educational opportunities, to looting and land acquisition. One might also easily accept the view that the asymmetrical living conditions caused by the capitalist economic system have contributed substantially towards violent careers of some individuals. However, material reasons do not explain the huge gamut of violent situations. More importantly, economic analyses are feeble explanatory devices for understanding the micro-dynamics of close-range violence. To illustrate these explanatory shortcomings one can zoom in on the empirical contexts which have traditionally been identified as the epitome of self-interested violent behaviour – the fighting motivations of soldiers in the second Liberian civil war and the punishment homicides of the Sicilian mafia.

These two historical examples have been chosen precisely because they have regularly been deployed to illustrate the centrality of materialist motivations for close-range violence (Arlacchi 1988; Gambetta 1993, 2009; Hoffman 2011; Käihkö 2017). However, this brief analysis will indicate that even in these two model cases, economics has not been the dominant factor accounting for the dynamics of violence.

2.4.1   *Social Pugnacity in the Liberian Civil War*

The two Liberian civil wars (1989–97 and 1999–2003) resulted in over 700,000 human casualties and the complete destruction of the country (Gerdes 2013). The second Liberian war involved three principal military organisations – Armed Forces of Liberia (AFL) who together with Charles Taylor's praetorian guard Anti-Terrorist Unit (ATU) fought and eventually lost to Liberians United for Reconciliation and Democracy (LURD) and Movement for Democracy in Liberia (MODEL) – all of which relied on financial and military support from the neighbouring countries (i.e., Sierra Leone, Ivory Coast and Guinea). This civil war has often been depicted as particularly vicious as it relied heavily on the use of child induced soldiers, criminals, and drug addicts who were involved in gruesome killings, torture, and rape of civilians. Charles Taylor's AFL and ATU were often singled out for their ruthless violence that was regularly deployed as a tool for personal gain. In this context a number of scholars have described the AFL and ATU as a business enterprise that contracted soldiers to fight and kill for money. Käihkö (2016: 144) argues that Taylor's government combined neo-liberalism with patronage and 'effectively subcontracted his war effort'. Hoffman (2011: 52) insists that all armed groups fighting in the civil wars of Liberia and Sierra Leone were composed of individuals who joined for economic reasons: 'The young men who made up the conflict's irregular fighting factions are in fact the real subcontractors of warfare today … the actual labour of war is more often done by a floating and available pool of unskilled local young men for whom war fighting has become one piece of a just in time mode of political, social, and economic production.' As Käihkö (2016) documents, the leaders of AFL were explicit about the financial inducements and the contractual nature of fighting: 'we talked about running a country and I remember we talked about "Liberia Incorporated", so that it ran more like a business rather than traditional concept of government' (Käihkö 2016: 106). In his interviews with former AFL leaders and ordinary soldiers Käihkö (2016: 148–51) emphasises that the recruitment and fighting had a fixed price tag:

Tamba's narrative offers insights into the realities of militia contracting in Liberia. During his two years of fighting with them in Lofa, Tamba was nominally serving under the Jungle Fire commander Yeaten. Yeaten could send him on missions, and would pay him $160 per attack, with the pay later increasing to $250. The militia attacks could take anywhere from a few hours to four days, giving a steady flow of cash to those willing to take the associated risks. As there could be weeks or at times months between attacks, many contractors like Tamba spent most of their time in resting areas behind the frontlines living a comparatively good life and spending their ostentatious income on women, food, and clothes.

When asked explicitly why he and others risked their lives, Tamba was unambiguous: 'We fought for money … how [do] you fight when you have nothing to eat' (Käihkö 2016: 152–3). Nevertheless, Käihkö (2016: 150–6) recognises that the financial inducement could not be the only reason for fighting and identifies logistics and the patrimonial loyalty to

Taylor (patronage networks) as other important sources of motivation. This research also indicates that the members of different military organisations seem to be motivated by different reasons: while the soldiers of LURD and MODEL regularly described themselves as 'freedom fighters' who brough peace to Liberia after many years of fighting, AFL and ATU soldiers lacked such narrative and tended to downplay ideological motives (Käihkö 2016: 153–4).

However, other studies paint a more complex picture of soldiers' reasoning. Morten Bøås and Anne Hatløy (2008) surveyed 491 ex-combatants who fought in the second Liberian civil war and their research shows that economic reasons were not among the primary motivations for joining the military organisations. In contrast to the dominant interpretations that posit 'greed' or 'grievance' as the key variable in motivation to join, Bøås and Hatløy (2008: 44–5) demonstrate that security concerns played the principal role in determining whether to join or not: 'most of the ex-combatants stated that their main motivation for joining an armed group was for security, either their own security or to keep their families safe'. The interviewees identified a number of reasons for joining the war effort with the two top reasons being 'feel more secure' (46 per cent) and 'keep family safe' (36 per cent). Although two thirds of recruits joined voluntarily, a substantial number of young people had been kidnapped or forced to join the military (32 per cent). Material reasons do appear as a source of motivation, but they are only fifth on the list of the main reasons identified with 21 per cent of respondents listing this as an important source of motivation. In addition, some ex-combatants were motivated by revenge (12 per cent), wanting to fight (10 per cent), or having nothing else to do (10 per cent) (Bøås and Hatløy 2008: 44–45). It is important to emphasise that the large majority of combatants were very young when they joined the military organisations with 64 per cent being less than 26 years old and over 60 per cent were still in school and living with their parents when they decided to join (Bøås and Hatløy 2008: 39–42). However, they were not from a marginalised population consisting of displaced and unemployed urban youths with a criminal background as claimed by the influential economic approaches (e.g., Collier and Hoeffler 2002; Mkandawire 2002). Instead, the majority of the combatants were ordinary young Liberians who suddenly found themselves in an unprecedented situation and had to make difficult decisions. This study indicates clearly that economic factors played a relatively marginal role in decisions to join the fighting: neither instrumental opportunism nor structural causes such as inequality or poverty were pivotal reasons. Instead, the changing social environment influenced individuals' choices where the focus was on protecting oneself and one's family and friends. Other recent studies confirm this line of argument. For example, Højbjerg (2010) emphasises the legacy of previous conflicts and the sense of external threat posed by different military organisations: many individuals joined AFL, LURD, or MODEL fearing that if they do not join their families would experience the same violence that happened in the first Liberian civil war (1989–96). Vastapuu (2018) explores the experiences of female combatants and child induced soldiers and also shows that security concerns played a much more significant role than materialist opportunism. Not only that, many child induced soldiers and women were abducted and forced to fight or serve various fighting forces but even those who joined voluntarily were rarely motivated by economic concerns.

Although much recent research has questioned the established views of the Liberian conflict as quasi-Hobbesian struggles over loot, money, and drugs these studies have not zoomed in on the social mechanisms that underpin the dynamics of close-range fighting. In other words, the existing scholarship tells us a great deal about the conflict in general, the main actors involved, and the legacies of the military and the civilian lives during and after the war and it shows clearly that economic reasoning was not the main driver of conflict. However, these studies do not tell us much about the micro-sociology of violence. From the Liberian example one can see that social pugnacity was generated by a variety of social processes and has in turn produced diverse responses.

2.4.2 The Italian Mafia and Close-Range Violence

The Sicilian mafia (Cosa Nostra) has been synonymous with unscrupulous violence since the nineteenth century. This organised crime syndicate is typically composed of several clans ('family') each of which controls its own territory. Its key activities such as protection racketeering, smuggling and trade of illicit goods and services, as well as the arbitration of disputes all rely on the use of excessive violence (Blok 1974; Gambetta 1993; Schneider and Schneider 2011; Varese 2011). The violence of the mafia has also traditionally been interpreted through economic categories: as a form of opportunistic materialism, as a consequence of deep inequalities, or through the economic functions organised crime provides in the absence of an effective state (Gambetta 1993; Schulte-Bockholt 2001). Hence neo-Marxist accounts see organised crime syndicates such as the Sicilian mafia as a direct result of structural inequalities produced by capitalism. The emphasis is often on the regional disparities between the wealthy north and the impoverished south of Italy and how the mafia operates 'as a normal facet of capitalism, no more outside its political economy than the other capitalisms to which we add such qualifiers as "merchant," "industrial," "finance," "proto," or "crony"' (Schneider and Schneider 2011: 3). The rational choice account focuses less on the structural inequalities of the capitalist system and more on the necessary services that the mafia provides to self-interested individuals. For Buchanan (1980: 132) organised crime can also be a tool for crime reduction: 'it is not from the public-spiritedness of the leader of the Cosa Nostra that we should expect to get a reduction in the crime rate, but from their regard for their own self-interest'. Varese (2011: 6) argues that mafias engage in 'extortion – the forced extraction of resources in exchange for services not provided'. Gambetta (1993: 1) defines the Sicilian mafia as 'a specific economic enterprise, an industry which produces, promotes, and sells private protection'. This cartel of semi-independent businesses ('families') addresses economic and security concerns of individuals living in a social environment lacking a stable state structure. In this context the mafia relies on the threat of violence to protect willing customers against potential theft, blackmail, or cheating by other traders. In Gambetta's interpretation the Sicilian mafia replaces the state as it can enforce contracts between traders. The mafia persists because it performs a necessary economic role: this organisation successfully privatises trust and, in this way, allows individuals to engage in economic transactions.

All these economic perspectives see violence as an instrument of control underpinned by egoistic behaviour. Mafiosi use excessive violence to establish and enforce protection racquets, to punish those who do not pay debts or follow their commands, or to send a threatening message to potential competitors, defectors, or spies. The gruesomeness of violence is intended to invoke fear and, in this way, prevent any challenge to this crime syndicate. In this context the Sicilian mafia has been involved in numerous assassinations including those of influential public figures and potential crime witnesses. For example, Cosa Nostra has killed 231 prominent individuals: 122 law enforcement agents, 45 politicians, 34 trade unionists, 14 magistrates, 8 journalists, 5 priests, and 3 other officials (Catino 2014: 208). The economic theories of organised crime rarely focus on the micro-social dynamics of violence and when they deal sporadically with this topic the tendency is to see mafia organisations as deploying very similar strategies of violent action. For example, both Varese (2011) and Gambetta (1993) see violence as a strategic choice that has no autonomy of its own. As Gambetta (1993: 2) puts it bluntly: 'violence is a means not an end; a resource, not the final product. The commodity that is really at stake is protection ... protection

[is] ... a lubricant of economic exchange ... The market is therefore rational in the sense that there are people who find it in their individual interest to buy mafia protection.' Similarly, the neo-Marxist and other structuralist theories of organised crime see violence as a by-product of capitalism where the 'mafia ... [is] integral to capitalist development, even if its "trademarked" means of production, the capacity of its members to exercise physical violence, contrasts with capitalists' general tendency to cede this capacity to the state' (Schneider and Schneider 2011: 16). Here too violence has no autonomy; it is only a consequence of structural developments. Moreover, these economic perspectives assume that the organised criminal syndicates engage in similar forms of violent action and are prone to almost identical types of violent behaviour.

Nevertheless, several recent sociological studies of the Sicilian mafia indicate that there is a pronounced variability in the deployment of violence between different criminal syndicates and even within the same mafia organisations over different time periods. These studies also show that economic factors are often not the main driver of violent behaviour. Thus, in his comparative historical analysis Catino (2014) shows how different organisational structures of criminal syndicates influence different dynamics and scale of violence. He dissects contrasting experiences of three main mafias: the Cosa Nostra (the Sicilian mafia), the Camorra (the Campanian mafia), and the 'Ndrangheta (the Calabrian mafia). His study indicates that the more centralised organisational structure produces mafias that engage in more violence at the top level of society and less violence at the bottom of the social pyramid whereas the less centralised organisations are characterised by the opposite trends in violence. In other words, the vertically shaped criminal syndicates such as Cosa Nostra and Camora have been responsible for more killings of state representatives and other influential notables while simultaneously controlling violence against ordinary individuals. In contrast, more diffuse organisations such as the Calabrian mafia tend to deploy less violence against state officials and engage aggressively against the ordinary population. Furthermore, while the vertical organisational structure is conducive to better control of conflicts within one territory and more targeted assassinations against the state representatives the horizontally organised syndicates lack capacity to fully police their territories and to confront the state authorities. As Catino (2014: 209) shows, the scale and type of violence also changes over time and as the Sicilian mafia gradually transformed over the years from a loose networks of 'families' into an effective centralised coercive organisation it increased the number of attacks against the state: 'In the 10 years before the creation of the

Cupola (1965–1975), the Cosa Nostra killed "only" 9 prominent individuals, while in the following 10 years (1976–1986) the death toll of high-profile victims reached 58, almost a 600% increase' (Catino 2014: 209). If the longer timespan is considered, the difference is even more striking: from 1957 to 1975 'when the Cosa Nostra had a provincial structure of coordination, the overall number of high-profile killings reached 24, with only one judge among the victims. In the 18 years after 1975, however, there were 87 high-profile assassinations, including 13 judges' (Catino 2014: 209). Hence the organisational structure shapes the character and scale of violence.

Varese (2011) has also questioned the idea that the mafia's violence is uniform and something that can be reduced to being only a means to an economic end. Instead, his comparative analysis of criminal syndicates in Italy, Russia, the USA, and China demonstrates clearly that most mafias operate more as political rather than economic organisations. Unlike Gambetta (1993) who sees criminal syndicates as business enterprises that sell protection, Varese portrays mafias as state-like entities with leaders that resemble politicians rather than entrepreneurs. One of the defining features of mafia organisations is their territoriality and as such their primary focus is on controlling and possibly expanding their existing territories. In contrast to business executives who are mostly extraterritorial and as such eager to maximise their profit, mafia bosses only move when they are forced to do so – under the direct pressure from the state or competing, stronger, mafias. The mafia organisations operate as political fiefdoms where mafia leaders build networks of loyalty through the threat of violence, control of information, and periodic transgressive events (e.g., public feasts, protection). In addition, all successful crime syndicates depend on the strength of their violent reputations. As Varese (2011: 14) points out: 'Reputation is a critical asset for mafiosi to carry out their jobs. The greater one's reputation for the ability to wield violence, the lesser one's need to resort to violence, since victims comply more readily.' The reputation is usually built through the information spread by those who have witnessed the cruelty of mafia violence. To maintain or enhance their violent reputations they rely on continuous inter-communal narratives, gossip, and rumours. Hence the mafias cannot move easily from one region or country to another as their reputations are grounded in the communities they control. In this context the social dynamics of violence is also shaped by territorial groundedness. While the settled and established crime syndicates such as Cosa Nostra in Sicily or Yakuza in Japan do not often have to engage in violent behaviour, the new or more mobile mafias such as the Solntsevskaya Bratva or the Albanian mafia in the US have to undertake more acts of violence and have to be more brutal to maintain or enhance their reputation.

Both of these examples indicate that the economic theories of close-range violence have a limited explanatory power. Although the second Liberian civil war and Sicilian mafia are regularly identified as the prototypes of violent behaviour caused either by self-interested opportunism or deep structural inequalities, a careful analysis shows that economic motivations do not play a central role even in these two cases. The two examples also reveal that violent pathways of individuals, groups, and social organisations are highly variable and multiple. The scale, intensity, and direction of violence are rarely shaped by narrow, uniform, and transhistorical instrumental goals and much more by the changing social and historical contexts. Although economic motivations matter, social pugnacity is shaped by a variety of social processes including the extent of organisational capacity, ideological penetration, and the envelopment of micro-solidarity.

2.5   Conclusion

The economic theories of violence have dominated much of social science in the past four decades. Although these approaches differ substantially with some focusing more on the motivations of individuals and others on the socio-economic structures that generate violent outcomes, all economic theories emphasise the materialist causes of violence. In this understanding violent acts happen because somebody can benefit from their use. Violence is conceptualised either as a second-order reality that can be deployed as a strategic tool or as a direct outcome of structural inequalities.[4] In this view violent action has no autonomy and cannot transpire from non-intentional, non-rational, or non-structural sources. These approaches have contributed to better understanding of violent acts which have traditionally been wrongly associated with collective irrationalities and individual pathologies. However, human beings are not only *homines economici* and as such many instances of violence have distinctly non-economic sources. While economic reasons can and do contribute to motivations and social contexts for violence, they are for the most part insufficient to generate and maintain protracted violent

---

[4] Lyall (2020) has recently developed an alternative and highly promising approach that focuses on the structural inequalities within military organisations. He argues that the degree of inequality within armed forces determines their fighting capacity. Hence more unequal military organisations experience more desertion, more casualties, and even more side-switching.

behaviour. Moreover, the economic theories offer little in a way of tracing the specific social mechanisms that underpin close-range violence. As they overemphasise the uniformity of human preferences and universality of material motivations they cannot properly account for the variability and malleability of violence in macro, meso, and micro contexts. To capture better the social processes that shape violent action it is crucial to go beyond economic determinism. In other words, economic factors can and do matter but mostly as a part of the larger contexts that include emotional reactions, ethical imperatives, organisational demands, ideological doctrines, and small group dynamics, among others.

3 Clashing Beliefs
The Ideological Fighters

3.1 Introduction

Acts of interpersonal violence have often been attributed to strong and uncompromising belief systems, religious fanaticism, or ideological rigidity. The mass media and more recently the social media often interpret acts of deliberate injuring or killing of another human being, previously unknown to the assailant, through the prism of specific beliefs, doctrinal creeds, and durable cultural identities. For example, from the nineteenth century to contemporary times a variety of secular and religious ideologies have been blamed for various acts of violence – anarchism, socialism, communism, fascism, Nazism, anarcho-primitivism, ethnic nationalism, Islamic fundamentalism, racism, Christian fundamentalism, neo-Luddism, Hindu fundamentalism, radical environmentalism, Jewish fundamentalism, Maoism, Trotskyism, white nationalism, and so on. The focus has regularly been on imputing causal links between a person's values and their acts of violence. Similarly, many wars, revolutions, genocides, and insurgencies have also been described as conflicts that were generated and sustained by incompatible belief systems. Thus, one often hears that competing nationalisms produced war, that different religions have caused a communal conflict and sectarian violence, that anti-monarchism and republicanism were behind specific revolutions, or that racism leads to genocide. In this chapter I explore the role religious and secular ideologies play in the individual and collective motivations for violence. The chapter critically addresses existing scholarship on the role of ideas, norms, and values in violent behaviour and articulates an alternative view of ideological power. I argue that the ongoing process of ideologisation rather than the fixed ideological doctrines shape the historical dynamics of violence. In this context ideological penetration helps justify violent acts and also mobilises a wider support base for violent action. Nevertheless, since human beings are complex and reflective creatures, ideological power alone is not enough to initiate and maintain social fighting. Instead, social pugnacity is regularly premised on the effective interaction of coercive bureaucratisation, ideo-logisation, and their envelopment in networks of micro-solidarity. The first part of the chapter offers a critical analysis of the existing approaches that emphasise the centrality of ideology for violence while the second part articulates an alternative interpretation of ideological power. The key theoretical points are illustrated with selected empirical case studies.

3.2   Religious and Secular Ideologies

On 22 May 2013, Lee Rigby, a British soldier, was hacked to death with a cleaver by two men near the Royal Artillery Barracks in Woolwich, southeast London. The attackers, two converts to Islam Michael Adebolajo and Michael Adebowale, also attempted to behead Rigby and once he was killed, they proclaimed:

The only reason we have killed this man today is because Muslims are dying daily by British soldiers. And this British soldier is one ... By Allah, we swear by the almighty Allah we will never stop fighting you until you leave us alone. So, what if we want to live by the Sharia in Muslim lands? Why does that mean you must follow us and chase us and call us extremists and kill us? When you drop a bomb do you think it hits one person? Or rather your bomb wipes out a whole family? ... Through many passages in the Koran we must fight them as they fight us. (*The Telegraph*, 8 June 2013)

The two men were arrested, brought to trial, and imprisoned for life. During their trial the judge, Mr Justice Sweeney, described their actions as 'the betrayal of Islam' to which the two attackers responded with: 'That's a lie' and 'Allahu Akbar' (*BBC*, 26 February 2014). This case resembles many recent episodes of terrorist violence where the perpetra-tors, the mass media that report these cases, and most of the audience that follow these events share the understanding that these violent acts were committed solely for ideological reasons. The phrases often used to describe these acts of violence imply the centrality of ideology – Islamic terrorism, militant Islamism, political Islam, Islamic extremism, and so on. In their justification of violence the perpetrators were explicit that they were avenging the death of Muslims 'by British soldiers' and that 'many passages in the Koran [say] we must fight them as they fight us'. Even when these acts are condemned as the betrayal of Islamic teachings, as Justice Sweeney has done in his verdict, there is near universal agree-ment that this violence was caused by specific interpretation or misinter-pretation of religious beliefs.

Even though the terrorists and the anti-terrorist organisations have mutually exclusive views about what these violent acts represent they mostly agree that religious identification plays a central role in the motivation for violence. In the variety of documents published by ISIS, Al-Qaeda, and Boko Haram religion features prominently as a motive for violent retribution. These and other violent organisations invoke selected verses from the Qur'an and Haditha to justify their use of violence against military targets and civilians. For example, the verse Al-Anfāl: 60 is often cited to legitimise violence against the enemies of Islam: 'Prepare against them whatever arms and cavalry you can muster, that you may strike terror in (the hearts of) the enemies of God and your own, and others besides them not known to you, but known to God. Whatever you spend in the way of God will be paid back to you in full, and no wrong will be done to you' (The Qur'an 2008). Another verse that features prominently in these documents and was also invoked by Rigby's killers is Surah 9:5: 'But when these months, prohibited (for fighting), are over, slay the idolaters wheresoever you find them, and take them captive or besiege them, and lie in wait for them at every likely place' (The Qur'an 2008). Holbrook (2010) has analysed a sample of thirty key texts used by the leading terrorist organisations and has found that the following Qur'anic verses appear most frequently in the jihadi literature: An-Nisa (4:74–5), At-Taubah (9:13–15, 38–9, 111), and Al-Baqarah (2:190–1, 216).

The anti-terrorist organisations and politicians who lead the struggle against ISIS, Al-Qaeda, and Boko Haram also emphasise the centrality of religious messages. For example, former US and UK leaders Barack Obama and David Cameron often referred to ISIS and Al-Qaeda as 'death cults' that have been led by 'twisted ideology'. In one of his speeches Obama stated the following: 'We cannot turn against one another by letting this fight be defined as a war between America and Islam. That, too, is what groups like ISIL want', using an acronym for the Islamic State terrorist group. 'ISIL does not speak for Islam,' he said. 'They are thugs and killers, part of a cult of death' (Baily 2015). Similarly, in the wake of the 2015 Paris terrorist attacks Cameron proclaimed that 'The United Kingdom will do all in our power to support our friend and ally France to defeat this evil death cult' and 'This evil death cult is neither a true representation of Islam nor is it a state' (*BBC*, 2 December 2015).

With the dramatic rise of this type of violence over the past two decades many social scientists have also identified ideological factors and especially religious identification as being the principal cause of violent behaviour. Some scholars draw on René Girard's theory of sacrifice and scapegoating aiming to show that religion and violence are inherently linked (Avery 2016). Girard (2005 [1972]) argues that religious institutions deploy violent acts to prevent the explosion of uncontrolled violence. The main function of human or animal sacrifice in religious rites is to stifle inter-communal violence: by concentrating violence within a single sacrificial object or a scapegoat the society contains potential violent reprisals that would arise from the competing desires of individuals. Others such as Juergensmeyer (2000), Stern (2003), and Stark and Corcoran (2014) have identified strong religious attachments as one of the key drivers of violent conflicts. They all focus on the cultural sources of violence and single out collective perceptions of humiliation and degradation as fuelling bellicose behaviour. Juergensmeyer (2000: 6) states that 'Although some observers try to explain away religion's recent ties to violence as an aberration ... these are not my views. Rather I look for explanations in the current forces of geopolitics and in a strain of violence that may be found at the deepest level of religious imagination.' In his view the acts of militant Islamist terror, just like other religiously inspired acts of violence, represent a form of performance for the global audience that helps empower the perpetrators. In this way the terrorist acts also address their constituents by presenting their acts as a retaliation for a long history of shared communal humiliation. Stern (2003) also emphasises the sense of humiliation that is framed in religious discourse as an important driver of violence. She sees religious terrorism as a form of cultural struggle that on the one hand bolsters the co-religionists and on the other hand generates a 'spiritual dread' in outsiders. Stern (2003: 22) also argues that 'religious terrorist groups are more violent than their secular counterparts and are probably more likely to use weapons of mass destruction'. Corcoran and Stark (2014) also single out religious beliefs as contributing to violent behaviour. In their understanding the monotheistic belief systems are more prone to confrontation as religious particularism promulgates an idea that there is a single truth and only one true religion. This attitude is less conducive to religious tolerance and can foster violent conflicts. In their survey of 'religious hostility', for 2012 alone they identified '810 incidents of religiously motivated homicides, in which 5,026 people died: 3,774 Muslims, 1,045 Christians, 110 Buddhists, 23 Jews, 21 Hindus, and 53 secular individuals' (Stark and Corcoran 2014: 27).

Secular ideologies have also been identified as a cause of antagonistic behaviour including close-range violence. For example, far-right ideologies were explicit in their glorification of violence and state power. For example, Mussolini (2005 [1932]: 230) often referred to the centrality of violence in the fascist movement: 'War alone brings up to their highest tension all human energies and imposes the stamp of nobility upon the peoples who have the courage to make it'; 'It is better to live one day as a lion than 100 years as a sheep.' Since the Nazi ideology also incorporated social Darwinist principles, violence was regularly justified in reference to the laws of nature. In *Mein Kampf* (2021 [1925]: 161) Hitler is clear about this:

The stronger must dominate and not mate with the weaker, which would signify the sacrifice of its own higher nature. Only the born weakling can look upon this principle as cruel, and if he does so it is merely because he is of a feebler nature and narrower mind; for if such a law did not direct the process of evolution, then the higher development of organic life would not be conceivable at all.

In this context he understood violence to be the essence of politics: 'The very first essential for success is a perpetually constant and regular employment of violence.'

These abstract ideological principles were also operationalised in practice as Nazis and fascists used violent means to enact their dystopian projects – from the onset of the Second World to the Holocaust and mass exterminations of all humans they considered to be undesirable in a Nazi state. These ideological vistas have also played an important role in face-to-face violence. As Bartov (1992) argues, Wehrmacht soldiers were imbued with these ideas and saw themselves as a master race fighting for its survival and protection of European civilisation against Judeo-Bolshevik barbarians. His analysis of diaries, letters, and military reports produced by the ordinary soldiers indicates that many fought for the Führer and Nazi ideology:

The most striking aspect of the soldiers' letters is the remarkable similarity between their terminology, modes of expression, and arguments and those which characterize the Wehrmacht's propaganda ... they perceived reality at the front just as he [Hitler] did in the safety of his bunker, sharing his fantasies of conquest and grandeur, or racial genocide and Germanic world rule. (Bartov 1992: 147–8)

Thus, in their diaries and letters soldiers often refer to fighting for a new world and better future while expressing willingness 'to sacrifice ourselves to a world-order which is not our own' in order 'to render a fraction of our thanks for the liberation of our beautiful homeland by our magnificent Führer Adolf Hitler' (Bartov 1992: 148–9).

Racist ideology has also inspired and justified both colonial violence abroad and the severe mistreatment of minority groups at home. Many scholars have emphasised the dehumanising portrayals of the Other as a precondition for mass extermination: 'The opponents in intercultural warfare ... often think themselves engaged in warfare with non-humans, variously conceived of as savage sub-human barbarians or being capable of superhuman feats – indeed sometimes at the same time' (Morillo 2006: 34). Racism offered rationalisation for the use of violence against the non-human Other – 'by dehumanising all adversaries … they can be killed, mutilated, and otherwise mistreated with clear conscience. Evidence of subhuman traits and racial inferiority, as well as alleged atrocities and supposedly implacable malice, all play part in this process' (Parker 2002: 56).

Other secular ideologies, from nationalism, anarchism, and socialism to animal rights have also been identified as motivating violent behaviour. For example, the spate of assassinations and dynamite bombings targeting political leaders and government officials in late nineteenth-century Europe and America was linked with the spread of anarchist movements and their advocacy of propaganda of the deed (the use of spectacular acts of violence to inspire mass revolution; Wilson 2020). Socialist and communist ideas have also inspired belligerence including wars, terrorism, insurgency, genocide, and revolutions – the 1917 Russian Revolution, the Cambodian genocide of the Khmer Rouge (1975–9), the insurgency of the New People's Army in the Philippines, the FARC guerrilla war in Columbia, and the Brigate Rosse (Red Brigades) in Italy among many others. Even the animal rights and environmentalism movements have generated violent responses with the Animal Liberation Front pursuing violent attacks on scientists involved in animal experiments and the destruction of laboratories that use animals.

However, the most influential secular ideology associated with violence has been nationalism. Nationalist ideologies have traditionally been linked to aggressive secessionism, terrorism, violent national unifications, and the creation of new states through violence. Nationalism has regularly been identified as a principal cause of wars and revolutions. Nationalist ideologies have also been associated with the persecution of minority groups and involved projects of ethnic cleansing and genocide. Hence many scholars have traditionally blamed nationalism for instigating a variety of wars and revolutions: 'European nationalism was a major force in the origins of both world wars' (Snyder 1968: 71); national unity 'is always effected by means of brutality' (Renan 2018: 11); 'the French revolutionaries bequeathed to the world, in essence, a radical formulation of the civic nationalist tradition' (Gerstle 2017: 148). More recently Wimmer (2012: 115) has attempted to show that 'the diffusion of nationalism and the nation-state themselves cause wars'. Wimmer and his collaborators have developed an extensive dataset of 464 wars fought since the early nineteenth century and have analysed the relationship between state formation and violence. In these studies, they show how nationalist mobilisation impacted on the collapse of imperial structures and how nationalism generated violence (Hiers and Wimmer 2013; Wimmer 2012). In the words of Hiers and Wimmer (2013: 212–13): 'we find that in all cases of imperial collapse nationalist movements played an important, and sometimes, crucial role ... we conclude that the rise and global proliferation of nationalist movements has been a crucial factor in reshaping the structure of the state system over the past two hundred years.' Several influential studies have linked nationalist ideologies to genocide. For example, Rummel (1997: 196) argues that the Armenian genocide was caused by the 'obsessive and deadly nationalism of the Young Turks before and during the First World War' while Melson (2003: 326) insists that 'in the Arminian genocide, the Holocaust, and Cambodian genocide, ideologies of nationalism, Nazi racism, and Maoism were crucial motivations of leaders and some cadres in the execution of genocide'.

There is no doubt that ideologies play an important role in mobilisation for violence and in the justification of violent behaviour. Since human beings are not emotionless automatons or solely interest-driven creatures they regularly engage in self-vindication and rationalisation of their own violent actions or of those they support. As meaning-oriented beings, humans usually generate, disseminate, and rely upon specific narratives that account for the acts of violence. Since most social orders proscribe or tightly regulate pugnacious behaviour the acts of violence require an explanation, or justification. This is particularly the case with close-range human-on-human violence when two bodies directly confront each other, or several bodies inflict damage on, or destruction of, another body. In this context the use of violence may also entail self-explanation and self-justification. When these acts of violence involve large numbers of individuals they usually rely on specific ideological narratives. As killing another human being often goes against the well-established normative codes that underpin most social orders these violent activities regularly require coherent ideological legitimation. Hence the killers of Lee Rigby instantly provided justification for his murder. They described it as an avenging act because he was a member of the organisation that is directly responsible for deaths of Muslims in Iraq and Afghanistan. They also emphasised that the religious doctrine they follow teaches them to act accordingly (i.e., Surah 9:5 'slay the idolaters'). On the surface this interpretation of cause and effect seems straightforward, and it usually is accepted as such by many. However, simple justification is not an explanation. The statements of perpetrators can never be taken at face value. To fully understand the individual motivations for violence it is necessary to go beyond what they say about their acts and to explore the wider social context of violence. While ideology is important to violent behaviour, neither religious nor secular ideologies operate as simple drivers of social pugnacity.

Firstly, the ideological interpretations of violence tend to reduce complex social processes to predetermined sets of inflexible and decontextualized beliefs. If ideology is the main driver of violence, then one would expect that many individuals who are exposed to the same doctrinal teachings would automatically behave in a similar way and would also act violently. Hence if Islamic teachings advocate that idolaters should be slayed then all true believers would follow this advice. However, this has not been the case and only a very small number of Muslims have embraced violent action. The same logic applies to the variety of secular ideologies – while socialism, conservatism, environmentalism, or anarchism have hundreds of millions of supporters throughout the world only tiny numbers of individuals have invoked these ideological principles as a motivator for their violent acts. Ideologies do not kill by themselves.

Both religious and secular ideologies have attracted huge numbers of followers precisely because they are malleable and allow individuals to interpret the same ideas differently. Hence the scriptural and foundational texts used to justify a particular course of action are open to different and often mutually exclusive interpretations. For example, Sura 9:5 that many jihadists invoke to legitimise their attacks on non-Muslims is regularly taken out of context, truncated, and even distorted. As Holbrook (2010) shows in his analysis of Qur'anic verses used by ISIS, Al-Qaeda, Boko Haram, and other extremist organisations Sura 9:5 is rarely quoted in full. The second part of this sura states clearly that violence is not inevitable: 'if they repent and fulfil their devotional obligations and pay the zakat, then let them go their way, for God is forgiving and kind' (The Qur'an 2008). The same contentious interpretation is visible in many secular ideologies where the key ideas found in the foundational texts have been interpreted in very different ways. For instance, in *The Communist Manifesto* (2005 [1848]: 89) Marx and Engels state that proletariat can win 'only by the forcible overthrow of all existing social conditions'. Some could interpret this statement as a call for violence while others would see it as a metaphor for change. Hence this text has served as an ideological springboard for radical revolutionary groups who argue that revolutionary violence is inevitable to abolish capitalist class exploitation but also for social democrats who have advocated reform and the evolutionary transformation of capitalism. Neither the foundational texts nor the ideological beliefs are fixed and static. They are constantly reinterpreted, and they evolve and transform in response to changing social and historical contexts.

Secondly, the view that ideologies determine individual and collective behaviour is a form of epistemological and ontological idealism that leaves no room for the political, economic, military, and other sources of action. Epistemological idealism is an analytical position which identifies knowledge with the structure of human thought (the knowledge only exists in one's mind) while ontological idealism represents the view that 'delivers truth because reality itself is a form of thought and human thought participates in it' (Guyer and Horstmann 2019: 1). In other words, it is the values and ideas that are perceived as being the primary drivers of individual and social action while material and political factors are attributed a secondary role. In this understanding human beings are viewed as norm-driven creatures who primarily act on their beliefs. However, human beings are much more than carriers of dominant values. This functionalist understanding is insensitive to individual differences as it does not recognise the will of individuals. Although shared values can influence behaviour, human beings are not marionettes that just automatically follow the norms of their groups. Instead, all organisations involved in violent activities experience internal tensions and disagreements some of which can lead to fierce ideological and political disagreement and splits. For example, in the early 1970s many Irish nationalists in Northern Ireland shared similar ideological views that advocated unification of the island of Ireland as a single sovereign nation-state. However, they profoundly differed on the questions of tactics, strategy, and the long-term planning of how to achieve this goal. While some advocated the use of violence, others opposed this strategy (i.e., IRA vs. the constitutional nationalist organisations such as SDLP). Furthermore, even among those who advocated the use of violence against British armed forces there was a pronounced difference on tactics and political goals which resulted in numerous political splits and formation of different militant organisations (PIRA, OIRA, real IRA, Continuity IRA, new IRA, Óglaigh na hÉireann, INLA, IPLO, etc.) (English 2003). Functionalist approaches are too static and too norm-centred to account for complexity and the changing character of social and individual action. As such they cannot explain the dynamics of social pugnacity.

Finally, the overemphasis on the fixed ideological doctrines as the key drivers of violence cannot help us explain the origins and the long-term dynamics of violent behaviour. Specific belief systems, ideological doctrines, and normative cultural creeds have been present for hundreds, or in some instances for thousands, of years and it is only in some historical periods that they have been invoked to justify violent action. The explanations that focus only on the contents of religious texts or manifestos that express the key principles of secular ideologies cannot elucidate much on the timing and the trajectories of violent behaviour. For example, the Bible and many other religious texts including the Torah and the Qur'an contain passages which invoke divinely sanctioned violence. Such passages could and have been historically used to legitimise violent acts. However, for much of history an overwhelming majority of individuals did not invoke these and similar passages to incite or conduct violent behaviour. Hence the specific timing matters. To understand how, when, and why such texts are used it is crucial to focus on the historical context. The twelfth-century crusading knights often referred to the religious texts to validate their war plans in the Middle East just as Soviet authorities have invoked Marxist ideas to crush their political opponents. As Ryan (2015) documents, during the Russian civil war (1917–22) Marxist principles were deployed by Bolsheviks to justify killings of the Whites. The government-controlled newspaper *Pravda* was explicit about this: 'White Guard organizations, conspiracies, or uprisings' will be shot, 'the class murderer, the bourgeoisie, must be crushed' (Ryan 2015: 811). In all of these cases and many others it was the political, economic, and other reasons that fostered the move towards violence and ideological norms have only been invoked when required to widen the popular mobilisation or to provide a justification for violent acts. It is not that ideological texts are the prime motivators of action, but they have proved useful in making sense of violence. This is not to deny the importance of ideological power. Ideology is not just a fig leaf for economic and political interests. Meanings and beliefs do matter to many individuals and they can motivate violent action. Nevertheless, violence is rarely the sole product of specific normative discourses. Smith (2005: 36) and other neo-Durkheimians who argue that 'social life can be treated like a text' are profoundly wrong. The fixed religious and secular texts cannot explain the enormous historical variation in human behaviour. Moreover, they are feeble in accounting for processes that make social pugnacity possible.

3.3   Ideological Penetration

It is clear that ideological power plays an important role in the popular mobilisation for violence and even more in the legitimisation of violent acts. However, it is less clear how exactly ideologies operate in the context of violent action. To better understand this process, it is necessary to move away from the conventional interpretations that centre on fixed doctrinal principles, offer functionalist and idealist explanations, or ignore the changing historical dynamics of ideological power. The ideological principles are rarely if ever the only driver of violent action. Instead, ideological power usually tends to align with other social factors to generate sustained violent behaviour.

As I have argued before, the focus should shift from ideology as a set of established and predetermined precepts towards ideologisation as a dynamic, ongoing, and relational historical process that shapes human violent action (Malešević 2017, 2019). Human beings have devised a variety of social mechanisms for justification of violence and have deployed them with more or less success throughout history. Nevertheless, ideologisation has historically expanded in influence with the development of organisational capacity. It is through the rise of state apparatuses, proliferation of private corporations, expansion of religious institutions and many other forms of organised power that ideologisation started deeply penetrating everyday life including the private sphere of ordinary individuals. The invention of printing, the development of compulsory education, the ever-increasing literacy rates, the proliferation of mass media, the emergence of civil society and the development of the public sphere are just some of the more significant processes that have stimulated the influx of ideologisation in ordinary life (Malešević 2017).

The spread of radical political movements associated with the American, French, Haitian, and the South American revolutions and the Napoleonic Wars have all ultimately changed the character of traditional social orders. They opened the space for democratisation of the public sphere and indirectly have also contributed towards further ideologisation of populations. The decline of religious authority and the Church's loss of monopoly on the interpretation of social reality has galvanised the emergence and propagation of diverse religious and secular ideologies including different strands of liberalism, socialism, conservatism, republicanism, and many other isms. These competing and often mutually exclusive interpretative horizons have all been associated with specific social organisations and movements that were competing for the allegiances of now ever more politicised and ideologised populations (Malešević 2002). This process was never haphazard but was shaped by rival organisational interests and ambitions. The variety of social organisations including the state, religious institutions, political parties, social movements, economic and professional associations, secret societies, revolutionary groups, and many other entities have articulated distinct blueprints for a better world and have devised different strategies for attracting new followers. In this sense ideologisation is a centrifugal phenomenon – its central doctrinal principles are formulated, developed, and disseminated from specific social organisations towards the wider public. Furthermore, this process thrives on conflicts with alternative ideological vistas. Not only do different social organisations aim to show that their ideological precepts are morally and epistemologically superior to those offered by organisations that espouse radically different ideas, but they also claim superiority vis-à-vis similar ideological discourses. For example, the early twentieth-century communist movements have fought intensely against fascism, but they have also invested enormous energies to combat ideologies that were much closer to them such as social democracy. Lenin (1919) was explicit about this in his description of social democrats as 'traitors to socialism': 'They represent that top section of workers who have been bribed by the bourgeoisie ... for in all the civilised, advanced countries the bourgeoisie rob—either by colonial oppression or by financially extracting "gain" from formally independent weak countries—they rob a population many times larger than that of "their own" country.' Thus, the social organisations develop ideological narratives aiming not only to mobilise mass support or legitimise particular social action but also to delegitimise competing ideological vistas.

In this context different ideological creeds have been associated with diverse modes of justification for violence. Some, mostly religious, ideologies have remained loyal to the traditional concepts of violence where killing of another human being was deemed to be a grave sin and was allowed only in specific contexts (e.g., legitimate defence as in the just war theory). The guiding principles here were derived from religious scriptures. For example, Christian democrats and other religious conservatives have been guided by biblical ideas such as the Ten Commandments – 'Thou shalt not kill' – and the New Testament – 'Put up again thy sword into his place: for all they that take the sword shall perish with the sword' (Matthew 26:52–3) and 'let him who is without sin cast the first stone' (John 8:7). In a similar vein Islamic conservatism is rooted in the Qur'anic postulates that value peace and discourage violence. A number of verses in the Qur'an emphasise the centrality of peaceful relationships including the notion of Dar es Salaam, a house of peace as an ideal society (The Qur'an 2008: 10:25) and the idea that God abhors any disturbance of peace (2:205).

However, some religious movements reformulated traditional Christian and Islamic teachings by further emphasising the sinful nature of violence. Hence Calvinists, Huguenots, and Jansenists among others all identified violence and killing as particularly sinful acts. For Calvinists, killing was not only linked with taking life but also with any harm inflicted on a fellow human being: 'To be clear of the crime of murder, it is not enough to refrain from shedding man's blood. If in act you perpetrate, if in endeavour you plot, if in wish and design you conceive what is adverse to another's safety, you have the guilt of murder' (Calvin 2016: 178). The peaceful Islamic movement Servants of God (Khudai Khidmatgar) which developed in Raj India in the early and mid-twentieth century advocated non-violent resistance and modelled their actions on the life experience of prophet Muhammad. The leader of the movement Abdul Ghaffar Khan would regularly invoke this example: 'The Holy Prophet Mohammed came into this world and taught us "That man is a Muslim who never hurts anyone by word or deed, but who works for the benefit and happiness of God's creatures." Belief in God is to love one's fellow men' (Stephen 2009: 12).

In contrast other, mostly secular, ideological projects have articulated new understandings of violence. Thus, many French republicans were adamant that the ends justify the means and that the use of violence was necessary to overthrow the ancien régime and to fight the external forces threatening the existence of a new and just society. This view was shared by republicans with different ideological creeds – Girondists, Montagnards, and Jacobins. Despite their doctrinal disagreements they all supported the idea that violence is a necessary part of the revolutionary experience. Hence Girondins such as Jacques Pierre Brissot argued that war with Austria and other enemies of the revolution was needed to keep the revolution alive: 'war is necessary to France for her honour ... war is a national benefit ... [the war is] a crusade for universal liberty' (Brissot 2007 [1791]: 26). In a very similar vein Robespierre justified the imprisoning and guillotining of 'internal enemies of the revolution'. In many of his speeches he pointed to secret plots to destroy the new republic and emphasised the need for an iron fist: 'Revolutions are made to establish the rights of man. Therefore, in the interest of these rights, it is necessary to take all measures required for the success of revolutions ... The revolutionary interests might require ... repression' (Scurr 2006: 270). He also said that:

The Committee of Public Safety sees betrayals in the middle of victory ... our work is criticized in ignorance of its motives; people want us ... to give the traitors time to escape ... I will tell you how treacherous and extensive is the scheme for bringing us down and dissolving us; how the foreigners and internal enemies have agents paid to execute it; I will remind you that faction is not dead; that it is conspiring from the depths of its dungeons ... it is weakness towards traitors that is ruining us ... People feel sorry for the most criminal individuals, for those who expose the homeland to enemy steel. (Robespierre in Lynch 2013: 50–1)

Other secular ideological projects developed different understandings of violence. For example, anarchist movements have been split between those who insisted that violence is crucial for radical social change and those who supported only peaceful revolutionary transformations. While

Pierre Joseph Proudhon advocated non-violent anarchist takeover of power, Errico Malatesta was adamant that violence of the vanguard minority is a precondition for successful revolution. In one of his speeches Malatesta (1921) makes a case for the necessity of force:

It is an axiomatic, self-evident truth that a revolution can only be made when there is enough strength to make it. However, it is an historical truth that the forces determining evolution and social revolutions cannot be reckoned with census papers ... Every new idea and institution, all progress and every revolution have always been the work of minorities. It is our aspiration and our aim that everyone should become socially conscious and effective; but to achieve this end, it is necessary to provide all with the means of life and for development, and it is therefore necessary to destroy with violence, since one cannot do otherwise, the violence which denies these means to the workers.

These and many other new articulations of violence have had an impact across modern societies as ordinary individuals became more receptive to different doctrinal models of violence justification. With the decline of religious authority, traditional views on violence were undermined by variety of novel ideological creeds and it is this cacophony of difference that has fostered further ideologisation across the social orders. Instead of a singular religious understanding of violence as the preserve of divine authority, secularisation has generated competing and conflictual visions of justification for violence. In this context the traditional interpretations had to reaffirm their doctrines and to develop a more persuasive defence of their positions. At the same time new secular and religious ideologies were challenging the established dogmas and propagating new models of ethics. For example, while the traditional Christian teachings see violence as a product of divine will and God's plan most secular ideologies treat violence as a product of human interactions. Hence while for the Calvinists shedding human blood was a cardinal sin and even contemplating harm to others was equivalent to murder, for Jacobins violence was permissible against those who threaten the revolution because it was sanctioned by the will of the people. Centrifugal ideologisation thus develops and expands in a changing environment. Relying on the existing and increasing organisational capacities it gradually penetrates the social order and infuses the everyday lives of ordinary individuals. With the democratisation of the public sphere ideologisation becomes embedded in different areas of social life: from state institutions, religious associations, and political movements to cultural organisations and civil society networks. Hence the understandings of violence oscillate and change depending on the level of organisational capacity and the scale of organisational penetration into the social order.

Although modernity creates conditions for the proliferation of very different narratives of violence, the strength of organisational capacity combined with political or economic monopoly can stifle this ideological variability. For example, the monopoly on the legitimate use of violence over particular territory has enabled nation-states to establish hegemonic dominance throughout the contemporary world. This structural ascendancy has played a decisive role in making nationalism the dominant operative ideology of the modern world (Malešević 2006, 2019). Similarly, the near hegemonic structural position of profit and free market oriented economic relations in production, trade, exchange, and industry has established capitalism as the dominant economic ideology of modernity (Milanović 2019; Piketty 2020). Both of these historical situations had direct impact on dominant understandings of violence: while nationalism justifies the use of violence in the name of protecting one's nation, capitalism justifies deep social inequalities and, in this process, tends to ignore or dismiss the non-physical experiences of violence. Simply put, in the nationalist discourses killing and dying for one's nation is not an act of violence but a morally superior and noble deed. Similarly, in the capitalist worldview the destruction of the environment for profit or forcing children to work in sweat shops that have a long-term negative impact on their health are not violent acts. The centrifugal ideologisation of violence allows for these different visions of violence to gradually penetrate and shape the everyday understandings of what is a justified form of violent action.

Furthermore, while in the pre-modern periods justification and mobilisation for violence would usually be confined to a single social stratum, religious group, locality, or kinship network, in the modern era ideologisation tends to affect entire social orders and can also have a global resonance. Traditional polities did not possess adequate organisational capacities to successfully penetrate their societies. As Hall (1986: 52) argues, pre-modern empires were capstone states that had neither interest nor capacity to infiltrate the local communal lives of their subjects. The rulers of capstone states feared that 'horizontal linkages' they 'could not see would get out of control'. Hence the state's 'concern was less with intensifying social relationships than in seeking to prevent any linkages which might diminish its power'. Moreover, in most cases the rulers did not require the consent of ordinary people to use violence. Some violent punishments against their subjects did require sanctification from the religious authorities and involvement in wars would often entail a degree of support from the nobility but the use of violence was a prerogative of the rulers (Haldén 2020). This all changed in the modern era where the use of violence is tightly controlled by the state and other social organisations but where justification for violence involves much wider sectors of the population.[1] In other words, the cumulative rise of organisational capacities together with centrifugal ideologisation generate a paradoxical situation where the rulers possess unprecedented coercive powers and can inflict much more violence than any of their pre-modern predecessors but unlike their predecessors, they require popular support for such actions. For example, Chinese and Roman emperors possessed vast despotic powers and could order summary executions at will, but they had no infrastructural capacity to swiftly implement their decisions in faraway provinces (Mann 1986, 1993). In contrast, the presidents and prime ministers of the US, UK, or France have superior infrastructural powers including gigantic coercive capacity, but they cannot use violence against their citizens and also need believable justification for participation in wars. Hence the ever-increasing ideologisation of population in modernity has created new conditions where there is more capacity for violence than ever before but where also all acts of violence require more justification and elaboration (Malešević 2017).

Ideological power is important because it makes violent acts meaningful. As harming or killing of other human beings goes against the moral prescriptions of most ideological doctrines it is paramount to justify and explain such acts. Hence most ideologies identify contexts as to where and when violence is permissible. For example, although killing in general is wrong, to kill in self-defence is acceptable. This principle is then extended to war situations which if characterised as defensive wars open the space for violence against 'the attackers'. The ideological discourses play a central role in framing a particular violent conflict as a 'just war' where injuring and killing of other humans becomes permissible. Similarly redefining the enemy as being non-human creates a situation where moral judgement can be suspended and violence is permitted.

The centrifugal ideologisation together with the increased organisational capacities of states allows the wider population to accept and naturalise these ideological tenets as given. Social psychologists have identified dehumanisation as playing a decisive role in making the injuring and killing of other humans possible and acceptable. Once the enemy is depicted as subhuman (animals such as rats, insects, bacillus, or objects, diseases, etc.) or superhuman (monsters, devils, witches, etc.) it is psychologically easier to treat that enemy differently to human beings (Bar-Tal 2010;

---

[1] When states manage to monopolise the legitimate use of force other organisations are proscribed from deploying violence. However, since this is a very recent development that can also be reversed or weakened (e.g., failed or collapsing states) other social organisations can also control the means of violence.

Haslam 2006). If the mental or physical constitution of the enemy is deemed to be outside of the parameters of humanity, then committing acts of violence is seen to be permissible. Haslam (2006) sees dehumanisation as a cognitive process through which others are denied humanity in two principal ways: through identifying the lack of characteristics that are uniquely human and through pinpointing the non-existence of ways of acting, thinking, and feeling that are associated with humanity. The former case represents an example of 'animalistic' dehumanisation while in the latter case the other is depicted as an object or automaton and this type of dehumanisation is 'mechanistic'. For Haslam (2006) dehumanisation is not necessarily a product of conflict situations but something that is based on universal social-cognitive processes and as such is present in everyday life.

However, most social psychologists recognise that wars and similar violent contexts foster intensified dehumanisation. For example, Bar-Tal (1989, 2010) identifies delegitimisation as a process of group categorisation whereby some groups are deemed to have extremely negative characteristics or whose behaviour is normless. This process involves dehumanisation but also outcasting (identifying the other as somebody who does not behave within acceptable norms), trait characterisation (attributing extremely negative personality traits – cowards, traitors, callousness), and reliance on political labelling (e.g., communists, fascists) to delegitimise the political aims of the other. These established strategies of delegitimisation help justify the use of violence as they sharpen the boundaries between groups, create a sense of moral superiority, and contribute to homogenisation of those committing violent acts. However, to be effective dehumanisation and other forms of delegitimisation must be successfully integrated into the propagandistic narratives that usually permeate situations of violent conflicts. Much research on dehumanisation has focused on war environments showing the central role played by mass media in disseminating propagandistic images of the enemy. For example, the Rwandan war and genocide of 1994 was preceded by the systematic and sustained depictions of Tutsis as non-human and non-indigenous invaders who occupied the Hutu land (this was articulated in the Hamitic thesis where Tutsis were deemed to be descendants of the cursed son of Noah; Hintjens 1999: 252). During the genocide, the newspapers and the two radio stations portrayed Tutsis as feudal parasites, cockroaches and snakes who have infested Rwanda. In particular the news broadcasts of Radio Télévision Libre des Mille Collines (RTLM) played a decisive role in dehumanising Tutsis and inciting violence. As Yanagizawa-Drott's (2014: 29–30) analysis of RTLM broadcasts and killing patterns shows, 'the main radio station broadcasting anti-Tutsi propaganda during the Rwandan genocide significantly increased participation in the violence against Tutsis' where '10 percent of overall participation can be attributed to the radio station's broadcasts', which amounts to around 51,000 perpetrators.

Nevertheless, what is missing in these psychological accounts of propaganda is understanding of the wider social contexts and the historical dynamics of ideologisation. The presence of universal cognitive capacities for dehumanisation is not enough to turn ordinary people into killing machines. Neither dehumanisation nor violence can be triggered at will. The propaganda can enhance, radicalise, and help justify dehumanisation but it cannot suddenly change public opinions. On the contrary propaganda can also backfire and provoke unwanted reaction and resistance. As I have argued elsewhere, instead of conceiving of propaganda as an omnipotent force that can easily and quickly sway public opinion, much war propaganda operates as a device of self-justification (Malešević 2010: 202–33). The effectiveness of propaganda and dehumanisation is premised on the pre-existing ideological penetration within a specific social order. In other words, dehumanisation and propaganda can only work when the population is sufficiently ideologised and as such receptive to propagandistic messages. Since ideologisation is a historical process which is dependent on the rise of organisational capacities, its trajectory has largely been upward. The ever-increasing ideological penetration has created conditions where propaganda and dehumanisation can aid social fighting and killing. This is not to say that the pre-modern humans were reluctant killers but only that the increased ideologisation has generated different and more embedded interpretative horizons for mobilisation and legitimisation of fighting and killing. This ideological shift together with the cumulative development of coercive organisational power and the tighter envelopment of micro-level networks of group solidarity has played a central role in the expansion of violence throughout history (Malešević 2017). Nevertheless, ideologisation is a messy and relational process that is shaped by variety of different drivers including structural changes, powerful agents, popular perceptions, and changing social conditions. To better illustrate how ideologisation operates and changes through time and space it might be useful to zoom in on two very different historical examples – the Crusades and the Sri Lankan Tamil Tigers. A brief comparative analysis of these two cases will exemplify how ideologisation shapes the dynamics of social pugnacity.

3.4   The Crusades and Social Pugnacity

The Eastern Mediterranean Crusades (1096–1271) have often been singled out as a typical example of violence caused by ideological fanaticism. For example, a leading historian of this period John France

(1999: 188) insists that 'In the Holy Land, Western Christians were only present out of deep ideological hatred of Islam.' Similarly, Runciman (1987: 32) takes the words of leading crusaders for granted and understands the Crusades as conflicts primarily driven by religious zeal: 'the struggle was now for glory of Christendom, for the rescue of the holy places, and for the destruction of Islam'. This is illuminated with the crusaders celebrating their victories with the choirs singing 'Glory be to God, Who has conquered the Saracens' (Runciman 1987: 32). Tyerman (2004, 2005) also argues that the crusaders went to Palestine to fight 'for essentially ideological religious reasons' and that they were motivated by 'spiritual indulgence, the time off purgatory, the prospect of heaven and, of course, relics, which were important'.

There is no doubt that religious beliefs played an important role in mobilising knights to fight in the Crusades and in justifying the territorial conquests in the Middle East. In 1095, Pope Urban II gave a highly influential sermon at Clermont that launched the Crusades. He was explicit that this was religious war against 'barbarians' who 'have killed and captured many and have destroyed the churches and devastated the empire ... I, or rather the Lord, beseech you as Christ's heralds ... to destroy that vile race from the lands of our friends. I say this to those who are present, it is meant also for those who are absent. Moreover, Christ commands it' (Bongars 1905: 382). Pope Urban II and many subsequent popes emphasised the centrality of religious inspiration for the Crusades. Not only were European knights obliged to recover the Holy Land and to protect their fellow Christians in Byzantium, but the popes also were clear that fighting in this religious war granted absolution of all sins and a secure place in heaven. In the words of Pope Urban II: 'All who die by the way, whether by land or by sea, or in battle against the pagans, shall have immediate remission of sins. This I grant them through the power of God with which I am invested' (Bongars 1905: 382). Other popes reaffirmed this promise although Innocent III made clear in 1198 that the remission of sins was a gift of God, not an automatic entitlement for crusaders (Asbridge, 2012).

However, ideological zeal was not the only source of motivation to assemble troops of soldiers to fight. Many knights were equally eager to acquire land and material possessions in Palestine. With the introduction of the principle of primogeniture across much of Europe many knights were left without inheritance. This principle established the right of the eldest son to inherit all of his father's land, possessions, and titles while the younger sons had to fend for themselves (Haldén 2020). Hence volunteering to lead soldiers in the battle for the Holy Land offered the opportunity of capturing territories from 'the Saracens' and even establishing small Christian kingdoms in the Middle East. The result of the first Crusade was the creation of four Roman Catholic polities in the Holy Land: the kingdom of Jerusalem (1099–1291), the county of Tripoli (1109–1289), the county of Edessa (1098–1146), and the Armenian Kingdom of Cilicia (1080–1375).

Once these polities came into existence the fighting motivation for the Crusades also attained a strong geopolitical dimension. The aristocratic rulers of these new polities were fighting to preserve their existence in the environment of the rising Muslim powers including the Seljuk Turkish expansion, the Mamluk invasions, and the conquests of the Ayyubids under Saladin, among others. With the gradual decline of the Byzantine Empire the viability of these polities became threatened, and the leadership of the Catholic Church was eager to mobilise more soldiers to fight in the subsequent Crusades. The control of the Holy Land had a geopolitical significance but was also an important status symbol for the Catholic Church and the European aristocrats who fought in the Crusades. It signified the strength of the Christian faith in the world that was until then completely dominated by Muslim rulers. Bearing in mind that in the eleventh, twelfth, and thirteenth centuries Christian Europe was largely an underdeveloped and politically marginal region of the known world, the military victories over the superior Muslim polities suddenly enhanced the position of Christendom in the region (Hillenbrand 2000).

Furthermore, the mobilisation for the Crusades impacted on the development of military power in Europe as those who volunteered to fight in the Holy Land were exempt from taxation, pardoned for their crimes, and received moratoriums on their debts (Tyerman 2004, 2005). The small Christian polities in the Middle East were deeply stratified with the dominant elite composed of the Catholic minority of Crusaders and their descendants. The rest of the population was culturally diverse including Greek and Syriac Orthodox Christians, Armenians, Sunni and Shi'a Muslims, Jews, and Samaritans. The non-Christian populations and particularly Muslims were marginalised second-class citizens (Hillenbrand 2000). The Church and the crusaders often dehumanised their Muslim enemies which helped them to justify their use of violence. Hence for crusaders the Muslims were not only barbarians, pagans, infidels, heretics, and idolaters but were also often depicted as 'hideous malformed monsters who conduct dastardly acts of villainy' and are often shown as 'performing acts of sexual depravity, extreme brutality, and evil trickery' (Morton 2016: 58–9). In Pope Urban II's influential sermon that officially launched the Crusades Muslims were described as a 'despised and base race, which worships demons' (Bongars 1905: 382).

The dehumanisation helped mobilise elite support for the Crusades and was also a useful tool for the legitimisation of violent acts against Muslim soldiers and civilians. Although the Church viewed all acts of killing as sinful, exceptions were made for the crusaders. Officially the Church preached that the killing of a non-believer prevented the possibility of conversion to Christianity. However, the just war theory and other theological compromises allowed for killings in a defensive wars and later also made a distinction between Christians and non-Christians: 'the act of killing a non-Christian was considered spiritually less reprehensible than killing a Christian' (Morton 2016: 49).

Nevertheless, on the actual battlefields these considerations were largely non-existent as crusaders were engaged in the slaughter of soldiers and innocent civilians. The later chronicles of the Crusades tend to justify mass scale violence through the prism of the enemy's alleged immorality and blasphemy: 'It was undoubtedly a just judgement that their blood was spilled in that same place where they have blasphemed God for so long'; crusaders chased Muslims 'with such hatred because they appropriated the Temple of the Lord and the Holy Sepulchre and the Temple of Solomon as well as other churches and polluted them with such shameful practices' (Smith 2017: 32). However, these religious and moralistic justifications together with the propagandistic dehumanisation of Muslims did not necessarily appeal beyond the aristocratic and clerical circles. Although the proto-ideological Christian narrative about the reclaiming the Holy Land had some resonance across different social strata, the Crusades were largely an elite-centred project. In other words, in this deeply stratified world ideologisation was rather shallow and confined to small sections of the aristocracy and top clergy. It is mostly within this select group that religious tropes were used to mobilise the support for wars and conquests and to justify acts of violence. In medieval Europe and the Middle East, the political and religious elites did not have to legitimise their actions to the wider society.

Instead, legitimacy drives were confined to their peers –fellow aristocrats and top clergy. The weak organisational capacities together with the low levels of literacy, and the lack of a society-wide public sphere, educational systems, and civil society networks meant that in the premodern world ideological penetration was very thin and limited. In this context the ideological narratives about violence relied heavily on dehumanisation strategies where the Muslim enemy was often portrayed similarly to how the European aristocrats depicted their own peasant subjects – as animals, monsters, and devils. Hence the crusaders killed their Muslim foes with the same attitude they held towards their serfs – as the *Froissart Chronicles* show, 'the knights did not have to treat their enemies according to the law of arms. The peasants were not human; their behaviour, as well as their appearance, betrayed them as animals' (Brown 2011: 271). Although in religious teachings all Christians were nominally prioritised over non-Christians, in reality one's social status often mattered more than religious affiliation. Thus, the aristocrats tended to avoid killing other aristocrats who were often ransomed and exchanged after the battle rather than summarily killed with the rest. They often fought together against the common enemy, would engage in trade and technological exchange, and even would convert to marry across the religious lines. Medieval poetry and chronicles clearly indicate that these cross-religious interactions were present and often trumped internal status and class divides.

The key feature of violence during the Crusades is that it was largely messy, chaotic, and unsystematic. Most casualties were the result of starvation, malnutrition, disease, and exhaustion and only between 15 and 20 per cent of knights died from weapon injuries (Mitchell 2004: 143). Each Crusade generated close to 20 per cent of deaths of clergy and knights from disease and malnutrition while the figures for the ordinary population, which were not recorded, were probably much higher (Mitchell 2004: 143). The epidemics, dysentery and febrile illnesses decimated populations on both sides. In this environment of uncertainty and insecurity dehumanisation fostered a degree of ideological unity between the aristocracy and the top clergy while also keeping the ordinary foot soldiers fearful enough to follow orders and keep in line despite the excessive losses.[2] The crusaders also tortured their enemies. This was often similar to how they treated their own disobedient or suspicious peasants. For example, a woman suspected of running away from her Frankish lord in Nazareth during the first Crusade in 1188 was burned at the stake as a sorcerer. Captured enemy soldiers were also tortured in a variety of ways including suspending captives on a gibbet, stretching them on the rack, using barnacles to crush their legs, and whipping prisoners on a pillory (Mitchell 2013). The use of torture is often a reliable indicator of weak coercive organisational capacity and a low level of society-wide ideological penetration (Malešević 2017).

---

[2] However, as Luft (2019) rightly argues dehumanisation is not a simple device of control that can easily transform one's behaviour. Instead, dehumanisation is usually accompanied by other processes that foster violent action: 'My research suggests this cognitive adaptation to violence goes hand-in-hand with a transformation in how ordinary killers perceive their victims. Dehumanizing propaganda can help with this process by providing participants with cultural narratives that frame violence as the morally right thing to do, and it can help them overcome their initial resistance to killing neighbours as a result' (Luft 2019: 1).

Hence ideology was important for the mobilisation and legitimisation of violence in the Crusades, but this ideological power was rather weak and narrow and heavily dependent on economic, geo-political, and military factors. Since ideological penetration was thin and mostly confined to the small segment of clerical and aristocratic elites dehumanisation and propaganda were its key ingredients.

3.5   The Social Pugnacity of the Tamil Tigers

In sharp contrast to the Crusades the violence of the Tamil Tigers was characterised by highly developed ideological penetration. Much of the scholarship on the Sri Lankan civil war (1983–2009) recognises that ideology played an important role as a generator of violence (Amarasingam 2015; Hellmann-Rajanayagam 1994; Lilja 2009). The Liberation Tigers of Tamil Eelam (LTTE) mobilised their support by advocating the establishment of an independent and sovereign Tamil state – 'free Tamil Eelam'. The LTTE leaders articulated a distinct interpretation of Tamil nationalism that was secular, revolutionary, and egalitarian. It draw inspiration from Indian nationalists such as Subhas Chandra Bose (Subhasism) and anti-colonial Dravidism and propagated national emancipation (Terpstra and Frerks 2017: 292). Although religious identification was one of the traditional key dividing lines between predominantly Hindi Tamils and mostly Buddhist Sinhalese, the LTTE opposed religious divides and supported the creation of a fully secular state. Furthermore, Tamil Tigers rejected Hindi traditionalism and patriarchal social relations and supported gender equality and the abolition of all vestiges of the caste system. The leaders of LTTE have often characterised the movement not only as nationalist but also as a form of 'revolutionary socialism' aiming to establish an egalitarian social order (Singh Bhasin 2001). The leading theorist of the LTTE Anton Balasingham described the movement's ideology in these terms: 'our total strategy integrates both the national struggle and class struggle, interlinks both nationalism and socialism into a revolutionary project aimed at liberating our people both from national oppression and from the exploitation of man by man' (Clarke 2015: 63). Similarly, when interviewed in 1986 the leader of the LTTE Velupillai Prabhakaran stated that their nationalist ideology aims to overcome the structural inequalities that generate hostilities between the minority Tamils and majority Sinhala: 'Both the common Sinhala and Tamil masses are oppressed and exploited, and they have similar socio-economic problems and aspirations. What divides them is the national conflict. The Sinhala ruling classes have generated this national contradiction to divide the

Sinhala and Tamil masses to reinforce their political power' (Singh Bhasin 2001: 1).

However, recognising that Tamil nationalism and socialism were important driving forces of conflict does not explain how exactly ideology shaped violent action in this case. Moreover, singling out the ideological doctrine alone obscures the relevance of other factors that also played an important role in galvanising violence including economic motives, coercive power, and changing geo-political dynamics. The scholars of the Sri Lankan civil war have analysed extensively the features of LTTE war economy and have demonstrated that the movement was successful in generating substantial revenue from international weapons smuggling, looting of government's humanitarian supplies, and compulsory taxation of the population under its control and even of those Sri Lankan public servants of Tamil origin who lived and worked in Colombo and other areas outside of LTTE control (Richards 2014). However, the most extensive resource accumulation was made through international networks including substantive contributions from the Tamil diaspora living in Europe, India, North America, and Australia (Jayasundara-Smits 2018). As Venugopal (2003: 22) shows, up to 80 per cent of the LTTE's annual budget of US$82 million 'was generated from diaspora contributions' including 'revenues generated from international trade, enterprise, and investments'. This efficient system of revenue collection was perfected over the thirty years of LTTE rule and as such it became self-reproductive, and in this way contributed to the continuation of civil war. The geo-politics also exacerbated the violent conflict. The changing strategic interests of neighbouring states (India, China, USA, etc.) as well as the fierce struggle between LTTE and the competing Tamil nationalist organisations (i.e., TELO, EROS, PLOTE, EPRLF) shaped the dynamics of violence. During the 1980s, the LTTE fought against the Indian peacekeeping force (IPKF) and managed to crash other competitors among the Tamil resistance groups (Richards 2014). These conflicts fostered greater ideological radicalisation and proliferation of indiscriminate violence against all those who opposed the LTTE leadership.

As the Tamil Tigers attained nearly monopolistic position they relied more on their coercive strength. The LTTE gradually transformed from a small guerrilla movement into a formidable para-state organisation. It enforced strict discipline among its members but also was effective at policing the wider Tamil community. The soldiers had 'to follow a strict moral code of conduct, which included prohibition of cigarettes and alcohol, while relationships with the opposite sex were also regulated' (Terpstra and Frerks 2017: 287). Their military performance was monitored and controlled through rewards and punishments. The new recruits swore an oath of allegiance and total loyalty to the LTTE and its leader Prabhakaran and were provided with a cyanide capsule to swallow in case of capture by the Sri Lankan army. Over the years the LTTE developed a highly coercive organisational capacity. It established and maintained a hierarchical and highly disciplined military structure with the ground forces, the navy, the air force, the intelligence, and the special suicide commando unit (the Black Tigers) (Stokke 2006). It combined this coercive organisational capacity with strong ideological penetration to bind the majority of Tamils around its political goals. It deployed coercive measures together with ideological persuasion to recruit new members and to widen its support base. Resistance and non-compliance were punished or delegitimised as a form of treasonous behaviour. The nearly total control of the population allowed the LTTE to penalise disobedience. As explained by an ordinary Tamil from Kilinochchi: 'the "one person per family" rule was prescribed in order to increase manpower for the war, and they forcibly recruited the youth into the movement. They kidnapped people and they imposed compulsory taxes. They collected funds forcefully, for example by abducting people and demanding ransom. They abducted or murdered people who were not in favour of the movement' (Terpstra and Frerks 2017: 288).

Nevertheless, most Tamils willingly complied with the strict orders and perceived the LTTE as the only legitimate armed force of Tamils. In the words of another ordinary Tamil: 'The LTTE was fighting to fulfil the aspirations of the Tamil people and seeking their freedom. People accepted them. The injustices and atrocities of the Sinhala army were increasing day by day. Under such a situation, the aim and activities of the Tigers were reasonable' (Terpstra and Frerks 2017: 297). The legit-imacy of the LTTE increased as they gradually transformed into an effective administrative machine that replaced the Sri Lankan state in the north of the island. They established their own public services includ-ing educational system, judiciary, health care, police, and welfare provi-sions (Stokke 2006). This high level of bureaucratic capacity enhanced the ideological penetration through Tamil society. In this context violence against the Sinhalese and particularly against the Sri Lankan military was legitimised through the ideological codes that emphasised the moral superiority of the LTTE struggle.

The much deeper societal ideologisation of Tamil society created conditions where moral supremacy trumped dehumanisation as the principal mode of political delegitimisation. In other words, whereas in the case of the Crusades ideological penetration was shallow and could never attain substantial cross-society and cross-class consistency, in the

Tamil case ideologisation was a society-wide phenomenon that affected nearly all its members. In this environment propaganda through dehumanisation was largely replaced by the idioms stressing moral superiority and the notion of virtuous violence. As Fiske and Rai (2014) rightly argue, violent behaviour does not always stem from dehumanising propaganda. Instead, many violent acts are the result of excessive humanisation, that is the notion that the person or a group who experience harm are fully deserving of such acts. 'People do not simply justify or excuse their violent actions after the fact, at the moment they act, people intend to cause harm or death to someone they feel should suffer or die' (Fiske and Rai 2014: 1). This 'virtuous violence' is motivated by strong moral principles and is aimed at regulating, redressing, or repairing existing social relationships. The perpetrators of violence do not harm their victims because they see them as less than human; instead, they expect their victims to feel pain or shame. Hence unlike the crusaders who often went to war with the images of Saracens as monsters and devils many LTTE combatants were well aware that the Sri Lankan soldiers were fully human, and they wanted them to experience retribution for injustice. The Tamil Tigers were willing to kill and die out of sense of moral responsibility to undo the injustice and to sacrifice themselves for their comrades, family members and close friends. This was not a form of moral disengagement, or 'moral holiday' as William James called it when individuals temporarily relax their ethical rules in order to enjoy a moment of transgression (Collins 2008: 476). While many crusaders may have been involved in indiscriminate violence this certainly was not the case with LTTE. Instead for most Tamil Tigers, injuring and killing Sri Lankan forces was an act of full moral engagement as they believed that their violence was justified and necessary. Thus, instead of dehumanisation they tended to humanise their enemy. In this context ideologisation and coercive bureaucratisation successfully enveloped the networks of micro-solidarity. The ideological penetration was fully visible in the micro-world of everyday life as ordinary Tamils perceived their personal losses and gains through the prism of LTTE ideology. This was most apparent in the cult of martyrdom of the Black Tigers. This special commando unit was trained to act as suicide bombers against Sri Lankan targets and their deaths were commemorated by the whole community. Their violent acts were deemed to be heroic acts of self-sacrifice for their nation. However, their martyrdom was framed through the discourse of kinship and friendship, that is a shared brotherhood, sisterhood, and comradeship. Hence dying for the freedom of Tamil Eelam was simultaneously an act of sacrifice for one's family and close friends. In this context the deep micro-level solidarities were fully interwoven into the wider ideological narrative of Tamil nationalism – by volunteering to die for Tamil Eelam a Black Tiger was also sacrificing his or her life so that family, friends, and their children and grandchildren could live in freedom. This ideologisation of the interpersonal domain was evident in the statements of ordinary Tamils who took part in commemorations of Black Tiger martyrdom: 'All the heroes are our brothers. So, the people and the Liberation Tigers together celebrated it impressively, displaying pictures and lighting lamps in the houses. The skills, abilities, and achievements of the heroes were revealed on the heroes' day. It is a day to be proud of' (Terpstra and Frerks 2017: 295). To sum up, the combination of high cumulative bureaucratisation of coercion and the deep ideological penetration within the Tamil social order together with the envelopment of micro-solidarity networks by the LTTE impacted deeply on the willingness of ordinary individuals to fight and die for the Tamil cause.

3.6   Conclusion

Ideology is a social glue that makes violent action meaningful. Moreover, shared ideological principles contribute to mobilisation and legitimisation of violence. However ideological doctrines do not by themselves generate violent outcomes. Our world consists of billions of individuals who subscribe to different religious and secular ideologies, yet only very small minority use violence to attain their ideological goals. Hence while social pugnacity often requires ideological motivation and justification, this is rarely a simple consequence of doctrinal teachings. Instead sustained violent action is usually a corollary of several processes including the expansion of effective organisational capacities, the envelopment of micro-solidarity networks, the changing historical conditions, the shifting geo-political environment, and so on. It is the confluence of these different processes that create conditions for the impact of ideology on the dynamics of violence. Social pugnacity is a consequence of these different processes. Nevertheless, it is through the process of ideologisation that individuals and social organisations become more receptive to the use of violence for political and other purposes. Ideological power resonates less as a fixed set of doctrines and principles and much more as a flexible and malleable process that allows social organisations and individual agents to situate and imprint their actions in the existing narratives and established moral codes. As Mann (1986: 22) rightly argues, ideological power resides in its ability to 'monopolise a claim to meaning' which often includes monopolisation of norms and aesthetic and ritual practices that accompany these belief systems. It is through the successful combination of ideologisation, bureaucratisation of organisational capacity, and the envelopment of micro-solidarity that one can influence the thoughts and behaviour of others and shape the trajectory of social pugnacity.

4   Enforced Fighting
Coercing Humans into Violence

4.1   Introduction

Coercion has always played an important part in making ordinary individuals into fighters. The ancient texts including Thucydides's *History of the Peloponnesian War* and Sun Tzu's *Art of War* point to the role of force in compelling ordinary soldiers to fight. For Thucydides, coercion is the cornerstone of soldering: 'We must remember that one man is much the same as another, and that he is best who is trained in the severest school' and 'The strength of an army lies in strict discipline and undeviating obedience to its officers' (Thucydides 2019 [400 BCE]: Book 2, 80, 92). Sun Tzu is even more precise on the role of force in making soldiers fight: 'If soldiers are punished before they have grown attached to you, they will not prove submissive; and, unless submissive, they will be practically useless. If, when the soldiers have become attached to you, punishments are not enforced, they will still be useless' (Sun Tzu 2017 [500 BCE]: 30). Hence once individuals are fully integrated into the military organisation they still need to be coerced into fighting: 'Throw your soldiers into positions whence there is no escape, and they will prefer death to flight. If they will face death, there is nothing they may not achieve ... If there is no place of refuge, they will stand firm ... if there is no help for it, they will fight hard' (Sun Tzu 2017 [500 BCE]: 37).

This emphasis on coercion is also present in modern wars. In the first sustained analysis of the behaviour of soldiers on the battlefield, Armand du Picq, a colonel in the French army, recommends coercive disciplining: 'What makes the soldier capable of obedience and direction in action, is the sense of discipline. This includes: respect for and confidence in his chiefs, confidence in his comrades and fear of their reproaches and retaliation if he abandons them in danger; his desire to go where others do without trembling more than they ... Organisation only can produce these characteristics. Four men equal a lion' (2006 [1881]: 55. 112). Force was also the backbone of fighting in the First and

Second World Wars. Not only were millions of unenthusiastic individuals conscripted to fight, kill, and die but their respective militaries devised a variety of punishments to deter instances of desertion or unwillingness to fight. Leon Trotsky's famous quote captures the experience of the First World War and the Russian civil war: 'An army cannot be built without reprisals. Masses of men cannot be led to death unless the army command has the death-penalty in its arsenal … the command will always be obliged to place the soldiers between the possible death in the front and the inevitable one in the rear' (Trotsky 2012: 411). More recent accounts also stress the coercive character of the military organisation. Conscription-based armies such as the Russian, Turkish, or Israeli periodically encounter resistance from unwilling conscripts facing the imminent prospect of violence. For example, in Israel 32.9 per cent of young people evaded conscription in 2019 most of whom invoked 'mental health reasons' (Asharq 2020). In Turkey, any attempt to evade conscription is rigorously punished and even voicing opinions against the draft is a criminal act punishable by six months to two years in prison (Rainsford 2005). Even the professional militaries such as the US or British also occasionally face discontent when soldiers are faced with protracted exposure to battlefields and hostile environments. For example, during their deployments in Afghanistan and Iraq the allied forces had to deploy coercive powers to discipline unruly soldiers and to keep them on the battlefields (Buncombe 2011).

Throughout history many military organisations have developed effective systems of control and punishment for unwilling recruits. Evading military draft has often led to long-term imprisonment and in some instances, individuals would ultimately face the firing squad. Many militaries have also instituted rigorous punishments and courts martial for misbehaviour on the battlefield with capital punishment regularly deployed as a measure for desertion or unwillingness to fight. Nearly all armed forces throughout the world have instituted military police to control the behaviour of soldiers on and off their areas of deployment (Bourke 2000).

Coercion is also deployed by a variety of non-state actors to force individuals to fight. From terrorist organisations, social movements, political parties, and paramilitary organisations to gangs and criminal cartels force has regularly been deployed to compel ordinary people to fight and kill. In this chapter I focus on the social dynamics of coercive power and specifically on the coercive mechanisms deployed by different social organisations to force individuals to fight. The first part explores the role of the state and its key coercive organisations such as the military and police while the second part zooms in on the coercive power of non-state organisations. The final section assesses the role of coercion in social pugnacity and argues that although coercive power plays an indispensable role in turning ordinary individuals into fighters, force alone is not enough to ensure continuous commitment to fighting.

4.2   Authority, Obedience, and Coercion

Much of the traditional psychological and psychoanalytical research has emphasised personality traits as being decisive in one's willingness to harm others. Adorno and his collaborators were the first to identify and empirically study the role of authoritarian personality in individual inclination to violence (Adorno et al. 1950). This research paradigm, which is still influential within social psychology, links violence with traumatic childhood experiences and attributes support for authoritarian politics to distinct personality traits. In this understanding individuals who score high on the authoritarian personality test (F scale) are considered to be significantly more prone to idolise authority figures and conform to demands from such figures. Building on Freudian premises this approach links punitive measures with resentment towards parents. This relationship is also linked with the unmet need for approval from one's parents. Hence for Adorno, willingness to harm others, acceptance, or support for such acts, is a product of authoritarian traits that are reproduced within authoritarian family structures.

This line of argument was developed further by a number of influential social psychologists who devised a variety of experimental techniques to test their key propositions. Thus, in a series of experiments Stanley Milgram and Philip Zimbardo explored how ordinary individuals conform to the demands of authority figures. Milgram's research attempted to measure one's willingness to obey persons of authority when instructed to inflict pain on unknown individuals ('the learners'). Following instructions from the experimenter, forty participants ('the teachers') administered what they believed to be electric shocks to 'the learners' and were willing to increase the intensity of the electric shocks when prompted by the experimenter. Milgram (1974) reports that all participants administered shocks at 300 volts and 65 per cent agreed to administer a staggering 450-volt shock. Milgram (1974) concluded that most human beings are prone to conform to authority regardless of the moral costs of doing so:

The extreme willingness of adults to go to almost any lengths on the command of an authority constitutes the chief finding of the study and the fact most urgently demanding explanation. Ordinary people, simply doing their jobs, and without any particular hostility on their part, can become agents in a terrible destructive process. Moreover, even when the destructive effects of their work become patently clear, and they are asked to carry out actions incompatible with fundamental standards of morality, relatively few people have the resources needed to resist authority.

Moreover, he was adamant that these results showed that the Holocaust was possible because ordinary individuals were simply obeying authority figures. For Milgram the willingness to take part in genocide is based on 'a common psychological process' demonstrated in his experiments (Blass 1999).

Philip Zimbardo's experimental techniques generated similar findings although his focus was nominally less on psychological traits and more on the situational contexts. In the famous Stanford prison experiment Zimbardo recruited a group of twenty-four middle-class student volunteers who were randomly assigned to roles of 'prisoners' and 'guards' in a mock prison. Zimbardo, who also participated in the experiment as a 'superintendent', found that students easily became comfortable with their assigned roles with a number of 'guards' deploying psychological torture on 'prisoners' whereas 'prisoners' blindly obeyed the authority and accepted the abuse. The experiment also indicated that one third of the 'guards' openly displayed 'sadistic tendencies' (Zimbardo 1972). Just like Milgram, Zimbardo concluded that obedience to authority is a universal characteristic of human beings. However, unlike Adorno and Milgram, Zimbardo argued that this universal capacity is not rooted directly in individual psychological traits but in the social conditions that shape human behaviour. This was particularly the case with the transformation of ordinary middle-class students who had no history of criminal behaviour into sadistic 'guards' (Zimbardo 1972).

These three well-known psychological studies had enormous influence on the understanding of human behaviour and especially on common views of people's willingness to harm other human beings. Despite their different focus all three studies have reinforced the popular view of humans as being inherently violent creatures. While Adorno and Milgram trace this propensity to violence to stable and fixed individual psychological traits, Zimbardo identifies social context as playing a key role in this process. However, even in Zimbardo's case the emphasis is on existing psychological attributes that are only triggered when an opportunity arises. The Stanford prison experiment was designed to show that changed social roles allow individuals to reveal their 'true selves' – their inherent but dormant sadistic impulses. In other words, all three studies reaffirm a rather pessimist perception of human beings whereby the propensity for violence is directly, or in Zimbardo's case indirectly, linked to individual psychological characteristics.

The three scholars who coordinated these influential studies were all adamant that coercive power played no role in the willingness to harm others. Although Adorno's study recognises punitive childhood practices as a significant contributor to the development of an authoritarian personality, his focus is on the distinct psychological traits and psychoanalytical conditions that stem from despotic family structures. While the authoritarian traits have deep roots in childhood the authoritarian adults are studied as individuals who make free choices to support, or engage in, violent behaviour. Similarly, Milgram's experiments pay little attention to the wider structural contexts and zoom in on universal psychological qualities as the principal drivers of behaviour. Milgram was explicit that coercion had nothing to do with the choices made by the participants administering the electric shocks:

Our studies deal only with obedience that is willingly assumed in the absence of threat of any sort, obedience that is maintained through the simple assertion by authority that it has the right to exercise control over the person. Whatever force authority exercises in this study is based on powers that the subject in some manner ascribes to it and not on any objective threat or availability of physical means of controlling the subject. (Milgram 1974: xx–xi).

Zimbardo too described his experiment in terms of voluntary participation where no participant was coerced into assuming their respective roles.[1]

Nevertheless, what these three studies show is not the universal psychological proclivity to inflict violence through individual choice but in fact they unwittingly demonstrate the significance of coercive power in making humans violent. The three studies do capture well the social dynamics of obedience, but they completely fail to understand the structural context of mass compliance with established rules. The Milgram and Zimbardo experiments took place in leading scientific institutions, were coordinated by highly esteemed academics, and were undertaken in the presence of other students, faculty, and staff. The experiments were

---

[1] All three of these studies have been criticised extensively for their methodological weaknesses and the lack of ethical considerations in their design and implementation. The Stanford prison experiment (SPE) has received the most severe criticism for 'the biased and incomplete collection of data, the extent to which the SPE drew on a prison experiment devised and conducted by students in one of Zimbardo's classes 3 months earlier, the fact that the guards received precise instructions regarding the treatment of the prisoners, the fact that the guards were not told they were subjects, and the fact that participants were almost never completely immersed by the situation' (Le Texier 2019: 1).

also conducted with an aura of scientific authority where academics were able to use methods legitimatised by the university and the state. In this context, coercive power was at the heart of the subjects' willingness to obey the rules. These coercive tools of organisational power might have been accepted voluntarily by the participants in the experiment but that in itself was not a sign of free choice. On the contrary individual compliance with the rules and procedures established and implemented by the dominant social organisations is one of the defining features of coercive organisational power. As I have argued previously, all complex social organisations possess and operate through coercive control (Malešević 2010, 2017). This is particularly the case with the bureaucratic forms of domination where, as Weber (1968: 1152) noted long ago, discipline is the defining feature of social order. Complex social organisations cannot operate effectively without the division of labour, delegation of responsibility, centralised decision making, hierarchical chains of command, and the consistent following of established rules. Hence all social organisations possess disciplinary mechanisms of control and coordination. Effective discipline is a precondition of organisational efficiency and to discipline human beings means to train them to obey rules or develop a particular form of behaviour. As a lack of discipline endangers organisational operationality all complex social organisations have to use punitive measures to control indiscipline and disobedience. Thus, social organisations are inevitably coercive entities. In some cases, such as with the military, police, prison services, or terrorist networks, this is obvious but coercive power underpins just as much most other complex social organisations – from hospitals, factories, religious institutions, private corporations, and political parties to scientific and educational institutions. All such social organisations are built on and operate through bureaucratic forms of rule including centralised and hierarchical command and control, elaborate systems of division of labour and delegation of tasks, and meritocratic models of recruitment and promotion. However, the very existence of these bureaucratic principles of operation is premised on the coercive capacity of these organisations: compliance with the established rules, obedience to commands issued by the central authority and line managers, organisational loyalty, and the disciplined execution of organisational tasks. The coercive capacity of social organisations is regularly enforced by formalised and informal penalties for disobedience. As human beings now live in a world completely dominated by complex social organisations, they simply cannot evade their coercive power. Therefore 'obedience to authority' is not a universal psychological phenomenon but a specific historical reality that characterises the contemporary world dominated by complex social organisations.

In this context the wider social structure is crucial in understanding the behaviour of 'authoritarian personalities' and students taking parts in the psychological experiments described earlier. These individuals were not individualised atoms operating in an organisational vacuum. Instead, their actions were shaped by the previous knowledge and experiences of coercive organisational contexts and by the organisational pressures of the academic institutions and scientific authorities that were legitimately conducting these coercive experiments. Hence obedience to authority was not a matter of simple individual choice and psychological givens but of the coercive organisational logic of the situation in which these participants were operating. The students were obeying the commands issued by what they would consider to be legitimate organisational authority. Milgram and Zimbardo assumed, yet never incorporated, free choice into their research design (Kaposi 2017: 396). Hence once trapped in the coercive social relation the participants could not simply disengage from organisational authority:

They may have believed that the experimenter telling them that they have "no choice" was acting truthfully, as he was the authority who would also torture or even kill some innocent in the other room. As a result, they may have not been able to extricate themselves from the situation because of the fact that they felt it torturing and never knew who would be tortured next if they refused to go on. And they may therefore really have been in a situation where any responsibility for what happened did not lie with them. (Kaposi 2017: 396–7)

Thus, the existing coercive organisational structures play a crucial rule in one's willingness to obey organisational superiors. Obedience to authority is not a universal psychological response but a context-dependent social phenomenon rooted in the historical realities of the coercive capacities of social organisations. To fully understand how social pugnacity works it is paramount to move away from de-contextualised psychological interpretations towards the historical sociology of coercive organisational power.

4.3   Forcing Individuals to Die and Kill: The Coercive Power of the State

The state is the most powerful coercive organisation. Modern nation-states are able to establish monopolies on the legitimate use of violence over their territories and to mobilise their citizens to participate in wars and other forms of organised violence. Although pre-modern states usually did not possess enough infrastructural powers to fully control their borders and frontiers, they still could deploy substantive despotic powers to force individuals to obey their authority (Mann 1986, 1993). The emergence of the state has historically been linked to the proliferation of warfare (Carneiro 1970; Tilly 1985). Tilly (1992) showed that war making and state making have been mutually constitutive processes. The expansion of protracted warfare in early modern Europe ultimately gave birth to the institutions of the modern state and civil society. War has also played a decisive role in the global transformation from a world of empires into a world of nation-states (Wimmer 2012). Although this was not a unidirectional teleological process, but a phenomenon characterised by numerous historical and geographical fluctuations, and periodic phases of rise and decline, the coercive organisational capacity of states has been on the increase over the last five thousand years and has dramatically accelerated in the last 300 years (Malešević 2010, 2017). The late nineteenth-century modernising empires and even more so contemporary nation-states have attained unprecedented coercive powers that are reflected in their ability to tax populations at source, to successfully control and police their borders, to collect information on their citizens, to create and enforce standardised education systems (eventually making primary education compulsory), and to regulate immigration and emigration, employment, health care and welfare provisions (Dandeker 1990; Malešević 2013; Mann 1993, 2013). With the development of science, technology, industry, transport, and communication networks, states were in the position to enhance their coercive organisational powers. The increasing organisational capacities allowed states to successfully monitor, regulate, and manage the populations under their control. This was achieved through the development and expansion of policing and judicial systems and the introduction and enforcement of society-wide military conscription. While police and courts became effective in coercively penalising undesirable behaviour the military draft ensured that a large number of citizens ended up in various theatres of war or as enforcers of violent acts against colonial subjects across the globe. The rise of police and the judiciary contributed to the pacification of social order and the creation of what Foucault (1975) called 'docile bodies' – individuals who gradually accepted and normalised their own state of subjugation. Once citizens became more acquiescent, they could also be drafted into the military and sent to fight in various wars or imperial conquests.

Paradoxically the greater coercive capacities of states were built in large part on their increased legitimacy. Both the French and the American revolutions contributed substantially towards legitimisation of state coercion. By institutionalising the idea of moral equality of all its citizens the new French republic was able to justify military conscription of millions of ordinary individuals. Facing attacks from the large-scale anti-republican forces of various monarchical European powers the republican leaders opted to utilise their egalitarian principles in order to institute a *levée en masse* – a requisition of all able-bodied men to fight for the nation (Conversi 2008). Hence the central ideas of the French Revolution (equality, fraternity, and liberty) implied that newly acquired freedoms and rights automatically invoke obligations towards the shared polity. If the nation includes all social strata, then everybody has the responsibility to defend its existence. In other words, as framed in the *levée en masse* decree issued in 1793, mass conscription is the nation defending itself:

From this moment until such time as its enemies shall have been driven from the soil of the Republic, all Frenchmen are in permanent requisition for the services of the armies. The young men shall fight; the married men shall forge arms and transport provisions; the women shall make tents and clothes and shall serve in the hospitals; the children shall turn old lint into linen; the old men shall betake themselves to the public squares in order to arouse the courage of the warriors and preach hatred of kings and the unity of the Republic. (Doel 2017: 49)

The decree was also very clear that avoiding and resisting the draft was not an option: 'No one may secure a replacement in the service to which they are called' and 'The Minister of War is responsible for taking all measures necessary for the prompt execution of the present decree' (Frey and Frey 2004: 150). The egalitarian ethics of inclusion and shared responsibility contributed to mass mobilisation and the new French republic was able to create an unprecedented military organisation comprising hundreds of thousands of soldiers. This policy of 'the nation in arms' propelled French victories in the Revolutionary (1792–1803) and Napoleonic Wars (1803–15). Although the conscript army lacked professionalism and military skills it could rely on its sheer size to rout much smaller professional militaries throughout Europe. Whereas the largest European armies rarely had more than 40,000 soldiers the Grande Armée recruited over 2.6 million individuals in the period from 1800 to 1813 (McNab 2009).

However, the process of recruiting so many ordinary people was far from smooth. Although the ideas of fraternity, equality, and liberty provided legitimacy for such an unprecedented undertaking, the ultimate success of conscription was still determined by the coercive power of the state. For one thing, mass conscription was not popular among ordinary people and many individuals attempted to evade the draft while others deserted after their recruitment. For example, in some regions of France up to 60 per cent of recruits deserted their military units while the ministry of war reported that 175,000 deserters applied for state support after the proclamation of amnesty (Forrest 1989: 70). The French state was also rigorous in punishing evasion and desertion and was particularly merciless towards any forms of organised violent resistance to the conscription. Whereas some regions experienced little opposition to the *levée en masse* other regions fiercely resisted the draft. This was particularly the case in Vendée and Brittany where between 1793 and 1796 up to 200,000 people were killed resisting the new republican government. This conflict started with Vendéans rejecting the conscription and the government's demand to fill their district's recruitment quota of 300,000 soldiers (Tilly 1964). The resistance to the draft was crushed violently and was justified with the ideas that revolution is built on 'inflexible justice' and that 'mercy is not a revolutionary sentiment' (Malešević 2017: 201).

The French military success prompted other rulers to implement systems of mass conscription and throughout the nineteenth and early twentieth century most independent polities in the world relied on military draft to recruit their soldiers. Even the US and UK, the only two large states without military draft, introduced conscription during the two world wars as their professional armies did not have enough recruits to fight the large armies fielded by the enemy. Although all states used effective propaganda campaigns to justify conscription and increase recruitment, mass compliance was attained through coercion: imprisonment for draft evasion and court martial with a possible death sentence for desertion. This ever-increasing coercive capacity of states played a central role in bringing millions of young recruits to the battlefields ultimately resulting in historically unprecedented death tolls. In other words, without substantially increased coercive organisational powers of states, including the capacity to legitimately implement mass conscription, there would not have been 85 million deaths from the two world wars and millions of other casualties resulting from other violent conflicts. Although many states have abolished conscription in the last few decades nearly all of them maintain the legal frameworks that allow for its reintroduction in times of war or major crises. For example, in the US conscription was officially abolished in 1973. Yet the law stipulates that 'almost all male US citizens and male immigrants, who are 18 through 25, are required to register with Selective Service' so that they can be called up into the military once conscription is reintroduced.[2]

In addition to states' capacity to coercively recruit citizens in times of war, states have also relied extensively on coercion during domestic

---

[2] See www.sss.gov/register/who-needs-to-register/.

revolutionary transformations and when colonising other societies. In both of these cases ordinary individuals were coerced to fight and kill other human beings. The major revolutions in France, the American colonies, Haiti, the Soviet Union, China, and Iran among others have all involved mass scale violence. The reorganisation and creation of new social orders resulted in civil wars, political killings, famine, hunger, ethnic cleansings, and genocides involving millions of casualties. Many of these human losses were the result of decisions made by government officials. In some instances, violence was a product of deliberate political rulings as was the case with the public executions ordered by the Committee of Public Safety during the Jacobin Reign of Terror in France, or the Great Purge of 1937–8 when Stalin ordered imprisonment and executions of over one million individuals accused of treason, sabotage, and counter-revolutionary activities (Ellman 2002). In other cases, mass casualties were the by-product of mismanagement and flawed decisions made by the rulers as was the case with Mao's Great Leap Forward when up to 45 million people died from famine and starvation (Bachman 2006). However, what is often missing in the conventional interpretations of these revolutionary events is the role of coercive organisational power in enacting these violent outcomes. The mass deaths and carnage do not transpire easily or automatically. This can only happen when hundreds of thousands of individuals are mobilised to perform these violent acts. Obviously if those involved consider such action legitimate, they are more likely to be willing participants. Nevertheless, even with a hefty dose of propaganda most ordinary individuals would still be reluctant to personally engage in such violent acts. While many might nominally support such activities for ideological or other reasons, being directly involved in mass scale violence is a very different prospect. Hence the key question is what are the central coercive mechanisms that make mass participation in violence possible?

Much of the traditional research has emphasised the psychological or economic motives for participation in mass scale violence. Individuals follow commands out of fear for their own lives or because they can benefit materially or symbolically from their involvement in violent acts. Although individual motivations matter a great deal, they are inadequate to account for the changing dynamics of participation in violence. Focusing only on the universal psychological, economic, or other individual motives cannot help us understand the historical, geographical, and situational variability of mass involvement in fighting and killing. For instance, all human beings experience fear when confronted with imminent threats to their life. Yet only some individuals decide to follow coercive commands and act violently on demand while others opt not to act violently despite the grave consequences to their own lives. Furthermore, even the same individuals can act very differently in different situations. For example, Fujii (2011: 151) describes the behaviour of a young Hutu man, Olivier, who was a perpetrator in the Rwandan genocide and who killed many Tutsi civilians and yet he also helped others to escape the killings. Similarly, Polish policemen who worked under German occupation were involved in arrests, deportations, and killings of local Jews yet also helped other Jewish families to escape the Gestapo: 'Michal Strzepka ... killed over a dozen Jews during his time at Radomysl Wielki PP station ... [yet] Strzepka, his wife, and daughter helped coordinate the relocation of the Berl family from village to village, provided them with food, information, and false papers, without receiving any payment in exchange' (Frydel 2018: 199).

The complexity of human behaviour is even more pronounced at higher levels of command. For example, the leading bureaucrats responsible for drafting and institutionalising discriminatory and genocidal policies under the Nazi regime such as Friedrich Wilhelm Kritzinger and Franz Schlegelberger, both of whom were the epitome of desk killers, also devoted a great deal of time, energy, and resources to save some Jewish families. Hence, they both helped their former boss Curt Joël and his family to evade the strict anti-Jewish laws that they themselves drafted and were highly instrumental in saving their lives. They also intervened on behalf of other Jewish colleagues by preventing their deportation or helping them transfer to other jurisdictions 'where it was easier to hide' their identity (O'Byrne 2018: 93).

In addition to this contextual variation in individual behaviour one can also identify differences in the enactment of coercive orders. Although military officers and government officials in Nazi Germany were usually given the same orders from the central authority to use indiscriminate violence against 'the enemy', their different interpretation and implementation of such orders often led to very different outcomes. For example, during the Barbarossa campaign the commander of the 12th Infantry division of the Wehrmacht fighting on the Eastern Front instructed his soldiers to kill all prisoners of war (POWs) without any mercy: 'Prisoners behind the frontline ... Shoot as a general principle! Every soldier shoots any Russian found behind the frontline who has not been taken prisoner in battle' (Bartov 1992: 84). In direct contrast another officer, General Joachim Lemelsen, ordered his soldiers not to shoot POWs and deserters as 'this is murder'. Instead, 'A Russian soldier who has been taken prisoner while wearing a uniform, and after he had put up a brave fight, has the right to decent treatment' (Bartov 1992: 86).

This contextual variability in individual behaviour indicates that the dynamics of organised violence cannot be reduced to fixed psychological, economic, or other motivations. Instead to understand how social pugnacity works it is necessary to shift the focus from individuals to collective action and structure. Collins (2008: 1) rightly argues that instead of zooming on violent individuals as given and static entities the focus should be on violent contexts: 'We seek the contours of situations, which shape the emotions and acts of the individuals who step inside them. It is false lead to look for types of violent individuals, constant across situations.' Violence is not an ingrained biological, psychological, or economic quality, it is a variable social process shaped by the changing individual and group dynamics as well as by specific organisational pathways. While Collins is absolutely right that violence is a situational phenomenon, he still unduly emphasises the role of agency in violent encounters. Nevertheless, to better understand the historical dynamics of coercive power and the ability of social organisations to force individuals to fight and kill it is paramount to explore the structural contexts too. Hence one of the key issues is that the coercive power of social organisations has its own logic and historical dynamics that can generate distinct violent outcomes.

This is not to say that structure trumps agency and that individual and group action is always determined by the social structures. Agency is often crucial in establishing and enacting particular organisational processes. For example, without Hitler and other leading National Socialists there would have been no Nazi Germany and its complex coercive-organisational apparatuses that mobilised millions of ordinary German citizens to fight, torture, and kill millions of civilians in the concentration and extermination camps, on the killing fields of occupied parts of the Soviet Union and Eastern Europe, or the starvation, disease and extermination through forced labour in the countries conquered by the Nazi military and police apparatus. However, once complex and durable social organisations are created and enabled to operate, they develop an organisational logic that operates on its own and often pulls passive, hesitant, and even unwilling individuals into its organisational cortex. Mann (1986) rightly argues that once states emerge as the dominant form of territorial organisation, they gradually cage individuals into their organisational shells. For 98 per cent of their existence on this planet humans were not constrained by social structures: they were nomadic foragers who lived in very small, flexible, and egalitarian bands. It is only the development of chiefdoms and more durable state formations that created the conditions for socially caging individuals into particular organisational forms. With the development of centralised states and permanent power structures the infrastructural capacities of states increase substantially so that they establish permanent organisational mechanisms for social caging. While states are the pre-eminent power containers, other social organisations such as private corporations, religious institutions, political parties, and many others also have the capacity to cage their members. The historical dynamics of social caging is crucial in understanding the logic of coercive power. The coercion is not an unexpected side effect of organisational development – it is its very core. Social organisations exist, develop, expand, and operate precisely because they possess coercive capacity to make individuals do things that they would ordinarily not do.

This organisational capacity has proliferated and expanded over time. Although some states and other social organisations have collapsed, have been colonised or integrated into other states and social organisations or have split into several entities the coercive organisational power as such has experienced relatively continuous and cumulative expansion (Malešević 2017). For example, most contemporary European states possess substantively more infrastructural power and organisational capacity than their much larger ancient counterparts. Although contemporary Italy is in territorial terms a much smaller state than the Roman Empire its infrastructural power and its organisational capacity is vastly superior to its Roman counterpart. The Italian nation-state possesses advanced transport and communication networks, can tax its citizens at source, has fixed and policed borders, has superior systems of surveillance and control, has a standardised and compulsory education system and nearly full literacy of its population, can successfully regulate migration, employment, welfare and health care provisions and many other capacities that the Roman Empire never possessed. The unprecedented development of infrastructural capacities has substantially increased the coercive capacity of states. Consequently, the speed and scope of coercive power has also expanded. This is particularly visible in the ability of state authorities to enforce their decisions quickly and over large territories.

For example, whereas the imprisonment of dissidents under the Romanov administration was sporadic and haphazard the Soviet state developed much more sophisticated coercive techniques and practices that allowed for the systematic imprisonment and deportation of any potential dissenters to the forced labour camps in the vast Gulag archipelago of Siberia and other parts of the Soviet Union. The substantially increased coercive power of the state played a central role in the imprisonment and deportation of more than 17 million individuals of which up to 3 million died (Applebaum 2003). Whereas the Romanov

administration was responsible for up to 4,000 deaths of political prisoners over a period of 85 years, Stalin's NKVD executed more than
700,000 political prisoners in less than a year (Pipes 2001: 67). This
means that the Soviet state was capable of killing '1,500 people per day'
'between August 1937 and November 1938' (Kort 2015: 236)
Furthermore, 'between 1937 and 1940 Soviet courts convicted more
than 7 million people of various offences' (Kort 2015: 236). The ever-
increasing coercive capacities also allowed the Soviet state to conscript
millions of recruits who could not evade the military draft or who did not
attempt to desert. Authoritarian states such as the Soviet Union and Nazi
Germany successfully combined despotic and infrastructural powers
(Mann 2012) to monitor, police, recruit, punish, and kill their
own citizens.

Non-authoritarian states have also dramatically increased their coercive organisational capacities in the twentieth and twenty-first centuries
which enabled them to pacify the domestic arena and to substantially
increase the surveillance of citizens, to expand the influence and number
of judiciary systems, to enlarge the prison population, and to militarise
the police force (Dandeker 1990; Go 2020). For example, the US has the
highest per capita incarceration rate and the largest prison population in
the world with 2.3 million inmates. The number of incarcerated individuals has increased tenfold in the last fifty years: from around 200,000 in
1972 to 2.3 million in 2018 (Sawyer and Wagner 2019). The number of
imprisoned individuals has also dramatically increased in many other
countries including Russia, Ukraine, South Africa, Poland, Mexico,
Brazil, Spain, and Kenya.[3] The number of criminal court cases has been
on the increase continuously for the last fifty years with most states
introducing new penal legislation and new criminal courts.

In addition to these structural forces that enhance the coercive power
of the state, there are also specific micro-sociological processes through
which coercion operates. Military scholars have regularly identified drill
as the defining feature of disciplinary control. Van der Haven (2016) and
McNeill (1997) have emphasised the role drill has historically played in
the development of social cohesion in the military through 'muscular
bonding' and the transformation of individual feelings of fear into a
collective sense of pride (see Chapter 9). However, drill has also been
highly instrumental in transforming ordinary civilians into obedient
soldiers. From Maurice of Nassau in the sixteenth century to contemporary times, military organisations have relied on drill to turn

---

[3] See https://worldpopulationreview.com/country-rankings/incarceration-rates-by-country.

individuals unwilling to fight into a disciplined combat machine. Drawing on the example of the Roman armies, Maurice introduced regularised marching and drill to transform disjointed individuals into highly organised military units committed to fulfilling the goals of their military organisation. The soldiers were taught to make coordinated movements on command so that they would always act in unison. The focus was on moving 'simultaneously and in rhythm' so that 'everyone was ready to fire at the same time' (McNeill 1984: 129). These coordinated rhythmic movements were practised outside of the theatres of war in order to create an effective military mechanism capable of acting on command and overpowering less organised opposition. However, drill was also introduced to break down potential individual resistance and to make sure that the soldiers cannot escape the battlefield: 'The trick was in the timing, and in preventing men from fleeing the battlefield entirely when they turned their backs on the enemy in order to reload in the rear. Oft-repeated drill, making every movement semiautomatic, minimised the possibility of breakdown' (McNeill 1984: 129). Hence drill practice and marching became integral to everyday life in the military as forcing soldiers to perform daily drills not only enhanced social cohesion but also made recruits more pliable and obedient to the military authorities. As Barkawi (2017: 148–9) emphasises, drill helps 'instill the habit of instinctive and automatic obedience to command' and 'through repeated practice and rigid attention to detail, instructors hoped that battle drill generated a "military conscience" in soldiers, one that would help them perform the correct actions in conditions of stress and danger'. Since the seventeenth century, drill has become an important coercive mechanism of disciplining individuals and embedding them into the military culture of fighting and killing. Close order drill has historically played a key role in helping socialise reluctant civilians and turning them into disciplined military subjects and this has enhanced social pugnacity.

This internal and external social caging that targets, moulds, and penalises human behaviour has also been deployed outside the borders of specific states. Imperial conquest and the colonisation of the globe has contributed further to the development and implementation of coercive power abroad. In many cases the use of new coercive capacities and novel disciplining techniques was pioneered in the colonies. While the development of civil society and free mass media has imposed constraints on the introduction of various coercive measures in the imperial centres, for the most part this was not the case in the colonial possessions where violence was often used indiscriminately. The colonial subjects were often forcibly recruited to fight in the colonial wars and occupation campaigns, to police other colonised populations, and to work as slaves or serfs in the extraction of resources in the colonies.

In the traditional historiography, the victories of British, French, or Dutch militaries in the First and Second World Wars have often been depicted as successes achieved by white European soldiers. In films, novels, computer games and other popular outlets the militaries that fought in these wars are almost uniformly represented as white Europeans. However, the historical reality was very different with millions of non-Europeans fighting in different theatres of war. Barkawi (2017: 7) documents that in the First World War over half a million Indian soldiers fought for the British Empire and they outnumbered soldiers from Australia and Canada while in the Second World War two million recruits from the Indian subcontinent fought 'from the China coast to Monte Cassino, sending divisions to East and North Africa, the Middle East, and Italy, while carrying the main burden of Britain's war against Japan in Malaya, Burma, and Northeast India'. Similarly, the French military relied extensively on recruits from the colonies to fight various wars. For example, the Armée d'Afrique was created in 1830 and was involved in numerous conflicts until the end of the Algerian war in 1962. The army recruited local populations including North African Arabs, Berbers, and French settlers and from 1913 the French state introduced a selective conscription that was applied to the native population of Algeria. Following the 1940 defeat the French government in exile (Free France) established in 1943 the French Expeditionary Corps, an army of 112,000 soldiers, mostly composed of North Africans. This army played a central role in the battles of Monte Cassino and significantly contributed to the French war effort (Caddick-Adams 2013). The Dutch military also relied extensively on indigenous recruits. For example, after occupation of the Netherlands by Nazi Germany in 1940 the Royal Netherlands East Indies Army continued fighting in Asia. Much of this force was composed of local recruits with over 28,000 indigenous soldiers and thousands of others in militia, territorial guard units and civilian auxiliaries (Vickers 2005).

The colonial powers often combined coercion with economic incentives to mobilise the local population to fight in conflicts abroad as well as to police their own societies. In most cases imperial governance used a divide and rule strategy to maintain control over vast territories and much more numerous local populations. For example, the British colonial authorities deployed the doctrine of martial races to differentiate sharply between ethnic, religious, and caste-based groups whereby only some groups were deemed a 'martial race' fit for military and police service and others were excluded. These essentialist categorisations made the divide and rule policies operational while also providing justification for privileging some groups over others. In most cases the groups categorised as 'non-martial race' and thus not fit for fighting were members of the traditional elite who were considered a threat to colonial rule. In the Indian subcontinent Brahmans and Bengalis were deemed 'non-martial races' while historically less privileged groups such as Sikhs, Punjabi Muslims, Gurkhas, Pathans, Dogras, and Garhwals were categorised as 'martial races' (Liebau 2017). Similarly, in East Africa the Kamba people were deemed to be a 'martial race' considered by British administrators as an obedient and 'mechanically-minded tribe' while the more numerous Kikuyu or Luhya were regarded as less loyal. The British imperial administrators consciously imitated their Roman predecessors in deploying the divide and rule strategy. As Henry Lawrence, a nineteenth-century military administrator emphasises: 'There is no doubt that whatever danger may threaten us in India, the greatest is from our own troops' (Barkawi 2017: 18). Hence, he recommended that the military mix different native soldiers together and to privilege some groups over others: 'oppose class against class and tribe against tribe' (Barkawi 2017: 23).

The *divide et impera* practice was also used by imperial governance to coercively police the domestic population and to force slave labourers to work for their imperial masters. For example, in Congo Free State (1885–1908), a colonial entity privately owned by the Belgian King Leopold II, the indigenous population was completely decimated by excessive state brutality and forced to collect natural rubber for export. The unprecedented violence in combination with the proliferation of infectious diseases, famine, and hunger all largely caused by the colonial activities resulted in up to 10 million deaths (Hochschild 1999). Much of the violence was committed by the colonial army the Force Publique which was run by the white European officers and black soldiers who were recruited from the domestic 'warrior tribes' such as Zappo Zap and Bangala and indigenous populations from Nigeria, Liberia and Zanzibar. In 1900 the Force Publique had around 19,000 soldiers who were responsible for enforcing severe labour practices and for punishing slave workers who did not meet their daily quotas. By treating labour as a form of taxation the colonial government was involved in mass scale violence ranging from the hostage taking of family members, body mutilation, torture, severe beatings and whippings, to killings and destruction of entire villages. The colonial administration created and ran a 'slave society' where the native population was coerced into labour to meet impossible quotas for daily rubber collection. The Force Publique and the business company militias were responsible for punishing those who could not meet their quotas or who tried to escape. Both of these offences were punishable by death. With the large number of victims, the soldiers of the Force Publique were expected to cut off the hand of a victim as a proof that they had administered the death sentence. Over the years the chopped-off hands became a replacement for the rubber quotas and were often used as a form of currency in Congo Free State.

4.4   The Coercive Power of Non-State Organisations

Although states are dominant purveyors of coercive power in the modern world many non-state organisations also possess substantial coercive capacities. Many violent non-state actors have proved capable of using force to transform ordinary individuals into committed fighters. The most recognisable non-state coercive organisations include drug cartels, gangs, private military contractors, armed religious organisations, paramilitary forces, insurgent movements, militias, vigilante units, and terrorist networks. For example, the largest drug cartels such as Sinaloa or Las Zetas in Mexico possess vast armed forces that number over 100,000 foot soldiers and as such are larger and more powerful than many military forces of nation-states.[4] Similarly, private military and security contractors such as Academii or G4S have enormous coercive capabilities including a workforce of hundreds of thousands. G47 employs 657,000 people many of whom are armed professionals (Kemeroff 2018). The largest insurgent movements such as the Taliban, Syrian National Army, Sudan Revolutionary Front, United Wa State Army, or Kachin Independence Army maintain substantial armed forces that in some cases involve up to 100,000 armed individuals. Even large-scale gangs often control tens of thousands of armed members – from Japanese Yakuza with 28,200 members to Hong Kong's Triads which number up to 160,000 active members (Wang 2017).[5]

Many of these violent non-state organisations operate similarly to the professional armed forces. They maintain a hierarchical structure with well-established chains of command and control, clearly delineated division of labour, a fixed system of recruitment and training, and the prospect of promotion within the organisation. This is not a surprise as all durable coercive social organisations rely on similar strategies to expand their size and influence (Malešević 2017). As Tilly (1985) demonstrated convincingly, there is a lot of similarity between the formation

---

[4] See www.washingtontimes.com/news/2009/mar/03/100000-foot-soldiers-in-cartels/.
[5] See www.japantimes.co.jp/news/2020/04/03/national/crime-legal/yakuza-group-membership-falls-15th-straight-year/.

of early modern states in Europe and the operation of criminal cartels. For example, state making was dependent on warfare where the rulers deployed protection racketeering to establish a monopoly on the legitimate use of violence: 'If protection rackets represent organised crime at its smoothest, then war risking and state making – quintessential protection rackets with the advantage of legitimacy – qualify as our largest examples of organised crime' (Tilly 1985: 169). Hence one of the key differences between the two is the nature of political legitimacy whereby the non-state armed forces are deemed to be illegitimate, while the state military and police organisations are 'protection rackets' with legitimacy.

Nevertheless, when some non-state actors prove militarily successful, they can transition the barrier to legitimacy. Hence many insurgent, terrorist, and paramilitary movements have proved capable of taking over the state apparatus or creating their own parastate structures and in this process have gained political legitimacy associated with established governments. This transition is possible precisely because the complex and durable non-state coercive agents possess coercive organisational capacities that resemble those of formal states and their military organisations. For example, the drug cartels such as Sinaloa and terrorist networks such as Al-Qaeda operate through flexible yet highly centralised bureaucratic organisational structures that in many ways are compatible with the hierarchical order that characterises legitimate state bureaucracies. Hence the Sinaloa cartel has traditionally operated through a four-layer structural model of organisation that ranges from the drug lords (*capos*) at the top, loyal lieutenants (*tenientes*) below them, then the hitmen (*sicarios*) in the middle and the falcons (*halcones*) at the bottom. While the drug lords are responsible for appointing the lieutenants and local leaders and making key decisions on the drug trade and other criminal activities, building and breaking alliances with other groups, and deciding on life and death issues, the lieutenants are responsible for the cartel organisation in their own territories including the recruitment of hitmen and falcons and the use of violence to pacify individuals and territories under their control. The third layer of responsibility includes hitmen who constitute armed operatives who are involved in variety of violent activities ranging from fighting with rival cartels and operating protection rackets, to kidnappings, theft, extortion, and assassinations. Finally, the everyday activities of the drug cartel are conducted by 'falcons' who observe and report on behaviour of rival cartels, police and military as well as on activities of ordinary people (Grillo 2012).

Al-Qaeda's organisational structure is very similar. The terrorist network is hierarchically structured with the small leadership responsible for all key decisions. Al-Qaeda documents emphasise that the organisation fosters centralised decision making but allows for the decentralised execution of commands (al-Hammadi, 2005). At the top of the organisation is a single leader (Amir) who 'is involved with operational, strategic, and tactical planning as well as logistical and organizational planning. The leader approves the annual work plan, the annual budget, and is in charge of changing them according to new developments' (Gunaratna and Oreg 2010: 1054). The leader is also involved in making decisions about promotions and demotions at the senior level. However, the leader and his deputy consult with the command council (*majil al shura*) which is the main decision-making body. The command council is responsible for authorising Al-Qaeda's regulations, policy plans, the annual budget and also elects individuals to different committees. The Amir is the head of the command council. The council also oversees the activities of the six committees which are hierarchically just below the *majil al shura* – the military committee, the political committee, religious committee, administrative and financial committee, security committee, and media committee. The military committee is one of the most important units within the organisation as it coordinates all military actions including the development of combat skills, military training, and acquisition of technical knowledge necessary for specific terrorist actions (Gunaratna and Oreg 2010: 1058). The military committee consists of four highly specialised units: (a) the general section with the main unit and the training unit both responsible for different aspects of internal fighting (mostly in Afghanistan and Iraq); (b) special operations unit that focuses on external terrorist actions including the establishment of sleeper cells in different countries; (c) the nuclear weapons section centred on acquiring and using non-conventional weaponry; and (d) the library and research section responsible for collecting information relevant to military actions. Gunaratna and Oreg (2010: 1054) conclude that 'Al Qaeda has evolved into a strict and clear-cut hierarchical structure organization'.

This organisational similarity with the bureaucratic model of the state coercive apparatuses is just as visible in the recruitment and training practices. The large-scale drug cartels, gangs, paramilitaries, and terrorist networks rely on volunteers,[6] but they also deploy various coercive

---

[6] Becoming a member of the gang is often a matter of individual choice. In many cases people join the criminal organisations to improve their socio-economic situation, to escape domestic abuse, to enhance their social status with their peers, to gain a sense of acceptance and communal belonging, or to experience excitement. However, in some situations membership is enforced by the gangs and those who reject the gangs are likely to be killed. Hence while one can often volunteer to join such organisations it is extremely difficult, and in many cases, impossible to leave such entities. For instance, some gangs such as the Aryan Brotherhood use the motto 'blood in, blood out' which means that a

practices to recruit their members. However, coercion is even more present in the training and everyday operations of these organisations. While the armed forces of recognised states are limited by legal provisions and normative codes in their use of force this is rarely the case with violent non-state organisations. The drug cartels and gangs regularly combine economic incentives with severe violence to recruit and keep their members within the organisation. In some cases, young individuals are offered money or drugs to join the organisation and once they become involved in the drug trade and other criminal activities, they cannot leave. As a Mexican official points out, the criminal organisations recruit boys as young as 12: 'The cartels recruit by first involving them in some drug trafficking, then in selling drugs and finally, in some cases for as little as $160 a week, they are given the job of tracking down people the cartel wants to assassinate.'[7] Gradually the young members become involved in other activities and are often trained to use weapons and fight. Once they become sicarios they are involved in regular fights and killings and there is no way out for these young men. As one 18-year-old member of Juárez Cartel (Vicente Carrillo Fuentes Organization) based in Ciudad Juárez in the Mexican state of Chihuahua describes his experience: 'Sicaritos are children who are assassins, 13 or 14 years old' who receive weapons and training from the cartels and are instructed to kill designated individuals (Burnett 2009: 1). Another former sicario emphasises that the young boys do not think much about their actions and are more focused on impressing their peers and cartel members: 'To be an assassin, you can't think … You just do it, grab a pistol and go kill somebody, or whatever. It doesn't matter if you die or not' (Burnett 2009: 1).

Many gangs and other criminal organisations deploy well-established violent initiation rituals that all new recruits have to undertake in order to become full members. For example, the US white supremacist prison gang 'the Aryan Brotherhood' numbering over 20,000 members maintains a violent ritual called 'making their bones' whereby a new recruit is expected to kill a rival gang member or a policeman (thus turning them into 'bones'). Other gangs such as the Almighty Latin Kings in the US or the Junky Funky Kids (JFK) in South Africa expose their new members to severe beatings. To officially join the JFK gang, one has to go through a tunnel of lined up gang members who use chains, belts, and wooden sticks to beat the new recruits. Similarly, the new members of the

---

member can leave only in a coffin. The gangs which control large swaths of territory and population are more likely to operate a very coercive system of membership recruitment.
[7] See www.mercurynews.com/2009/11/05/mexican-drug-cartels-recruiting-youths/.

Almighty Latin Kings have to endure severe beatings from other members in order to be 'jumped into' the organisation. Potential female members might experience an even worse initiation ritual: gang rape by the members through which the new recruit is 'sexed into' the gang (Miller 2002).

Once the new members are fully integrated into the gang they are often subjected to violence. Any indication of disobedience to senior gang members is likely to provoke beatings and other forms of severe punishment and in some cases death. A vague suspicion of being a police informant or spy for another criminal organisation can also result in torture and death. Even everyday disagreements and instances where another gang member feels that he or she was disrespected can generate violence to the point of losing one's life. The frequent change of leadership, splits within the gang, and conflicts with other gangs all generate a continuous environment of violence. The regular activities of these criminal organisations such as the trafficking in narcotics, people, arms, counterfeit goods, and money and so on all involve the use of violence on an everyday basis. Thus, the non-state organisations rely extensively on coercion. They possess and deploy the coercive power that stems from the organisational capacity in a similar way to how the state military and police operate. However, they also deploy more despotic power and arbitrary violence in their everyday operations as they are not constrained by the normative and legal codes under which the militaries and police have to work. Hence the coercive power plays a central role in making ordinary members fight and kill for their organisations. To track how exactly the coercive power and social pugnacity work among non-state actors I will briefly explore two different but highly compatible contemporary examples – the everyday violent practices among the gangs of the Northern Triangle of Central America and the coercive recruitment of children in Uganda's Lord's Resistance Army.

4.4.1   Coercion and Social Pugnacity of Central American Gangs

Salvador, Guatemala, and Honduras are often identified as countries with extremely high homicide rates – in 2018 Honduras was at 44.7 while Guatemala was at 22.4 and Salvador at 36 per 100,000 inhabitants. In 2015 El Salvador was at 103 and Honduras was at 88.5 which were among the highest homicide rates in the world.[8] Most of these deaths and other forms of violence were generated by the activities of the two

---

[8] See www.statista.com/statistics/696152/homicide-rate-in-el-salvador.

large-scale gangs – Barrio 18 (Mara 18, Calle 18) and Mara Salvatrucha (MS 13). Although both gangs originated in the US in the mid-to-late twentieth century, they expanded dramatically in El Salvador and Guatemala after over 200,000 Central Americans who grew up in the US were deported in 1996 to the Northern Triangle of Central America. Over the last two decades the two gangs have deeply penetrated the three Central American societies and have established firm control over territory and population throughout the region. Barrio 18 has over 70,000 members in El Salvador alone and they are involved in a variety of criminal activities. Both gangs deploy a very strict hierarchical system of organisation where any signs of disrespect, disloyalty, or disobedience are severely punished. For example, Barrio 18 has instituted a rule where even a minor indication of insubordination to the gang leader or a lack of 'proper respect' to other gang members is punished by 18 seconds of harsh beating while the more serious transgressions may result in a death penalty. The 18 seconds' beating ('beat-in') is also used as a ritual of initiation for new members. Although the organisation is deeply hierarchical it is also very decentralised: Barrio 18 is run by the established members, *palabreros* (or *veteranos*) who coordinate activities of semi-autonomous but hierarchically organised cells. The lower layers of authority are leaders of *canchas* and each *cancha* is divided into *tribus* (tribes) (Dudley 2015). The organisation maintains a different structure in different countries. For instance, in Honduras Barrio 18 is more centralised with different layers of hierarchy. There is a distinction between full gang members who are integrated in all criminal activities and the affiliates who are involved in some activities such as intelligence or moving illicit goods. Furthermore, the full members are structured vertically from gang leaders (*toros*) who control a specific 'clique' (*clica*) to the lower-level leaders (*homies*) who command several 'soldiers' (*soldados*) each (Serrano 2020: 1).

Mara Salvatrucha (MS 13) is more a centralised and even larger criminal organisation which relies extensively on coercion. For example, in El Salvador MS 13 has 246 cells (*clicas*) while the rival Barrio 18 has only 28 *tribus* (Dudley 2015). MS 13 has a more rigid structure with the ruling council (*ranfla* or *mesa*) composed of veteran members who coordinate regional and local cells (Manning 2016). The lower levels of authority include programmes managed by mid-level leaders who run the gang cells (cliques). The organisation also uses violence for initiation rituals with 13 seconds of beating (*el brinco*) of new initiates by three to five established members. In many cases, particularly in El Salvador and Honduras, the new initiates are also expected to murder a 'chavala' (member of a rival gang) in order to become 'homeboy', that is, to gain full membership of MS 13. For example, a police report from the US describes how MS 13 admitted a new member after he killed a rival gang member: 'Detectives obtained detailed information about an alleged MS-13 meeting on January 8 at an auto repair shop in Everett. At the meeting, Joel Martinez, nicknamed "Animal," allegedly became a homeboy after murdering Irvin De Paz, 16. Herzzon Sandoval, who MS-13 ranks call "Casper" and prosecutors say is the Eastside Loco clique leader, presided over the meeting' (Manning 2016: 1). Once an individual becomes a full member, he can never leave the gang. MS 13 also deploys severe beatings as a means of disciplining transgressions of existing members. Hence the organisation operates a code where each act of misbehaviour is penalised with a specific form of punishment. The list of potential violations includes a variety of misdemeanours from 'missing meetings, to being drunk in public and pulling out a gun, to losing clique property' while more serious misconduct such as 'failing to come to the aid of a fellow homeboy', an attempt to escape the gang or to inform the police are all punished by death (Manning 2016: 1).

Violence is also utilised to enhance group solidarity. As all members are expected to participate in all forms of criminal activity including beatings and killings the shared experience of violence helps establish stronger bonds between the gang members. 'In the MS13, all members must do "missions," and during a mission, all members must participate. In some cases, this means repeatedly hacking a victim with a machete. Refusal means almost certain death since the member or aspiring member is a potential witness' (InSight Crime 2019: 49). Violence is also deployed to police the social and territorial boundaries that the gang controls as well as to enforce the collection of revenue through extortion (collecting *renta*). MS 13 has maintained a reputation as an extremely violent gang which kills anybody who challenges its authority or is willing to cooperate with the government to provide testimony against the gang members. The gang also relies on violence to control intra-gang fighting. The conflicts between cliques and individual members might involve mediation by the senior leadership and in some instances punishments for transgression include hefty fines, beatings, or even death. Violence is also deployed as a political tool. For example, in El Salvador MS 13 and Barrio 18 have been able to win concessions from the state through the regulation of homicide rates. During the truce periods agreed with the government the homicide rates in the country have plummeted and in exchange the Salvadorean government agreed to provide payments to the gang or to organise prison transfers for the senior gang members (InSight Crime 2019: 48). Both MS 13 and Barrio 18 use violence for most of their everyday activities and violent acts shape all life stages of their members. The coercive power of these organisations is at the heart of their existence and it is this coercive structure that turns their members into brutal fighters and killers. Violence underpins all aspects of membership: 'potential members commit violent acts to be considered for membership and ultimately to gain entry; they are then beaten into the gang in a ritual that has left more than one permanently scarred; they move up the gang ladder by "putting in the work" and showing "commitment," euphemisms for committing violent acts in the name of the gang' (InSight Crime 2019: 48–9).

4.4.2   Coercive Power and Close-Range Violence in the Lord's Resistance Army

Many insurgent and militia groups recruit underage boys and girls to fight – there are over 300,000 children drafted into a variety of military and paramilitary organisations throughout the world. However, Uganda's Lord's Resistance Army has gained a notorious reputation for its relentless coercive recruitment of children and the fact that most of its combatants have been forcibly recruited as children. It is estimated that between 10,000 and 14,000 LRA combatants were underage boys and girls who were taken away from their families at gunpoint and forced to fight for this paramilitary organisation (Briggs 2009; Singer 2006). Other sources indicate that up 25,000 children[9] were abducted by the LRA although not all of them were subsequently recruited into the rebel force (Allen et al. 2020). Nevertheless, the overwhelming majority of LRA soldiers – 90% – were recruited into the armed force as children (Kaplan 2009: 98). Initially the LRA could not recruit enough soldiers and opted to focus on children to keep the insurgency going (Oloya 2013: 61). In many cases children were recruited to fight while their parents, siblings, teachers, neighbours, and others who resisted their recruitment were killed in the process. In some cases, the children were forced to kill their family members and friends to survive. For example, one former LRA combatant, Bosco, recalls his traumatic experience when he, as a six-year-old boy, had to kill his five-year-old sister as she was too young to keep up with the LRA march:

---

[9] Following Oloya (2013: 20) I avoid using term 'child soldiers' as this wrongly implies that such individuals had fixed age identities. Instead Oloya recommends a concept which better recognises the processual character of individual experience – 'child induced soldiers'. This concept 'defines the starting point of the torturous journey, initiated in childhood, that takes these children into the world of organised violence, and from which, if they survive, they often emerge not as children but as young adults'.

The commander pointed the barrel of his gun at me and said: 'Cut her and do it quickly!' I thought: 'Please let me die.' Then I heard the rapid fire right over my head. That's the moment when my heart sank, and I knew I was going to do it. I raised my arm to haul out, and my sister started to cry. And I started to cry as well and said: 'Please forgive me, Juli. I have to do this.' The commander tapped my shoulder once more. And I raised my arm and I drove the machete through my sister's neck. (Ruta 2013)

The LRA emerged from the Holy Spirit Mobile Force led by the Acholi spirit-medium Alice Auma who led a rebellion against the Ugandan government led by Yoweri Museveni between August 1986 and November 1987. Auma claimed to be channelling a voice of a dead army officer called 'Lakwena' (the messenger) believed by many of her supporters to be a manifestation of the Holy Spirit in Christian teachings. In 1988, after the Holy Spirt movement was defeated by the government forces, Joseph Kony, another self-proclaimed spirit medium, reorganised the resistance against the Ugandan government with a new armed force – Lord's Salvation Army that in 1992 became Lord's Resistance Army. LRA established its base in North Uganda and was also active in Southern Sudan, Central African Republic, and eastern DR Congo. LRA's ideology represents a blend of Christian fundamentalist millenarianism (with the emphasis on the Ten Commandments) and Acholi nationalism (Kaplan 2009: 107–12; Oloya 2013: 58–9). These ideological principles were combined with Kony's charismatic authority as most LRA members believed that their leader possessed supernatural powers. For example, one former LRA combatant also recruited as a child describes the common view of Kony among the LRA members:

He [Kony] is not a Muslim, or a Christian, he is his own religion. He can sit and then talk from very far away and give orders. And then he can look at you and tell you he knows what you are thinking. Everybody is afraid of him. But we all admired him. He promised us that he will take over the government and then we would be able to live in big houses and drive cars. We were forced to watch those who wanted to escape being killed. Nobody wanted to escape then. (Kaplan 2009: 109)

Hence ideological principles and charismatic appeal were also underpinned by the coercive power of this paramilitary organisation and its authoritarian leader.

Just like Barrio 18 or MS 13, LRA relies extensively on violence to recruit its members and to make them effective combatants who fight and kill for the organisation. The fact that over 90 per cent of new recruits were children allowed LRA to use violence as an effective means of socialisation into the realm of armed struggle. In this way LRA was able to mould very young minds into loyal combatants. As one former LRA member explained, 'So Kony is strong because he abducted children, and completely made them forget their home experience ... we who were abducted as children knew nothing. All we knew was that combat is a good thing. As a young child you are treated according to your size, given small rewards that fits your thinking and size to entice you' (Oloya 2013: 61). By normalising the use of indiscriminate violence including severe beatings, rape, torture, and killings the LRA created violent individuals who themselves then reproduced the same violent patterns of action. As Oloya (2013: 85) states: 'killing was deliberately trivialised, it was casual, without any apparent reason' and as such 'trained the children not to be afraid of killing, inuring them to the sight of blood'. Once fully integrated into the LRA the children would also be trained to act violently against other new child recruits. Another former LRA member, a 16-year-old girl abducted as a child recalls how recent young recruits were moulded through the shared experience of violence. She described the case of a child recruit who attempted to escape LRA and was caught:

They made him eat a mouthful of red pepper, and five people were beating him. His hands were tied, and then they made us, the other new captives, kill him with a stick. I felt sick. I knew this boy from before. We were from the same village. I refused to kill him, and they told me they would shoot me. They pointed a gun at me, so I had to do it. The boy was asking me, "Why are you doing this?" I said I had no choice. After we killed him, they made us smear his blood on our arms ... They said we had to do this so we would not fear death and so we would not try to escape. (Kaplan 2009: 111)

In addition to regular use of violence against dissenters and deserters LRA deployed other forms of coercive power. For example, child recruits were required to undergo physically intense military training (*pwonyo mony*) and to march relentlessly for hundreds of kilometres with little or no food or water (Oloya 2013: 81). The girls regularly experienced sexual abuse by the senior commanders and as soon as they began having periods, they were given away to be 'wives' to the officers. For example, Kony has fathered numerous children with 'young brides' many of whom were simply raped by him (Oloya 2013: 90–2). The LRA also established a rigorous disciplinary system where young recruits were expected to undergo a purification ritual (*wiiro kom*) through which children were expected to transition from the civilian into the military world – 'washing the civilian mind'. Following the purification ceremony, the new recruits were expected to pursue ascetic lifestyles with prohibitions on unsanctioned sex, smoking, drinking alcohol, using drugs, gambling, and eating a variety of foods (pork, honey, eggs, and some fruits). Breaking any of these prohibited activities would automatically result in corporal punishment (Oloya 2013: 89). Hence the coercive power underpinned almost all aspects of life in the Lord's Resistance Army – the child induced soldiers were recruited through indiscriminate violence, were initiated into the armed force through violent practices and rituals, were trained to be violent, were expected to kill and torture their enemies and also to use violence against any disobedient fellow combatants.

4.5   The Social Logic of Enforced Fighting

The conventional view, inspired by neo-Darwinism, sees fighting as an automatic and natural reaction to external threat – the fight or flight response. However, while human beings just as other species possess the universal proclivity for self-preservation there is nothing automatic and natural in their experience of fighting. Instead of being an inherent biological and psychological response social pugnacity is a complex, highly dynamic, contextual, and variable social process. Moreover, large-scale protracted fighting is only possible through the existence of durable social organisations such as states, armies, police, paramilitaries, militias, gangs, and many other established purveyors of violence. As Collins (2008: 28) points out, 'historical comparisons show that social organisation is a huge component in determining the amount of violence that takes place. The history of armies is the history of organisational techniques for keeping men [and women] fighting.' Hence the scale, extent, and timing of fights are determined by organisational dynamics. The social organisations are the backbone of protracted fighting and the historical record shows clearly that wars, revolutions, genocides, and other forms of organised violence proliferate on the back of ever-increasing organisational capacity of states and non-state actors (Malešević 2017; Mann 1993, 2013). Furthermore, one of the defining features of organisational power is coercion – social organisations rely on their coercive capacities to make individuals fulfil the specific tasks that contribute towards realisation of goals set by the social organisation. Thus, for organised purveyors of violence that means making individuals into effective fighters. In this context coercion plays an indispensable role in recruiting individuals into violent organisations and in creating a social environment where they have to fight and kill other human beings. As many leaders of different violent organisations have recognised through-out history, without the presence and continuous threat of force ordinary individuals would not fight at all. Hence, much of the fighting that has taken place in history was enforced fighting. Both state armed forces and non-state violent organisations have devised a variety of techniques, rituals, and social practices to transform ordinary individuals into effect-ive fighters. Violent acts and coercive power have defined all aspects of combat and the preparation for fighting – from coercive recruitment and oppressive training techniques to the policing of participation in conflicts and the punishment of dissent and desertion. Although coercive power was not the only element deployed to make individuals into fighters it has historically been the most significant tool for mass scale participation in violent events.

Nevertheless, despite its historical centrality in transforming ordinary people into efficient combatants, coercive power has rarely been deployed as the sole mechanism to increase fighting efficiency. Both state and non-state actors have usually combined force with other incentives including ideological justification, material inducements, the prospects of status enhancement, emotional blackmail linked to one's networks of micro-solidarity, the attainment of specific political rights, and the possibility of greater social, economic, and political inclusion, among others. Although coercive power is a mainstay of social pugnacity the continuous commitment to fighting entails more than simple force. For example, to be able to conscript millions of individuals to fight in the two world wars the states had to combine coercive pressure with society-wide ideological penetration where the war goals had to resonate with the grassroot perceptions of what the fighting was aiming to achieve. It is only through the synchronous action of coercion, ideology, and micro-solidarity that the majority of ordinary individuals understood participation in these wars as a moral absolute that had to be realised. While coercive power was deployed to recruit and keep soldiers in the theatres of war (through rigorous punishments for desertion, insubordination, or defeatism) ideological framing was used to depict the violent conflicts as the national struggle for survival (through the propagandistic portrayals of national heroism of soldiers and dehumanisation of the enemy). Both of these large-scale processes were successful only when couched in the language and practices of everyday life with a focus on deep kinship, friendship, and comradeship ties. In these discourses all citizens were ideologically and organisationally entangled into moral and emotional commitments to each other. The soldiers were primed to fight on the account that they were protecting their loved ones from a merciless enemy bent on their destruction while the civilians were expected to support the war effort on the account that their loved ones, the soldiers, were sacrificing their lives for their very survival. Thus, in both cases the ideological and coercive powers tapped into the microcosm of group solidarity. The circular logic of fighting beseeches both sides through emotional and moral blackmail. If you as a soldier are unwilling to fight this means that you do not love and care for your family and friends who will die because of your selfishness and your moral flaws. The same logic is deployed in addressing the civilians: you as a civilian have to unconditionally support this war at a time when our soldiers are sacrificing their lives for you, and any resistance or unwillingness to fulfil your war responsibilities indicates your selfishness and moral failings.

Non-state violent organisations also combine coercive power with ideological tenets both of which have to be embedded in the networks of micro-solidarity. However, the ideological creeds used by the paramilitaries, gangs, militias, insurgencies, or terrorist organisations may not be as developed or institutionalised as they are in the case of nation-states and their coercive apparatuses – military, police, and the judiciary. Usually, states have a much larger population under their control and more robust ideological apparatuses at their disposal including mass education systems and government-controlled mass media that shape much of the public sphere. While some non-state actors such as terrorist groups or separatist insurgencies emphasise their ideological doctrines – ranging from religious fundamentalism and anarchism, to socialism and nationalism, other violent organisations such as gangs, drug cartels, or private military contractors minimise the visibility of ideological power. Nevertheless, ideological tenets play an important role even in violent non-state organisations that downplay its presence. For example, despite popular views that see gangs and drug cartels are rapacious entities whose members are motivated by greed alone much of the sociological scholarship indicates that such criminal organisations operate within specific shared value systems built around notions of individual and collective honour, moral reciprocity, and status hierarchy (Bourgois 2003). Even the most violent non-state organisations such as MS 13 and Barrio 18 just as LRA possess and utilise distinct doctrinal teachings that govern their everyday conduct – from the mystical idea of preservation of *el barrio* (one's community) in MS 13 and Barrio 18 to the LRA's Christian millenarianism. In this case too, the ideological discourses resonate with the members only when couched in the language of micro-solidarity. Hence most non-state violent organisations deploy the kinship and comradeship idioms that frame membership in the violent organisation through the prism of brotherhood and fraternity. For example, MS 13, Barrio 18, and many other gangs successfully combine coercive, ideological, and micro-interactional powers to forge an image of the organisation as an entity defined by deep social ties of the micro-group. Concepts such as 'mara' and 'barrio' invoke a sense of intense solidarity:

What seems to bind all these groups is that they are looking for a sense of place: a space where they can get protection and nurturing – both positive and negative; a space where others are supportive of one another; a space it can call its own, henceforth its near constant references and symbols that beckon the homeland. That space is what they call el barrio ... the construction and the maintenance of el barrio is fundamental to all gang members. Efforts that put anything above this idea run into stiff resistance. (InSight Crime 2019: 23)

Therefore, protracted intergroup fighting entails the presence of coercive power which is regularly articulated in the form of specific violent social organisations. Whether such organisations are created and maintained by states or by non-state actors they often operate in a similar way aiming to maximise their coercive capacity and to expand their reach, scope, and influence. In this process they have developed a variety of social mechanisms to mould ordinary human beings into effective combatants. In this sense violence begets violence: the coercive social organisations create violent realities where individuals are forced to fight and kill. However, social pugnacity cannot be sustained by force alone. To be fully operative and influential in the long term, coercive power requires a degree of legitimacy. Much of this legitimacy is attained and maintained through ideological embedding in the spaces of micro-level solidarities.

5   Fighting for Others
The Networks of Micro-Bonds

5.1   Introduction

The principal aim of this chapter is to explore the social context of fighting for other people. The traditional instrumentalist accounts emphasise that individuals are self-preservers who are unlikely to fight for others unless they are forced or induced to do so by genetic, material, or symbolic benefits. Hence for many cognitive evolutionary psychologists sacrificing oneself for others is possible only if such acts will increase one's inclusive fitness, that is, the direct or indirect ability of an individual organism to pass on its genes to the next generation. For rational choice theorists collective action is always rooted in self-interest and one will fight for others on the assumption that others will do the same, thus enhancing the possibility that shared action will bring about greater benefit for all. Nevertheless, recent studies have questioned these well-established views by indicating that biology and instrumental rationality largely play a marginal role in the context of close-range violence. More important are emotions and moral ties as they impact substantially on one's decision to fight for others. Many individuals develop strong networks of micro-solidarity which motivate different forms of collective action in the context of violent encounters. In this chapter I analyse when, how, and why individuals fight for others. The focus is on the dynamics of social pugnacity. I argue that one's willingness to fight is a contextual phenomenon shaped by specific ideological and organisational logic. Nevertheless, despite its temporal and spatial variability, micro-group solidarity is a universal practice that underpins nearly all durable violent conflicts. In other words, fighting for others is a foundation of social pugnacity. The first part of the chapter traces the evolutionary trajectory of human sociability and looks at the structural transformation of micro-bonding in different historical contexts. The second part briefly explores the social and physical dynamics of micro-solidarity in the context of close-range fighting. The final, and longest, part analyses the workings of micro-level solidarities in the fighting practices of the three very different armed forces – American volunteers in the Spanish Civil War, Indian soldiers in the First World War, and members of the Wehrmacht in the Second World War.

5.2   The Power of Micro-Solidarity

Fighting is often perceived as an individual biological response. When people are attacked it is assumed that they automatically fight for self-preservation. When they attack others, the assumption is that this too is motivated by biological givens – to increase one's own or direct progeny's capacity for survival. For cognitive evolutionary psychologists and other sociobiological approaches risking one's own life to save others only makes sense in the context of the organism's capacity for genetic self-reproduction: if the organism cannot survive, the tendency is to privilege kin over non-kin and close kin over distant kin (Gat 2006; Martin 2018; Pinker 2011). Even when fighting is conceptualised through the prism of economic or symbolic self-interest this too is perceived to be a part of a wider biological incentive for survival. Thus, rational choice and other economics centred approaches see fighting as a self-interested activity that operates according to specific cost-benefit calculations. When individuals fight for others, this is done to increase one's own chances of survival or to materially benefit from the acquired resources and status enhancement that successful fights can bring (Kalyvas 2006; Laitin 2007; Wintrobe 2006).

However, these instrumentalist accounts offer sociologically unrealistic images of human action. Human beings are much more than simple benefit maximisers. More importantly, rational calculations and biological motivations play a rather minor role in the process of fighting. In other words, to understand the dynamics of close-range fighting the focus has to shift towards wider social contexts that make social pugnacity possible. Human beings are not isolated ahistorical atoms driven solely by their biological and economic needs. Instead, most cases of violent action are the product of specific social and historical contexts. Even when an individual is acting alone this action is always shaped by knowledge, past experiences, perceptions, and expectations involving other people. In sociological terms no significant human action is ever a product of a solitary individual. Even the most egotistic individuals inevitably fight for others. In some cases, this involves a conscious decision to protect another human being (a family member, a close friend, a trusted comrade, a well-liked neighbour, an admired individual, etc.). In other instances, fighting might be motivated by one's willingness to impress others, to conform with the values and actions of one's group, to please a respected authority, to enhance one's social position and status within a group, to preserve the honour of one's kin, and for many other socially relevant reasons.

Human beings are social creatures, and their actions are shaped by their social environment. Human sociability itself is not a biological given or a fixed state of being but something that has evolved and developed over millions of years. As anthropological and archaeological research indicates, the predecessors of *Homo sapiens* such as *Homo Australopithecus*, *Homo habilis*, and *Homo erectus* had different patterns of sociability. For example, *Australopithecus* resembles modern chimpanzees in mating and cohabitation patterns where males largely remain close to their place of birth while females move to neighbouring groups. This early hominid species was polygamous (Moorad et al. 2011). In contrast *Homo habilis* and *Homo erectus* seem to have been the first hominids that practised monogamous relationships (Werner 2012). The researchers believe that *Homo habilis* tended to live in small groups of around eighty-five members (Aiello and Dunbar 1993). Since *Homo erectus* evolved into a species with increased body and brain size they were capable of developing more complex social organisation. Recent research indicates that individuals of this species 'lived and moved in cooperative multi-male groups' consisting of around twenty individuals (Hatala et al. 2016). Other scholars have emphasised that with the evolution of hominids the group size gradually increased, but it generally remained under 150 individuals, a number also associated with the arrival and expansion of *Homo sapiens* (Gowlett et al. 2012). The changing technological environment of *Homo erectus*, characterised by their ability to use fire for cooking and to build and deploy small tools to gather food and for protection had an impact on their sociability. Being exposed to large predators in open savanna settings impacted on the development of social cooperation and coordination. Nevertheless, it seems very likely that group formation was still in a rudimentary state as individuals tended to move in order to avoid threats from the carnivores inhabiting the savanna (Carotenuto et al. 2016). Some anthropologists argue that these ever-present hostile environments have contributed to stronger group bonding either in terms of gender (Willems and van Shaik 2017) or kinship (Wong 2013). Other scholars have interpreted the 1.77 million-year-old fossil finds in Dmanisi, Georgia as an indicator that *Homo erectus* had already developed a sense of compassion. The fossil of a toothless man's skull suggested that he was fed and cared for by his immediate social group. This level of long-term commitment might be a sign of strong social bonds (Castro 2015).

With the emergence of *Homo sapiens* between 200,000 and 300,000 years ago, social ties developed and strengthened further. One of the reasons for increased sociability was the longer period of growth and maturation of human offspring. *Homo erectus* progeny had faster brain growth rates than humans and as such did not require the development of child-rearing skills and the long-term commitment that are part and parcel of human upbringing (Simpson et al. 2008). By spending years together on raising and protecting offspring which could not survive on their own, human beings have developed intense networks of micro-level solidarity.

Once *Homo sapiens* attained the capacity to use language, around 50,000 years ago, this new skill further enhanced human sociability. Being able to express emotions and to formulate ideas allowed early humans to enforce their social ties through the exchange of shared symbols of communication. Some researchers have also identified social grooming as a potent cohesive mechanism that stimulated the development of group solidarity (Dunbar 2017; Suvilehto et al. 2015). Although all primates practise social grooming, humans have substantially expanded the repertoire of this social practice. While primates and other social animals use grooming in part to clean each other and maintain their appearance and in part to develop strong bonds,[1] human beings use social grooming exclusively to develop, preserve, and enhance their social ties. Human beings have developed variety of social grooming practices including face-to-face physical interaction (e.g., shaking hands, hugging, patting, stroking, cuddling, or engaging in play fights) and non-physical forms of grooming (e.g., spoken language and written communication). These different types of social grooming are related to the strength of social relationships (Takano and Ichinose 2018). The tendency is to have more physical interaction with people who are closer to us: from very close and frequent physical intimacy of lovers to hugging, patting, stroking, and kissing on the cheek with one's close friends and family members. However, as Dunbar and Lehmann (2013) show, the intensity of social grooming impacts on the size of the group. Humans cannot maintain close, protracted, and intense relationships with large numbers of others. Instead, our cognitive capacities to maintain stable social relationships rarely extend beyond 150 individuals (Dunbar 1992), while our deep emotional commitment is likely to involve a much smaller

---

[1] Some primates spend much more time in social grooming than is necessary for hygienic purposes. For example, gelada baboons spend close to 17 per cent of daytime activity on social grooming even though only 1 per cent would be enough for cleaning purposes (Dunbar 2021).

number of people. Hence in their social grooming practices humans have to prioritise some individuals over others. Much of recent research confirms that there is a strong linear link between the size of a group and the length of time invested in social grooming (Dunbar and Lehmann, 2013; Lehmann et al. 2007). With the development of language, human beings were able to differentiate their social grooming practices whereby close family and friends could receive more face-to-face physical interaction while other socially significant individuals would mostly be the objects of non-physical grooming.

Dunbar (2017, 2021) argues that laughter has also contributed to the development of stronger social bonds among humans and that it may have evolved before language. Just as social grooming, laughter stimulates the release of endorphins in the brain which help individuals to relax by lowering the heart rate. Laughter is a social activity that often supplements grooming and, in this way, increases social bonding. The evolution and development of other social practices including singing, gossip, and storytelling have also contributed substantially towards enhancement of micro-group solidarity. Collective singing involves a degree of coordination and harmonisation that enhances cooperation and cohesion while also generating emotional bonding. As anthropologists have demonstrated, gossip is a nearly universal social phenomenon often deployed to enhance group cohesion, while storytelling has allowed individuals to develop a sense of collective purpose (Boehm 2019; Gluckman 1963).

Human sociability has also evolved through collective action. With the discovery of fire and the use of hearths small groups of people were involved in everyday activities including shared preparation of food, cooking, and eating and spending time together near the common source of warmth and light. Early humans were dependent on cooperation with others and gathering of food was usually a collective endeavour. Later on, with the increased reliance on hunting, collective action became a cornerstone of successful acquisition of protein-rich foods. The experience of hunting which ordinarily would include group of people who live together played an important role in heightening social bonds. The exposure to imminent danger when facing large and hostile animals fostered closer attachments among small groups of humans. Such dangerous and life-threatening situations also stimulated the development of stronger emotional ties and moral commitments between the members of a group. Shared hunting experiences encouraged the rise of small group solidarity where individuals were expected to support and fight for others.

For much of prehistory, human beings lived in small foraging groups. These nomadic, egalitarian, fluid, loose, and kinship-based communities would typically involve 30–50 people in the case of simple bands or up to 200 individuals forming small tribes.[2] The tribe is usually composed of several bands and would share a dialect or language and other aspects of culture. These foraging groups dominated the landscape of Earth for 98 per cent of our existence as a separate species. In this context it seems clear that human beings have evolved to live in very small groups.

With the emergence of sedentary lifestyles and the establishment of the first civilisations, human social habitats expanded dramatically: instead of living in small, face-to-face kinship-based groups human beings became members of polities consisting of hundreds of thousands and even millions of citizens. For the last 5,000 years large empires have dominated much of the globe and their rulers have put great deal of effort into reorganising social life. The imperial projects were based on highly hierarchical structures that often deliberately impeded the functioning of existing micro-groups. By coercively mobilising ordinary citizens for mass construction projects or military conquests these imperial structures often destabilised, dispersed, and sometimes destroyed the established networks of micro-solidarities. For example, the first dynasty of Imperial China, the Qin (221–206 BCE) introduced a variety of organisational measures to centralise power and to undermine local group attachments. The rulers standardised weights and measures, issued new currency, built new road networks and land irrigation systems with coerced labour, and introduced a new taxation model. They also developed a new structure of household organisation with standardised land allotments that were capable of supporting military units. This centralising project was deliberately aimed at undermining the existing networks of extended kinship. As clearly stated in a document issued by a governor of the Qin commandery this was a deliberate policy:

Anciently, the people everywhere had their own local customs. They differed in what they found beneficial and in their likes and dislikes ... This is why the sage-kings created laws and regulations, with which to straighten and correct the hearts of the people ... The purpose of all laws, statutes, and ordinances is to teach and lead the people, rid them of dissoluteness and depravity ... and turn them toward goodness. (Burbank and Cooper 2010: 49)

Many other ancient empires including the Egyptians, the Romans, Achaemenids, Abbasids, Fatimids, and others have also attempted to weaken the established patterns of micro-solidarity. In contrast many

---

[2] The term 'tribe' is highly contested in anthropology. Some scholars dispute its usefulness and see it as a product of colonialism (Friend 1975) while others find it useful and argue that there is no adequate conceptual replacement that would capture all aspects of this phenomenon (Crone 1986).

later empires such as the British, French, and Dutch among others have focused on using increased organisational and ideological capacities to penetrate and envelop the micro-world (Malešević 2019). Nevertheless, as this process was often deeply hierarchical and culturally exclusive its outcome was asymmetrical with greater success at the centre and mostly failure in the imperial peripheries.

It is only with the rise and proliferation of the nation-state model that micro-level solidarities were better integrated into the organisational and ideological structure of the polity. However, even in nation-states micro-level attachments are not amalgamated with the state structure: instead, the states have to continuously engage in ideologisation and bureaucratisation of their respective populations (Malešević 2013). If this were not the case the rulers would not have to constantly mobilise their citizens by invoking the idioms of unity and metaphors that portray nations as extended families. Although these calls for national unity and shared sacrifice are more pronounced in times of deep social crises (e.g., wars, pandemics, major natural disasters, economic depression) similar ideological notions are also visible in periods of stability. The politicians, government officials, leaders of civil society, and many others tend to rely on imagery that projects group solidarity across a much wider plane then it usually occupies. Hence left-wing leaders and trade unionists might invoke the unity of all workers, the feminist movements tend to speak of universal sisterhood, religious authorities often refer to the brotherhood of co-religionists (umma, kirk, shared church), and right-wing associations might address their supporters in terms of ethnic or racial unity.

Nevertheless, in all of these cases and many others, when solidarity is projected beyond the face-to-face level and is addressed to an abstract community involving millions of anonymous individuals it inevitably becomes an ideological device. These discourses draw upon existing emotional attachments and moral commitments generated in the micro-interactions of face-to-face networks of solidarity and attempt to project that cohesion onto a wider ideological canvass. Thus, in nationalist discourses people's genuine feelings of affection and moral obligation towards their parents are translated into love for motherland or fatherland. In the language of nationalists real kinship ties are cast onto the wider backdrop of nationhood that is envisaged as symbolic kinship (i.e., the nation is our mother or father). Other ideological discourses use a similar matrix with the same aim – tapping into the real emotional bonds and moral allegiances that are produced in the micro-word and deploying them to enhance commitment to the specific ideological project. In this sense Althusser (1971: 121) was right that all ideologies aim to interpellate individuals as members of specific collective categories.

Ideological projects hail and in this process transform and constitute individuals as members of specific groups: 'all ideology hails or interpellates concrete individuals as concrete subjects'. For example, by addressing individuals as Catholics, proletariat, Germans, or heterosexual men ideological discourses foster transformation of individuals into subjects that represent particular structural configurations. However, what is missing in this account is a clear differentiation between the micro-level solidarities that are created and developed in face-to-face interaction and the broader structural contexts that have to rely on developed organisational capacity and elaborate ideological homogenisation. In other words, Althusser is wrong that everything is ideology and that these ideological state apparatuses are always linked with the capitalist mode of production. Instead, ideological processes can be generated by a variety of historical forces and their penetration into the micro-world is not inevitable but something that entails a great deal of organisational work.

Thus, for much of their existence on this planet human beings have lived in a very small groups and have developed strong bonds of solidarity within such groups. Since the formation of the first states ten to twelve thousand years ago their leaders have attempted to either weaken these micro-level solidarities or to envelop these bonds and project them onto the wider ideological and organisational canvass. In many respects this organisational attempt to tap into micro-solidarities has never ceased: all large-scale social organisations continue to penetrate small group bonds and to deploy the language of micro-solidarity to forge ideological unity within their organisational structures. This is visible in a variety of organisational contexts – from religious organisations (e.g, our brethren in faith) and private corporations (e.g., the company as a big family), to state institutions (e.g., community of employees as friends) and civil society groups (e.g., comrades in a common struggle for justice). Nevertheless, the discourses of micro-solidarity have historically been most pronounced in social organisations involved in fighting. To fully justify the principles involved in fighting and killing that go so much against the norms of most societies it was necessary to tap into the micro-world and redefine wars, revolutions, genocides, uprisings, or acts of terrorism as instances of fighting for significant others. To mobilise individuals to willingly participate in violent actions or to consent to such acts taking place it was crucial to invoke the imagery and energy of micro-group solidarity. Thus, when young recruits are mobilised to fight in a war the central message is not that this is a political conflict initiated and overseen by the rulers of two or more states but that they are fighting to defend their families and close friends against the 'merciless enemy'.

Once on the battlefield the soldiers develop strong bonds with the members of their squad, platoon, or company and the military organisations rely extensively on these networks of micro-solidarity to keep the fight going regardless of the circumstances. Similarly, participating in acts of ethnic cleansing, genocide, or terrorism is almost never framed in terms of political or ideological agendas of organisations perpetuating these violent acts. Instead, terrorists and *génocidaires* are primed to see themselves as protectors of their families, friends, and comrades in arms. Even people who fight and kill during uprisings and revolutions tend to interpret their actions through the prism of sacrifice for others. To fully understand why micro-solidarity is such a powerful motivator it is important to explore its dynamics in social pugnacity.

5.3   Micro-Solidarity and Close-Range Fighting

Human beings are tactile creatures who tend to express their emotions through physical interaction. Micro-sociologists and social psychologists have provided ample evidence that human beings often express their emotional highs and lows through physical interaction with others (Collins 2004, 2008; McClelland 1985, 2014; Wohlstein and McPhail 1983). When an individual is very happy, she is likely to touch, hold on to, or hug other people, and joy is also shared with signs of physical support by others. Similarly, when receiving a very sad news or experiencing emotional turmoil one expects to receive comforting long hugs, patting on the back or shoulders, holding hands or upper body, handshakes, and other forms of physical interaction. Human beings are often consoled and heartened by physical gestures from other humans. In extreme situations when there is no opportunity for physical contact individuals might engage in continuous waving movements that resemble parents rocking a baby in their arms or in the crib. The example of this behaviour comes from Auschwitz and other Nazi concentration camps where some inmates exhibited severe emaciation and weakness due to starvation and were not able to stand up. The Nazi guards pejoratively called such inmates 'Muselmann' (Muslims) as their 'swaying motions of the upper part of the body' resembled 'Islamic prayer rituals' (Sofsky 1997: 329). These extremely weak individuals were moving rhythmically so as to re-enact the physical touch of another human being that they were craving.

The physicality of human interaction is also visible in public events such as when fans start hugging, holding, and kissing each other after their team scores a goal or wins a game. Many celebratory occasions involve people holding hands, singing, dancing, and patting each other on their shoulders. As Collins (2004: 66) argues, these body-on-body actions intensify one's feelings and enhance interaction rituals through which human beings find fulfilment: 'the strongest human pleasures come from being fully and bodily absorbed in deeply synchronised social interaction'. Face-to-face interaction is crucial to this process as it allows for the participation in a shared emotional experience; it focuses mutual attention of those involved and can ultimately generate physical rhythmic synchronicity all of which contribute to development of interpersonal solidarity. For Collins (2004, 2020), this physical interaction is a precondition of group solidarity. Although human beings can create and maintain social bonds at a distance it is very difficult to keep such links durable and strong without periodic physical interaction. For example, DiMaggio et al. (2019) and Ling (2008) show that new technologies such as online communication and the regular use of mobile phones do not replace the physicality of human interaction but rather supplement it with an additional layer of contact. The tendency is to communicate online and via mobile phones with the same individuals that one usually interacts with in physical encounters. Although the use of social media allows for regular interaction with people who are located far away the strength of social ties is still determined by periodic face-to-face interactions even if they involve video calls and other forms of IT mediated communication. As Collins (2020: 496) points out, 'Our enforced natural experiments [such as the COVID-19 pandemic], as well as ongoing studies of interaction in the IT era, show that the ingredient of physical co-presence is chiefly important because it enables the key processes, establishing a mutual focus of attention, and monitoring all the sensory signs of emotion, action, and rhythm, for the degree to which they are shared or at cross-purposes.'

While face-to-face interaction is important for all forms of microgroup solidarity, it is indispensable for fighting. Obviously, one cannot be involved in a close-range physical fight without being in close proximity with other human beings.[3] However, fighting is not only about exchanging punches and injuring or killing one's opponent. Instead fighting involves social and physical interaction that develops before, during, and after the fight. Social pugnacity also involves not only the fighters and the objects of their violence but also one's external social referents: individuals whom the fighters aim to please, impress, scare, protect, obey, and relate to in many other ways. In some important

---

[3] Of course, humans can be attacked and killed at distance by snipers, aerial bombings, cannon fire, drones, or projected missiles but this is a different phenomenon from close-range fighting.

respects a close-range fight is a microcosm of wider social relationships. For example, when one observes a street brawl the focus is usually on individuals who are responsible for starting the violent encounter – a drunk partygoer, an angry football club supporter whose team has just lost the game, a petty criminal who regularly participates in street fights, a teenager who is testing the limits of the law and so on.

The agency-centred theories of crime tend to interpret these acts of violence through the prism of different individualist factors: from the lack of self-control to instrumental behaviour focused on personal gain, the strain caused by one's inability to achieve one's goals or the competing definitions of situations resulting in labelling some acts as being criminal. In contrast the structure-centred approaches emphasise socio-economic inequalities, cultural transmission, social learning practices, and the social construction of deviance (Ray 2018). Although many of these approaches are successful in accounting for some aspects of violent behaviour, they are not able to explain the sheer variety of human responses to violence. Moreover, as these approaches differentiate sharply between legal and illegal forms of violent acts, they often decontextualise and de-historicise wider human experience. For example, violence generated in a war context (e.g., soldiers fighting other soldiers on the battlefield) or in combat sports is not regarded as an object of criminological analysis as these acts are deemed to be legal by the state authorities. At the same time, any action that contravenes the legal definition of violent crime is automatically deemed to be a violent act. Interestingly the focus here is not on the physicality of violence but on the legal definition of a threat as articulated by the state apparatuses. Combat sports regularly involve exchange of punches and severe injuries while fighting on the frontlines generates mass human casualties, yet neither of these two are defined as acts of violent crime. In contrast throwing a shoe or spitting on a police officer will likely not cause any physical damage but may be treated as a violent attack from a legal perspective.

These state-centric understandings of violence through the prism of crime are inadequate to capture the complexity and changing character of violence. For one thing the state authorities prioritise scrutiny over social action that might be seen as a threat to the existence and functioning of the state itself. Hence insults and attacks on government representatives such as ministers, police, or military usually invoke more severe punishments than violence against ordinary individuals. Similarly committing acts of violence in the name of the state (e.g., clandestine human intelligence activities) is not considered to be crime and is often rewarded. The same applies to soldiers fighting in war where killing of an anonymous enemy soldier is not deemed to be a criminal/violent act but a noble deed.

For another thing the uniform criminalisation of violent acts leaves little or no room for understanding differences in one's subjective experience of violence. The same act of violence might have very different outcomes as some individuals may recover quickly or even dismiss their experience of violent attack while others might be traumatised for life. Finally, understanding violence through the prism of crime makes no provision for the temporal and spatial dimension of violence: the definition of what constitutes a violent act changes through time and in some cases is culturally specific (Malešević 2017). For example, many religious texts deem blasphemy to be a form of violence against God and as such entailing the death penalty (e.g., Leviticus 24:16 in the Bible). These teachings have underpinned many legal systems throughout the world for centuries and are still used in many countries such as Saudi Arabia, Pakistan, and Iran where blasphemy is still punished by death. In many European countries such laws have been repealed and blasphemy is not considered to be a form of crime/violence. At the same time other forms of behaviour which have not previously been considered as violent – such as spousal battery – have been criminalised and penalised. Hence the definition and understanding of violence changes through time and through different cultural contexts. All of these social complexities that underpin the dynamics of violence through time and space have a direct impact on the phenomenon of social pugnacity.

Social fighting is a process shaped by the wider context and as such always involves more people than those present in the altercation. Fighting is a social phenomenon influenced by broader macro-organisational and ideological forces as well as by specific micro-social dynamics. In both of these contexts violence is moulded by one's relationship with other human beings. Even when a fight involves only two individuals the act of violence is still wrought by the presence of many (invisible) others. Human beings are creatures that fight and kill for others.

To explore how this process works in the context of close-range violence one can look at three very different historical experiences – the micro-group dynamics of social fighting among the international volunteers of the Spanish Civil War (1936–9), among the Indian soldiers who fought in the British Imperial forces during the First World War (1914–18), and the frontline behaviour of Wehrmacht soldiers during the Second World War (1939–45). Although these three case studies involve very different ideological doctrines and organisational structures the patterns of micro-group dynamics relating to fighting show a great deal of similarity. This is most clearly visible in the letters written from the frontline where the combatants vividly describe their experiences of fighting.

5.4   Close-Range Fighting in Different Wars: Three Case Studies

To better understand the social dynamics of fighting it is important to explore the everyday experiences of soldiers in different wars. By zooming in on three very dissimilar military organisations that were driven by profoundly different ideological doctrines one can untangle the workings of micro-level solidarities across a variety of battlefield experiences. In this section I briefly analyse three cases defined by sharp ideological differences (American socialist volunteers in Spanish Civil War, deeply religious Hindu, Muslim, and Sikh soldiers fighting in the First World War, and the far-right Wehrmacht military driven by racist Nazi ideology).[4] Although these ideological and organisational differences shape social relations among soldiers and influence their behaviour on the battlefield the analysis of soldier's personal letters also reveals many similarities across these diverse military organisations.

5.4.1   *American Volunteers in the Spanish Civil War*

The Spanish Civil War involved a number of different military organisations spearheaded by the two main adversaries – the People's Army of Spain/Spanish Republican Army (Republicans) and the Falange Española Tradicionalista y de las Juntas de Ofensiva Nacional Sindicalista (Nationalists). Both sides were supported by many political groups in Spain and abroad and also relied on international volunteers. However, the Republicans had a substantially larger cohort of international volunteers fighting for their cause.[5] By the end of the war in 1939 more than 40,000 individuals from all over the world had

---

[4] For more information about the data used in this chapter see the Appendix.

[5] The international forces that fought with the Nationalists were rarely fighting as identifiable national units and were mostly integrated into the Falange Army. The exceptions to this were Irish Brigade (700 soldiers) and the French Jeanne d'Arc company of the Spanish Foreign Legion (500 soldiers). More than 20,000 individuals from different countries fought with the Falangists (Keene 2007; Othen 2008). This does not include the regular military forces of fascist Italy and Nazi Germany both of which provided military support. As Kirschenbaum (2015: 6) points out: 'Italy contributed more than seventy thousand troops, and both Germany and Italy sent hundreds of artillery pieces, tanks, planes, and pilots, including the infamous German Condor legion responsible for the April 1937 destruction of Guernica'.

volunteered to fight for the Republicans with the majority of volunteers coming from France, Italy, and Germany (Thomas 2003).[6] There is no doubt that the majority of international volunteers were motivated by ideological principles – to protect the secular, democratic, and egalitarian Republic against the militarist, monarchist, conservative, and clerical dictatorship. Many volunteers were active members of left-wing organisations which were instrumental in mobilising the units of volunteers and organising their participation and transport to Spain. The communist, socialist, anarchist and other left-wing movements together with the Comintern, Soviet Union, and Mexico provided arms, military advisers, and logistics. Nevertheless, ideology and organisation were not the only reasons why individuals decided to join the war and why they continued fighting even when it became apparent that the Republican forces would be defeated, and that many volunteers would lose their lives.

Micro-group solidarities played a crucial role in the recruitment of volunteers and in keeping them fighting on the battlefields of Spain until the end of the war. The legacy of war also kept many war veterans bound into the strong networks of solidarity for many years and often until their deaths: 'the Spanish civil war often remained a defining moment of their own life stories and personal networks – something that they often separated (or tried to separate) from the larger Stalinist context' (Kirschenbaum 2015: 10). Although recruitment was organised by left-wing political organisations, the majority of recruits did not join as individuals but with their friends or family members. Many volunteers had previously fought in the First World War and had substantial combat experience. Other volunteers had fought in the British, French, and Dutch colonial wars, the Irish War of Independence, or the Balkan Wars of 1912–13 among others. These individuals were more likely to join together with their comrades from previous wars with whom they already shared strong interpersonal bonds. The fact that international brigades were organised into national units allowed individuals to maintain already existing social ties and to forge new bonds that remained strong long after the Spanish Civil War.

The letters written home by the volunteers who fought in the Abraham Lincoln Brigade show that many American combatants were reluctant to socialise with the local population and preferred to spend time with their

---

[6] The international brigades had representatives from 53 countries most of which were organised in their own national battalions and brigades such as the German Thälmann Battalion, the Italian Garibaldi Battalion, or the American Abraham Lincoln Brigade (Thomas 2003).

American comrades. For example, 'Jason Gurney, who served with both the Americans and the British, noted that few of his comrades knew much of anything about the country they had pledged to save from Fascism and rarely made friends beyond their own circle' (Eby 2007: 102).

Although most American volunteers were strongly motivated by ideological principles including anti-fascism, anti-militarism, socialism, and communism many decided to join because their friends were volunteering too and because they saw the rise of fascism across Europe as a direct threat to their own micro-groups – their families. Hence their letters indicate clearly that many American volunteers came together with their friends or family members: 'you must all remember many fine comrades are going; with that your task becomes greater' (Nelson and Hendricks 2013: 44); 'I've been palling around with a guy from my neighbourhood, Hy Stone' (Nelson and Hendricks 2013: 41); 'I have just finished a 500-mile trip to the south of France with some of my friends' (Nelson and Hendricks 2013: 44). When describing their reasons to join, the tendency is to invoke ideological commitments together with the perception that the war in Spain represents a direct threat to their families and friends. For example, in a letter to his father one American volunteer explains that although his decision to join the war was difficult, it was premised on his belief that his participation will help stop his brothers becoming involved in another world war: 'unless these forces are stopped, we are sure to have another war in which Milty, Harvey, Roland, Howard, Elmer and I would surely be dragged (Nelson and Hendricks 2013: 30). Similarly, other volunteers invoke the potential threat of fascism to their family and friends in the USA: 'Yes, Ma, this is a case where sons must go against their mothers' wishes for the sake of their mothers themselves' (Nelson and Hendricks 2013: 32); 'because if we crush Fascism here, we'll save our people in America' (Nelson and Hendricks 2013: 34).

Other volunteers would often refer to the wider groups that their families and friends represent. Thus, Jewish volunteers describe their participation as a struggle against fascism that could spread to the USA and as such would be a grave danger to Jewish population: 'And don't you realize that we Jews will be the first to suffer if fascism comes? ... So, I took up arms against the persecutors of my people – the Jews and – my class – the Oppressed. I am fighting against those who establish an inquisition like that of their ideological ancestors several centuries ago, in Spain' (Nelson and Hendricks 2013: 32). In a similar vein, African American volunteers justified their actions in terms of fighting against racist ideology that underpins fascism:

why I, a Negro, who have fought through these years for the rights of my people, am here in Spain today? Because we are no longer an isolated minority group fighting hopelessly against immense giant ... All we have to do is to think of the lynching of our people ... We will build us a new society – a society of peace and plenty. There will be no color line, no jim-crow trains, no lynching. That is why, my dear, I'm here in Spain ... Here we're laying the foundation for world peace, and for the liberation of my people. (Nelson and Hendricks 2013: 34)

Thus, in all of these cases the emphasis is clearly on jointing the war in order to fight for others – one's family and friends, one's social class, or one's ethnic, racial, or religious group.

Even when there is no reference to specific micro-groups the volunteers regularly invoke others as their point of reference – entire humanity. So, one can read in their letters that they fight as 'an active part of a great progressive force, on whose shoulders rests the responsibility of saving human civilization' (Nelson and Hendricks 2013: 33) or 'Those who feel that I must justify my action [for joining the war], I refer them to the bloody hand of Hitler, no further justification is needed. The dead babies on the streets of Madrid are more articulate than any master of words' (Nelson and Hendricks 2013: 43).

While the decision to join was often couched in the language of attachment to one's micro-group at home the actual shared experience of fighting fostered the formation of new form of micro-solidarity – the comradeship of those who fight together. This is not to say that the war comrades replaced the existing social ties of family and friendship. Instead, the new comrades gradually became integrated into the established bonds of micro-solidarity. This was an ongoing process shaped by the changing dynamics of battlefield experiences. Hence in some letters the primary reference is still to the significant others at home: 'you asked me a question which I repeat in every letter – Do I still love you! TREMENDOUSLY! Why even when we were being bombed and strafed, I looked at my watch and thought of where you were at that hour' (Nelson and Hendricks 2013: 185–6). In other letters the attachment to the family is combined with newly created bonds on the frontline where the combatants aim to bring closer their two micro-groups: 'I am thinking of Louise [a daughter] now. Her birthday is tomorrow ... what I want to do in this letter is to write ... about some of our comrades. It is the thought of these comrades that makes you willing to face again the hell you have already faced' (Nelson and Hendricks 2013: 187–8). Or: 'we were in a fierce battle that day – one lasting days – we were outnumbered, outclassed in arms, worn out tremendously after a month of heavy fighting, we were strafed, bombed, shelled without a moment's let up. ... Henry Mace of Cincinnati did a good job that night – he held the hill with a handful of men ... I love you for your simplicity and the purity of your soul. And how I do love you honey!' (Nelson and Hendricks 2013: 379).

Many American volunteers vividly describe this process of intense group formation through the shared experience of social pugnacity:

The things that have happened during the past two weeks I will never forget [the battles]. They were the most eventful of my whole life. The death of my comrades moved me more than I can describe ... Above all, the spirit and courage of our American comrades gives me joy. I thought that such courage existed only in books. But I've seen acts of bravery I'll never forget. I've seen comrades killed protecting others. I've seen our wounded smile confidence into our comrades still fighting. It's these things that give you confidence in a final victory. It's these things that make you fight on in spite of the horror and brutality. (Nelson and Hendricks 2013: 190)

Or: 'My mind always goes back to some of the boys who "got it" or who are missing. Some of these fellows were very close to me. I can't cry anymore like I did at Brunete. My eyes are quite dry. But I wish I could cry and get the relief it gives you. Whenever I think of these fellows my heart grows heavy. You will never know what fine fellows they were' (Nelson and Hendricks 2013: 382).

The battlefield experience was a formative moment in the lives of many American volunteers. The unprecedented social environment of the frontline where one is exposed to constant life-threatening situations and dependent on the continuous support of others had a profound impact on the dynamics of group formation. While common sense would suggest that such situations of danger would foster a strong shift towards self-preservation and egotistic behaviour the sociological reality is that under these conditions human beings display more altruism than ever. This is also recognised in the letters of the American soldiers from Spain many of whom provide numerous examples of self-sacrifice for others. For example, in a letter to his family one soldier recalls how a commander of the machine gun company continuously exposed himself to danger to save others: 'when we were forced to drop, he was still up, looking around to see that we were all down. Then he dropped. How he missed being hit that day, I'll never understand.' Later on 'he was under machine-gun fire. Finally, he was hit ... as he was being carried on a stretcher to the ambulance, he clenched his fist and said, "Carry on boys". Then he died' (Nelson and Hendricks 2013: 187). Similarly, a volunteer scout disobeyed command in order to protect others:

He had an easy job behind the lines, but refused to stay there. He insisted on being with the boys in the front ... He [became] a lead scout, always in advance of the battalion, and in most danger ... [once the unit was under severe fire from the enemy located in a nearby hose] and he volunteered to go out with bombs and blow up the house. Just as he was ready to go, we got word that we were to go some other place ... he was shot in the head ... he was out in front, a grenade in his hand, ready to throw. He died instantly. (Nelson and Hendricks 2013: 188)

Another soldier wrote:

We were given orders to go over the top of Mosquito Hill. As we went up, Harry Hynes was killed. Ernie Arion was killed. I was wounded. We were laying a barrage and it was a trifle low. Gene went flying down the hill with Fascist bullets nipping at him – he showed me the marks later – to give orders to lift the barrage higher, just in time. I couldn't, with my leg broken. Gene save my life; then he came back with water, wet my lips, and bandaged my leg and stopped the flow of blood. He went around that day ... tending for wounded men, hourly risking his life for us by going for water. (Nelson and Hendricks 2013: 197)

The very intense sense of micro-group attachment that most soldiers developed on the frontlines was a product of an environment where one is constantly exposed to the life-threatening situations. However, this was not an instant development; instead, tight group bonds were built gradually through the shared physical and emotional experiences before, during, and after the battle. As Collins (2004) and McClelland (2014) rightly point out, continuous face-to-face interaction involving close physical contact stimulates the development of strong emotional ties. The synchronicity of bodies feeds into and enhances the emotional harmonisation. Living together in close proximity, sharing beds, food rations, and free time, discussing their past lives and reminiscing about their families and friends back home all contribute to the development of strong social ties. Military training and practice together with the integration into the hierarchical military structure all foster social bonding. Hence the soldiers do not arrive on the battlefield as individuals but as members of already established micro-groups. As King (2013: 37) shows, micro-group solidarity is often built through shared collective action. Soldiers develop emotional attachments through shared interaction and particularly through successful collective performance: 'a group is cohesive insofar as it is successfully able to act together, and cohesion refers to its collective performances ... successful performance typically strengthens the affection the group members have for each other'. This gradual development of micro-group solidarity is clearly visible in the case of the Abraham Lincoln Brigade. The combatants regularly make references to the physicality of their shared experiences in the everyday life on the front. The letters describe these situations:

Charlie W ... and I had been buddying up for the past week. We have been sharing poncho and blanket, fox holes and food. Yesterday evening the shells began falling fast and furious. Charlie ran to a little fox hole and I started following. (Nelson and Hendricks 2013: 93)

I think that time we spent in that little valley was the most formative period of our lives. We had erected little tents and saw no one but ourselves ... Gene and Van de Ross used to squeeze into one of our little pygmy tents and you should have seen what a tight squeeze three big men like ourselves made. We spent all our time laughing at each other and at everything under the sun ... there would soon to be little enough laughter. But it was the laughter of men – men who were not afraid to die, but who loved life. (Nelson and Hendricks 2013: 195)

The experiences of American volunteers in the Spanish Civil War indicate clearly how central micro-group dynamics is for social pugnacity. Moreover, despite the ever-present dangers and the high possibility of losing one's life most combatants prioritised their micro-group over self-preservation. Battlefield fighting is primarily a fight for others.

5.4.2   Indian Soldiers in the First World War

The patterns of social fighting among the American volunteers in the Spanish Civil War were far from unique. The battlefield experiences they describe in their letters resemble the those of many other soldiers across different wars (Grossman 2004; Holmes 1985; Lippard et el. 2018; Malešević 2010, 2017). Although different societies and different historical contexts are shaped by diversity of social and cultural practices there is a strong element of cross-cultural and cross-temporal continuity in the patterns of micro-group solidarity. Fighting for others regularly tends to overpower self-protection on the frontline.

To illustrate this point one can briefly explore the dynamics of micro-group solidarity in a very different part of the world, in a different conflict and among individuals who were motivated to join by very different reasons – the Indian soldiers who fought in the First World War. Analysing the letters[7] from Indian recruits it is possible to identify some striking similarities. Even though these individuals had a very different cultural background including profoundly different value systems and practices and had different motivations to join the war, once on the

---

[7] Since the majority of Indian soldiers were illiterate, their letters were often dictated to the scribes (i.e., literate Indian soldiers or military administrators) and also read aloud to their family members and friends back home in India. The letters were censored for any sensitive information that could be used by the enemy and in their letters, soldiers often indicate that they are not allowed to write about particular aspects of their war experience (Omissi 1999:180, 222, 231).

frontline they displayed similar patterns of social fighting. In other words, they too fought for others.

The British Indian Army was mostly composed of illiterate peasantry from the north and north-west of the Indian subcontinent. Relying on the social Darwinist theory of 'martial races', the British colonial administration prioritised recruitment of Punjabi Muslims, Sikhs, Gurkhas, and other groups that they considered to be 'warrior races' (Barkawi 2017: 40). This all-volunteer force initially included around 215,000 soldiers and by the end of the First World War it grew to 573,000 members (Heathcote 1995; Morton-Jack 2018; Omissi 1999). Unlike the American volunteers of the Spanish Civil War who mostly joined for ideological reasons the Indian recruits were predominantly labour migrants who joined for salary and secure employment or were landless Untouchables for whom the army was a vehicle of status improvement. Some volunteers such as high-caste Rajputs, joined the army to preserve their martial tradition (Barua 2005). The army fought in Europe, Africa, and the Middle East.

The organisational capacity of the British Imperial administrative and military apparatuses made the mass mobilisation of Indian recruits possible. Without this military structure in place Indians would not have participated in the First World War. Ideological commitments played a marginal role during the recruitment phase but gradually gained significance as soldiers became more integrated into the military organisation and had substantial experience of fighting. Nevertheless, religious ideological discourses dominated over more secular commitments to the imperial project. Although soldiers regularly refer to the imperial authority of the King and show filial obligation to the Sirkar (i.e., government),[8] the fighting, killing, and dying is usually interpreted through the well-established religious categories of Islam, Hinduism, or Sikhism. The long-term exposure to the carnage of war has often enhanced the religious beliefs of soldiers. Hence the letters of Indian soldiers are full of religious ideology: 'but we must do as God decrees' (Omissi 1999: 109); 'the time of death is fixed for each man and that time can never be altered ... if God spares me, we shall meet again. If not, well, we are given life only to reach death in the end' (Omissi 1999: 128); 'Death comes to us one day, wherever we may be. Live in confidence and serenity; God will give victory to our King' (Omissi 1999: 183); 'do not

---

[8] Soldiers often used a similar formulation to express a sense of responsibility towards the government – they have to fight because 'they have eaten the salt of the Sirkar' (Omissi 1999: 20).

be alarmed or disturbed, and when you go into battle, call on the name of God ... God will sustain you' (Omissi 1999: 286).

Although organisational capacity and ideological penetration contributed to social pugnacity the micro-group solidarities proved decisive throughout the war. As in the case of American volunteers in Spain, the Indian recruits joined mostly not as individuals but with their friends or family members. For example, in a letter to his grandfather one soldier refers to his friends and siblings as 'brothers' who have joined together and fight as one: 'we four are the true sons of our Rawat fathers – Bhawain Negi, Nian Singh, Nata Singh, Gokul Singh. If we die it will be in France or Europe or on the battlefield' (Omissi 1999: 109). Another soldier describes the importance of being together on the frontline with his brother and how he was affected by his death:

My mother, when we two brothers came to the war, we were both of us in one place and were always meeting together. If my brother went out on any duty, I used to wander after him until I saw him again, and when I saw him, my heart would thrill with joy. And he too would so wander after me. ... we had great love for each other. But the last day came. He passed away very quickly, and to whom can I now look here ... my brother is dead ... Now I am dead. All the grief that is in the world is now upon me. (Omissi 1999: 143)

The pre-existing social ties proved crucial in bringing soldiers to the frontline and even more so in keeping them fighting until the end of the war. The British recruitment policy was in part built on the principle to preserve existing social ties and use them as a source of motivation to fight. Hence squads, platoons, companies, and regiments were often populated by members of the same family, friendship network, clan, caste, or religious group (Barkawi 2017). These pre-existing micro-attachments were particularly important in the beginning of the war when Indian military units that fought in France suffered heavy casualties.[9] The scale of human losses generated shock among the Indian troops who were not used to this type of warfare. Hence a pronounced sense of desperation was present in their letters. Nevertheless, despite the hopelessness of their situation they continued fighting on the premise that they were doing this for their families back home. This attitude is visible in their letters from France: 'It is very hard to endure the bombs, father. It will be difficult for anyone to survive and come back safe and sound from the war. The son who is very lucky will see his father and mother, otherwise who can do this ... The numbers that have fallen

---

[9] The total losses of the Indian Army were high (49,000 sepoys) and many of the casualties happened in the first year of the war (Omissi 1999: 4).

cannot be counted' (Omissi 1999: 27–8). 'My dear brother ... the war is still going on. Hundreds and thousands are engaged, and it goes on day after day ... There can be no confidence of life or of seeing again the dear children or of seeing you once more ... If I live I will write again' (Omissi 1999: 30). 'This is a devils' war. When will it end? If I recover, I shall not remain a soldier but serve my parents' (Omissi 1999: 39). 'I have been wounded in the head but hope to get better soon. My fate now is very lucky [in] that I am alive, and all my brethren have been killed ... In the time of calamity these four things are tried – faith, fortitude, friend and wife' (Omissi 1999: 45–6).

The importance of home-based micro-solidarities is also noticeable in letters where soldiers ask their siblings or close friends not to join the war so as not to expose themselves to the danger: 'I have heard that you have come to the war. I am very angry with you. It was more than enough that I should be there, and it is a pity that you too have to come. ... Work so as to spare your life, and not do anything foolish ... Tell Shiraz Khan to keep the brotherhood well-united and save their lives' (Omissi 1999: 54). Similarly, another soldier implores his friend not to enlist: 'When we attack, they direct a terrific fire on us – thousands of men die daily ... The battleground resounds with cries. So far as is in your power do not come here' (Omissi 1999: 59). Or: 'For God's sake don't come, don't come, don't come to this war in Europe. ... I am in a state of great anxiety: and tell my brother Muhammad Yakub Khan for God's sake not to enlist' (Omissi 1999: 61).

Despite heavy casualties the soldiers regularly helped each other on the battlefield, and in the process often endangered their own lives. For example, Subedar Mir Dast was awarded the Victoria Cross, the highest military award for holding the line under attack and saving eight wounded officers at Ypres. During this attack with poisonous gas, he was also wounded and gassed. He briefly reflects on this experience by emphasising the importance of his micro-group: 'I have been twice wounded, once in the left hand ... the other injury is from gas ... The men who came from our regiment have done very well and will do so again' (Omissi 1999: 77). In a similar vein, a Sikh commander died sacrificing his life for his unit: 'Chur Singh has suffered martyrdom in the war ... He drew his sword and went forward. A bullet came from the enemy and hit him in the mouth. So did our brother Chur Singh become a martyr' (Omissi 1999: 126). Or: 'We have been fighting for fourteen months, and the fighting has been very fierce ... Our troops have been accounted the stoutest of all the troops. At this time, they are in such heart that they would stay the tiger unarmed. [Every man] fighting with heroic bravery becomes himself a hero ... [we] exalt the name of race, country, ancestors, parents, village, and brothers' (Omissi 1999: 142). As Barkawi (2017: 63) emphasises in the context of both world wars the officers were fully aware how important micro-group ties were for their soldiers: 'New officers in the Indian Army were warned about "bhai bundi", or brotherhoodliness, the idea that men with village or kinship ties will watch out for another.'

Just as in the case of American volunteers in Spain, Indian soldiers write about the creation of new micro-group solidarities forged in the hardship of war. The focus here is on the shared life in the trenches and the physicality of everyday interaction: 'The fire of bombs descends all night long, and the rain of machine guns never stops. I live in a dug-out … Everybody sleeps, eats, and drinks underground. These trenches used to belong to the French, but now belong to us … There is a great discomfort in the trenches, and lice swarm on the men' (Omissi 1999: 201). 'We are always in the trenches … the guns fire all day like the thunder in [the month of] Sawan … The shells are passing over our heads as we sit in the trenches' (Omissi 1999: 227). 'The battle is raging violently, and various new ways of fighting have been introduced … No one can advance beyond the trenches … At the present time we are suffering … However after two years' experience, we have grown used to all these troubles' (Omissi 1999: 231). The protracted trench warfare exhausted the soldiers, but the shared experience of difficulty enhanced their micro-group attachments:

We are in the open, and it is very cold with continual snow and rain, and we are suffering a good deal. The horses are up to their necks in mud … We have put our little tents in the mud. We are all very worn out, and our feeding arrangements are unsatisfactory. We have no opportunity of bathing. … We are in a regular hell and tired of life, yet our souls are so shameless they do not leave our bodies. (Omissi 1999: 283)

The soldiers often illustrate the significance of micro-group attachments through references to the group status. For example, soldiers write about their units' difficult battles and many casualties but also emphasise the great esteem that that their units now have: 'Our regiment made a charge and suffered great losses … 300 were killed or wounded. Our regiment has won a good name for itself' (Omissi 1999: 105). 'Our reputation is good enough as it is, but it would have been greatly enhanced [if they had not lost many officers]' (Omissi 1999: 106). 'We were the first to go into action. We took five villages from the enemy … Our regiment in particular made a great name for itself … God protected us, each one' (Omissi 1999: 282). 'We are Rajputs, and it is our privilege to fight bravely in battle, and if we are wounded or die, we gain renown and honour' (Omissi 1999: 298). Some soldiers emphasise the unit's commitment to fighting in order to maintain or enhance their reputation: 'We will do our best to uphold the family traditions and the reputation of our tribe' (Omissi 1999: 227). In some cases, group status is related directly to one's caste and the soldiers understood their fighting commitments through the prism of increased caste position:

> Our caste is very low down the scale, just because we do not serve in the Army. Everyone knows I am an officer, but no one knows who the Buranas are … we are inferior just because we are not soldiers. Now, it rests with God and you to raise the name of the Buranas … The whole object of military service is to raise the reputation of one's caste, and that is what we have to do. (Omissi 1999: 296)

All of these examples indicate the centrality of fighting for (significant) others.

Despite profound differences in time, space, and social values between American volunteers in the Spanish Civil War and Indian soldiers in the First World War there is a great deal of similarity in their experiences of fighting. In both cases micro-group solidarity played a crucial role in bringing soldiers to the battlefields and keeping them there despite enormous human costs. In both instances fighting for others regularly trumped self-interested behaviour.

5.4.3   The Wehrmacht in the Second World War

While American and Indian soldiers were all volunteers, the military forces of Nazi Germany combined conscription with volunteering. Although initially volunteers were the majority in the Wehrmacht, the onset of the war in 1939 changed this balance and the number of conscripts increased dramatically.[10] Hence unlike the Waffen-SS which remained predominantly a volunteer force, the rest of the Wehrmacht was mostly composed of drafted soldiers. It is estimated that during the Second World War 18.2 million men served in the Wehrmacht with around 13 million in the army, 3 million in the air force, 1.5 million in the navy and the rest were foreign volunteers and conscripts and auxiliary forces (Müller 2016). There is no doubt that both ideology and organisation were the cornerstones of the Wehrmacht's power. As Sait (2019), Rossino (2003), and Bartov (1992) demonstrated convincingly, Nazi ideology did not only inspire Waffen-SS forces but was just as important throughout the entire German army. The racist and conquest-oriented

---

[10] Between 1935 and 1939, 2.4. million were volunteers and 1.3 million were conscripts. By the end of the war, conscripts constituted the overwhelming majority of Wehrmacht forces (Müller 2016).

imperial project, radical anti-Semitism, the struggle for the *Lebensraum* (living space), the glorification of *Volksgemeinschaft* (people's community), and many other key Nazi ideas all motivated the actions of the Wehrmacht forces. The initial military successes of the Nazi German army also owed a great deal to the creation of effective organisational capacity that made *Blitzkrieg* (lightning attack) possible. Without the large and sophisticated military machine, ordinary recruits would not have found themselves in a situation which ultimately led to the deaths of millions of other people. Nevertheless, even in the Nazi case, ideology and organisation were not enough to sustain the long-term war project. Instead, the military expansion and later contraction were in large part determined by the strength and weaknesses of micro-level solidarities.

One of the earliest studies of social cohesion among the Wehrmacht forces indicated that the attachment to the 'primary group' was the principal motivation behind the unwillingness of the German soldiers to surrender even when it was clear that they had lost the war (Shils and Janowitz 1948). The central argument of this study was that Nazi propaganda played a marginal role in soldiers' commitment to fighting. Instead, the focus was on the strength of micro-group ties. As Shils and Janowitz (1948: 314–15) argue:

> Where conditions were such as to allow primary group life to function smoothly, and where the primary group developed a high degree of cohesion, morale was high and resistance effective or at least very determined regardless in the main of the political attitudes of the soldiers. The conditions of primary group life were related to spatial proximity, the capacity for intimate communication, the provision of paternal protectiveness by NCOs and junior officers and the gratification of certain personality needs, e.g., manliness, by the military organisation and its activities.

Other scholars have challenged this finding by insisting that the ideological commitments of the Wehrmacht soldiers were more important (Bartov 1992; Rossino 2003). Bartov (1992) argues that the primary group model is inadequate to explain individual determination to fight until the end. The key issue here is that the enormous losses that the German army experienced forced commanders to continuously recruit new conscripts and reorganise their units. This situation generated 'highly heterogeneous units' which did not have time to create new 'primary groups'. As Bartov (1992: 38) points out: 'Having seen their old comrades, the members of their "primary groups", killed or wounded, the few survivors of the first winter in Russia could neither form into new groups due to the constant and rapid manpower turnover, nor even briefly enjoy a sense of strength by being sufficiently reinforced.'

While Bartov is right that the primary group model is flawed,[11] this in itself does not mean that the micro-level solidarities did not play an important role in fighting. While ideological power is an important motivator of social action, and was crucial in the mobilisation of German soldiers, ideology cannot simply replace micro-level ties. Instead, ideological power works best when it can effectively tap into the existing micro-group bonds (Malešević 2017, 2019). Although Bartov offers valuable critique of the primary group model his bird's-eye view leaves no analytical room for understanding the complexities of micro-group formation. Both Shils and Janowitz and Bartov subscribe to the essentialist view of social groups. While the former perceive 'primary groups' as given, stable, and largely unchanged social forms the latter assumes that with the high casualty rates 'primary groups' automatically 'disappear' (Bartov 1992: 33). However, groups, just as social pugnacity itself, are not fixed objects but entities in motion – processual phenomena that involve reflective individuals who continuously evaluate their group attachments. In this sense a micro-level solidarity does not stop with the death of some or many of micro-group members. Instead soldiers often fight precisely because they have strong attachments to the individuals who have lost their lives – to keep their memory and the memory of their attachments alive. 'Groupness' is a dynamic and variable phenomenon that is built on actual face-to-face interactions but also on the memory of such interactions. In this sense Wehrmacht soldiers fought not only for living comrades but also for those who had perished during the war (Shepherd 2016).

Furthermore, even short periods of time can generate intense emotional commitments. The shared experience of battlefield often forges strong bonds in a matter of months and even days (see Chapter 10). New recruits cannot symbolically or physically replace fallen comrades, but they can be relatively quickly integrated into the existing networks of micro-solidarity. This is not only a question of organisational capacity but also of willingness to develop emotional commitments to others. Moreover, micro-group solidarities are also built around a sense of attachment to one's family and friends back home. Even when military units are severely decimated, the remaining soldiers and new recruits retain their emotional attachments to their significant others and it is

---

[11] For my criticism of the primary group model as developed by Charles Cooley (1909) and applied to the military units see Malešević (2017: 286–7) and Chapters 7 and 8 in the present volume. Bartov does not focus on the processes that make micro-solidarity possible. Instead, he overemphasises the organisational aspects of military units including inadequate training of recruits and the chaotic leadership structure (see Bartov 1992: 52–5).

these micro-level solidarities that keep them fighting. They are still fighting for others.

More recent scholarship indicates that the motivation to fight for many Wehrmacht soldiers was not significantly different to that of other combatants (Fritz 2010; Holmes 1985; Nietzel and Welzer 2012; Shepherd 2016). Many members of the regular armed forces differentiated themselves from the Waffen-SS whom they considered to be ideological fanatics eager to die for Hitler and the National Socialist project.[12] In their accounts from the battlefield – as documented in their letters, diaries, memoirs, and secret recordings – one can identify a similar pattern of commitment to comrades, friends, and family. Analysing numerous tapes of secret recordings of Wehrmacht soldiers who were prisoners of war (POWs) in England, Nietzel and Welzer (2012: 319) conclude: Frontline soldiers felt an almost exclusive sense of duty to their comrades and their superiors who formed their social units … As a rule German soldiers were not "ideological warriors". Most of them were fully apolitical.' This commitment to micro-level solidarity is also apparent in many letters that soldiers sent from the frontlines: 'the secret behind our incredible success and victories' stems from 'the great comradeship [that] binds us German soldiers together' or 'one must help the comrades stuck in the mud, that one simply belongs there, that one cannot be torn away, because one feels oneself out there almost at home' (Bartov 1992: 34). Or: 'One must bear it and hold on to that which remains: the good spirit of comradeship and which surrounds me with much love' (Fritz 2010: 202).

The dominant fraternal themes encountered among the Americans in the Spanish Civil War and Indians in the First World War are just as present among the Wehrmacht soldiers. Hence many German soldiers were recruited together, their shared experience of the battlefield formed the patterns of their group solidarity, while living together in close proximity under extremely difficult conditions helped forge strong emotional ties.

The Wehrmacht operated a regional and localised recruitment system that consciously aimed to maintain existing group ties. Thus, the army recruited soldiers from regional conscription zones (*Wehrkreise*): 'This policy meant that not only were troops trained and grouped into units together, but also that the wounded could expect to re-join their old

[12] These soldiers also shared the view that Waffen-SS forces suffered much higher casualties but as Overmans's (2004) analysis of German military casualties during the Second World War shows, the Waffen-SS fatalities were not much higher than those of the regular army.

comrades once they recovered' (Bartov 1992: 30). As Fritz (2010: 183) explains: 'replacements never travelled to their units as individuals – as in the American army – but as coherent groups (*Ersatzbataillone*, or *Marschbataillone*)'. In their letters recruits often express satisfaction that their military training and first fighting days were spent with people they knew well: 'Fuchs ... spoke of his intense joy at being in a unit with men from his region and village, a pleasure that contributed to the growth of a close fighting spirit' (Fritz 2010: 183). In addition, a number of young recruits already had experience of membership in various youth associations (Hitler Jugend, Deutsches Jungvolk, Edelweiss Pirates, etc.) where they developed a sense of strong group attachments. Some recruits would also join together with their friends from these organisations. This element of continuity in the bonds of comradeship is visible in soldiers' descriptions: 'I was full of enthusiasm when I joined the Jugenvolk at the age of ten ... They seemed to me to be holy. And then the trips! Is there anything nicer than enjoying the splendours of the homeland and in the company of one's comrades?' (Fritz 2010: 186).

The military units were shaped as paternalistic and hierarchical entities where officers would lead their soldiers into the battle but were also responsible for the 'care for their needs, creating thereby a sense of belonging to a family' (Bartov 1992: 31; Fritz 2010: 183–4; Schulte 1989). The army establishment consciously emphasised the development of strong unit cohesion with the focus on the squads, platoons, and companies: the idea was to create bonds of 'tight bunches of men who suffered, fought, and died together' (van Creveld 1982: 68). The recruits soon developed this sense of group attachment and this is clearly reflected in their personal letters: 'I've become such an integral part of my company that I could not leave it ever again' (Fritz 2010: 183); 'my unit was my home, my family, which I had to protect' (Fritz 2010: 46).

As in the cases of American volunteers and Indian soldiers, the Wehrmacht recruits were initially more focused on their micro-level solidarities at home: their family and friends. This was particularly pronounced in times of hardship and heavy casualties when images of family life at home brought comfort but also a sense of strong emotional attachment: 'Images whirled through my thoughts; my hometown, the old castle high on the sandstone cliff, the colourful fields of flowers, on the edge of the city, my father and sister at home' (Fritz 2010: 168); 'as the moment of attack grew closer, my terror was rising. I wanted to confide something of my anguish to my mother' (Fritz 2010: 167). One young recruit emotionally recollects the last visit of his mother to his troop training centre: 'Early tomorrow morning at this time mother will leave again ... How strange this last get-together! Sad and dreamlike.

I will remain strong. Tears come to mother anew ... I take hold of her loving, concerned, workworn hands ... No words. A last kiss, and I am outside in the clear cold November night' (Fritz 2010: 40). In some cases, this micro-level attachment to home was framed in ideological terms where family and the nation become one. For example, in a letter to his wife a soldier identifies Germany with his family: 'For in our hearts is Germany, the Germany that must live. Germany, that is you and the children. You are the homeland for us, and we carry you in our hearts. We fight and sacrifice and bleed for you. We never weaken for a second, for you must be protected. Back in our trenches, we think of home. I hold your last dear letter in my worn hands.'[13]

The shared hardship of the frontline moulded group cohesion. For example, the unbearable cold and hunger on the Russian Front did not lead to individualist struggle for self-preservation but instead served to enhance group ties. As German soldiers report from the frontline: 'Shoulder to shoulder we fulfil our duty, like the old comrades, and are firmly resolved to fight and triumph, so that our models, the fallen comrades, will not be sacrificed in vain. Their death is my duty ... Better to fight honourably and die than to steal life' (Fritz 2010: 201). Even when soldiers were dying of hunger and cold on the Russian Front their focus was much more on their two micro-groups – one at home and the other on the battlefield – than on themselves. Hence in a letter home one soldier describes the harrowing conditions of the Russian winter: 'The cold is ongoing. The poor wounded have to be brought in by sledge at night in order to avoid being seen by the enemy, and so they freeze all over again before they reach us. Because the Russian is always attacking, driving his hordes ever onwards, there are always wounded and dead for us' (Shepherd 2016: 209). Under these conditions some soldiers contemplated or resorted to cannibalism but even in this extreme situation self-cannibalism was more likely: 'as there was no shortage of human corpses, some men in Wilhelm Beyer's unit contemplated cannibalism – even, if necessary, on their own body parts' (Shepherd 2016: 270).

The strength of micro-bonds was most perceptible in the carnage of the battlefield when the death of a close comrade would regularly invoke deep emotional response. For example: 'As I returned to my command post in the village I gaped at the dead comrades. I was so shaken that I almost cried' (Fritz 2010: 58); 'the pain of our buddies comes alarmingly close to us, the eternal same thoughts of such an hour: why him, why not me?' (Fritz 2010: 202); 'As I read the lines, it was as if I myself

---

[13] https://research.caslvin.edu/german-propaganda-archive/schul03.htm.

had been struck' (Fritz 2010: 202). The sense of emotional attachment and moral obligation extended beyond the battlefield and soldiers who were injured and sent back home or moved to other military posts regularly felt a strong need to go back to their units on the frontline: 'I had to get back to the front. I could not bear to sit around … when I knew what my comrades were going through. I had to get back'; 'I could no longer live any further in France amid this quit and richness. I had to get back to my friends and brothers at the front. Perhaps it was the call of the dead comrades that compelled me to return here … I am proud to be at the focus of the battle' (Fritz 2010: 206).

Just as in the case of American and Indian combatants, social ties were built and enhanced not only through shared experience of fighting but also through living together in close proximity and sharing the hardships and solaces of everyday life. The daily physicality of face-to-face inter-action, working, eating, sleeping, and fighting together all fostered intense group ties. As one soldier describes daily routine on the frontline:

In the rain, the tents stare at us stiff and clay-like while we hurry to dig out the marshy field … In the darkness we bump into and press against each other … Soon we chew on dried-out bread with the eternally same salted canned meat … We are so tired we can't think … The breathing and confusing dreams become deeper, we press against one another for a little warmth. (Fritz 2010: 4)

This shared everyday hardship moulds a strong sense of unity that is later displayed at the battlefields where soldiers fight for each other but also for their comrades who have perished in previous battles:

You look at each other, you survivors, with whom you lay together, in the same foxhole day in and day out, at night stood watch shoulder to shoulder, with whom you laughed together, cooked, ate, slept, fought with and made up with … What binds the living so strongly and so loyally to those who are dead? Often misinterpreted, by a few completely understood, bound by chains of necessity: Comradeship? (Fritz 2010: 185)

There is no doubt that the actions of Wehrmacht soldiers were deeply shaped by the ideological postulates of Nazi doctrine. This is clearly visible in their letters, conversations, diaries, and many other documents (Bartov 1992; Rossino 2003; Sait 2019), and even more so in their merciless behaviour against civilians and POWs across occupied Europe. Nevertheless, being involved in a genocidal and conquest-oriented project is not necessarily incompatible with feeling a strong sense of moral obligation and emotional attachment to one's micro-group. In this sense, on the micro-level the social pugnacity of German soldiers was not profoundly different from the soldiers of other armies in many other wars: they often killed and died for their significant others.

5.5   Conclusion

The conventional wisdom has it that the individual combatants involved in wars, revolutions, insurgencies, terrorist actions, and other forms of organised violence primarily fight for themselves – from self-preservation to attaining specific material or symbolic benefits. Many social scientists also subscribe to a more refined version of this position. For the cognitive evolutionary theorists fighting is a means 'for the achievement of primary biological ends' (Gat 2006: 38) and as such it only makes sense in terms of self-reproduction or the extension of one's own gene pool. The utilitarian theories of violence interpret fighting as a form of self-interested behaviour centred on one's survival or acquisition of material and political resources: as Humphries (2005: 510) insists, 'to understand causes of contemporary civil wars one should forget about the political and cultural arguments and focus instead on the greed of rebels and especially their trade in natural resources'. The culturalist interpretations understand fighting through the prism of shared norms and values – 'Cultures need to coax and trick soldiers into participating in combat' (Goldstein 2001: 331). However, none of these approaches can adequately capture the complexity of social behaviour in the combat zone.

To fully understand the dynamics of fighting one has to look beyond the fighting itself. Paraphrasing the famous line from Kipling one could say 'what should they know of fighting who only fighting know?'[14] The phenomenon of social fighting cannot be reduced to the very narrow event associated with the actual physical confrontation of two or more human bodies. Instead, social pugnacity is a phenomenon involving a variety of organisational, ideological, and micro-interactional processes that make the acts of direct confrontation possible and meaningful. The combatants have to be mobilised, armed, trained, transported, fed, and clothed by specific social organisations all of whom shape their attitudes and behaviour before, during, and after fighting. Furthermore, a variety of social organisations, civil society groups, and friendship and family networks are also involved in the socialisation of individuals into their combatant roles. This is a long-term process framed by specific ideological categories developed and reproduced by educational systems, mass media, public sphere, peer groups, kinship networks, and many other social actors. In this context social pugnacity includes much more than killing and dying on the battlefields – it is a social process that exists

---

[14] Rudyard Kipling's poem 'The English Flag' (1891) contains this line 'And what should they know of England who only England know?'

both before and after the actual physical confrontation. Human beings are social creatures that constantly respond to other people and shape their behaviours and beliefs in reference to others. In this context social fighting is nearly always defined by human relationships with other humans. In other words, individuals rarely fight for themselves alone and instead tend regularly to fight for others. These others can be abstract categories predefined and systematically propagated through the recognisable ideological tropes reproduced by specific social organisations such as a state apparatus, a military organisation, an insurgent movement, a terrorist unit, and so on. In these ideological framings one is primed to fight for imagined communities of others – members of our nation, ethnic group, race, religious affiliation, gender, status, caste, or class group (umma, proletariat, universal sisterhood, sons of soil, etc.). Nevertheless, the combatants are much more likely to respond to representations of concrete others whom they know and whose affections they share – their close friends, lovers, family members at home, and their comrades on the frontline. Hence the experiences of close-range violence across the world and throughout different historical and cultural contexts show that fighting is rarely about self-interest and more often about the protection and preservation of significant others. It is only when social organisations deploy ideological discourses that successfully mimic the language of micro-solidarity that they can motivate combatants to fight.

6   Avoiding Violence
The Structural Context of Non-Fighting

6.1   Introduction

Human-on-human violence is often perceived as a transcultural and transhistorical phenomenon. Hence most people assume that war and other forms of organised violence have always existed and have been present in all social orders throughout the world. However, both historical and anthropological research indicate that organised violence developed very late in human history (over the last 10,000 years or so) and that throughout history many social orders have shunned violence in many of its forms. Anthropological research has corroborated that there have been hundreds of societies with different levels of organisational complexity that have rarely experienced fighting and that have also devised elaborate ritualistic and other practices to avoid violence within and outside of one's group. Hence in this chapter I explore why fighting is a historically specific practice that affects some societies much more than others. I also analyse why some individuals, small groups, and social organisations are less prone to fighting or actively opposed to violence than others. The chapter also zooms in on the structural contexts that hinder the development of ideological and organisational mechanisms that foster social pugnacity. I argue that the phenomenon of non-fighting operates according to similar sociological processes as those that make fighting possible – non-fighting, like fighting, does not come naturally but is a product of micro-interactional, organisational, and ideological work.

6.2   The Micro-Sociology of Non-Fighting

In popular culture fighting is often depicted as an instinctual reaction. The widely shared assumption is that once facing a direct threat human beings will try to flee or resort to violence. However, historical and anthropological studies indicate that human responses to violent threats are much more complex and diverse than the simple 'fight or flight' formula allows. In fact, much of recent scholarship shows that fighting does not come automatically to most humans and that the non-fighting is the norm. As Collins (2008) argues, an overwhelming majority of confrontations do not end in violence and even individuals with a reputation for violent behaviour do not engage in fights all the time:

whatever the motive or interest that individuals and groups might have for fighting, the overriding empirical reality is that most of the time they do not fight. They pretend to get along; they compromise; they put up a peaceful façade and manoeuvre behind the scenes; they bluff, bluster, insult, and gossip, more often at a distance than to their opponent's face. When they do actually come to violence, the determining conditions are overwhelmingly in their short-term interaction. (Collins 2008: 337)

Collins emphasises that human beings are not very good at violence because confrontations generate fear and tension which prevent effective fighting. Hence the precondition for any efficient fighting is the capacity to circumvent these emotional barriers. That is why individuals who find themselves in violent conflicts often tend to use narcotics and alcohol or require other organisational, technological, or ideological supports to fight (see Chapter 10).

Collins is right that fighting does not come automatically to humans and that most individuals are not natural born fighters. However, he is wrong in treating non-violence as a habitual human condition. Both fighting and non-fighting entail a great deal of commitment and work. Pacifism is not the default position of the human race; it is a process that involves individual and social action. Just as fighting necessitates organisational and ideological prompts and is shaped by different historical conditions the same applies to non-fighting. Non-violence is not a spontaneous and passive condition but a product of individual and collective action and specific beliefs and practices. Those who advocate or pursue non-violent action often do so vigorously and with a lot of commitment. As Martin Luther King Jr. (2011 [1964]) emphasised: 'Nonviolence is a powerful and just weapon. Indeed, it is a weapon unique in history, which cuts without wounding and ennobles the man who wields it.' In other words, the phenomenon of non-fighting also requires sociological explanation as historical and contemporary records show that some individuals, groups, and societies are more likely than others to avoid fighting but also to actively practise non-violent policies for resolving disputes. Non-violence is both a micro- and macro-sociological phenomenon although the two often overlap.

On the individual and micro-group level, non-fighting might involve such practices as actively evading military conscription, practising conscientious objection to violence, deserting from armed organisations, avoiding shooting at the enemy on the battlefield, or actively pursuing different forms of non-violent resistance. In some of these situations, individuals and small groups avoid violence for moral, religious, or other principled reasons while in other cases non-fighting is a product of emotional reactions or cognitive decisions that transpire in specific situations. However, just as fighting is not an easy act for most people the same applies to active non-fighting. Individuals who decide to evade, abscond from, or leave violent organisations such as the military, police, vigilante groups, militias, or gangs often face draconian punishments and ostracism from other members of their society. For example, draft dodgers, deserters, and even conscientious objectors have often ended up in military courts and many have also faced firing squads.

In the eighteenth and nineteenth century, deserters from the military were often flogged or branded with tattoos indicating their cowardice. By the end of the nineteenth century and into the early twentieth century most countries introduced regulations that mandate the death penalty for those who desert the frontline, and some still apply this rule for draft evasion too. During the Second World War, Soviet authorities issued an order that officers should shoot all deserters on the spot while their family members were to be arrested (Roberts 2006: 132). Nevertheless, despite severe punishments and the mandatory death sentences that some armies operate, desertion and draft evasion have been widespread practices throughout the world. In the wars that the USA fought since the early nineteenth century, the desertion rate tended to be relatively high – from 12.7 per cent in the War of 1812, to 8.3 per cent in Mexican–American war (1846–8), to around 10 per cent during the American Civil War. The Union Army had up to 200,000 deserters and the Confederate forces lost 100,000 soldiers to desertion (Adams-Graf 2017). During the Second World War, over 21,000 US soldiers were sentenced for desertion but only 49 were given the death sentence (Adams-Graf 2017). The Vietnam War was characterised by a very high level of draft evasion and a substantial rate of desertion. It is estimated that over 500,000 US soldiers deserted their positions in Vietnam and up to 14 million people have evaded draft through deferral, exemption, disqualification, or conscientious objection (Adams-Graf 2017; Cortright, 2005). At one point in 1972, 'there were more conscientious objectors than actual draftees' (Cortright 2005: 5). With the abolishment of military draft and the introduction of completely professional militaries the desertion rates have been much lower in most Western militaries including the US armed forces. Nevertheless, both the Iraq and Afghanistan wars generated a significant number of desertions. From 2003 to 2007 approximately 5,000 US military personnel deserted the Iraq War every year with a peak in 2006 with 8,000 deserters (Adams-Graf 2017). Researchers have identified a variety of reasons for desertion including individual motives (such as mental breakdown, fear, exhaustion, inability to obey commands, etc.) and collective dynamics (including the composition of military units, presence of conscripts, social heterogeneity, factional polarisation, and strength of local attachments among others) (Bearman 1991; McLauchlin 2015).

While the deserters, draft evaders, and conscientious objectors often face legal state sanctions including imprisonment and even a death sentence, non-fighting is also penalised and vilified by civil society groups and personal networks. Hence those who purposefully disengage from fighting on the battlefields, in gang conflicts, violent insurrections, genocidal projects, or other forms of violence often face ostracism from their immediate groups including their co-fighters, friends, family, neighbours, and the wider society. The decision to stop fighting or to leave a violent gang can often result in immediate death. Some gangs operate the rule 'blood in, blood out' which means that joining and leaving a gang entails violence. To join a gang, one often undergoes a ritual of 'beat in', or in some cases 'kill in', that is, one is has to experience violence or to participate in the beating or killing of the gang's enemy (see Chapter 4). Leaving the gang is even more difficult as one is often suspected of being a potential threat to the gang. Hence many potential leavers are simply murdered to signal to the others that none can leave a gang. This draconian policy tends to work effectively as only small number of gang members have managed to leave or defect to other gangs. For example, Fong et al. (1995) show that only 5 per cent of prison gang members defect from their gangs and one of the main reasons for defection is 'refusing to carry out a "hit" on a non-gang member'.

Similarly, unwillingness to take part in violence against civilians during insurgencies, revolutions, or genocides may also result in exclusion from the group or physical or social acts of punishment, while testifying against those responsible for such acts of violence can result in death. For example, both the Provisional IRA in Northern Ireland and the Red Brigades in Italy have operated a policy of limb punishment shootings (kneecapping) for anybody who was deemed to be a police informant or was willing to testify against these organisations in court. It is estimated that up to 2,500 individuals were kneecapped in Northern Ireland during the Troubles (1968–98). The kneecapping was not only a physical form of punishment, but it also marked an individual with a deep social stigma indicating treason and disloyalty to one's community (Williams 1997). The active non-participation in acts of violence against civilian population as in ethnic cleansing, population displacements, or genocide can also result in severe physical or social penalties or instant execution. The experience of Rwandan genocide shows that ordinary Hutus who refused to participate in genocide would often be killed on the spot by the Interahamwe militia. As Prunier (1999: 247) emphasises, 'Either you took part in the massacres or you were massacred yourself'. In other situations, the non-participation in killing might only result in social stigma. For example, in the Second World War, some German officers allowed soldiers not to take part in the genocide. As Browning (1992) shows in his book *Ordinary Men*, some Nazi officers did not punish their soldiers for their decision not to kill during the Holocaust and mass slaughter of East European civilians. Members of the Reserve Police Battalion 101 were given the option not to take part in the mass killings of civilians, although only a handful made this choice.

Conscientious objection has also played an important role in preventing fighting. Although this principle was invoked for centuries, it is only recently that military organisations have accepted conscientious objection as a legitimate reason to avoid participation in fighting. Hence two UN resolutions (1995/83 and 1998/77) accepted in the 1990s state that 'persons performing military service should not be excluded from the right to have conscientious objections to military service' and that 'persons performing military service may develop conscientious objections' (UN Commission on Human Rights 1998). Following these resolutions many militaries throughout the world have developed alternative forms of military service where conscientious objectors undertake an equivalent civilian service that does not involve use of guns and other military devices. Nevertheless, for much of history, conscientious objectors were severely punished for their stance including regular executions. Many states still do not recognise conscientious objection and regularly imprison individuals who object to obligatory participation in military. During the First World War, many conscientious objectors were imprisoned, forcibly brought to the battlefields, or court-martialled and sentenced to death. In the UK, for example, 62,301 individuals were registered as conscientious objectors with one third being imprisoned and 34 sentenced to death (with most sentences later being commuted to prison terms)[1] (Casquete 2008). In the USA during the First World War, 450 conscientious objectors were found guilty and sentenced by military courts with 17 receiving a death sentence, 215 sentenced to life or 20-year prison terms, and the rest receiving long prison terms (Kohn 1987). During the First World War, 72,354 individuals applied for

---

[1] www.iwm.org.uk/history/conscientious-objectors-in-their-own-words.

conscientious objector status while in the Vietnam War no less than 171,000 people were granted such status (Levi 1997).

The early forms of conscientious objection were centred on religious beliefs that prevent individuals from doing harm to other humans. Hence both the UK and the USA made a provision from eighteenth century onwards to allow for a limited form of conscientious objection – in the UK Quakers were exempt from military service since 1757, while US individual states would often allow Amish, Mennonites, Jehovah's Witnesses, Seventh-day Adventists, Quakers, and Church of the Brethren among others to avoid military draft. More recently the provisions have also been made for some sects of Judaism, Buddhists, Hinduists, Jainists, and Bahai believers and variety of non-religious beliefs including pacifism, humanism, anti-militarism, and anti-imperialism among many others.

Despite gradual acceptance of conscientious objection as a legitimate ground for non-fighting, in some countries many conscientious objectors face social stigma within their societies. This is particularly pronounced during periods of war when their actions are often deemed as treasonous and cowardly behaviour. Thus, many conscientious objectors often face severe criticism and social exclusion for their unwillingness to fight.

Draft evasion, desertion, unwillingness to take part in violence against civilians during genocide, insurgencies, and revolutions, avoiding gang wars, and conscientious objection are all very different forms of non-participation in fighting. These acts of non-violence are often rooted in different individual motivations and diverse social conditions. Some individuals refuse to fight and kill because these practices go against their beliefs. For others, unwillingness to fight might be an act of self-preservation, an emotional response to a specific situation, or a result of disillusionment with the social organisation involved in fighting. Nevertheless, despite these pronounced differences there are also some common sociological processes that characterise non-fighting on the micro-level.

Firstly, the scale of non-fighting is often determined by the organisational capacity of entities involved in violent conflicts. Social organisations that possess greater coercive power are more likely to stifle instances of non-fighting. In this context modern bureaucratic systems operate more effectively than the traditional patrimonial models of organisation. Whereas pre-modern European armies lacked organisational capacity to maintain discipline and punish disobedience, most contemporary military organisations in Europe have well established mechanisms for the control of their soldiers. For example, eighteenth-century army contingents in Ireland were often characterised as inefficient and ill-disciplined with high levels of desertion and general unwillingness to fight. Some reports describe soldiers as being continuously drunk and incapable of performing their roles: in 1750 'the departure of a regiment from Limerick with its drummers incapable due to drink, and its officers carried on litters' (Garnham 2005: 91). The army was prone to absenteeism with high levels of corruption 'at every level, from the provision of uniforms and equipment to the building of barracks'. In addition, troops were dispersed throughout the country in small units which 'made training and the maintenance of discipline a near impossibility' (Garnham 2005: 91–2). The patrimonial model of organisation generated an unstable and unreliable system of recruitment, training, and pay that undermined the cohesiveness and fighting capacity of the army. Garnham (2005) emphasises that the army was often composed of underaged, physically unfit, and unmotivated recruits. The undersized units were also over-reliant on Catholic soldiers who were less loyal to the British state. Hence non-fighting was a direct product of weak organisational capacities of a military organisation that could not enforce its commands.

Similarly, the example of the post-2003 US sponsored and equipped Iraqi army demonstrates how weak organisational capacity contributes to the inability and unwillingness to fight. This was evident in military conflicts with ISIS in 2013 and 2014 when many Iraqi military units quickly collapsed during the war. Abbas and Trombly (2014) describe how the Iraqi army's second division broke down during the ISIS attack and in the process experienced huge territorial losses in Nineveh province. Despite having modern military equipment and a sizeable number of soldiers the second division collapsed quickly due to its patrimonial structure and very weak organisational capacity:

On paper, the 2nd Division appears modern in structure with overwhelming advantage in manpower and firepower. In practice, these units are undermanned, underequipped, and undertrained, due in large part to misallocated resources. Prior to 2012, the 2nd Division commander, Staff General Naser al-Ghanam, tried and failed to enforce military discipline and discourage corruption, much to the chagrin of the rank and file. (Abbas and Trombly 2014: 1)

The patrimonial system of governance undermined all attempts to reform the military:

In the Iraqi army, leadership at the division level maintains enough sway over logistics and pay to embezzle and extort lower ranks. Many officers see their units as businesses with reliable revenues rather than combat outfits. "You don't earn a [commanding position]: you buy it," a Captain in the Iraqi army said. (Abbas and Trombly 2014: 1)

Hence when attacked by a well-disciplined and highly motivated force such as ISIS the soldiers of the second division just ran away from their posts.

In direct contrast, well-established modern bureaucratic systems tend to operate a very effective model of recruitment, training, and coordination. For example, most efficient military organisations such as the Shayetet 13 commandos of the Israeli Defence Forces, or Recces, the South African Special Forces Brigade, are composed of exceptionally skilful, extensively trained, and highly motivated individuals. These military units possess great coercive capacity which is successfully deployed internally to discipline their members and externally to fight effectively in combat situations. Both organisations operate a highly selective and competitive system of recruitment and new recruits have to undergo prolonged and extremely demanding training. While potential Recces recruits have to complete a week-long selection process during which they are not allowed to eat or sleep and have to face numerous physical and mental challenges, Shayetet 13 recruits have to undergo twenty months of rigorous training. These bureaucratic systems successfully maintain elaborate division of labour and a hierarchical chain of command which together with status and material inducements generate highly motivated fighters.

Secondly, the willingness to fight is also shaped by ideological commitments. However, the focus here is less on individual motivations and more on the spread of specific ideological discourses and practices within the social organisations involved in fighting. Just as with organisational capacity, social entities that possess greater ideological penetration within their membership are more likely to generate committed fighters. In most successful cases, deeper ideological penetration is dependent on the higher organisational capacity and social organisations that combine the two tend to have less desertion. For example, China's People's Liberation Army (PLA) has historically combined ideological and organisational powers to instil greater fighting capacity among its recruits. The army gained popularity during the civil war (1927–49) against the Kuomintang armies as it was able to articulate a very different ideological doctrine that resonated with the ordinary population. Mao's Three Rules of Discipline and Eight Points of Attention (1928) struck a chord with the large Chinese peasantry and contributed significantly towards their willingness to join the Communist army. In contrast to the Kuomintang forces who disrespected the civilian population, often confiscated their possessions, and looted their houses without permission, the Chinese Red Army strictly followed the Three Rules thus avoiding conflicts with the local population. The Three Rules were: 1. Obey orders in all your actions; 2. Do not take a single needle or piece of thread from the masses; and 3. Turn in everything captured. In addition, Mao proclaimed the following 'Eight Points of Attention' which also operated as ideological precepts that were obeyed by the army: 1. Speak politely; 2. Pay fairly for what you buy; 3. Return everything you borrow; 4. Pay for anything you damage; 5. Do not hit or swear at people; 6. Do not damage crops; 7. Do not take liberties with women; and 8. Do not ill-treat captives (Uhalley 1985). Many of these rules were strictly enforced and any Red Army soldier found looting property of peasants would be shot on the spot. The PLA's legitimacy is still rooted in this ideological legacy of civil war (and the War of Resistance against Japanese Aggression (1937–45)) and ordinary soldiers are motivated by these nationalist principles. The army possesses enormous organisational apparatus and in combination with deep ideological penetration is capable of maintaining 2.8 million soldiers in its ranks.

However, shared ideological principles can also motivate individuals not to fight. For example, during the Vietnam War, the US military possessed exceptional technology, high coercive capacity, and a substantial degree of ideological penetration within its forces. Yet, the character of the war impacted profoundly on the level of ideological commitment among recruits. As the war continued for years without victory or a clear exit strategy, the US army had to conscript large number of young nonprofessionals and the ideological messages that the army disseminated about the 'fight against communism' and 'safeguarding of democracy' started to backfire. With the rise of the anti-war movement in the USA and the ever-critical daily media portrayals of the war, the US army found itself on the back foot while many of its soldiers started openly sympathising with the anti-war movement.

At the same time, the Vietcong forces remained highly motivated to fight. US intelligence produced a number of documents about the high 'will to fight' among the Vietcong and increasingly low levels of support for military action among US soldiers. Hence two intelligence reports from 1970 and 1974 respectively document the continuous commitment to fight until the end. In 1970:

Hanoi still considers that it has the will and basic strengths to prevail ... Despite Hanoi's obvious concerns with its problems, the Communists almost certainly believe that they enjoy some basic strengths and advantages which will ultimately prove to be decisive.

And in 1974:

Hanoi continues to demonstrate its determination to impose Communist control on the South. There has been no apparent curtailment in Hanoi's support for [the war] ... Finally, even if there is not a major offensive during the next year, it is clear that at some point Hanoi will shift back to major warfare in its effort to gain control of South Vietnam'.[2]

Finally, although organisational and ideological context plays an important role in non-fighting just as in fighting, the social dynamics of violence avoidance is strongly linked with networks of micro-solidarity. The combatants rarely decide to avoid draft, desert from the frontline, or avoid gang fighting on their own. In most cases this is a collective decision influenced by attitudes of small networks of friends or family members. The small group network ties play a crucial role in the avoidance of violence just as they might motivate individuals to join armed groups and fight. As indicated in Chapter 5, micro-level solidarities impact deeply on one's decision to enlist in the variety of armed organisations – from regular military forces to insurgencies, terrorist cells, gangs, or revolutionary secret societies, among others. The research indicates that joining such organisations is regularly a collective act: networks of friends and family members often collectively join military forces, gangs, terrorist cells, or revolutionary groups (Attran 2011; Hassan 2011; Malešević 2017; Vertigans 2011). Individuals participate in violent acts to impress, or please others, or to conform to the norms of their micro-groups of close friends and family members.

The same logic applies to non-fighting. Although some non-fighting might be driven by solitary decisions and strong pacifist beliefs, most human beings opt for avoidance of violent conflict through group dynamics. For example, the common practices of draft avoidance and desertion during wartime have regularly been shaped by the collective action of small networks. The scholarship on the American Civil War shows that desertion was more likely to happen in squads and platoons that were more socially homogeneous (Bearman, 1991). Similarly, Shils and Janowitz (1948) and Rose (1951) have identified interpersonal relationships within platoons and military companies as proving decisive in preventing or fostering surrender during the Second World war. More recently McLauchlin (2015, 2020) and Bou Nassif (2015) have explored the group dynamics of desertion and defection during civil wars and found that unit composition and social cohesion determine the patterns of desertion and defection. In a comprehensive study of draft evasion and desertion during the Syrian Civil War in 2014 and 2015, Koehler et al. (2016) have shown that this high-risk behaviour was shaped by strong network ties. Although individuals make decisions to avoid recruitment

---

[2] www.rand.org/pubs/research_briefs/RB10040.html.

or to desert by themselves it is their embedment in small group networks that is critical to how these decisions are made. The decision to leave the Syrian army were directly linked to a sense of attachment to family and friends who either encouraged soldiers to desert or defect or were perceived to be under direct threat and the desertion was the most secure route towards helping family and friends. For example, one ex-soldier explains how he decided to desert the Syrian army after a phone conversation with his sister:

She reportedly told the soldier that insurgents were on their way to a military position in Tadmur (Palmyra). While on the phone with her, he recalled hearing people at the mosque in the background screaming "Allah Akbar!" When asked about the incident, the soldier's sister reported on the conflict in Palmyra and his deceased friends. The soldier resolved to leave the military right after that phone conversation. (Koehler et al. 2016: 449)

In another case the desertion happened after prolonged decision making and conversation with family and friends who initially opposed desertion but eventually agreed and supported this joint decision:

He contemplated desertion very early in the conflict. Although he did not tell his family explicitly, his father knew he was thinking about leaving the military. Yet, his father was against taking the risk of desertion and instead insisted that his son was not to kill anyone while on duty. The eventual deserter explained that it was thus initially difficult for him to decide to desert, especially with his family living in a regime-controlled area, as he was worried about the regime's possible retribution against them. (Koehler et al. 2016: 450)

The same micro-group principle applies to gang desistence. In most instances leaving the gang is an extremely dangerous act that can result in one's own death but also the deaths of family members. Hence gang desistence is deeply linked with networks of micro-solidarity. Many individuals attempt to leave the gang with their family members or close comrades. As Miller (2002) and Sanchez-Jankowski (1991) show, many gangs are composed of multigenerational members and leaving the gang often entails an agreement with other family members: '32 percent of the fathers of gang members who were interviewed stated that their children belonged to the same gang to which the fathers had once belonged' (Arciaga-Young and Gonzalez 2013: 8). In addition, gang desistence may be a result of family obligations: 'Familial ties and victimization experiences were cited far more often than institutional affiliations as reasons to terminate the ties to the gang' (Decker and Lauritsen 2002: 105). In some cases, becoming a parent impacts on one's decision to leave the world of violence: 'For many young men, fatherhood acts as a significant turning point, facilitating a shift away from gang involvement, crime and drug sales; a decline in substance abuse; and engagement with education and legitimate employment' (Moloney et al. 2009: 312).

Thus, on the micro-sociological level, the dynamics of non-fighting operates similarly to that of fighting: in both cases social action is shaped by the organisational, ideological, and interactional contexts. Just as they are willing to fight, kill, and die for others, humans are also willing to avoid violence and desert from fighting to please or accommodate their significant others. In other words, social pugnacity is a scalar phenomenon ranging from active non-fighting to the complete immersion in violence.

6.3   The Macro-Sociology of Non-Fighting

Collins (2008) is absolutely right that as individuals, human beings are not very competent at violence. Efficient fighting entails skills, knowledge, experience, and endurance. Most of all, to be effective fighters humans have to be recruited, trained, and managed. Hence protracted and coordinated large-scale violent action requires the existence of social organisations capable of mobilising and training many individuals. The historical record shows clearly that the proliferation of violence coincides with the development of large-scale social organisations and especially the state. While hunter-gatherers may not have been intrinsically peaceful, they simply did not possess adequate organisational and ideological tools to mobilise and coordinate millions of individuals for combat. Much of recent archaeological and palaeontological research indicates that foragers avoided violent confrontations and that the institution of warfare develops and proliferates only with the creation of sedentary lifestyle. The archaeological records show that there is no evidence of sustained organised violent conflicts with large numbers of casualties among the simple hunter-gatherer populations before the Neolithic revolution (Ferguson 2013; Fry 2013; Wendorf 1968). The archaeological studies on skeletal remains indicate that most cases of violent deaths and injuries were caused by interpersonal disputes. It is extremely rare to find evidence of group violence in the Palaeolithic period: most records of human remains point to conflicts involving two or three individuals. Even cave paintings rarely depict human-on-human violence: 'Palaeolithic art shows no drawing of group conflict, and there is virtually no indication from late Palaeolithic skeletons of murderous violence' (Guthrie 2005: 422). Hence the expansion of organised violence has historically been linked with the creation of para-state (i.e., chiefdoms) and state structures (empires, city-states, and patrimonial kingdoms). It is no historical coincidence that the development of civilisation and the proliferation of war emerge at the same time – around 10,000 to 12,000 years ago (Bowden 2013; Malešević 2017; Mann 1986).

The same principle applies to contemporary hunter-gatherers. There is no doubt that these populations are not 'the remnants of the ancient past' as often portrayed but are profoundly different societies that have experienced long-term historical changes. Nevertheless, these societies exhibit some similar organisational features that have characterised ancient foragers. One of these features is the personalised nature of violent disputes. As Fry and Söderberg (2013: 270) show, most forms of violence among contemporary foraging populations involve disorganised and personalised disputes between individuals: 'More than half of the lethal aggression events were perpetuated by lone individuals, and almost two-thirds resulted from accidents, interfamilial disputes, within-group executions, or interpersonal motives such as competition over a particular woman.' Anthropologists have identified a variety of practices that contemporary foragers use to avoid violent confrontations including wrestling matches, mock ritualistic confrontations, spear throwing and dodging, fire rituals, reciprocal blow striking to one's head and shoulders, chest pounding, verbal confrontations, song and dance contests and so on (Fry and Szala 2013: 464; Hoebel 1967: 92). For example, several Australian nomadic groups use fire rituals to avoid violent confrontations: the Warumungus of Northern Territory and Warlpiri of Western Australia rely on ritualistic fire torches to settle conflicts between two or more people who have a dispute. The individuals run at each other with flaming torches trying to hit the opponent while also avoiding the flame targeted at them. Once the ritual is completed the conflict is deemed to be settled (Curran 2019; Fry and Szala 2013). Similarly, other foraging populations such as Dogrib, Ingalik, Slavey of North America, and Siriono and Ona of South America rely on publicly organised wrestling rituals to resolve disputes within the community (Hoebel 1967). Instead of violent fighting, wrestling matches are used to diffuse conflicts and to decide on disputes.

The avoidance of unnecessary conflicts is a principle that is practised not only within a single group but also between neighbouring groups. Many ethnographic studies provide ample evidence on a variety of foraging societies that shun violence and never attack neighbouring groups. There are still over seventy known hunter-gatherer populations that rarely engage in intra- or intergroup fighting. Some of the most extensively studied cases of such peaceful societies include Semai of Malaysia, !Kung of Namibia, Angola, and Botswana, Copper Inuit of Canada, Paliyan of India, Siriono of Bolivia, Zapotec of Mexico, and Mbuti of Congo. For example, the Zapotec population promotes egalitarian principles and gender equality, and children are taught to avoid all forms of violence. The parents shun physical disciplining of their children and insist on correcting their misbehaviour through communication and dialogue. Consequently, studies on Zapotec children aged three to eight have shown that most children are reluctant 'to participate in play fighting and real fighting' and this attitude 'strengthens with age' (Fry et al. 2009: 22). The society relies on community councils, which can meet on a daily basis, to resolve conflicts. Gossip is also used to shame aggressive behaviour (Stephen 2005). Consequently, Zapotec avoid violent conflicts with other groups.

The cultural values of Semai also emphasise non-violent conduct. The principle of *punan* underpins much of the Semai's attitude to violence. *Punan* stands for a belief which is underpinned by a specific set of rules that promote non-violent conflict resolution. The idea of *punan* is liked with the notion of making another person unhappy by frustrating their desires. This act would then increase the chance of conflict between the two individuals and might lead to violence. Thus, Semai rely on the *punan* principle to organise their everyday life (Dentan 1968). They rely on public shaming to avoid violence. The periodic disputes are often settled at public assembly sessions (*becharaa*) which can last for several days until the dispute is resolved. In addition, just like the Zapotec, Semai children are raised in a spirit of non-violence: there is no physical disciplining or forcing children to bend their will to adults. The focus is on group participation and inclusion of all while competition is discouraged. When attacked by outsiders Semai prefer to flee and hide instead of engaging in a fight. Although they generally mistrust foreigners when confronted with aggressiveness, they usually try to shame the attacker's actions or escape the conflictual situation (Robarchek and Robarchek 1998). Both Semia and Zapotec societies are characterised by very low homicide and suicide rates.

It is only with the emergence of complex social organisations such as chiefdoms and states that war and other forms of organised violence dramatically expand throughout the world (Malešević 2017; Mann 1986). In the prehistorical context, non-fighting is a much more prevalent phenomenon than fighting. This is not to say that the pre-state societies did not engage in violent conflicts at all but only that the wide-ranging confrontations of entire societies necessitate the presence of substantive organisational (and ideological) capacity. In structural terms, the non-fighting historically precedes fighting, and more fighting is also linked with the development and expansion of social organisations. In this sense, large-scale pugnacity is a by-product of social development. One of the defining features of civilisational advancement through time has been the proliferation of warfare. From the Akkadian empire (2334–2154 BCE) to the British imperial project (1583–1960), war and violent conquest went hand in hand with the rise of complex social organisations, technological improvements, economic growth, political development, cultural achievements, and social progress. The state apparatus has played the central role in transforming ordinary individuals into the cogs of their fighting machines. As Mann (1986) shows, this was a deeply coercive process through which reluctant and unwilling populations were gradually caged into the organisational structures of the state. The social caging made human beings dependent on state power as the state provided protection and continuous access to economic resources at the expense of individual liberties. With the unification of China under the Qin (230–221 BCE), state power expanded to such an extent that the rulers were able to mobilise hundreds of thousands and possibly millions of individuals to fight in protracted wars. The centralised state apparatus was also behind unprecedented projects such as the Great Wall of China and the construction of the massive canals linking the capital city of Xianyang with the provinces (Zhao 2015). Similar processes characterised the Roman Empire which also managed to cage millions of individuals into its state apparatuses while also mobilising enormous military force. The Roman legions conquered and controlled vast territories from Britain and North Africa to the Middle East and the military was also capable of building the infrastructure from paved roads, bridges, and colosseums, to aqueducts and drains. Other imperial orders deployed similar organisational techniques of social caging (Le Bohec 2013).

With the onset of modernity, the social cages of the state penetrated nearly all spheres of social life. As Tilly (1992) shows, in the early modern period European state formation intensified on the back of protracted wars. To keep these conflicts going the rulers were forced to modernise their state apparatuses. Needing more soldiers, resources, and funding they embarked on the expansion of civil service and administrative institutions, fiscal reorganisation and new taxation policies, new modes of banking and economic development, new systems of military recruitment, development of science and technology, and the building of country-wide systems of transport and communication. These enhanced caging mechanisms were in part introduced through force and in part through bargaining with the nascent civil society. Hence the long-term consequence of increased state power was the rise of civil liberties including improved citizenship rights, freedom of speech, assembly, and press, the rise of parliamentarism, and the introduction of some welfare provisions. By the late nineteenth and early twentieth century most states had managed to establish legitimate monopolies on violence, taxation, education, and judiciary over the territories under their control. These monopolies together with the ever-increasing reliance on new military technologies and novel systems of recruitment made fighting a widespread activity. For one thing the advanced systems of organisation were deployed to recruit millions of soldiers to fight in large-scale wars. For another thing the new technologies, including the use of long-distance weaponry, made fighting less psychologically and morally demanding as soldiers were less likely to see and empathise with their human targets on the other side. Finally, fighting in interstate wars gained greater popular support as wars were now legitimised through nationalist ideologies: with the monopoly on education, nation-states were able to institutionalise nationalist principles as the dominant operative ideology of modernity (Malešević 2006, 2019). Thus, killing in the name of the nation became a noble deed. The historical trajectory of organised violence clearly indicates that conditions for social pugnacity increase with the rise of organisational capacities, greater ideological penetration of societies, and the development of science and technology that mediate fighting and killing through distance.

Nevertheless, the monopolisation of violence by nation-states has another corollary: while the concentration of coercive power within the state apparatuses has increased external capacity for fighting in interstate wars, this process has simultaneously also decreased fighting within the nation-state. By monopolising the legitimate use of violence within their own territory, modern states have managed to pacify their domestic realms (Centeno 2002; Giddens 1985; Mann 1986). Hence the intensified state formation has also created organisational and ideological means for systematic non-fighting. In ideological terms, fighting outside of the state apparatus (military, police, secret service actions, etc.) has been delegitimised and proscribed. Most contemporary states prohibit or strictly regulate the use of weaponry in the civilian sphere and nearly all states possess legislation that criminalises the use of violence outside of state action. In addition, the use of non-sanctioned violence by ordinary individuals has also been delegitimised by civil society.

While pre-modern social orders largely tolerated personalised violent conflicts, in the contemporary world all such acts are legally outlawed and also considered to be socially unacceptable. For example, in ancient Greece just as in medieval Europe personal retaliation for perceived wrongdoing was tolerated and sometimes even encouraged. As Griffiths (1991: 90) shows, in ancient Greek society personal acts of revenge against transgressors were completely acceptable: 'embedded in the Greek morality or retaliation is the right of vendetta. An act of homicide, whether deliberate or accidental, against a member of a clan (genos) demanded the shedding of blood for blood'. Similarly, Bloch (2014 [1961]: 126) documents how blood feuds were widespread throughout medieval Europe and how retaliation for wrongdoing was considered to be a central moral obligation: 'Among the Frisians the very corpse cried out for vengeance; it hung withering in the house till the day when, the vengeance accomplished, the kinsmen had at last the right to bury it.' In direct contrast the legal systems of contemporary nation-states prohibit all forms of retaliatory violence where homicidal acts have regularly been categorised as 'unlawful killing'. Although some legal systems differentiate murder (killing with malice) and manslaughter (killing without malice) all such acts are strictly punished with long-term prison sentences, life imprisonment, and in some countries even the death penalty. For instance, in the US state of Texas if an individual is convicted of 'capital felony' he or she can be sentenced to death. The capital felony crime is defined legally as an act where the offender 'intentionally or knowingly causes the death of an individual' involving such events as 'murder of a public safety officer or firefighter in the line of duty; murder during the commission of specified felonies (kidnapping, burglary, robbery, aggravated rape, arson); murder for remuneration; multiple murders; murder during prison escape; murder of a correctional officer; murder of a judge; murder by a state prison inmate who is serving a life sentence for any of five offenses; or murder of an individual under six years of age'.[3]

The state's monopolisation of violence combined with ever-increasing organisational capacity have contributed significantly to the decrease in many forms of violent crime over the last several centuries. As Eisner (2003) and Spierenburg (2008) show, homicide rates experienced substantial reduction in Europe between the sixteenth and early twentieth century. The data for some parts of Western Europe indicate 35 deaths per 100,000 in the thirteenth and fourteenth century while in the sixteenth century this number is much lower – 20 and by the beginning of the twentieth century the average rate was around 2 per 100,000 (Eisner 2003; Spierenburg 2008). Other parts of the world have also recorded a significant decline in homicide rate over the last three centuries although this decline was less linear than in the case of Western Europe. North America and the USA especially had higher homicide rates in the nineteenth century (particularly in the 1850s). The USA also experienced periodic increases of homicide in 1900s and 1960s. However, the overall trend for the past several centuries has been one of long-term decline in

---

[3] https://tarlton.law.utexas.edu/texas-death-penalty.

the rate of homicides. The data indicate that this has been the case with most other forms of violent crime. Hence just as historical increase in fighting was a product of organisational development the same applies to non-fighting. Whereas the proliferation of social organisations specialised in fighting generated more mass destruction such as in wars, revolutions, and genocides, the organisational monopoly of state power has pacified the domestic sphere thus contributing substantially to non-fighting. By removing weaponry from everyday life, by delegitimising the use of violence outside of state control, and by increasing the organisational capacity for policing the domestic sphere the state has created conditions for the expansion of peaceful resolution of conflicts among ordinary citizens.

In addition to organisational power, non-fighting was also shaped by ideological power. On the one hand the state authorities have created legislative systems that prohibited unsanctioned fighting. These legal provisions were enhanced by ideas and values that promote peace and discourage the use of violence within society. Such ideas were regularly propagated in state-controlled educational institutions, mass media, and the public sphere. It is no accident that most modern societies perpetuate the idea of the past as 'a foreign country' (Lowenthal 1985) and in many cases our pre-modern ancestors are depicted as savage brutes that were always at war with each other. On the other hand, this ideological narrative of violent past vs. peaceful present has also been promulgated by various groups within civil society. Since the Renaissance and Enlightenment, the European past has regularly been portrayed as backward and violent with medieval Europe often identified as the pinnacle of barbarism. These ideas have gained enormous popularity in the twentieth and twenty-first century. The academic books, novels, films, TV programmes, and computer games that reproduce these simplified and historically unfounded visions of the past tap into popular perceptions and successfully reinforce already existing views of the incessantly violent pre-modern world. For example, Steven Pinker's bestseller *Better Angels of Our Nature* (2011) is a typical representative of a very popular genre that uncritically glorifies the contemporary period as the 'most peaceful era in our species' existence' while simultaneously denigrating previous historical periods as relentlessly and excessively brutal. Leaving to one side the empirically unfounded generalisations of such works, what is more relevant here is how they reinforce the already established ideological narratives of state superiority. By sharply delineating between the barbaric past and civilised present these narratives buttress the notion that contemporary nation-states are the only legitimate purveyors of violence. In this way both the state and civil society contribute to the delegitimisation of fighting within the confines of nation-state. However, by differentiating sharply between internal and external use of violence these narratives also help legitimise fighting between nation-states in times of war and other forms of organised violence. The legal provisions against personalised acts of violent crime together with the state and society-wide dissemination of non-fighting ethics have had a profound impact on popular attitudes against all forms of violence. Although populations of many societies have gradually become insensitive towards acts of violence over the past several centuries it is really after the Second World War that one notices a strengthening of global movement against all types of violence.

The development and spread of various religious and secular ideologies that advocate non-violence has provided a structural impetus for non-fighting. Although many traditional religious and philosophical teachings contain reference to avoidance of violence and some such as Jainism, Taoism, Lemba religion, Mennonites, Quakers, and Amish explicitly advocate non-fighting, the pacifist ideas gained global popular support only after the Second World War. The end of war against Nazism and fascism galvanised de-colonial struggles around the world and also stimulated the development of civil rights movements advocating full citizenship rights for minority groups. Many of these political groups have embraced pacifism as the most efficient political strategy to achieve their goals. Inspired by the pacifist teachings of Mohandas Gandhi, Martin Luther King Jr., James Bevel, Thích Nhất Hạnh, and Nelson Mandela among others these anti-establishment movements have been successful in challenging the status quo. Despite focusing on different aims and being composed of diverse groups of individuals these movements utilised similar ideological principles of non-violent resistance.

Drawing on traditional Hindu and Buddhist idea of *ahimsa* (non-violence against all living beings) Gandhi articulated a unique approach to civil disobedience – *satyagraha*. This theory of non-violent resistance is grounded in the idea that violence cannot be used for peaceful ends: instead for Gandhi means and ends are indivisible and as such all conduct should involve non-violence. The *satyagraha* resistance campaign was built around rules that emphasised peaceful conduct and empathy while also insisting on firm commitment to non-violent principles. For example, two of the central rules of the *satyagraha* campaign state the following: 'Never retaliate to assaults or punishment; but do not submit, out of fear of punishment or assault, to an order given in anger' and 'If anyone attempts to insult or assault your opponent, defend your opponent (non-violently) with your life' (Chakrabarty 2006: 196).

Gandhi's philosophy of non-violence has influenced many leaders of civil rights movements who encouraged their supporters to prioritise peaceful campaigns of resistance over violent confrontations against oppressive rule. In this sense *satyagraha* and its regionalised adaptations from the USA and Northern Ireland to South Africa and beyond have contributed to the ideological reframing of conflicts through the prism of non-fighting.

Nevertheless, the most influential post-Second World War ideological current that has contributed to the idea of the non-violent conflict management is the spread and institutionalisation of human rights. Although conceived during the Enlightenment and formulated in the wake of the French and American revolutions it was the 1948 Universal Declaration of Human Rights that initiated the global proliferation of human rights. The allied victories in the Second World War spearheaded a new set of moral principles that privileged certain fundamental rights 'to which a person is inherently entitled simply because she or he is a human being'. The geo-political dominance of liberal democratic states such as the USA, UK, France, and West Germany contributed to the expansion of human rights principles and policies all over the world. With the collapse of the Soviet political order in the early 1990s the human rights agenda attained nearly hegemonic position. Thus, today even authoritarian states have to justify their actions in reference to being fully committed to protecting human rights. Since human rights are centred on preservation of life and liberty of individual human beings, they nominally instigate non-violent conduct in the resolution of conflicts. For example, several key articles in the Universal Declaration of Human Rights directly challenge actions that ordinarily involve violence: articles 3, 4, and 5 all denigrate violent action. Article 3 states that 'everyone has the right to life, liberty and security of person' meaning that killing, imprisoning, and threatening human beings is an infringement of human rights. Article 4 is even more explicit in forbidding slavery, slave trade, and servitude while article 5 focuses on torture and demeaning forms of punishment ('No one shall be subjected to torture or to cruel, inhuman or degrading treatment or punishment'). These principles have guided the action of many states and civil society groups and in this way have also contributed to the delegitimisation of violent fighting.[4]

---

[4] However, as David (2020) shows convincingly, any attempts to externally impose and institutionalise human rights norms and practices, such as through mandatory memorialisation rituals, can also backfire and generate violent resistance from those who perceive such impositions as a form of ideological colonisation.

These ideological shifts had a significant impact on popular opinions and as various surveys show populations all over the globe have become intolerant towards many forms of violence including capital punishment, domestic violence, animal abuse, and torture. This increased sensitivity towards violence has been also reflected in the mass media, education systems, entertainment industries, and the public sphere. The use and even the depiction of violence in the public context has become more regulated, compartmentalised, and policed. This change has been reflected in legislative prohibitions such as on corporal punishment in schools, on physically disciplining one's own children, regulation of child-on-child violence, and banning of animal cruelty in entertainment industries. In addition, the traditional, mostly patriarchal, policies of highly gendered child upbringing have also been delegitimised. The idea that boys should be raised as tough individuals who show no emotion and as such would be ready in the future to fight for their country as brave warriors has also been undermined. The ever-increasing gender sensitivity has also delegitimised the idea of fighting.

With these organisational and ideological transformations, non-violent resistance has gained wider support throughout the globe. Moreover, as Chenoweth and Stephan (2011) show, non-violent civil resistance has often proved more effective in generating long-term social change than violent campaigns. Chenoweth and Stephan's analysis, based on a dataset of 323 mass level violent and non-violent campaigns from 1990 to 2006, indicates that in this period the non-violent campaigns of change were significantly more successful that their violent counterparts:

among 312 campaigns, non-violent resistance methods have been more than twice as effective in achieving limited and full success among antiregime campaigns. Nonviolent and violent resistance campaigns have the same rate of full success in antioccupation campaigns, but the use of nonviolent resistance makes partial success (i.e., autonomy or power sharing) more likely. (Chenoweth and Stephan 2011: 72–3)

This study focuses on the variety of non-violent forms of political action including protests, boycotts, civil disobedience, general strikes, and other forms of resistance and shows that non-violence often trumps reliance on fighting in terms of moral acceptance, social commitment, or physical costs of participation. Avoiding violence also widens the participation and expands the movements' support base.

In addition to the macro-organisational and ideological processes that have contributed to the proliferation of non-fighting, this long-term structural change has also affected patterns of group solidarity. The historical transformation of social order has generated new forms of group dynamics. The gradual shift from imperial structures and patri-monial kingships to the nation-state model of governance has provided an impetus to transformation of residential, kinship, class, and status-based patterns of group solidarity. For example, while in the pre-modern world band, clan, tribe, extended families, or lineage were the principal units of group solidarity, in the contemporary world collective attach-ments generally tend to be smaller such as conjugal families, residential friendship networks, school or work-based peer groups, or lifelong deep comradeships. The expansion of the internally pacified nation-state model has reshaped micro-group attachments and has also impacted on the proliferation of non-fighting within such groups. The changing ideological and organisational landscape has transformed interpersonal relationships. For example, while in the pre-modern world aristocrats were often entitled to torture and kill their disobedient serfs and slaves or to legitimately rape their female helots including the *jus primae noctis* ('right of the first night'),[5] contemporary nation-states proscribe the use of violence on the basis of one's status or gender. Similarly, the preva-lence of blood and clan feuds and vendettas of the pre-modern world has been replaced with state-regulated punishments in modernity. In both of these cases the changed character of micro-level solidarity plays a crucial role in the rise of non-fighting. While in the former the shift towards more egalitarian principles delegitimises status-based violence, in the latter legal individualisation undermines the collectivist norm of blood revenge. The historical decline of rigid and inherited status-based forms of violence has reinforced voluntarily formed networks of micro-group solidarity as in friendships and comradeships. In a similar vein, the shift from the traditional forms of social control such as blood feuds between clans and extended families towards state-mediated conflict resolution between individuals has reshaped the micro-group dynamics in everyday life. While before, fighting was a moral obligation of all members of the clan or extended family, today a violent attack on a close friend or a family member does not require violent retaliation against an entire family or clan. Instead, the focus is on the individual responsible for violent attack. Most individuals understand and respect this principle not only because any attempted revenge would be rigorously punished by the state, but also because they often share modernist principles where guilt

---

[5] The right of the first night or the right of the lord (*roit du seigneur*) refers to the legal right of the lord to spend the first night with the bride of his vassals. This practice seems to have been present in China during the Lai dynasty and in the Western Xia state, in Anatolia, Hawaii, and possibly medieval Europe. However, a number of historians dispute that this right was implemented in medieval Europe at all (Classen 2004).

for violent acts is individualised and where the state, and not the clan or family, is deemed to be the ultimate arbiter of justice. Hence organisational and ideological changes have impacted profoundly on the willingness to fight at the micro-interactional level.

The social, political, economic, and cultural changes that have taken place in the last two centuries have created new organisational, ideological, and micro-interactional mechanisms for the proliferation of both violent and non-violent action. The regulated division of labour, complex hierarchical systems of rule, coordinated and disciplined social action, development of science, technology, and industrial production, development of robust communication and transport networks together with more literate population have all created new conditions for the expansion of organised violence but also for organised non-violent action. Just as military and police apparatuses of states have enhanced their capacity to fight so have the practitioners of non-violent resistance developed new organisational strategies to achieve their goals. Hence the non-violent resistance campaigns in the twentieth and twenty-first century have been better organised and coordinated and have devised novel systems of mobilisation and political action. The most successful forms of non-violent action include civil disobedience, boycotts, sanctions, picketing, strikes, marches, protest events (including artistic performances), tax resistance, and community education campaigns among many others. One of the most successful early non-violent campaigns of resistance was the Salt March (Salt Satyagraha) led by Gandhi from 12 March to 5 April 1930. This act of civil disobedience against the colonial rule in India was a well-organised campaign of tax resistance that centred on contesting the British salt monopoly. The movement was spearheaded by a small number of dedicated followers of Gandhi (78) who embarked on a long march through India advocating against the British salt monopoly. By late March and early April this movement had attracted millions of supporters many of whom followed Gandhi's example in breaking the British salt laws. The protesters engaged in salt making themselves and encouraged other participants to do the same. Following the arrests of Gandhi and over 60,000 of his followers by the colonial authorities the protest continued for the whole year and gained substantial international visibility thus making the Indian independence movement recognisable around the world. Although the British rulers did not accept their demands the movement was highly successful in mobilising long-term resistance against imperial governance and in gaining global support for its non-violent actions (Weber 1998). The relative successes of this non-violent campaign was built on the combination of effective organisation (which coordinated acts of disobedience across the Indian subcontinent), coherent ideological doctrine (anti-imperialism and Indian nationalism as developed and articulated by Gandhi), and the ability of the movement to penetrate the microcosm of everyday life in the British Raj (focusing on salt, an ingredient used by all the population, the movement was able to mobilise millions of individuals for its cause).

Similarly, the African National Congress (ANC) under Nelson Mandela relied extensively on civil disobedience to bring down the apartheid regime. Influenced by Gandhi's example, the ANC initiated their own Defiance Campaign against Unjust Laws on 26 June 1952. This date was later designated as the National Day of Protest and Mourning. The campaign emphasised non-violent acts of civil disobedience including strikes, protests, burning of apartheid documentation (i.e., passes for Africans), trespassing the 'whites-only' areas and public facilities, bus boycotts, violating curfews for Africans, and so on. The movement was well organised and relied on thousands of trained volunteers who wore ANC armbands to demonstrate the strength and size of their political organisation. With ever-increasing coerciveness of the apartheid state the ANC members deployed a variety of novel tactics to overwhelm the police and the court system. For example, they declined to defend themselves in courts or to be represented by a public solicitor so as to increase the number of imprisoned people to the extent that the state could not cope. They also refused to pay fines for minor breaches of law in order to be imprisoned and thus increase the number of prisoners and thus overwhelm the prison system (Lodge 1983; Reddy 1987).

Just like the Salt March in India this campaign was only the beginning of a long-term struggle against the oppressive regime. Although the apartheid state withstood this mass-scale resistance movement and in the process increased its coercive reach (i.e., introducing draconian penalties for non-violent protests) the Defiance campaign successfully mobilised a multi-racial resistance movement throughout South Africa. The membership of ANC increased from 7,000 to over 100,000 and the campaign received wide international coverage and visibility (Reddy 1987). The use of non-violent means to attain tangible political goals proved highly beneficial and the ANC continued to rely on this strategy until it finally destroyed the apartheid regime in 1994. Similarly to the Salt March, this campaign combined increased organisational capacity (well-organised and coordinated series of specific actions by the ANC throughout the country) with a coherent and clearly articulated ideological programme (racial equality and social justice as vocalised by Mandela and other ANC leaders). The movement also proved adept at linking their organisational structure and ideological doctrine with the micro-level solidarities of ordinary people in South Africa (by honing on their everyday experiences of humiliation and racial discrimination).

The strategy of avoiding direct confrontations and deploying peaceful methods of resistance ultimately proved effective in both of these cases with India gaining independence from Britain in 1948 and South Africa attaining a fully democratic political system in 1994. By withdrawing their consent and willingness to cooperate, citizens undermined the organisational capacity of the state and also delegitimised its character. As Scott (1998) points out, large-scale social organisations cannot operate relying only on legal procedures, rules, and regulations. Instead, their very existence is dependent on the continuous compliance and cooperation of their members. If members only follow the established regulations and do nothing else – such as in work-to-rule industrial actions – the organisations cannot operate: by 'performing only duties stated in their job descriptions' employees generate a situation where 'the work grinds to a halt' (Scott 1998: 310). The same principle applies to non-violent campaigns of resistance – by increasing the number of individuals who do not cooperate and do not give consent to government actions the state organisation cannot function effectively or at all. The mass non-compliance affects not only the ideological legitimacy of the regime but also destabilises its organisational capacity. If these actions are well embedded in the everyday practices of ordinary people, in their own micro-universes, then the non-violent campaigns are more likely to succeed (Chenoweth and Stephan 2011).

6.4   Conclusion: Making Non-Fighting Possible

The leading scholars of social movements such as Tilly (2003, 2008) and Tarrow (2012) argue that violence is not a sui generis phenomenon but an instrument of contentious politics. It is a means or strategy for political action and as such it can take variety of forms from civil disobedience and general strikes to riots, uprisings, insurrections, revolutions, and wars. As Tilly (2008: 5) specifies, contentious politics involves 'interactions in which actors make claims bearing on someone else's interest, in which governments appear either as targets, initiators of claims, or third parties'. In this understanding, violence and non-violence only represent a continuum of possible strategic tools that individuals and social movements can use to attain desired political goals.

Although this perspective has been very valuable in debunking the traditional perception of violence as an irrational phenomenon driven by fanaticism, the contentious politics perspective has also overemphasised the utilitarian character of violence. Violence is not just a means to an end, it is a distinct sociological phenomenon that operates according to different rules and once released it often generates a logic of its own (Collins 2008; Malešević 2010, 2017; Schinkel 2010). This sui generis quality of violence affects both the micro-interactional and macro-historical realities. For example, protracted wars generate profound changes in social order and impact on long-term transformations of gender relations, patterns of social stratification, ethnic and racial hierarchies, citizenship rights, welfare policies, and so on (Goldstein 2001; Mann 1993, 2012). In a similar vein, many individuals directly exposed to violence have traumatic experiences which shape their personalities and their relations with other people for years. The impact of violence on social relations does not cease with the end of hostilities or with the healing of physical wounds. Violence lasts much longer than other forms of social action. Thus, violence is not just a strategic tool, it is a distinct and autonomous phenomenon that generates specific long-term responses – from emotional reactions to political action, and particular cultural or ideological framings.

Furthermore, the contentious politics perspective offers a too symmetrical view of antagonistic practices. While it is true that political action can take a variety of forms that range from very violent to completely non-violent, it is important to differentiate between violence and non-violence. Organising a general strike and killing thousands of people in a terrorist attack are very different political acts with very different social consequences. The variability of social action does not automatically imply that all forms of political action operate in a similar way. On the contrary, as I have attempted to show in this chapter, non-violent action has a rather different logic and distinct trajectories to that of violent behaviour.

Non-violence is not just a static starting point in the wide repertoire of contentious politics. Instead, it is a complex set of processes that involve a great deal of work. Non-fighting is not something that is automatic, a state of being that involves no action. Rather non-fighting, just as fighting, entails organisational, ideological, and micro-interactional activity. Although peaceful conduct between human beings is much more common than instances of violence, this conduct is a product of elaborate social action. In this sense social pugnacity has a scalar quality – it allows for a variety of social actions that can range from active non-violence to extreme violence.

Collins (2008) is absolutely right that violence is not an instinctive and simple response to a situation of social disorder or a lack of central authority. The Hobbesian vision of primordial war of all against all is not a sociological reality. Human beings are complex creatures that regularly display a variety of behaviours and the tendency is, whenever possible, to opt for non-violent over violent forms of action. Thus, sustained violent action regularly involves organisational coordination and coercive pressure, ideological support and delegitimisation of non-fighting, and strong embedment into the existing micro-solidarities.

What Collins, just as Tilly and Tarrow, ignores is that non-violence is not a default position of humanity. Non-fighting is not a passive and given state but an active response, often based on conscious decision making and coordinated collective action. Hence just as myths about violence and fighting have been dissected and deconstructed by several sociologists (Collins 2008; Ray 2018; Schinkel 2010), the same should be done for the experience of non-fighting.

The avoidance of violence is a social phenomenon that appears in a variety of macro-historical and micro-interactional contexts. Individuals decide to evade military conscription, to desert from the armed forces and gangs, or to stop shooting at armed adversaries in a similar way as they choose to join such organisations and to fight and kill. These decisions are often rooted in very similar sources of motivation: a sense of attachment to one's micro-group, a strong ideological commitment, and the organisational capacities that make these choices realisable. In both cases, violence and non-violence are a product of social action and something generated through actual or symbolic interaction with others.

On the macro-level the practices and principles of non-fighting can become so pervasive that they penetrate entire social orders. Once ideology, organisation, and micro-solidarity are so intertwined with the habitus and social structure of non-violence, the non-fighting becomes a norm. This is quite visible in many historical and contemporary contexts – from the peaceful hunter-gatherer communities that publicly shame their members for any acts of aggression to the modern nation-states that monopolise the legitimate use of violence over their territories and largely criminalise private acts of fighting. The macro-sociology of non-fighting shows that the increased organisational capacity together with the pervasiveness of specific ideological doctrines play an important role in the entrenchment of non-fighting as a practice and a belief system. While social movements and other associations provide robust organisational vehicles for non-violent action, the ideologies of peaceful resistance imbue these organisations with non-violent discourses and in the process also delegitimise violent behaviour. The success of such movements is largely determined by their ability to fuse their organisational and ideological power with the existing networks of micro-solidarity. Hence the most efficient resistance campaigns, from the Indian independence movement to the anti-apartheid struggle in South Africa, have effectively combined pacifist and human rights ideologies with the forceful and flexible organisational structures that have manged to penetrate the remote Indian villages and poorest shantytowns of South Africa and mobilise mass support for non-violent action. The organised avoidance of violence can be very successful political strategy. As Chenoweth and Stephan (2011) show, in the recent period non-violent campaigns have regularly proved to be more effective devices of social change than revolutions, wars, terrorism, and other forms of organised violence.

7   Social Pugnacity in the Combat Zone

7.1   Introduction

Social pugnacity is a complex and contextual phenomenon. As argued in the previous chapters its dynamics is shaped by variety of factors including coercive-organisational capacity, the extent of ideological penetration, and the intensity of micro-interactional bonds. Although people can fight for economic, political, ideological, and other reasons social pugnacity can never be reduced to individual motivations only. Instead, a combat experience has its own social dynamics that is shaped by the changing social environment. This relates not only to Clausewitz's (2008 [1832]) well-known fog of war that always generates uncertainties and unpredictable behaviour, but even more importantly violent conflicts impact profoundly and are in turn impacted by the changing group dynamics. Wars, revolutions, insurgencies, and other forms of organised violence are dependent as much on the strength and endurance of the macro-organisational structures as the micro-group ties. The link between these two is often established through shared ideological narratives. However, it is not completely clear how this process operates in practice. Do form, size, or shape of the armed organisation influence one's willingness to fight? Are fighters involved in clandestine political movements or criminal syndicates motivated by the same principles as those fighting in formal military organisations? What specific role do organisational structures, economic incentives, coercive pressure, and ideology play in individual and collective decisions to fight?

In this chapter I aim to answer these questions by exploring the organisational, ideological, and micro-interactional dynamics of two ostensibly very different armed forces: the Provisional Irish Republican Army (IRA) and the Army of the Serbian Republic in Bosnia and Herzegovina (*Vojska Republike Srpske*, VRS). Although I explore the disparities between these two coercive organisations my focus is largely on the significance of their organisational and ideological powers and how they relate to micro-level group solidarities. The aim is to look at the formal organisational structures and official ideological discourses and then compare those with how ideology and organisation operate in everyday reality. Hence by exploring the structural features of these armed forces and by zooming in on the motivations of combatants to join, and fight for, these armed forces we can also find out about the organisational and ideological composition of the two military formations.

7.2   Why Do Combatants Fight?

The classics of military studies such as Sun Tzu, Machiavelli, Jomini, Clausewitz, and du Picq have all explored the question of an individual's motivation to fight. They have also all recognised that most ordinary people are unlikely to fight unless incited or pressured to do so. As du Picq (2006 [1880]: 55) emphasises, 'man does not enter battle to fight, but for victory. He does everything that he can to avoid the first and obtain the second'. Sun Tzu (2017 [500 BCE]: 27) also identifies incentive as a key factor that make combatants fight: 'Treat your men as you would your own beloved sons. And they will follow you into the deepest valley'. Although most military organisations have faced a problem of recruitment throughout history this became more prominent when militaries composed of aristocrats and mercenaries were replaced with all-citizen armies. With the introduction of mass conscription and development of the nation in arms in the nineteenth and twentieth centuries, the question of motivation to fight come to the fore. In this context many military organisations have invested heavily in finding out how to increase fighting efficiency and for that purpose have stimulated research on combativeness. The early sociological studies on this phenomenon can be traced back to the Second World War and its immediate aftermath when scholars attempted to identify under which conditions soldiers were more likely to fight. Although much of this scholarship focused on the actions of US soldiers (Marshall 1947; Stouffer 1949), some researchers also explored the fighting motivation among Wehrmacht units (Shils and Janowitz 1948). These early studies, often conducted under war conditions, have emphasised 'the primary group' as playing a decisive role in motivation to fight.[1] Hence while Stouffer (1949) and Marshall (1947) showed that strong group attachments

---

[1] The primary group model draws on Charles Cooley's (1909) sociological theory of group formation. He identified family, playgroups, and community of elders as the principal forms of primary groups that imbue specific morals and values to all individuals during their primary socialisation. For a critique of this approach see Malešević (2017).

among the American forces were instrumental in maintaining unit cohesion, Shils and Janowitz (1948) argued that the unwavering commitment of Wehrmacht soldiers to fight even when it was clear that the war was lost can be explained by the strength of their 'primary group'. In their own words:

The behaviour of the German Army demonstrated that the focus of attention and concern beyond one's immediate face-to-face social circles may be slight indeed and still not interfere with the achievement of a high degree of military effectiveness ... primary needs were met adequately through the gratification provided by the other members of the group. (Shils and Janowitz (1948: 315)

This focus on social cohesion within military units dominated much of the scholarship until the 1980s. Studying a variety of wars and military organisations the general consensus was that most combatants fight less for the lofty ideological goals or specific economic inducements and more for their 'brothers-in-arms'. Stewart (1991: 17) summarises these findings:

Disparate men from varied socioeconomic backgrounds, of different ethnic origins and levels of education are expected to become not just a collective of individuals but a unit in which an individual will sacrifice his life and die in order to preserve the group. Because of well-developed friendship or camaraderie, men will fight individually as a part of a unit to defend the group as a unit.

However, by the early 1990s this approach had been challenged by a number of historians, political scientists, and economists who offered alternative explanations for the sources of individual combativeness. Several historians and political scientists such as Bartov (1992, 2001, 2018), Rossino (2003), and Leader Maynard (2014, 2019) argue that ideological commitments are a principal motivator for fighting. Rossino (2003) and Bartov (1992) focus on the Wehrmacht's conquest of Europe and insist that this ideological project underpinned the motivation of German soldiers. Analysing letters, diaries, and memoirs of German officers and soldiers they argue that strong ideological beliefs were not only present among the political and military leaders but also among ordinary soldiers. The dominant doctrinal narrative in Germany at this time combined 'unique ideological goals of National Socialism with the traditional military-political objective of establishing a German empire in Eastern Europe' (Rossino 2003: xiv). Thus, many soldiers were indoctrinated well before they joined the German military: 'the obedient and uncritical participation of millions of soldiers in "legalised" crimes was significant also in that it probably ... reflected the moral values these young men had internalised before recruitment' (Bartov 1992: 7). Leader Maynard (2019) broadens this debate further by focusing on a variety of violent conflicts aiming to show that ideological commitments underpin individual and group action in war, genocides, uprisings, and terrorism. He identifies four principal mechanisms that make ideology a decisive driver of violence – commitment, adoption, conformity, and instrumentalisation.

Among the ideological factors nationalism is often singled out as being the principal source of combatants' motivation to fight. For example, van Evera (1994), Keegan (1994), and Gat (2006) see nationalism as being one of the main causes of wars. In this context nationalist motivation is understood to play a central role in the decision to join armed forces and fight for one's nation or ethnic group. More recent, empirically very rich, comparative studies by Wimmer (2012) and Hiers and Wimmer (2013) identify nationalism as the key variable in the worldwide proliferation of wars since 1816. These studies emphasise the nationalist aspirations of social movements and non-state armed forces in waging violent conflicts for national self-determination.

More recently some scholars have shifted this debate towards the economics of violence. The focal point for this type of research has been the struggle over natural resources in recent civil wars such as the poppy in Afghanistan, coca in Colombia, diamonds in Sierra Leone and timber in Cambodia. Although self-preservation and economic gain have been identified already by many classical studies the new research has highlighted the specific mechanisms of self-interested behaviour in the combat zone. Hence Segal and Segal (1983) and Moskos (1975) challenge the 'primary group' thesis and argue that social cohesion in theatres of war is largely produced by pragmatic decisions concerned with one's survival: they are 'mandatory necessities arising from immediate life-and-death exigencies' (Moskos 1975: 37). Recent contributions extend this line of reasoning further by specifying the key mechanisms that underpin individual decision making on the battlefield. The rationalist theories of civil war focus on the material and symbolic benefits derived from joining violent conflicts. The focus here is on the credible commitment problem among the leaders and soldiers involved in fighting: the soldiers agree to fight on the assumption that others will do the same but either individual can renege on this agreement (Fearon 1994; Keefer 2012). Furthermore, the unpredictability of the combat zone can generate the free rider problem where some individuals benefit from the fighting of others while minimising their own risk of exposure to violence (Kalyvas and Kocher 2007). The instrumentalist approaches to fighting also zoom in on issues such as division of materials and symbolic acquisitions in conflict, and the incentives to misinterpret or block access to information regarding the costs and benefits of participation in violent conflict (Keefer 2012).

The combatants might also face 'issue indivisibility', that is, a situation where it is difficult to reach compromise as rational actors cannot agree that the issue over which they are fighting is divisible (Fearon 1994; Fearon and Laitin 2003).

Finally, another strand of scholarship has highlighted the role of coercion in mobilising and forcing individuals to fight. The argument that most soldiers fight because they are forced to do so has been a staple of military thought for centuries (Clausewitz 2008 [1832]; du Picq 2006 [1880]; Machiavelli 1985 [1532]). More recently social scientists have identified how coercion works in practice and how this impacts on soldiers' motivation (Bolten 2012; King 2015; Malešević 2010; Rush 1999). The focus here is on how organisational discipline, self-control, regulations, and coercively imposed rules mould social action within military units. While there is general recognition that authoritarian states rely more on force than their non-authoritarian counterparts, coercion has been singled out as being the crucial mechanism of soldiers' recruitment for centuries. Moreover, the existence of military police and hierarchical chains of command, which are present in all armed forces throughout the world, indicate how coercion is embedded in military structures. The significance of force can be observed through data on the executions and imprisonment of deserters and those who disobey officers' commands to fight. For example, during the Second World War, up to 15,000 German soldiers were killed for defeatism or desertion (Bartov 1992: 96) while in the Soviet Union over 158,000 individuals were executed for desertion (Niebergall-Lackner 2016: 2).

However, even in non-authoritarian militaries, desertion and disobedience are severely punished, including the death penalty. Thus, fear of such extreme punishments looms large in any soldier's decision on whether to fight or run away from the battlefield.

Much of the research on soldiers' motivation to fight has centred on formal military organisations. There is a widespread view that such formal organisations (i.e., conventional armies, navies, or air forces) operate according to well-established and formalised structures that can adequately address all four sources of soldiers' motivations to fight: coercion, economic self-interest, ideological goals, and small group attachments. In other words, in contrast to less formal armed units (such as insurgencies, terrorist groups, paramilitaries, etc.) regular military forces are perceived to be much better at enforcing discipline, providing regular pay and other material inducements, delivering sustained ideological support, and even generating an organisational environment for the development of micro-level solidarity networks (Moskos 1975; Siebold 2007). Recent work by King (2013, 2015) has emphasised professionalism itself as being the main driver of soldiers' motivation to fight in a formal military organisation such as the British Army (i.e., 'successful collective performance').

In this chapter I aim to challenge such views through the comparison and contrast of two organisationally and ideologically different military formations – one nominally formal but rather unconventional (VRS) and one clandestine (IRA). Furthermore, my ambition is to move away from the narrow focus on individual combatants towards the social dynamics of pugnacity. Since willingness to fight is a social rather than a psychological process, this chapter focuses in particular on the structural contexts that generate such motivation. Hence the aim is to explore what role ideology, coercive organisational structure, and small group solidarity play in these two armed forces. Although this research project also gathered information on the material incentives this motive did not feature as a significant factor for our respondents. Since neither VRS soldiers nor IRA volunteers received any substantial financial compensation throughout the conflicts the focus here is firmly on the other three sources of motivation to fight.[2]

7.3   Situating the Two Conflicts

The war in Bosnia and Herzegovina (1992–5) and 'The Troubles' in Northern Ireland (1969–97) were the two most destructive violent conflicts of late twentieth-century Europe. The two conflicts were very different in terms of the size, timescale, the extent of casualties. and the wider geopolitical contexts. 'The Troubles' were defined by protracted but low-level violence resulting in 3,532 fatalities and over 47,500 injured.[3] In contrast, the Bosnian and Herzegovinian war was significantly shorter but much more destructive resulting in 104,732 fatalities and numerous injured individuals (Zwierzchowski and Tabeau 2010).[4] The Bosnian conflict was also characterised by systematic abuses of civilians including mass-scale rapes, torture, ethnic cleansing, and genocidal campaigns, while the violence in Northern Ireland was more

---

[2] This is not to say that some members of these military organisations were not in part motivated by other material incentives including the protection of their homes or in some instances the opportunist pillaging of abandoned goods (see Bougarel 2006: 481).

[3] https://cain.ulster.ac.uk/index.html.

[4] The total number of casualties of war in Bosnia and Herzegovina is highly disproportional as most victims were Bosniaks (Bosnian Muslims) who account for 68,101 fatalities while the total number of fatalities for Bosnian Serbs is 22,779, for Bosnian Croats 8,858 and for others 4,995. The Bosniaks are also substantially overrepresented among the civilian casualties (25,609 vs. 7,480 for Serbs, 1,675 for Croats and 1,935 for others) (Zwierzchowski and Tabeau 2010).

sporadic with the primary target being members of the military, police, and paramilitary organisations while civilian casualties were often regarded as 'collateral damage'.

The social and political context of the two conflicts was also very different. While the 'Troubles' transpired in an environment of a stable political structure of the liberal democratic British state, the war in Bosnia and Herzegovina followed the collapse of the state socialist Yugoslavia. While the former conflict was confined to a province within a powerful state with a large military and police force that could contain the extent of violence, the latter involved variety of state and non-state actors within Bosnia and neighbouring states fighting over the control of the territory. In sociological terms, the two cases are also different in a sense that class divisions played much more important role in Northern Ireland than in Bosnia and Herzegovina. The ethno-religious and political divides tend to overlap with the class divisions in Northern Ireland where the Irish nationalists/Catholics have traditionally been discriminated by the British Unionist/Protestant state in terms of electoral representation, policing, employment, and housing rights (O'Leary 2019). In contrast and despite a long history of class divides along ethno-religious lines Bosnia and Herzegovina attained a substantial degree of cross-ethnic equality during the state socialist period (1945–92). The sociological studies conducted in the late 1980s indicate that Bosnia and Herzegovina had achieved ethnic parity across most important societal sectors including key governmental posts, civil service, leadership of industry, police, education, housing, and employment (Katunarić 1991; Malešević 2006: 224).

Nevertheless, the two conflicts also share some important similarities. In both cases one encounters competing claims over territory framed in terms of mutually exclusive ideological projects. In Northern Ireland, the main dividing line is British Unionism vs. Irish Nationalism where the former focus is on maintaining the status quo with Northern Ireland continuing to be a part of the United Kingdom while the latter rejects partition of the island and advocates unification with the Republic of Ireland. In Bosnia and Herzegovina, the divide is also centred on territorial dispute and incompatible ideological projects: the Bosnian Serb and the Bosnian Croat nationalists support partition of the country with an aim of unification of the territories under their control into Serbia and Croatia, respectively. In contrast the Bosniak nationalists support centralisation of the country.

The two armed forces analysed in this chapter, IRA and VRS, were the key military organisations involved in the pursuit of ideological projects associated with Irish and Serb nationalisms, respectively. Although the

Irish Republican Army was created in 1917 this name was later adopted by many republican groups with the Provisional IRA outflanking its competitors (i.e., Official IRA) and becoming the main armed force of the republican movement in 1972. Initially the IRA was a large movement focused on protection of Catholic areas, retaliation for violence, and a guerrilla campaign against the British state and its military and police. In these violent actions, the IRA was involved in bombings and assassinations of the British security force installations and personnel and have also been responsible for killing many civilians. However, with the greater coercive response by the British state from 1970s onward the movement transformed its organisational structure, becoming a clandestine, smaller, and more decentralised organisation. With the introduction of internment without trial by the Northern Ireland government in 1971 and the immediate arrest of over 342 suspects considered to be members of IRA, the movement was forced to reorganise their activities[5] (English 2003: 139).

From the mid-1970s until 1997 the IRA was a clandestine organisation often categorised as a terrorist group involved in variety of violent campaigns in Northern Ireland and England. With the development of the peace process and signing of the Good Friday Agreement in 1998, the IRA declared a ceasefire and has gradually ended its military involvement by decommissioning its weaponry and officially announcing the end of its campaign in 2005. Due to the clandestine nature of this organisation and the prolonged campaign, it is difficult to know the exact number of IRA volunteers. However, it is estimated that up to 10,000 people had been members until 1986 and probably many more until 1997 (Bishop and Mallie 1988: 112).

The Army of the Serbian Republic (VRS) was established in May 1992 and until its abolition in December 2005 operated as the principal armed force of *Republika Srpska* (RS). As this military organisation was a direct successor of the JNA (*Jugoslavenska Narodna Armija*, Yugoslav People's Army) in Bosnia and Herzegovina (BiH) much of its organisational structure was inherited from the JNA. More specifically, the VRS was composed of former JNA officers born in BiH, units of Territorial Defence from the BiH municipalities with a majority Serbian population, as well as various paramilitary formations that accepted integration into the VRS (Milovanović 2011: 5). The General Staff was composed entirely of former professional JNA high ranking officers: four generals, seven colonels, and one captain. The new armed force also adopted the

---

[5] Between 1971 and 1975 around 2,000 people were detained without trial.

military doctrine of the JNA including its tactical, operational, and strategic dimensions. The size of the VRS varied from 80,000 to 120,000 by the end of the war (Finlan 2004; Milovanović 2011; O'Ballance 1995). Although the new armed force included small numbers from minority groups (including some Croats and Bosniaks) and a small contingent of international volunteers (mostly from Russia and Greece) the overwhelming majority of soldiers were ethnic Serbs from Bosnia or other regions of the former Yugoslavia.

Despite their obvious differences, the IRA and VRS were non-conventional military organisations focused on realising specific ideological blueprints as well as establishing and maintaining control over contested territories. In both cases nationalism was a driving source of legitimacy and organisational capacity was generated to accomplish their ideological goals – united Ireland and all Serbs living in a single state, respectively. The interviews with the former combatants of these two military organisations help elucidate the social dynamics of combat experience and its relationship with the wider structural forces of ideology, coercive organisations, and micro-group solidarity.

7.4   VRS's Coercive Capacity: The Incoherent Army

The defining feature of any armed force is its coercive capacity. The success of military organisations in war or insurgencies is often determined by their ability to enforce discipline, establish clear and efficient chains of command and control, and create organisational mechanisms to recruit combatants to fight as well as to keep them engaged in theatres of war (Biddle 2004; King 2013). Hence to force individuals to fight one needs robust organisational capacity in place.

On paper, the VRS would fulfil such criteria. In organisational terms the VRS was regarded as an effective, functional, well-organised, and logically structured modern military force built on the principles of Weberian (legal-rational) bureaucracy. For one thing VRS was a direct inheritor of the JNA which in itself was generally regarded as one of the most powerful and well-organised European military forces (Gow 1992; Žunec et al. 2013). For another thing commentators have regularly emphasised how VRS maintained much existing JNA personnel, weaponry, and military equipment. Hence in contrast to the other two military forces involved in the Bosnian war, ABH (Army of BH) and the HVO (Croatian Defence Council), VRS had well established hierarchical structures, professional officers, and a clearly defined division of labour and could rely on an abundance of military resources (Magaš and Žanić 2001). Furthermore, the fact that for much of the war the VRS controlled nearly 70 per cent of Bosnian territory was also taken to be a reliable indicator of its organisational superiority.

However, when one digs a bit deeper into its organisational dynamics what comes across is the profound weakness of this armed force which was often incapable of coercing its soldiers to fight. This finding can be gleaned from the official statements and even more so from the interviews with the combatants. Hence according to General Manojlo Milovanović (2011: 7) who was the deputy chief of staff of the VRS, the officer corps consisted of 21 per cent professional officers and 79 per cent reserve officers. Nevertheless, nearly all significant command roles were entrusted to the professional staff only: 'Most commanding responsibilities from the regiments' commanders onwards, including specific commanding operational and strategic responsibilities were [exclusively] assigned to the professionals' (Milovanović 2011: 7). Whereas the majority of VRS commanding officers were professional staff, educated and trained in the Yugoslav (JNA) military schools and academies, rank and file soldiers – the conscripts – were overwhelmingly of non-professional background. Following several waves of mass mobilisation starting in May 1992, out of the total number of VRS soldiers 98 per cent were conscripted recruits. In most important respects throughout the war the VRS tended to rely extensively on its professional cadre who were not only responsible for the command, tactics, strategy, and organisation but also bore the brunt of action on the frontlines. The staggering degree of this reliance (or dependence) on the professionals is illustrated by the fact that out of the total casualties of the VRS during the 1992–5 war, 38 per cent were officers (Milovanović 2011: 13). This statistic suggests that the VRS establishment could not trust or rely on the ordinary recruits to fight the war but had to deploy professional officers to the theatres of war.

Leaving to one side the Clausewitzian point about the chaotic character of all modern warfare where the 'friction' and the 'fog of war' generate uncertainty, haziness, unreliability of information, and make all armed forces less effective, the VRS's organisational structure was in most instances unusually feeble. Although the VRS inherited much from the JNA, these two militaries were built for very different purposes and had very different ethnic structures and ideological goals and the transition to new armed forces was anything but smooth. In fact, as the JNA military structure was dependent on the Yugoslav and Bosnian multi-ethnic officer corps who were trained to defend their state from possible external attacks by NATO or the Warsaw Pact countries, much of this knowledge was not particularly useful in waging a civil war or in fighting with armed or unarmed civilians. Furthermore, from its inception the VRS struggled to fill many significant military roles, as many highly skilled individuals evaded conscription and those who were conscripted did not have the requisite military training or were reluctant to fight. This was particularly pronounced in the Serb controlled parts of Bosnia where 'most of the combatants were mobilised by force' (Bougarel 2006: 479) and where a majority of soldiers were recruited in the countryside while many urban middle-class men of recruiting age managed to escape the frontlines through emigration abroad or through the use of nepotistic networks (Backović et al. 2001; Judah 1997; Oberschall 2000; Ron 2003). The VRS was also riddled with a pronounced tension between (the former JNA) professional officers and the conscripts who generally did not trust high-ranking officers and tended to be much more loyal to their local (non-professional) commanders. This was borne out by the interviews with former VRS soldiers: 'We respected officers that stayed [and fought] with us but there were instance of those [officers] who would run away ... and then the soldiers would stop trusting [the officers]' (Zoran 1, VRS).

Another conscripted solider emphasises this disconnect between the higher ranked officers and ordinary soldiers. In his view the officers paid no attention to soldiers: 'You see them on TV later depicted as heroes, but they treated us just as numbers ... people could not go home for a year or so ... we had to fend for ourselves ... nobody would visit us ... you had to protect yourself and that is it' (Zoran 2, VRS).

When asked about relationships between officers and soldiers one former combatant insisted that there was no relationship at all: 'I did not see many honourable, honest [officers] ... they were a separate caste, they did not socialise with us ... and I did not know any of them before the war ... Suddenly [with the outbreak of war] they became important and they would show this in an ugly way' (Jovo, VRS).

This attitude was just as much present among the volunteers who also did not have a very good opinion of the professional officers. One such volunteer describes the attitude towards his superiors: 'There was no respect [for the professional officers] ... they would visit the troops every 10–15 days from the command HQ which was about 10 km away ... we would pay attention to their visits ... as the local commanders were pushing us to show them some respect' (Dragan, VRS).

Some soldiers highlighted the strong legacy of JNA culture among professional officers: 'There were some fools who were typical communist officers ... on one occasion on the battlefield [during an intense enemy attack] we were ordered to lay down in line. I hid behind the rock and this officer was shouting at me to stay in the line ... saying that I have to follow his order even if I were to get killed ... so I thought I will not die for you, you moron ... such a JNA [attitude]' (Dejan, VRS).

Although some units were well ordered and disciplined, interviews indicate that in many units there was a chronic lack of discipline. Some platoons were composed of soldiers who did not undergo even the basic military training and the new recruits had to learn how to use weapons on the frontline. Others emphasise the lack of enforcement of discipline: 'Generally, I don't think that there was much discipline ... the military leadership was not particularly repressive towards soldiers ... I cannot say that everybody did what they wanted but there was no strict military discipline ... of course one had to obey specific regulations, higher ranking officers and so on ... but nobody was rigorously sanctioned for non-disciplined behaviour' (Milan, VRS).

When explicitly asked about the state of discipline in their unit other soldiers describe it as 'poor' (Zoran 1, VRS) or 'non-existent' (Saša, VRS). These two ex-combatants describe their experience in the following terms: 'We were in a platoon that did not belong to any other larger military unit ... no corps or divisions ... nobody paid attention to us ... so I ran away from that unit' (Zoran1); 'It was chaos, nothing like the movies, the small cliques emerge, you are on good terms with some guys, you protect each other ... when action starts with shooting you lose compass, you don't know where to go, the order comes in but nobody listens, a catastrophe' (Saša, VRS).

In particular the interviewees highlight the lack of expertise and experience in military units headed by reserve officers: 'They were not professional officers ... reservists, leaders ... literally those who could not escape [the recruitment], just as me ... everybody had to go, without experience, perhaps some had attended the school for reserve officers, they might have had some bookish knowledge, but they didn't know anything about organisation, they were trying to save their skins' (Saša, VRS).

Another big issue hampering discipline was rampant drunkenness among soldiers. This was particularly visible in the units solely composed of volunteers: 'I joined the volunteer unit ... they gave us uniforms, guns, munition and put us on the bus to Jajce ... We came up there in the evening ... and 90 to 95 per cent of soldiers were under the influence of alcohol' (Dragan, VRS).

Some soldiers indicate that periods of truce were often interrupted by drunk soldiers: 'there was brandy, [local people] would sell brandy ... one would get drunk ... this would happen ... somebody would express his frustrations, tensions ... a drunk man ... what can you expect from such a man' (Zoran 1, VRS); 'Somebody started shooting because he had drunk a bottle of brandy' (Dragan, VRS).

These micro-organisational difficulties expressed in the chronic lack of discipline, and the distrust of higher ranking (former JNA) officers was also present on the macro-level. During the war there was a pronounced tension between the leaderships of the VRS and RS personified in the open conflict between General Ratko Mladić and President Radovan Karadžić[6] (particularly in the later period). In addition, the soldiers' dissatisfaction with the leadership also resulted in a serious mutiny in 1993 in Banja Luka. The former combatants were aware of these tensions and reflected on them during the war:

We were well aware about this [the Mladić–Karadžić conflict] ... we had a feeling of betrayal, all soldiers were behind Mladić and the expectation was that Mladić will arrest the civilian leadership of the state because of criminality and other things ... but it seemed that he just secured his position and did not do anything ... even though the complete army was behind him, and in my unit and perhaps others we were forced to sign something ... and we were like Praetorians, they knew how we think ... we were hoping that something would happen ... the fracture ... but nothing happened ... and this was not only once but also in 1993 when this same Mladić came in and destroyed the mutiny ... he did the same when Karadžić removed him from his post ... and when the army stood by him, when he had the chance to do something but did nothing. (Nenad, VRS)

Hence despite its nominal features as a modern bureaucratic system, in reality the VRS had a relatively feeble organisational structure and as such could not successfully coerce its soldiers to fight. The military lacked organisational capacity to enforce discipline, was internally deeply divided and disordered, and as such was not particularly effective as a military force. Coercion was important, and to some extent effective, in the mobilisation of the ordinary recruits. However, since the VRS had rather weak organisational capacity, coercive power was not the decisive factor in soldier's motivation to fight.

7.5 IRA's Coercive Capacity: The Bureaucratic Network

In popular imagination the IRA actions are often associated with the passionate commitment, spontaneous deeds, and creative improvisation that characterise many insurgencies. Nevertheless, much of the recent research indicates that this organisation in many ways resembled a conventional military force. The IRA was conceived as a military organisation that imitated the structure of established armies including the British Army (BA) and the Irish Defence Force (IDF). Hence it was structured similarly to these two armies with brigades, battalions, and companies

---

[6] Ratko Mladic and Radovan Karadzic are the convicted war criminals responsible for the genocide in Srebrenica and the mass scale killings during the 1992–95 war in Bosnia and Herzegovina.

that were responsible for control over different territories. For example, in 1970s the Belfast and Derry brigades were composed of several battalions which in turn were divided into companies covering specific areas of the two cities. Thus, in Belfast the first battalion covered Upper Falls, Ballymurphy, and Andersonstown, the second battalion controlled the Lower Falls, Clonard, and the Divis Flats, and the third battalion covered The Bone and the Short Strand (Bowyer Bell 2000). The Derry Brigade was significantly smaller, but it too was territorially organised with specific battalions covering four different parts of the city under its control: Bogside/Brandywell district, Creggan, Waterside, and Shantallow (Toolis 2015). Both brigades had centralised Command Staff responsible for decision making and coordination of military actions. The hierarchical and professional character of the organisation was in part built on the existing military culture of its members: many volunteers were previously soldiers in the BA or IDF and as such were familiar with the command structure, regular training, marching, saluting, and other conventional military practices (Moloney 2002). For instance, the IRA's Chief of Staff from 1969 to 1972 was former Royal Air Force corporal Seán MacStiofáin (born in London as John Edward Drayton Stephenson) (Hunter 2001).

The IRA changed and evolved from the late 1960s to 1997. Initially its organisational structure was less hierarchical with the commanders and majority of ordinary members being involved in military operations. Over the years as the organisation expanded it become more hierarchical and bureaucratic. In the 1990s the IRA operated a complex organisational structure with clearly defined division of labour. Hence just as in the conventional military organisations, the majority of IRA members were not involved in actual fighting but were responsible for administrative, logistical, financial, and other supporting roles. Instead of direct exposure to violence most members were performing other roles – from intelligence, surveillance, and planning, to storage and management of weapons. For example, in the Derry Brigade most individuals were active in bureaucratic roles as well as the engineering department, the financial department, and the department of internal affairs dealing with informers (Toolis 2015).

The organisation also had constantly to adjust so as to evade arrests and disruption of their activities by the British government. In this context, the IRA maintained a flexible yet hierarchical system of governance: where a specific commander was imprisoned or interned, he would automatically lose his rank and would be replaced by another individual[7]

---

[7] With the high number of arrests in the 1970s the average term of office in the Belfast Brigade was just eight months.

(Moloney 2002). From the mid-1970s to the 1990s, the IRA became a highly bureaucratic organisation in every sense. The emphasis was on rules, regulations, and disciplined action. This was also clearly specified in the IRA training manual, the Green Book published in 1977 where members are instructed to strictly follow the chain of command: 'You obey all orders whether you like them or not ... The Army as an organisation claims and expects your total allegiance without reservation ... All volunteers must obey orders issued to them by a superior officer regardless of whether they like the particular officer or not' (O'Brien 1999: 352).

This coercive organisational pressure was recognised and respected by the ordinary members who often emphasised the difference between the highly disciplined structure of the IRA and the more lax organisation of its youth wing Fianna Éireann. In the words of a Belfast volunteer: 'While you were in the Fianna you were, we'd a certain amount of autonomy in the Fianna ... but you also knew all the stuff you weren't allowed to do. So, once you joined the army then that was a whole different kettle of fish' (IRA volunteer E).[8]

This emphasis on hierarchy, delegation of tasks, discipline, and the strict chain of command is voiced by another former IRA combatant:

You were a volunteer, and my attitude as a volunteer was that you had to be told what to do and be able to take orders, not to question orders. ... Once you got a run down on things that you were supposed to do or were going to do you could have been asked 'well is everything ok, has anybody else any questions, anybody not too sure of anything'. So, there was that wee bit of freedom in asking some things you weren't just too sure of, you know. But to be told to do something and to do it, that was the protocol.

Everything had to go through the structure, you know ... There was a structure set up there and the structure always came into play because you always took your orders from your people who you were under and that's the way it was. You just couldn't decide yourself to go and do something. No. You couldn't, no you don't do that ... So obviously there was a protocol there that everything went through the structure. (IRA volunteer D)

A very similar assessment was made by an IRA volunteer from Derry who sees hierarchy as the key feature of this organisation:

---

[8] The data from the interviews with the former combatants were collected as a part of the project 'The Mediated Settlement of Armed Conflicts in Northern Ireland and Bosnia-Herzegovina' coordinated by Niall O'Dochartaigh and me in 2011–13. The interviews with the former IRA members were conducted by Niall O'Dochartaigh from 2011 to 2014. See more about the methodology and data collection in the Appendix.

It's just not a democratic organisation, it's classed as an army, it's a guerrilla army and if you're not prepared to deal with the structure, the command structure would be your OC [Officer Commanding] and whatever and you're not prepared to listen then there's no open discussion ... it's recognising and respecting the actual structure and if you're not prepared to respect then you leave you know or you're shown the door, you know. (IRA volunteer N)

The coercive character of this hierarchical command structure was enforced through formal systems including 'court martial' and range of punishments for disobedience. In the words of a former IRA member from Belfast:

You would have been accountable to your local command. They were accountable to the battalion command. ... I mean there was always accountability, sometimes the accountability would have been more ruthless than what you would have expected but I suppose it was the IRA's way, the army way of ensuring discipline, kept you alive and also kept you focused, kept you functioning. (IRA volunteer B)

In addition to clearly defined hierarchies, discipline, and the established chain of command the IRA also focused on recruiting competent individuals and assigning their appropriate role in the organisation:

... in terms of your command structure. There would have been various people with areas of responsibility, you know, your senior officers and stuff. Some of them you would have had a lot of respect for and others you wouldn't have had a lot of respect for ... in terms of leadership there were obviously some leaders who were very much more inspirational, who would have held your attention and held your respect. Some much more so than others ... a lot of the time it would have been their clarity of thought, their methodology. Whenever somebody was going to do something the way that they would approach it, making sure that all avenues are covered. Is this done? Basic sort of, it's basically management skills that you would find in any other role. Some people had excellent management skills, others don't have the same level of management skills and possibly they're only [in] that job because the guy before them got arrested or the guys who were better than them got moved somewhere else to a different area or a different chain of command or whatever. (IRA volunteer J)

The focus on professionalism meant that personal relationships had to be subordinated to the organisational chains of command and control. This was not easy as many volunteers knew each other well before they joined the IRA:

I had to conduct a meeting one night, and my mate said 'we were really taken by you Jim, you're not Jim now like. You walked up in front of us all, "ok lads I want you all to stand to attention. Tomorrow night I want 6 of you up here and 6 of you down there". You kind of fall into that kind of role and there's people naturally progress up and there's people who don't. (IRA volunteer Q)

Hence, in contrast to the popular perception of the IRA as an informal, spontaneous, and passion driven organisation the reality is that this armed force was defined by a highly bureaucratic structure. For much of its existence the IRA had a clearly developed system of command and control characterised by substantive coercive capacity and elaborate division of labour. The organisation was able to impose a hierarchical system of decision making, successfully manage internal dissent, and enforce discipline through formalised punishments. The IRA also evolved over the years and developed a flexible model of command which delegated responsibility across the entire organisation. Nevertheless, while coercive pressure was important for the very existence of IRA it was not the main factor in mobilising volunteers to join and fight for this organisation. In other words, coercion played an important role in maintaining the organisational structure of the IRA but was less effective as a mobiliser for fighting.

7.6   VRS Ideology: A Nationalist Military with Non-Ideological Soldiers

There is a general tendency to view the military of the Republic of Srpska as a highly ideological army (Cigar 2001; Žanić 2007). This is apparent in two senses: through the inherited legacy of the JNA and through its role in the ideological formation of RS. The VRS was formed from the ashes of the JNA in Bosnia and Herzegovina and as such was composed of officers and other professional soldiers who were educated and socialised in the JNA institutions. As the JNA was commonly characterised as an ideologically rigid social organisation dominated by highly doctrinaire top-ranking officers (Dimitrijević 2001; Gow 1992) it is no surprise that a substantial degree of this ideological severity was passed on to the VRS. For example, just as in the JNA, and unlike most militaries in democratic states, the VRS maintained a strong association with the ruling party. Although nominally the armed forces were depoliticised as high-ranking officers were banned from membership in political parties, the military leadership was fully in tune with the ideological vistas of the ruling party in RS – the Serbian Democratic Party. As Bougarel (2006: 428) emphasises, this was also the case with the other two militaries that fought in the Bosnian war, ARBiH (with strong links to the Bosniak SDA party) and Croatian HVO (with even stronger links to HDZ) as all three armed forces inherited a substantial part of the JNA's legacy 'to the extent that they too participated in the state-party systems'.

The second, and perhaps more significant, ideological role is the general perception of the VRS as one of the cornerstones of the Serbian nationalist project, the result of which was the establishment of RS. This is explicitly stated in all significant military and RS government documentation as well as in surveys of RS citizens (Bougarel 2006; Pravilo službe VRS 1993). All recruits were expected to be familiar with the VRS handbook for soldiers – *Pravilo službe Vojske Rrepublike Srpske* (The Rules of the [Military] Service of VRS).

The central reference point in this ideological narrative is that both RS and VRS were established in response to the violent break-up of federal Yugoslavia as a means to protect the Serbian population from becoming an ethnic minority dominated by the Bosniak majority in an independent and unitary Bosnia and Herzegovina. As former VRS General Milovanović (2011: 1) states, 'unprotected Serbs had to organise their military as they had no other means of protection'. Furthermore, RS and the VRS were understood to be both a guarantor of security for the Serbian population in BiH but also an institutional device to protect and treasure Serbian cultural traditions including the language, Cyrillic script, Serbian Orthodox religion, and specific cultural practices (e.g., slava, kumstvo, epic poetry, etc.). In this context the military doctrine of VRS included clear references to these ideological idioms: 'the moral fibre of VRS is to be built and developed on the Serbian heritage, tradition, patriotism, awareness of war goals, religion, professionalism of its command cadre and the sense of justice and humanity in relation towards the wounded, dead and captured soldiers and their family members' (Milovanović 2011: 6). As the war progressed, the ambition was to generate a greater degree of ideological unity and these key principles were formulated and implemented by professional officers responsible for ideological indoctrination: 'The centralisation of war efforts was coupled with an effort towards ideological homogenisation: officers in charge of morale were appointed at every level in the military hierarchy' (Bougarel 2006: 482).

In broader terms VRS ideological goals fully corresponded with the political programmes of SDS and other Serbian parties in BiH. In this view unlike the monarchist pre–Second World War Yugoslavia which safeguarded Serbian interests, its communist post-1945 counterpart was for the most part seen as being highly detrimental to the development of the ethnic Serbian population. Moreover, the creation of a relatively loose federal state in the 1970s (the 1974 Constitution of Yugoslavia) was understood as being designed to weaken the Serbian position within the federation and foster further secessionist ambitions among the non-Serbian populace. According to this position the collapse of the Yugoslav state was triggered by the collusion of the Western powers and secessionist movements all of whom conspired to make ethnic Serbs living outside

Serbia into a deprived minority. Hence the VRS and RS were seen to be an expression of popular will among Bosnian and Herzegovinian Serbs who aspired to live in a unified state with all other Serbs from the former Yugoslav federation. In other words, ethno-nationalist principles were utilised to justify the creation and existence of both VRS and RS. More specifically VRS asserted the right to use force through nationalist ideology as it was seen by its leadership to be the legitimately constituted armed force of the Serbian nation and its newly established state – RS.

There is no question that both Serbian nationalism and ideological inflexibility played a substantial role in VRS war activities. For one thing, the idea of establishing a continuous territory for the Serbian state was the raison d'être of VRS's existence. For another thing, despite the nominal commitment to its depoliticisation the VRS's internal structure for the most part reproduced the ideocratic nature of the JNA where instead of the Communist Party (LCY) the Serbian Democratic Party (SDS) maintained complete dominance (Bougarel 2006). However, this is not to say that the VRS was an ideologically strong social organisation. On the contrary, as our data show, ideology in general, and nationalism in particular, were a much weaker force than ordinarily assumed.

Firstly, there was a pronounced ideological tension between professional officers and the SDS political leadership which was in charge of the VRS. While the former JNA officers were educated and socialised in the milieu of the multi-ethnic Yugoslav socialist state that glorified the postwar legacy of communist partisan resistance (against fascist invaders and their *chetnik* [Serbian nationalist and monarchist] collaborators) the political leadership was openly hostile to this legacy and highly sympathetic to the anti-communist *chetnik* tradition. This ideological polarisation was also present among ordinary soldiers. As several of our interviewees acknowledge, individual soldiers were politically divided in terms of their ideological preferences. As one respondent put it, soldiers had very different political preferences: 'Some loved Slobo [Slobodan Milošević], some Vuk [Drašković], others Radovan [Karadžić] or this or that [political] option' (Zoran 1, VRS).

Secondly, despite the nominal presence of ideological grand vistas such as the 'preservation of Serbian people and their culture' or 'the unification of all Serbs into a single state' the contours of the VRS's ideological aims were far from being clear. The political and military leadership were split on the issues of central war aims: some advocated preservation of a rump Yugoslavia (with Serbia, Montenegro, and the VRS controlled territories of BiH); others were keen on the establishment of 'Western Serbia' through the unification of the Republika Srpska with the Republic of Serbian Krajina (in Croatia); while yet others preferred the creation of a fully independent RS and a minority accepted a wide autonomy within an independent BiH state. Moreover, ordinary soldiers were confused as to what the overarching aim of the war was:

Military aims were never defined and the political goals were not communicated to the soldiers. (Nenad)

We never knew the strategic reasons for why, how and how far [we have to go] to encircle some territory ... nobody ever came and told us the aim is this and that ... even when the unification of territory where Serbs live is mentioned ... if that is the case and if everybody agrees and even if it is against the whole world[we would go for it] ... but nobody ever told us this. (Zoran 1)

This lack of clear ideological ambitions and military goals generated a great deal of resentment among the ordinary soldiers:

On one occasion the soldiers were angry because the ceasefire was signed ... Bihać battlefield in 1994 ... when we entered Bihac Jimmy Carter had a meeting with Karadžić and we had to withdraw, 4 km then 8 km ... many people died ... there were problems ... (Zoran 1)

Some soldiers were openly hostile to what they perceived to be political trade over territories:

'...you hear some news that [this territory] was sold, these soldiers withdrew, those attacked, somebody sold out... and this affected our motivation. (Dragan)

When Dayton was signed ... I was disappointed that we lost territories that I considered to be Serbian ... Drvar, Grahovo, Petrovac ... but this was simply agreed at that meeting ... that is politics. (Nenad)

There were many better options ... but the politics did not do its job properly ... the politics was the worst factor in the whole war ... what the military accomplished until 1993 ... they [the politicians] could not capitalise on, to agree [something better]. (Zoran 1)

Although many analysts acknowledge this ideological polarisation and the lack of clearly defined political, military, and ideological goals there is still a tendency to assume that ethnic nationalism was a powerful motivating force among VRS combatants (Cigar 2001; Gaub 2011; Žanić 2007). However, the in-depth analysis of interviews with the soldiers demonstrates a more complex picture. To understand these complexities, it is crucial to distinguish between the conscripts (the overwhelming majority of soldiers) and the (relatively small number of) volunteers. Whereas, as a rule, most volunteers were initially driven by strong nationalist ideals this was not the case for the conscripts who generally exhibit less enthusiasm about the Serbian nationalist project. For example, some volunteers describe how and why they joined VRS:

I was living in Germany and already in 1990–91 the divisions emerged [between individuals who started distinguishing] who is who ... Serbs were going to Serbian pubs, others to their own ... and over there I listened to various people, attended meetings, listened to the Serbian traditional epic songs, etc. and something boiled in me so I said I am going there ... I have a father and a mother, they are alone ... and I came back home and volunteered [to join VRS]. (Dragan)

To be honest ... in 1992 ... there was some allure so we all went [to VRS] with pride ... it was different in 1995 ... but I still felt need, the patriotic need, to go. (Novak)

Some soldiers emphasised the legacies of the First and Second World Wars:

In WWII, my family were victims of genocide ... they are from Kozara, and I know what happened in 1941–42, camps, suffering of Serbian people and simply there was our internal revolt not to experience that again ... that is why we got involved ... what determined my decision to join was the awareness that my people are threatened. (Milan)

I thought we were right ... because of what happened in WWI and WWII, and all that history ... I felt that Serbs experienced the biggest loss after Yugoslav collapse and that we have the right to settle scores for what they've done to us ... and to secure some space for us. (Nenad)

In contrast many conscripts were less enthused by nationalist rhetoric:

I did not believe the war would break out ... we were raised in that spirit ... my best friend was a Muslim ... you could not choose who will be your mother and father ... before the war, even in 1991 and 1992 I did not know who was who [a Serb, Croat or Muslim]. (Jovo)

Half of my friends were Muslims and Croats ... even today when they come from Sweden or Denmark we are together ... so nobody thought about ethnicity. (Saša)

I was never a nationalist ... I never felt some kind of hatred towards others ... because somebody is a Muslim ... even though I've seen [terrible things] in war. (Dejan)

Some soldiers were completely indifferent to ideological aspirations:

Some liked Radovan [Karadžić] or other political options and we loved Partybreakers [the Belgrade rock band] ... we were not interested ... only fun [zajebancija], nobody was into those serious stories ... I was not interested in any of that of whether your country will join EU, or whether it will be called like this or like that ... there were fatcats who sat, ate and talked about these stupidities ... but I had no interest in any of that. (Zoran 1)

Some conscripted soldiers emphasised the role mass media played in mobilising public support for the nationalist cause: the media 'pumped up the Serbdom ... nationalist rush ... and you think you are going to supposedly defend your people' (Dejan). Among the conscripts there was also a sharp divide between the urban and rural cohorts with many individuals who grew up in the multi-ethnic urban environments expressing less ideological commitment to war than those who were raised in a mono-ethnic countryside: 'those guys from the city [Banja Luka] did not look so much towards nationalism, or religion, but these from the villages were more likely to be arrogant and proud of their Serbian-ess, they gave more attention to these things ... [the two groups] did not get on well ... the city raja and those from the outside ... we had different values. We were raised differently' (Saša).

Although nationalist motivations did play a substantial role for some soldiers throughout the entire conflict, a majority were less inclined to express their war experience in such general ideological terms. What seems to be a more important source of motivation was a sense of loyalty and attachment to one's specific micro-group. This was usually articulated in two ways: as a feeling of moral obligation towards close family members and friends at home and as a sense of responsibility and attachment towards their comrades at the frontline. Hence when asked about their decision to join, most responses focus on sentiments of obligation towards their friends and family: '[I joined VRS] because I felt responsibility towards my father and mother' (Dragan); 'all my friends joined, my relatives, uncles ... nobody was eager to go but, my god, you have to accept the reality of changed environment' (Nenad); 'the better off people sent their children abroad ... but these who stayed ... it was as it was ... when you fraternise with people ... it would be shameful to say I am leaving [abroad]' (Zoran); 'I felt I had to defend my family' (Mile); I was born in Banja Luka ... and all my friends from the housing estate, and from the school joined [VRS] so did I too' (Nenad).

Both conscripts and volunteers were often mobilised or would join VRS together with the people they already knew, and these friendships were often strengthened through the shared experience of the battlefields: 'We were people of the same generation – 18, 19 years of age ... however, there were many units with the mixed aged groups 40, 50, 60 ... but you also had entire families within a single [military] unit ... father, son, uncle, cousins' (Milan); 'We were the same generation, kids of the same age in the same shit ... four people sharing one small tin can (pašteta)' (Zoran 1).

While most respondents joined the VRS out of a sense of obligation towards their family and friends, once on the frontline their continuous commitment to remain there was primarily linked not to ideological grand vistas but a sense of solidarity towards their comrades. Many interviewed soldiers express these sentiments clearly:

We felt solidarity towards each other ... when somebody was injured ... everybody would look after him to do the best he can to help. (Dragan)

There was always one for all ... usually 7 to 10 people together ... you felt you will give a life one for another, and that is how our relationships have developed. (Zoran 1)

I was ready to die for them and they would do the same for me ... I would not be able to sleep otherwise ... but there were people who would just come [to fight] for the weekend ... and would go back home to Belgrade instantly. (Zoran 2)

[Difficult war experience] brings people together ... you develop these bonds, you help each other. (Saša)

We were like brothers ... for 64 days I could not go home, there is no hygiene ... great friendships, you would not be able to survive without this ... I was carrying a wounded comrade ... they were shelling us ... your life was in peril, but you keep carrying him, if it hits you, it hits you. (Zdravko)

Our friendships are still strong ... when I meet my friend [from war] Dragan, who has four children today, who is now serious and grey I kiss him like a brother. (Dejan)

This strong sense of localised attachment would regularly surpass general nationalist sentiments. For example, some soldiers perceived their officers as being morally inferior and lacking any sense of solidarity:

These generals, they were awful people, they would hide in a hole and then would give us speeches ... when everything was over. (Mile)

When they declared the mutiny [in 1993 Banja Luka] ... lieutenant colonel [Rajko] Šarenac gave a speech ... telling us that 16th battalion was treasonous ... I stood up and said ... how can they be treasonous my relatives are there, in that brave unit, you are not telling the truth ... then he shouted you are the infiltrator, etc. (Dejan)

This lack of national solidarity was also occasionally visible when soldiers confronted the local Serb population:

At some point we were given 50 marks voucher [from the VRS] so we would go to the local store in the midst of war activities and they [local Serb shop owners] would tell us they do not accept these vouchers ... no matter that he is a Serb he cannot tell us that they do not accept these vouchers ... there were a lot of conflicts between us and the locals in these places we defended ... there was no love lost here ... he has a shop and I am defending him ... and he still charges me. (Dragan)

Although the VRS was established to implement a specific ideological goal and was infused with a strong doctrinal ethos of Serbian ethno-nationalism this ideological zeal was much less present among ordinary soldiers. Rather than being unwavering ideological warriors most of these conscripts joined the army and continued to fight out of a sense of moral responsibility and emotional attachment towards their family and close friends. In other words, ideology was important in sustaining the VRS military structure, but it was less significant as a source of soldiers' motivation to fight. This finding fits well with the recent scholarship on the relationship between nationalism and violence which raises serious doubts about nationalist ideology as a being a significant source of combat motivation (Collins 2013; Malešević 2013). What really mattered for social pugnacity were the bonds of micro-solidarity: the combatants' friends and close family members at home as well as their comrades on the battlefield.

7.7   IRA Ideology: Between Nationhood and Comradeship

Similar to the case of VRS, the IRA is often perceived to be a militant organisation driven by strong and uncompromising ideological doctrine – Irish nationalism. As Smith (1995: 108) argues, the IRA was an ideological movement where 'the nature of the internal dynamic contained within republican ideology ... dictated that any solution which failed to live up to the absolute truth of the "republican code" would be a violation of the movement's birth right'. The key principles of IRA's ideology were articulated in its 'Green Book', a training manual for all IRA members who were required to study this manual before they were sworn in (Coogan 1987: 679–712).

The opening line of the 'Green Book' defines the IRA not only as a military force but also as a legitimate government of the Irish Republic:

Commitment to the Republican Movement is the firm belief that its struggle both military and political is morally justified, that war is morally justified and that the Army is the direct representative of the 1918 Dail Eireann Parliament, and that as such they are the legal and lawful government of the Irish Republic, which has the moral right to pass laws for, and to claim jurisdiction over the territory, air space, mineral resources, means of production, distribution and exchange and all of its people regardless of creed or loyalty. (Green Book I:1)

The other central principles that underpinned the IRA's actions include commitment to establishing a united Ireland comprising all 32 counties, and continuing to carry out 'a campaign of resistance against foreign occupation forces and domestic collaborators' in order to end '800 years of oppression'. In addition, the movement was focused on 'creating a Socialist Republic' and rejecting the monarchy and British imperialism.

The IRA was also hostile to the governments and mainstream parties in the Republic of Ireland which were regularly described as 'Free-State Governments' established by the 'Treaty sell-out' (Green Book I:3).

One of the key ideological precepts of the IRA was the glorification and preservation of Irish nationhood. In this context the Irish nation was conceptualised in perennial terms as an entity that has existed for more than a thousand years: 'The nationhood of all Ireland has been an accepted fact for more than 1,000 years and has been recognised internationally as a fact.' In this context the IRA has valued the revival of Irish language and other cultural practices: 'Culturally we would hope to restore Gaelic, not from the motivation of national chauvinism but from the viewpoint of achieving with the aid of a cultural revival the distinctive new Irish Socialist State: as a bulwark against imperialist encroachments from whatever quarter' (Green Book I:4).

The organisational structure of the IRA was established and operated in a way that would reflect the movement's claim that it uniquely represents the will of the Irish people and is the only legitimate government of the Irish Republic. The key legislative body entrusted with decision-making authority was the General Army Convention where all IRA organisational units could send delegates. The Convention would elect a twelve-member Executive which was responsible for selecting the Army Council composed of seven members. The Army Council was the principal operational body involved in everyday activities (English 2003; Moloney 2002). The movement emphasised the democratic character of its rule although only members of the IRA were involved in the process of decision making. Since the IRA was a clandestine organisation its actions and policies were regularly articulated in public life by its political wing – Sinn Féin. However, the relationship between the IRA and Sinn Féin was often ambiguous and riddled with periodic disagreements as the IRA leadership perceived their organisation as the sole legitimate government of the Irish Republic.

As a clandestine organisation, whose key representatives had no access to the mass media, the IRA leadership had to devise alternative ways of disseminating their massages to their supporters and to the wider public. In this context, ideology played an important role in justifying violent actions and the leadership devoted great deal of attention to the articulation and proliferation of their ideological messages. The continuous ideological justifications were also an important mechanism for preventing defeatism and potential desertion from the movement.

While the mainstream mass media in the UK and later also in the Republic of Ireland deemed their actions as terrorist and sectarian the IRA aimed to project the vision of its movement as secular and inclusive of all cultural traditions in Ireland. Hence 'the Green Book' describes the republican movement as part of the global anti-colonial and revolutionary forces: 'The position of the Irish Republican Army since its foundation in 1916 has been one of sustained resistance and implacable hostility to the forces of imperialism, always keeping in the forefront of the most advanced revolutionary thinking and the latest guerrilla warfare techniques in the world' (Green Book 1:4). The IRA portrayed its activities as a defensive war of liberation which is not aimed against Protestant and Unionist populations but against the British state. It also rejected the Cold War divides by depicting its struggle as a part of the global liberation movement:

It is against such political economic power blocks East and West and military alliances such as NATO and the Warsaw Pact. It stands with our Celtic brothers and the other subject nations of Europe, and with the neutral and non-aligned peoples of the Third World; it seeks a third, socialist alternative which transcends both Western individualistic capitalism and Eastern state capitalism, which is in accordance with our best revolutionary traditions as a people. (Green Book 1:4)

Despite these universalist claims, the IRA was generally associated with a strong anti-Loyalist, anti-Protestant, and anti-Unionist orientation and the overwhelming majority of its members were from Catholic backgrounds. For much of its existence the Provisional IRA was an organisation centred on protecting Catholic areas and fighting the B-Specials (Ulster Special Constabulary), British Army, and loyalist paramilitaries.

Nevertheless, despite these strong ideological currents that underpinned the IRA's existence as a political and military organisation its ordinary members were less driven by ideological goals. The movement itself developed from the highly localised popular dissatisfaction with the position of Catholics in Belfast and Derry in the late 1960s and early 1970s. The focus here was on the protection of individual neighbourhoods from the intrusion of the RUC and loyalist paramilitaries. This was also recognised by the leaders of IRA such as Billy McKee who was the first commander of the Provisional IRA in Belfast. He emphasised the local concerns over ideology: 'it was just what you'd call Catholic defence. When the Troubles started here there was practically no IRA ... a big lot of [those who joined] were not Republicans; they were people who maybe had never been involved in anything' (Malešević and Ó Dochartaigh 2018: 317).

The majority of volunteers joined the IRA for variety of non-ideological reasons among which a sense of responsibility towards their friends, family, and the local community prevailed. The focus was clearly on local concerns such as the perceived injustices by the government officials, B-Specials, or the British Army. Many volunteers were spurred on to join as they viewed the IRA as the only force capable of preventing and stopping loyalist attacks on their neighbourhoods. The individuals were mostly recruited in the neighbourhoods by the activists they already knew. As Ó Dochartaigh (2010) shows, many new members of the IRA were less interested in the ideological aims of the movement and more in the immediate situation of their neighbourhoods and the protection of the Catholic areas of their cities. The wider nationalist ideas such as the reunification of the island or establishment of a socialist republic, the key ideological precepts of the IRA leadership, were trumped by local, residential, kinship-based attachments. The regional IRA leaders would often voice their concerns about this ideological tension. For example, the leader of the IRA in Derry, Sean Keenan, described the situation in the late 1960s and early 1970s in the following terms: 'it was necessary to have fighting men there at the time and we didn't have the time to teach them the niceties of republicanism … But I believe that eventually those boys will realise what the fight is all about and that it's not against Protestants' (van Voris 1975: 294).

Even though all new recruits underwent prolonged ideological training and education many of them retained their original motivation to join and fight with an organisation that would help them protect their communities, families, and friends. This localised sense of responsibility towards significant others grew in importance with the greater involvement of the British Army in pacifying the Catholic working-class areas of Belfast and Derry. Many new members of the IRA come from these working-class neighbourhoods. For example, the escalation of violence in the context of the Bloody Sunday massacre in 1972 when the British Army shot twenty-six and killed fourteen civilians during a protest march against internment without trial galvanised support for the IRA in Derry. As one IRA volunteer states, it was such violent acts that motivated many to join the organisation: 'Probably one of the deciding factors would have been constant harassment of British troops at the time on the streets. It generally created an atmosphere of violence and the desire to fight back and not to accept that type of state' (English 2003: 122).

Many young volunteers had very little if any understanding of the ideological doctrine that underpinned the movement. This is well illustrated in the recollection of a 16-year-old Belfast volunteer:

I went down to Kingdom hall; it was like a community hall and myself and two other people were sworn in. The flag and the gun and swear allegiance to the Republic sort of thing. Didn't understand what it all meant, it was all like, well it was patriotic words, but I felt patriotic, I felt like this is, I'm joining something that's good ... they said 'why do you want to join' I said 'I want to fight the British, I want to free Ireland' because somebody told me that when they ask you that's what to say. 'I want to fight for Ireland, Ireland's freedom'. You were kind of tripping out these wee patriotic things. (IRA Volunteer Q)

Since the IRA leadership was aware that many new recruits lacked even rudimentary knowledge of the movement's aims, the emphasis was on their ideological indoctrination. However, this process was riddled with difficulties and a degree of passive resistance on the part of new members:

You would be brought along, as I say, put through sort of an education recruitment process just to test you more than anything to see were you Republican, what you knew about Republicanism and what you knew of what was current at that time, what the war was about, were you just wanting to join it for the fun of it, the craic or because your mates was in it and stuff like that. So, it was like a wee bit of a weeding out process. (IRA Volunteer B)

Many new volunteers had joined with their friends and family members and these networks of micro-solidarity were maintained and even enhanced through the conflict. However, many individuals also forged new comradeship through shared experience of fighting and experiencing common hardships. In the words of an IRA volunteer:

When I joined ... I wouldn't have been particularly close to these lads [other Fianna members], they would have been, maybe played for different teams or soccer or Gaelic or hurling, GAA teams, or went to different schools. So, you'll always gravitate towards your school mates and all that sort of thing ... then when you join your Slua [unit] and you get involved in your Slua work, you start becoming closer. Then some started becoming your friends, closer friends than school mates. (Joint interview with IRA Volunteers G and H)

Or:

Then ... you went into what was called a unit and a lot of people knew each other. Within the unit there was about 12 in it, it was a pretty large unit, and we would have all known each other from our school days or don't live that far away from you. So, we would all have known each other, we all became friends and then that sort of friendship and comradeship would have built up among, as you're going along. (IRA Volunteer D)

However, the republican movement was successful in tapping into these networks of micro-solidarity by linking old and newly formed friendships with the wider ideological goals. This was often attained indirectly: instead of protracted ideological indoctrination through the speeches of leaders or the republican leaflets and other literature, many volunteers embraced the ideological messages through the experience of shared fighting:

The bonds that you would develop with people who you're working with on active service would, yeah it would, you would develop a relationship with them unlike any that, outside of that. In ordinary life you would never experience that sort of bond. And there are even people that, people at times that you didn't particularly like on a personal basis, but you knew that you could rely on them. You knew that they were rock solid and that they wouldn't let you down. So, it was a strange sort of a bond but those type of things developed. (IRA volunteer J)

The proximity of shared life on an everyday basis together with regular exposure to external threats and the dangers of being killed, wounded, or imprisoned all played an important role in forging deep bonds between the combatants:

You have to have a sense of your comrades and that's very, very important and the sense of comradeship that comes from actual involvement in stuff, that you then come to, there are bonds which are built from your activism. (IRA Volunteer J)

Similarly to the case of the VRS, ideological commitments were not the most significant motivator for joining the IRA or for continuing to fight despite the extremely hostile conditions. In most cases local attachments and micro-group solidarities were more important sources of motivation to fight. This is not to say that Irish nationalism was irrelevant for participation in combat but only that the ideological narratives had to envelop the existing networks of micro-level solidarity to make a long-term impact on the IRA combatants. Although the military organisation derived its legitimacy from the ideological creed formulated in the Green Book and other key documents of the movement the ordinary volunteers were receptive to these ideological messages only when they were successfully couched in the language of comradeship, kinship, neighbourhood, and friendship.

7.8   Social Pugnacity between Organisation, Ideology, and Micro-Solidarity

The motivation for fighting is often understood in strictly individualist terms. Many scholars tend to analyse willingness to fight through the prism of individual choices: economic self-interest, strong ideological commitment, personal response to external coercive pressure, or a strong sense of identity with one's fellow combatants. However, by overemphasising these individual choices one can never grasp the complexity and sociability of the fighting experience. Hence to better understand the dynamics of fighting in the combat zone it is crucial to shift the focus from individual decision making towards the social and historical contexts that make fighting possible. In this sense social pugnacity is a phenomenon shaped by organisational capacity, ideological penetration, and the envelopment of micro-level solidarities (Malešević 2013, 2017).

The experiences of combatants who were members of the IRA and VRS show clearly that their actions were moulded by structural forces as well as by everyday agency of people involved in the conflict. Since the IRA volunteers and VRS recruits received no meaningful financial incentives to fight, the motive of economic self-interest was dismissed instantly in the interviews with the ex-combatants.

Coercive pressure was important in the case of the VRS where most recruits were conscripted and where evading the call for mobilisation could result in imprisonment. However, coercion did not play decisive role on the battlefields where soldiers were rarely reprimanded or disciplined for their disobedience. In fact, the VRS organisational structure was unusually feeble with the army being largely divided between the professional officers and ordinary recruits. The weakness of VRS coercive capacity was also apparent in the willingness of ordinary soldiers to continue fighting despite pronounced dissatisfaction with the military establishment. In most cases the combatants were inclined to fight with their comrades and in this process expose themselves to continuous danger of being killed or sustaining incapacitating injuries.

Despite being a much smaller, non-conventional, and clandestine organisation, the IRA maintained a stronger coercive organisational capacity and as such was able to enforce discipline and a hierarchical division of labour. This coercive capacity was particularly visible in the execution of military operations. However, the coercive power was not a decisive variable in determining motivation for fighting. The republican movement could not prevent individuals leaving the IRA or even changing sides and becoming secret British informers.

In both cases ideology features prominently in the justification of violent actions undertaken by these two armed forces. Nationalism in particular is emphasised strongly in the official documentation of VRS and IRA. The key precepts of ideological doctrine are clearly formulated in booklets that all recruits had to study: the 'Green Book' in the case of IRA and 'The Rules of the [Military] Service of VRS' (Pravilo službe VRS). Nevertheless, while ideological power and its organisational penetration were highly important for the two respective militaries, the official ideological discourses were not the primary sources of motivation for fighting for the majority of combatants. Instead, ideology had potency only when it was successfully embedded in the existing networks of micro-solidarity. The process of ideologisation matters much more than the ideological doctrines. In both cases combatants joined their respective military organisations out of sense of responsibility towards significant others – their close friends, family members, trusted neighbours, childhood comrades, peer groups, and so on. The IRA volunteers emphasise their local neighbourhood loyalties and interpret their struggle through the prism of protection of their local communities. Once they had shared experience of protracted violent actions and everyday exposure to danger the IRA members also developed lasting micro-group bonds with other volunteers. In a very similar vein, the VRS recruits joined their military organisation with the view that they were defending their families, friends, and local communities. Even though some of them had an opportunity to escape the military draft by travelling to Serbia or abroad they felt that such acts would undermine the moral standing and even safety of their families within their local communities. The shared battlefield experience enhanced these micro-level bonds which now incorporated not only the significant others from home but even more so the new comrades with whom they shared the everyday calamities of war. Hence in the combat zones the micro-level attachments and 'fighting for others' have regularly trumped self-interested behaviour. The micro-group bonding has proved more significant than the often-proclaimed ideological vistas such as 'united Ireland', 'anti-imperialism', 'anti-monarchism', and the 'creation of a Socialist Republic' in the case of IRA combatants or 'the protection of Serb nation', 'defence of Serbian Orthodox Christianity', or realising 'the project of all Serbs living in a single state' in the case of VRS soldiers.

None of this is to say that ideological power does not matter. On the contrary, ideology in general and nationalism in particular are potent legitimising forces that both of these military organisations invokes and relied on. The key tenets of nationalist ideology were utilised extensively by both the IRA and VRS to identify the common aims and ambitions for the military action. The key ideological creeds provided a necessary social glue for organisational cohesion and for leadership unity. The ideological narratives were also deployed to make a sense of the conflict and to legitimise the use of violence. The ideological penetration is important for justification of organisational goals and the hierarchical structures of decision making. Ideological principles legitimise the violent struggle and the organisational structures created to lead such a struggle. If combatants did not see such organisational hierarchies as legitimate they would not join these armed forces nor would they continue fighting in situations of extreme hardship. Hence the strength of all military organisations rests on their ability to develop coercive organisational capacity that is underpinned by a substantive degree of ideological legitimacy. For the ideological narratives to be recognisable and appealing to the ordinary combatants they have to successfully tap into the existing micro-level bonds. This 'translation' of micro-level solidarities into the ideological power of specific social organisations is sustained by strong organisational capacity. Nevertheless, even when organisational capacity is not at full strength, as was the case of the VRS where the structure of military organisation was ambiguous and lacked a degree of trust among ordinary recruits, the ideological envelopment of micro-solidarity can maintain the patterns of social pugnacity. Hence despite the pronounced organisational weaknesses, VRS soldiers continued to fight for their comrades and their families and friends back home.

This comparative analysis shows surprisingly that a small, clandestine, and insurgent movement such as the IRA can operate a more bureaucratic system of governance in a Weberian sense than a formal military organisation such as VRS. The IRA was more formalised, had a better developed system of command and control, was more disciplined and had a more elaborate division of labour than its more regular military counterpart, VRS. In some respects, this was linked to the asymmetrical power structure under which the IRA had to operate – the dominance of the British security apparatus and more powerful military and police forces present in Northern Ireland together with the continuous surveillance and intelligence gathering on IRA activities. Therefore, the republican movement would not have lasted so long if it had not been structured as an efficient, centralised, yet flexible entity that operated according to legal-rational mode of authority. Being a relatively small military organisation, the IRA was also more successful in utilising the existing micro-level bonds to enhance its organisational capacity. In direct contrast, the VRS's organisational weaknesses proved a major obstacle for increasing ideological penetration within the micro-level bonds. The ultimate outcome of this organisational failure was the near collapse of the VRS in 1995 (see Chapter 8).

The combat zone is a dangerous, unpredictable, and unstable social environment that moulds human behaviour. However, the combatants' willingness to fight is not determined by their individual choices but by the wider social dynamics. The combatant does not arrive at the battlefield as a tabula rasa, an individual automaton that reacts to the external stimuli. Instead, combatants are already influenced by their previous experiences of life with other people that is framed by specific organisational and ideological legacies. They also do not fight alone but with other combatants with whom they share a strong sense of emotional and moral attachment. The combatants also reflect on their future and the possibility of not ever seeing again their family members, close friends, and lovers. All of these complex past, present, and potential future social experiences shape the attitudes and behaviour in the combat zone. The combatants, just as other human beings, are creatures defined by their sociability. Social pugnacity is rarely if ever a fight for oneself but primarily a fight for significant others.

8 Organisational Power and Social Cohesion on the Battlefield

8.1 Introduction

Most scholars and military practitioners agree that social cohesion plays a crucial role on the battlefield. If soldiers do not trust their comrades and officers, they are unlikely to fight well or at all. Nevertheless, there is no agreement on the question: What are the key sources of group cohesion? Some authors emphasise the psychological variables and focus on the cognitive aspects of in-group bonding while others identify shared social action and professional performance as the principal causes of the willingness to fight. In this chapter I question the centrality of these two explanatory paradigms by shifting the debate towards the structural contexts. More specifically I argue that the success or failure of micro-level social cohesion is determined by its relationship with organisational power. In other words, social cohesion is rarely an autonomous phenomenon that can be completely divorced from the organisational capacity of armed forces. In many cases these two are mutually interdependent processes the workings of which often determine the long-term trajectories of a particular conflict. By zooming in on the case studies of the Croatian Army (HV) and the Bosnian Serb Army (VRS) during the 1991–5 Wars of Yugoslav Succession, I show how unit cohesion and social pugnacity are enhanced and sustained by organisational development. Hence, despite the initial similarities in the level of fighting motivation in the armies, the long-term structural input proved decisive for military success: the HV maintained strong army-wide networks of micro-group solidarity and won the war whereas the VRS never developed such models of social cohesion and ultimately lost large swaths of territory finding itself on the verge of complete collapse. The different experiences of these two military organisations indicate clearly that social cohesion and social pugnacity are not just psychological phenomena defined by the micro-level social action but are a long-term processes regularly shaped by the wider structural forces.

8.2 The Sources of Social Cohesion

Recent debates on the sources of social unity in the military have largely focused on the significance of the so-called standard model of military group cohesion (Siebold 2007). This model differentiates between task cohesion and social cohesion. Task cohesion refers to the 'shared commitment among members to achieving a goal that requires the collective efforts of the group' (MacCoun and Hix 2010: 139). The focus here is on a shared common goal and motivation to act as a team in finding the best way to attain that shared aim. In contrast, social cohesion is a phenomenon associated with the mutual affinity between members of a military unit. It is a phenomenon that relates to 'the extent to which group members like each other, prefer to spend their social time together, enjoy each other's company, and feel emotionally close to one another' (MacCoun and Hix 2015: 139). The standard model also distinguishes between horizontal and vertical cohesion whereby the former entails bonding between ordinary soldiers within the crew, squad, or platoon while the latter refers to attachments involving individuals across hierarchical chains of command (leaders and their subordinates) (Griffith 1988). Some scholars also identify another layer of cohesion – the organisational cohesion which relates to 'the members of the group and the next higher command level' and the institutional cohesion involving bonds 'between the members of the group and the larger institution of which it is a small part' such as an army, air force of the navy (Siebold 2011: 458). Many military psychologists and some sociologists argue that this standard model of military group cohesion can explain the willingness and efficacy of fighting in the combat zone. In particular they focus on the strength and weaknesses of the unit level cohesion (Siebold 2007, 2011; Stewart 1991: 89–120; Winslow 1997: 57–68). The most influential representative of this position, Guy L. Siebold insists that peer bonding is 'the essence of military group cohesion'. For Siebold (1999, 2011: 449) group cohesiveness is defined as 'the degree to which mechanisms of social control operant in a unit maintain a structured pattern of social relationships between unit members, individually and collectively necessary to achieve its purpose'. In other words, military group cohesion relates to 'the extent to which the members come together to form the group and hold together under stress to maintain the group' (Siebold 2011: 450).

Psychological studies of cohesion explore the relationship between group unity and military performance (Beal et al. 2003; Chiocchio and Essiembre 2009; MacCoun and Hix 2010; Siebold 2011). Their findings indicate that the two phenomena are strongly linked. However, as

MacCoun and Hix (2010) emphasise, the link is weighted towards the performance rather than cohesion: it is successful performance that enhances unit cohesion rather than cohesion being a precondition of effective military performance. Some of these studies also found that task cohesion was a better predictor of military performance than other forms of military cohesion (Chiocchio and Essiembre 2009; MacCoun and Hix 2010). Other psychological research downplays task cohesion and emphasises the intensity of group ties. For example, Siebold (2011: 451) argues that there is no need to differentiate between social and task cohesion as tasks only relate to the activities of the group:

this conceptualization of cohesion does not need to distinguish social cohesion from task cohesion ... In contrast, this conceptualization separates the cohesion of the group (including the trust between the members and their capacity for coordinated action) from the action or tasks of the group itself. The success or failure of the group action or tasks in turn feeds back into the group cohesiveness.

In this context the focus shifts towards different layers of group cohesion – the primary group cohesion involving peer and leader bonding and secondary group cohesion relating to institutional and organisational bonding. Both layers of cohesion entail bonds built on trust and long-term cooperation (Siebold 2007).

Other researchers have questioned these findings and even more the psychological interpretations of the impact military unit cohesion has on fighting performance. The earlier critics such as Madej (1978) and Bartov (1992: 29–58) focused their attention on the role of military skill and ideology respectively while downplaying the unit cohesion. As discussed in the previous chapter, Omer Bartov's analysis of Wehrmacht soldiers' letters, diaries and memoirs showed that due to enormous battlefield fatalities many military units did not have time to build long-term bonds and they still fought relentlessly until the end. Victor Madej's research has also raised doubts about the relationship between cohesion and performance. However, for Madej ideology was not as important as military skill, discipline, and the superior organisation all of which increased the fighting capacity of the Wehrmacht. Other critics have emphasised the pragmatism of soldiers and material benefits (Collier 2000; Moskos 1975; Ross 2006).

Nevertheless, the most sophisticated recent critique of the standard model of military cohesion was articulated by Anthony King (2006, 2007, 2013, 2014). King develops an alternative, sociologically grounded, explanation of military performance that downplays psychological variables and centres on social action. King has shifted the debate from motivation towards performance. In his view, rather than treating interpersonal motivation as being a synonym for combat performance, it is necessary to clearly differentiate between these two phenomena as high group motivation does not necessarily result in effective performance. If unit cohesion is prioritised over military tasks, it can in fact be counterproductive to organisational aims. There are many examples from the history of warfare when armies lost battles precisely because their soldiers were more loyal to their squads, platoons, and companies than to the war goals of their military forces (Fuller 1990; Janis 1985; Wilcox 2016; Winslow 1997). For example, during the First World War both Italian and French militaries experienced defeats with soldiers demonstrating greater attachment to their units than to the military aims of their respective armies as a whole (Fuller 1990; Wilcox 2016).

The porous link between performance and cohesion is also visible in the cases where soldiers demonstrate high motivation to fight while having weak social ties within their military units. The typical examples include the private military contractors and highly specialised soldiers operating advanced military technology while working alone or in very small teams of professionals (fighter pilots, military drone operators, aerial sensor operators, etc.) (Boyle 2020; Singer 2004). Hence King questions the idea that greater social cohesion inevitably leads to better military performance. He argues that the standard model of military group cohesion cannot account for the complexity of social behaviour on the battlefield. More specifically King insists that the conventional, psychological, understanding of cohesion has to be redefined in order to capture its dynamic quality. In other words, for King (2013: 36) cohesion is not only about 'inter-personal attraction' but primarily about 'the successful coordination of actions' in the combat zone. In his words: 'Cohesion refers to the ability of the soldiers in an infantry platoon to act together and to achieve their mission in the face of the enemy; cohesion is demonstrated when soldiers are able to shoot, move, and seek cover together or in mutually supportive ways … cohesion refers to collective combat performance itself.' Being firmly grounded in the neo-Durkheimian tradition King does not reject the significance of social cohesion. On the contrary he is adamant that group unity is integral to all military activity. However, he completely reconceptualises cohesion: instead of psychological affinity between individuals cohesion is redefined as a Parsonian collective action: 'To extrapolate from Parsons, it might be claimed that cohesion refers most accurately to collective action itself, and specifically, to successful collective performance, not to sentiments which encourage that performance' (King 2013: 37).

The contributors to this ongoing debate have all made important and insightful interventions. There is no doubt that researchers should focus on the role that performance, cognitions, and emotional attachments to one's comrades play in the formation of social cohesion. However, to fully understand the changing dynamics of micro-solidarity and its impact on social fighting one has to widen this debate. The question of why soldiers fight cannot be reduced to a rather narrow set of variables such as the psychology of interpersonal attraction or the military performance itself. Firstly, both of these perspectives, the motivation and performance focused models, are overly instrumentalist in the sense that they aim to provide a diagnosis of a social phenomenon by looking exclusively at its military value. In other words, rather than exploring military units and small group cohesion as particular forms of group dynamics, the emphasis has been firmly on how these processes contribute to the performance of the military goals. In this context, and despite their pronounced differences, the two dominant perspectives are quite similar in that they both single out military efficiency as the ultimate telos of this process. However, to fully understand why soldiers, or other human beings for that matter, fight, one has to move away from such a narrow focus on military utility. Whether we explore the nature of social ties or we look at the social dynamics of performance, in both cases one is bound to analyse universal social processes that involve activities that are not unique to the military. Both performance and peer bonding are universal phenomena present in a variety of social contexts. The research on the behaviour of soldiers, revolutionaries, terrorists, *génocidaires*, insurgents and guerrilla fighters, rioters, members of militias and paramilitary units, violent gangsters, and many other groups involved in social fighting shows clearly that they exhibit many very similar social features (Collins 2008, Della Porta 2013; Lawson 2019; Malešević 2017; Tilly 2003; Üngör 2020). To capture this rich social dynamics of fighting it is necessary to move away from the focus on narrow military utility. Any attempt to explain the willingness to fight entails engaging with standard sociological processes that are far from being the sole prerogative of the military. As argued throughout this book, social pugnacity is a universal social phenomenon that takes a variety of guises. Since the dynamics of fighting is shaped by different historical, cultural, and social processes it is also a highly variable experience. In this context, the overemphasis on military efficacy and exceptionality is unlikely to help shed light on this universal human experience.

Secondly, both of these dominant approaches are also similar in the sense that they tend to privilege micro over macro contexts. Whereas the interpersonal motivation approach singles out a variety of psychological variables as crucial for understanding group bonding, the performance-centred perspective zooms in on micro-level social action. Nevertheless, any attempt to understand small group dynamics without analysing the broader structural and historical contexts is bound to be reductionist and incomplete. The key feature of any such small unit is the fact that it operates and exists within a large-scale social organisation (e.g., military, revolutionary movement, system of militias and paramilitaries, death squad, insurgency, etc.) that itself interacts with other social organisations (e.g., the state, other militaries, private corporations, religious institutions, international bodies, etc.). In this context both performance and interpersonal bonding are inevitably influenced and shaped by the wider structural forces, including the organisational and ideological currents of specific militaries and other coercive organisations (Malešević 2017; Mann 1993, 2012; Üngör 2020; Wilson 2020). Just as motivation for fighting cannot be reduced to individual choices, the same applies to small group action. Neither interpersonal attraction nor collective performance can develop and take hold without the larger organisational structures. Soldiers or guerrilla fighters can increase their fighting capability through enhanced interpersonal bonds or through shared social action, but both of these processes only happen in the context of violent conflicts initiated and waged by specific macro-level organisations – the state, the paramilitaries, the guerrilla movements, the regular armies, and so on.

Thirdly, these two dominant perspectives focus almost exclusively on the contemporary experience of Western military organisations and as such are unable to account for the sheer diversity of combat experience across time and space (Haldén 2018; Käihkö 2018). As Käihkö (2018: 571) emphasises, there is a need to engage with 'the armed groups that are non-Western, non-state, and non-modern' as 'most armed groups currently waging war [throughout the world] belong to the first two categories' while the analysis of historical cases from different periods of time can help us recognise the enormous diversity of human experience with fighting. Haldén (2018) develops a similar argument in the historical context: the overused examples of the US and British militaries do not tell us much about the historical variety of military cohesion and even less about the historical trajectories of social change. Instead analysing the social dynamics of early medieval war bands as well as modern militias and guerrillas in Africa, South America, and Southeast Asia can help us explain better the historical context and cultural variability of fighting. As argued in the next chapter both the collective performance and the intersubjective affinities of combatants are historically and culturally variable. Although human beings share similar emotional, cognitive, and moral characteristics and capacities they express them differently and different violent experiences generate diverse patterns of social pugnacity in the combat zone.

These three shortcomings of the dominant perspectives in the study of social cohesion are rooted in the conventional understanding that the unity of large-scale military organisations depends solely on the psychological and the micro-social foundations of individuals that compose military units. However, for much of human history it was the social structures that have proved central in sustaining and in some cases even generating micro-level solidarities (Malešević 2013, 2017: 285–92). Hence, rather than emerging spontaneously from below, group cohesion has often been nurtured and maintained from above.

This is not to say that the networks of solidarity can be created at will or simply engineered at the top of a particular military establishment. Instead, the most successful organisations develop social mechanisms that tap into the existing pockets of micro-solidarity and link them to their wider organisational aims. Sometimes this process involves deliberate manipulation and even intentional deceit but, in most cases, it emerges and operates as regular organisational dynamics centred on maintaining and expanding the influence and reach of a specific organisation. As these processes unfold and as organisations grow and expand, the direction of existing micro-level solidarities regularly changes. The most efficient organisations, such as nation-states or large-scale religious organisations, influential social movements, and even some private corporations have historically proved highly capable of linking micro-level solidarities with their organisational aims. For example, the nation-state has been established as the dominant model of territorial organisation in modernity by successfully combining its organisational capacity with the ideological power of nationalism. In this context, the nation-states utilise the emotional imagery of face-to-face group interaction by projecting kinship and friendship metaphors onto the wider organisational plane. Hence, rather than asking citizens to fulfil specific organisational demands necessary for the survival of that organisation, the representatives of nation-states regularly invoke familiar kinship and friendship-based images of the need to make sacrifice for the honour of one's motherland or to protect 'our brothers and sisters' (Malešević 2013: 81–7). Similarly, clandestine political organisations from Euskadi Ta Askatasuna (ETA), the Liberation Tigers of Tamil Eelam, and the Provisional IRA to Al-Qaeda and ISIS have all ideologically framed their military activities in the language of micro-solidarity. Hence while ETA, LTTE, and PIRA invoke the notion of shared ethnic community (our Basque, Tamil, or Irish comrades respectively), Al-Qaeda Central

(Al Qaida fi al Khorassan) and ISIS make constant references to the brotherhood and sisterhood of umma.

The dominance of micro-sociological and psychological approaches in the study of military cohesion is also rooted in the near universal perception that human sociability is a given and an automatic phenomenon. Psychologists such as Siebold see group bonding as an intrinsic feature of human life. He defines bonding as 'the social relationship, both affective and instrumental, of changeable strength (weak to strong) between service members and their group, organization, and service institution. The locus of bonding is in the relationship, not in the actions or interactions between the service member and the group, organization, or institution, although such actions or interactions are influenced by and feed back into the relationship' (Siebold 2007: 288). He is explicit in conceptualising sociability as something that has an 'essence' which is manifested in psychological ties that individuals develop with each other within a group: 'The essence of strong primary group cohesion, which I believe to be generally agreed on, is trust among group members (e.g., to watch each other's back) together with the capacity for teamwork (e.g., pulling together to get the task or job done)' (Siebold 2007: 288). This perspective is deeply problematic as it reifies and essentialises social action. Instead of understanding human beings as dynamic creatures the tendency is to presume the existence of psychologically given 'human nature' and inflexible and biologically given social bonds (Käihkö 2016: 6; 2018; Malešević 2017: 286–7). In this sense the micro-sociological perspective as developed by King and others is a major improvement. King (2007: 641) rightly argues that if cohesion is understood as 'emotional essence, which pre-exists practice' then it is impossible to observe and analyse the changing dynamics of social bonds. Nevertheless, despite these valuable criticisms King's functionalist micro-sociology is also wedded to an overly ahistorical and thus static notion of group sociability. There is no doubt that cohesion is developed and maintained through social action, as argued by King, but social action cannot be reduced solely to the military performance of combatants. Instead, sociability is a historical and structural phenomenon that is shaped by the organisational legacies over longer periods of time.

Since both Siebold and King perceive humans as intrinsically social they inevitably subscribe to the view that micro-level cohesion precedes organisational unity. However, as recent studies from primatology and paleo-anthropology indicate, this is a highly problematic assumption. Turner and Maryanski (2008: 135–67) and Turner and Stets (2005: 20–35) show that the early humans were quite far from being the gregarious species traditionally depicted. These studies emphasise pronounced differences between apes and monkeys. Whereas monkeys are generally highly social this is not the case with gorillas, chimps, or orang-utans who are more solitary creatures. Turner and Maryanski (2008) see this as an evolutionary strategy for long-term survival. In contrast to most other simians who continued living in trees that were relatively safe and rich with fruits, and as such could sustain large packs, the savannah-roaming apes had to disperse in order to survive. Hence our predecessors, the walking apes who emerged in the African savannah, developed very weak social ties between adults. Hence, in order to gather enough food and to avoid dangerous predators, the early humans tended to move in very small and highly flexible groupings. For millions of years our predecessors lived in tiny foraging bands whose membership was highly fluid and changeable. In this context, sociability develops quite late in human evolution: rather than originally living in 'primary groups' human beings have become fully-fledged social beings only with the development of social organisations (Malešević 2017: 41–66; Mann 1986).

The key point here is that group cohesion, whether in terms of psychological bonds or joint social action, is not intrinsic to human beings. Rather than emerging as an automatic or innate response to an external threat, the social cohesion of military units is often a structural product – the outcome of long-term organisational and ideological processes. With the rise of permanent state structures 10–12,000 years ago, organisational power has become decisive in forging, maintaining, and enhancing human sociability (Mann 1986). The proliferation of imperial polities and religious proto ideologies in the last 5,000 years has contributed substantially towards the development of permanent settlements where human beings could establish stronger kinship and residential networks (Burbank and Cooper 2010; Kumar 2017, 2021). These structural changes often went hand in hand with the ideological transformations that fostered the idea that human beings are naturally gregarious creatures. This idea was further entrenched and radicalised with the rise of Renaissance humanism, the Enlightenment, and Romanticism. With nation-states gradually replacing empires as the dominant mode of territorial rule in the world the organisational power has further increased. With the ever-expanding infrastructural capacities of states individuals have become caged in its organisational webs (Mann 1986, 1993, 2012).

Nevertheless, this is not to say that social structures completely determine social action. On the contrary, since human beings are not naturally gregarious creatures all social organisations have to commit a lot of energy and resources to maintain organisational unity. This is usually achieved by successfully tapping into the micro-level solidarities and depicting the large-scale organisations as one's close friends, family members, lovers, and cherished comrades. Military and other violent organisations are no exception. Instead of just relying on 'natural psychological affinities' or shared group performance they devote a great deal of attention to forging, maintaining, and harvesting micro-group solidarities for organisational ends. None of this is to deny the genuine emotional ties that individuals develop in platoons or squads. The point is that such bonds are rarely if ever only the result of natural human reactions but are something that also has a strong organisational underpinning. Thus, to provide a more complete explanation of social cohesion and social pugnacity it is crucial to explore how social organisations such as the armed forces develop, maintain, and use different organisational and ideological mechanisms to create or enhance micro-level solidarity.

Although both King and Siebold recognise the significance of military organisation in helping forge micro-level attachments they still see social cohesion largely as a bottom-up phenomenon. For example, Siebold (2011: 455) argues that 'the primary group cohesion model' trumps 'the secondary group cohesion model' meaning that 'military cohesion was best assessed at the small group level such as the squad (about ten members) or platoon (a little over thirty members)'. King, too, identifies the platoon as the epicentre of solidarity although as a neo-Durkheimian he distinguishes between the mechanical solidarity of traditional militaries and the organic solidarity of the modern armed forces: 'in contrast to the mechanical solidarity of the infantry platoon in the citizens army unified by its common social background, the professional platoon is united by professional ethos and its functional interdependence' (King 2013: 357). The problem with both of these accounts is that they are oblivious to the central role that structural forces play in this process. Rather than assuming that the military organisations just bring the 'natural' micro-level solidarities together it is paramount to explore how and when social organisations are capable of facilitating formation of group cohesion at the top. In other words, there is nothing natural and self-evident in group formation: all forms of group solidarity entail substantial organisational work.

The main issue for all organisations, including the military, is to make an organisational unit resemble a naturalised social group. Hence one's analytical gaze should be firmly on this structural process whereby bureaucratic units became normalised as human groups. For example, Siebold's model of the 'primary group' does not differentiate clearly between groups and military units. In contrast to squads or platoons, which are formal organisational units constructed and maintained by bureaucratic mechanisms of specific military organisations, groups are informal, dynamic, and variable entities. While membership in any platoon is dependent on the organisational needs of the military and as such largely random (i.e., almost any recruit can inhabit any platoon), group membership is built on a personal sense of attachment between individuals. Hence, whereas a platoon is a bureaucratic and interchangeable unit of military organisation, group membership is built around emotional and friendship ties. While the former is valued for its organisational functionality, professional detachment, and military utility, the latter entails personal loyalties, emotional attachments, and a sense of care and responsibility. Thus, rather than simply assuming that platoons operate as 'primary groups' it is important to analyse how military organisations succeed in transforming 'cold' bureaucratic units into naturalised 'warm' entities with kin-like properties. This is far from being an automatic process. Instead, any attempt to naturalise and normalise administrative units into 'primary groups' faces major internal and external obstacles and requires a great deal of organisational and ideological work.

Some armed forces have developed a variety of organisational mechanisms aimed at forging and then utilising micro-group attachments for military purposes. One such programme is the US Army's COHORT system which is centred on linking micro-group bonding to military performance by keeping the same soldiers 'together from the initial training through overseas tours to discharge (or reenlistment)' (Knickerbocker 1982: 1–3). The COHORT system was created in the 1980s in order to 'develop a unit personnel replacement model that will give the army more cohesive, and better trained soldiers, who have confidence in each other, and who will be more likely to withstand the intensity of the first battle of the next war' (Pully and Tatum 1988: 8). Another successful US Army initiative developed along similar lines is the Buddy Team Enlistment Option which is designed for the simultaneous recruitment and joint training of up to five friends. As explained on its website this programme is created only for new recruits whereby 'a recruit and his or her friends may enlist in the same Military Occupational Specialty (MOS) and attend Basic Combat Training (BCT) and Advanced Individual Training (AIT) at the same time'[1] (Powers 2016: 1–2).

Other military organisations, including British and French armed forces, have developed similar programmes either to encourage military

---

[1] See www.goarmy.com/benefits/additional-incentives/buddy-team.html.

recruitment or to better integrate individuals into the military structure. For example, British SAS troops have traditionally used the 'four-man module, two pairs of "buddies"' structure (Ladd 1986: 104). Furthermore, militaries have also changed their policies in theatres of war whereby the weapons that have traditionally been manned by a single individual (e.g., anti-aircraft systems) are now operated by several soldiers thus benefiting from micro-group cohesion. As Collins (2008: 56) points out:

> Group-operated weapons rely on solidarity at the most micro level; the effective combat team is one in which the soldiers are paying attention to each other more than to the enemy. Group-oriented weapons are important, then, not so much because of a specific technology but because they facilitate a mood of solidarity ... group-operated weapons facilitate troops falling into an interaction ritual with each other, entraining their bodies into a collective enterprise and a common rhythm [thus inspiring ...] the confidence and enthusiasm to fire even when others succumb to the debilitating tension of combat.

There is no doubt that the soldiers operating such weapons experience a genuine sense of attachment to each other. However, the key issue here is that this sense of micro-level solidarity is largely generated and maintained by the military organisation itself.

In all of these cases one can clearly see the crucial role organisations play in fostering, developing, and sustaining micro-level solidarities. Hence, social cohesion is not an inherent property of human life but something that often entails a great deal of organisational and ideological work. One of the key arguments of this chapter is that social cohesion on the battlefield and social pugnacity depend more on the integration of the micro-social dynamics with the wider organisational structure than on simple psychological affinities or shared performance. To explore how this process works in practice and to provide some validation of the main argument it is necessary to develop specific case studies. Hence, I compare and contrast the structural dynamics of social cohesion in two armed forces: the Croatian Army (*Hrvatska Vojska*) and the Bosnian Serb Army (*Vojska Republike Srpske*).

8.3   Military Organisations in the Yugoslav Wars of Succession

The breakup of Yugoslavia in a series of wars (1991–9) has received a great deal of scholarly attention. However, researchers have largely focused on the geopolitical picture by zooming in on the collapse of state socialism, the end of the Cold War, the uneven processes of democratisation, the rise of nationalist mobilisation, and the role of political elites in fomenting violence (Baker 2015; Gagnon 2004; Malešević 2002; Ramet 2006). The establishment in 1993 of the UN International Criminal Tribunal for the former Yugoslavia (ICTY), responsible for prosecuting serious crimes committed during the wars, shifted the analytical focus towards the human rights violations that took place during these wars. Scholars have studied the key perpetrators of war crimes and have also examined the experiences of victims and survivors of genocide and ethnic cleansing. With the availability of extensive documentation collected for these trials, researchers have produced an abundance of valuable studies on the role of political leaders and paramilitary organisations in the crimes committed during the war (Baker 2015; Gordy 2013; Vukušić 2019). However, there has not been much systematic research focusing on the behaviour of ordinary soldiers during the war, and there is still a paucity of evidence on their motivations and actions in the combat zone. Moreover, it is not clear how and why the dynamics of social pugnacity changed during the war. The analysis of interviews with former soldiers of the Croatian Army (HV) and the Bosnian Serb Army (VRS) will help us shed more light on this issue.

The wars in Croatia and Bosnia and Herzegovina were deeply entangled. What in March 1991 started as a conflict between the Yugoslav People's Army (*Jugoslavenska Narodna Armija*, JNA) and the Croatian Army (*Hrvatska Vojska*, HV) was by April 1992 transformed into an all-out war involving a number of additional warring parties: the Bosnian Serb Army (*Vojska Republike Srpske*, VRS), the Serbian Army of Krajina (*Srpska Vojska Krajine*, SVK), the Croatian Council of Defence (*Hrvatsko Vijeće Obrane*, HVO), the Army of Bosnia and Herzegovina (Armija Bosne i Hercegovine, ABH), the People's Defence of Western Bosnia (*Narodna Odbrana Zapadne Bosne*, NOZB), and numerous paramilitary formations. Military alliances shifted during the war according to the changing priorities of political leaders. Initially, the Croatian and Bosnian militaries (HV, HVO, and ABH) fought together against various Serb military formations (JNA, VRS, SVK). However, from October 1992 to February 1994, Croatian and Bosnian military organisations were at war with each other throughout Bosnia and Herzegovina. This war came to an end in March 1994 with the signing of the Washington Agreement, and the former adversaries were united again in fighting the Serb military formations. In August 1995, HV initiated Operation Storm that resulted in the complete defeat of SVK and also undermined the capacity of VRS to control much of its territory in North-western Bosnia. This military operation forced Serb political and military leaders to agree to a comprehensive peace agreement in Dayton, Ohio in November 1995 which officially ended the wars in Bosnia and Herzegovina and Croatia (Baker 2015; Gagnon 2004; Malešević and Ó Dochartaigh 2018).

For much of this period (1991–5), Croatian (HV) and Bosnian Serb (VRS) armies were the largest and best-armed military organisations involved in the two violent conflicts: the VRS had between 80,000 and 120,000 soldiers while, by the end of the war, the HV numbered over 250,000 soldiers (Divjak 2001: 155; Milovanović 2011: 5–7; Špegelj 2001: 32; Žunec et al. 2013: 33). These two armies were based in two different countries (Bosnia and Herzegovina, and Croatia) which were officially not at war with each other.[2] Nevertheless, for much of the war, they were direct opponents. The most intensive periods of confrontation between these two military organisations include 1992, when the two armies clashed in Northern Bosnia and Western Herzegovina, and the second half of 1995, when HV together with the Army of Bosnia and Herzegovina defeated Serbian troops and captured much of North-western Bosnia leading to ceasefire and the end of the Croatian and Bosnian wars.[3] The two military organisations were established and strived to implement mutually exclusive ideological goals. The principal aim of the HV was to liberate the whole of Croatia, initially from the JNA and later from its direct offshoot, SVK. In addition, HV was involved either directly or indirectly (through its sibling organisation, HVO) in the Bosnian conflict aimed at carving out a separate territory for Croats living in Bosnia and Herzegovina. In that process it fought both the VRS and the ABH. In contrast, VRS's principal war aim was to establish a territory within Bosnia and Herzegovina that would be inhabited and dominated by the Serbian majority which then could join Serbia or rump Yugoslavia. However, despite these contrasting ambitions, both military organisations were ideologically driven by similar ethno-nationalist principles aimed at creating states for their respective ethnic groups while trampling the rights of minority groups or actively aiming to eradicate minorities from the territories under their control. The two militaries

[2] Although HV's main adversary was the Serbian Army of Krajina (SVK) the two Serbian military forces were both offshoots of JNA and as such were largely financed and supplied by the Belgrade based central command of the Yugoslav Army (Vojska Jugoslavije). The government of rump Yugoslavia (Savezna Republika Jugoslavija) provided $4.73 billion to the governments of breakaway Serbian regions most of which went for the financing of VRS and VSK (Cigar 2001: 210). In addition, both VSK and VRS fought against HV. As Žunec et al. (2013: 22) rightly point out, JNA, VRS, SVK, and VJ were all in a political sense part of the same military.

[3] In 1995 HV captured 4,000 kilometres of land that was controlled by VRS (Cigar 2001: 223).

largely relied on ordinary conscripts to fill their ranks. Hence, VRS was created in May 1992 as the military force of the Bosnian Serb state (*Republika Srpska*). It was composed of the small number of Bosnian Serb officers who served in the JNA and the young Bosnian Serb recruits who were required to undertake mandatory military service. In this context former JNA officers born in Bosnia and Herzegovina together with the conscripts and other military personnel operating on the territory of Bosnia and Herzegovina (i.e., Territorial Defence and some paramilitary groupings) were all integrated into the VRS. As the war intensified, the VRS called up individuals from the JNA reserve forces under Bosnian Serb control. The army also accepted a number of volunteers, but their proportion rarely exceed more than 2 per cent of all soldiers (Milovanović 2011). The VRS also inherited a substantial number of weapons from the JNA: up to 800 tanks, 4,000 mortars and artillery weapons, up to 100 aircrafts and 50 helicopters.

The Croatian Army (HV) was formally constituted in September 1991. It developed out of an armed semi-police force National Guards (*Zbor Narodne Garde*, ZNG) which was created in April 1991. Initially, the HV was composed of volunteers and conscripts with the officer corps combining defectors from the JNA, police officers, Croatian born officers and soldiers from the French Legion and other foreign military organisations. By May 1991, the armed forces consisted of 60,000 soldiers including 3,017 officers who defected from JNA (Špegelj 2001; Žunec et al. 2013). Although initially the new military had a chronic shortage of weaponry and resources, it gradually acquired some weapons by successfully occupying JNA military depots and garrisons in Croatia and by importing weaponry from abroad. By 1995 HV had expanded substantially with up to 250,000 soldiers and a well-established system of command and control throughout Croatian territory. A large majority of HV soldiers were also conscripted, although CA had more volunteers than BSA (Špegelj 2001; Žunec et al. 2013). In addition to fighting a largely defensive war in Croatia, HV was also involved in the offensive war in Bosnia and Herzegovina directly or indirectly by providing organisational support, weaponry, officers, soldiers, and finance to its 'sister' army – the Croatian Council of Defence (*Hrvatsko Vijeće Obrane*, HVO). Although starting on a back foot, HV developed gradually into a strong military force which in December 1991 recaptured large parts of western Slavonia and by 1995 defeated VRS (and VSK) and in this process acquired control over most of Croatia and substantive parts of Bosnia and Herzegovina.

By looking at the origins and development of these two military organisations one would expect the VRS to be a much more effective and cohesive force than the HV. For one thing VRS was the direct successor of the Yugoslav People's Army which at its peak was considered to be one of the largest military forces in Europe[4] while HV was for the most part an ad hoc-created entity that emerged in the midst of war (Gow 1992; Špegelj 2001; Žunec et al. 2013: 52). For another thing, unlike HV which had little military expertise and a chronic shortage of weaponry and resources, VRS started off as a much better equipped and professionally trained force, at the core of which were highly skilled former JNA officers. In this context the expectation was that the VRS would be a more powerful and more efficient military organisation capable of defeating its organisationally weaker adversary. Nevertheless, the outcome of the 1991–5 war showed otherwise: it was HV that ultimately proved victorious.

Why this outcome? There are many explanations for this trajectory of war ranging from the wider geopolitical factors, to economic and ideological reasons. Many analysts have focused on the role of the EU, US, and other Western governments in providing political, economic, and military support for Croatia while the Serbian government received only lukewarm backing from its international allies (e.g., Russia, Greece, and China) without receiving any concrete help. Others have emphasised the economic collapse that Serbia faced during the war with the UN imposed embargo from April 1992 to October 1995 which resulted in the dramatic fall of production, wages, and living standards and unprecedented hyperinflation all of which had an impact on the direction of military operations.[5] Some commentators have identified the ideological divide that had a substantial impact on the war with Serbia being governed by the ex-communists while the Serbian controlled regions in Bosnia and Croatia were ruled by radical right-wing politicians. This ideological polarisation was particularly visible in the latter stages of the war when Milošević's government was involved in political conflicts with the Bosnian and Croatian Serb leaders the result of which was the temporarily imposed blockade on the Bosnian Serb leadership (Špegelj 2001; Tus 2001; Žunec 2001). The Serbian society was also deeply divided on the military activities outside of Serbia with some opposition groups protesting against the war, or the direction the war was taking, while others rejected the draft notices. As Backović et al. (2001: 336) show, 'there was

---

[4] As Žunec et al. 2013 (2013: 52) document, JNA's peacetime force was composed of 250,000 soldiers while the wartime size of the military force was between 1 and 1.5 million.

[5] For a comprehensive review of different theories aiming to explain the collapse of Socialist Federal Republic Yugoslavia see Jović (2001).

mass draft dodging' among young men called up to serve in the military operations: 'in a closed session of the Assembly of Serbia, it was announced that the response of reservists in Serbia as a whole was 50 per cent, but in Belgrade only 15 per cent'. Furthermore 12,000 individuals were charged for draft dodging in 1991 alone while up to 150,000 had moved abroad to escape the draft.[6]

While all these factors certainly contributed to the outcome of the war, what has largely been neglected is the changing dynamics of social cohesion and pugnacity on the battlefields. I argue that HV won in part because it was able to generate and then utilise the social cohesion of its forces in a much more effective way than VRS. In this context HV soldiers were substantially more motivated to fight than their counterparts in VRS (and SVK). Nevertheless, this is not to say that the soldiers of VRS had no strong micro-level attachments. On the contrary, in the early days of war many VRS platoons and companies displayed a strong sense of comradeship and some of this micro-solidarity was maintained throughout the war. However, unlike HV which proved capable of utilising the organisational and ideological capacities to foster and enhance social cohesion during the course of the war, VRS did not develop adequate organisational mechanisms to stimulate or utilise the small unit solidarity of its soldiers. Hence as the war unfolded, HV was able to gradually create conditions for the organisational enhancement of social cohesion whereas VRS lagged behind and ultimately never established such an organisational structure.

8.4   VRS and HV Compared

The conventional views see the victory of HV as being rooted in the character of war it waged: the defensive war for the independence of a country attacked by powerful external forces. In this narrative VRS and SVK are regularly perceived as aggressors engaged in territorial conquest (Špegelj 2001; Tus 2001). However, these views tend to simplify what was a highly complex and at times contradictory conflict. For example, HV was also involved in the territorial conquest in Bosnia and Herzegovina while VRS was perceived by much of the Serb population living in Republika Srpska as a defensive force standing in opposition to ever threatening NATO forces, the expanding HV and the emerging

---

[6] The former military leaders from both warring sides (HV's General Martin Špegelj and JNA/JA General Veljko Kadijević) agree that the poor mobilisation levels in Serbia and the Serbian controlled areas of Bosnia and Croatia played an important role in the direction of the war. See Špegelj (2001) and Kadijević (1993: 23–91).

Army of Bosnia and Herzegovina (ABiH). These views are reflected in the interviews with the ex-combatants on both sides. Both the HV and VRS former soldiers emphasise that they joined their respective military forces for similar reasons: to defend their country, people, place of residence, families, and friends. For example, former HV soldiers emphasise that they fought 'to protect my country, my town ... our town was attacked' (Saša HV); 'you feel you have to do something ... you fight for [your] life, your town and people around you ... my town was under attack' (Vlado HV); 'I was spurred by the patriotic feelings ... I was sorry for the children ... and I did not want that my child fights [in some future war]' (Vjeko HV). Very similar motives were present in the responses of the VRS soldiers: 'I volunteered to protect my mother and father' (Dragan1 VRS); 'the decisive issue was my realisation that our people are under threat' (Milan VRS); 'I felt it was my patriotic duty to fight' (Nenad VRS)' 'I had to defend my family' (Mile VRS).[7]

Another marked similarity in the initial experiences of the two armed forces' members was a strong sense of comradeship within the military units. In some instances, these intense micro-level attachments came from the fact that the soldiers knew each other before the war, and they joined the military together. In other cases, this in-group solidarity was generated through the shared experience of warfare. For example, many HV soldiers talk about their previous friendships: 'we were all-volunteer unit and more or less we all knew each other from before ... from the same neighbourhood ... we were troupe of friends ... we knew each other from school' (Saša HV); 'at the beginning we all knew each other, friends and such ... it looked as if we just moved from disco to the front ... we shared everything, helped each other as much as we could ... we were all like a family' (Vjeko HV). Other soldiers, who did not know their platoon members, talk about strong social ties forged in the war:

I was only 18 years old and had some friends from the childhood and such but in the first ten days, maybe even less, five to six days, I formed such strong ties with people that was unbelievable ... that you can be linked so much with the people that you know for only five days ... later this seemed normal to me ... we were dependent on each other ... if you don't trust a man next to you, he protects you while you sleep and if he runs away you are the first to die ... so you have to trust him ... our ties were really strong. (Ivan1 HV)

The initial experiences of VRS soldiers were very similar. Many of the conscripts were young men joining together: 'We were people of the

---

[7] The information on the methodology and data collection for this study is available in the Appendix.

same generation – 18, 19 years of age' (Milan VRS); 'we were the same generation, kids of the same age in the same shit' (Zoran VRS); 'we felt solidarity towards each other ... when somebody was injured ... everybody would look after him to do the best he can to help' (Dragan VRS). Just as with HV, the platoons of VRS were characterised by intense social ties that were forged in the shared experience of war: 'I was ready to die for them and they would do the same for me ... I would not be able to sleep otherwise' (Zoran 2 VRS); 'we were like brothers ... for 64 days I could not go home, there is no hygiene ... great friendships, you would not be able to survive without this ... I was carrying a wounded comrade ... they were shelling at us ... your life was in peril but you keep carrying him, if it hits you it hits you' (Zdravko VRS); '[shared difficulties] bring people together ... you develop these bonds, you help each other' (Saša VRS); 'there was always one for all ... usually 7 to 10 people together ... you felt you will give a life one for another, and that is how our relationships have developed' (Zoran VRS).

Although initially both militaries attracted substantial numbers of volunteers, some of whom were foreigners while others came from the diaspora, the composition of the two armed forces was quite similar: there was an overwhelming dominance of conscripts led by the former JNA professionals on both sides (Žunec et al. 2013). Although HV also relied on the National Guard volunteers, some of whom had a police background, and former French Foreign Legion soldiers, while VRS incorporated some paramilitaries, these individuals remained a small minority within each armed force. This quite similar starting position coupled with the VRS weapons superiority all mitigated against the HV victory. Yet HV ultimately prevailed as the dynamics of social cohesion in these two cases changed substantially over time. However, this was less linked to the character of war or the soldier's perception of progress made in war but primarily, I would argue, due to ability of one side to successfully utilise its organisational capacity to increase cohesion and social pugnacity. In other words, unlike VRS which for the most part proved incapable of generating or utilising pockets of locally based networks of micro-solidarity, HV gradually established a military force that forged and then successfully used the micro-level social cohesion of its units.

At the heart of this process were substantive structural changes. Although for much of 1991, Croatian defence consisted of mostly disorganised forces composed of weakly integrated units some of which were controlled by political parties,[8] local leaders, and informal networks, by

---

[8] For example, the extreme right-wing Croatian Party of Rights (HSP) established its own paramilitary force – Croatian Defence Forces (Hrvatske Obrambene Snage, HOS). This

1995 HV had developed into a well-functioning military force that instantly recaptured all of the Croatian occupied territories, completely defeated SVK and was also able to force retreat of VRS units from much of North-western Bosnia. During the operation Southern Move in early October 1995 the HV and HVO forces were in position to capture other parts of Northern Bosnia including the largest city of Republika Srpska, Banja Luka, but the Croatian political leaders in agreement with the US and EU governments decided to stop this military campaign and allow VRS troops to withdraw (Ripley 1999).

This is not to say that HV military success was rooted in savvy decisions made by Croatia's political leadership. On the contrary, as leading HV generals Martin Špegelj and Anton Tus show, HV succeeded in spite of Croatia's highly incompetent political leadership which often interfered with military planning (Špegelj 2001: 35; Tus 2001). For example, instead of allowing the military to continue with the defensive operations in Croatia in 1992 in order to recapture the occupied territories the political leaders decided to devote most of their military resources and energies to the war in Bosnia and Herzegovina instead.

In this context the preference was given to the political loyalty over military expertise. However, the initially unfavourable situation on the frontline forced the political leaders to rely on military professionals who developed a formidable organisational structure. In the first phases of the war the military organisation was largely built by skilled defectors from the JNA[9] (Tus 2001), while in the latter stages of the war much organisational work was undertaken by 'the new generation of officers who had risen through the ranks in combat and were accepted by their peers as leaders' (Tus 2001: 50). In addition, in the final stages of the war HV has greatly benefited from the military expertise of the US based private military company – L3 Military Professional Resources Inc. As Singer indicates, the 1995 Storm offensive which crushed Serbian forces in Croatia and Bosnia had all the hallmarks of US military doctrine (Singer 2008: 5). Although Singer and other commentators emphasise the centrality of the coordinated use of force (integration of air power and artillery with quick movement of infantry) this does not explain fully the instant disintegration of VRS and SVK forces which previously seemed to be quite robust. The better coordination and strengthening of the

---

armed group was active on the various battlefields in Croatia and Bosnia and Herzegovina and was later integrated into the Croatian Army.

[9] As General Anton Tus commented on the JNA renegades who jointed HV, 'we had first-class people – military professionals and commanders fully equal to the war situation we faced. General Stipetić and Colonel Franjo Feldi were considered to be the best operations officers of the former 5th district' (Tus 2001: 49).

military capabilities of the HV does not explain such a dramatic and almost instant decline of the VRS. Hence considering all the different phases of war, I would argue that HV military success was in large part grounded in the increased and organisationally mediated cohesion and social pugnacity of HV's military units which was followed by the almost simultaneous decline in the organisational capacities and dissipation of micro-level solidarities of the VRS and SKV.

Although both armed forces started off with similar types of soldiers and officers and had similar levels of unit cohesion, HV proved capable of fostering and integrating small unit solidarity with the larger organisational demands which was not the case with the VRS. For example, as General Tus (2001: 50–1) documents, HV gave up on 'the classroom models' and abandoned 'the classic army units of divisions and corps' which were replaced with a 'large number of battle, tactical and operational units, and battlefield commands'. This drastic change of operational zones was critical in bringing units together: 'smaller units were successfully linked, and the command hierarchy began to be respected'. Furthermore, the HV's military successes were not rooted in its technological superiority. On the contrary, as Žunec (2001: 82) shows, in 1995 HV was still a 'primitive military force, with small technical resources' and in this way was quite similar or even in some respects inferior to the VRS. Despite the popular perception shared in the region that, by 1995, HV was well armed and equipped from abroad, this was not the case: 'there had been no essentially new procurement of arms or military equipment, nor had any new military personnel been trained' (Žunec 2001: 73). Hence the main point of difference was the increased organisational capacity: unlike VRS where the initial unit cohesion gradually dissipated or simply was never integrated within the wider organisational structure, HV proved capable of successfully aligning the micro-level solidarities with the wider organisational goals and thus increased its social pugnacity. Unlike VRS, HV was capable of harnessing and transforming micro-level attachments into the organisational machine of its military force. The key issue here was that unlike VRS which inherited much of the JNA's structures and did not invest in organisational innovation, HV had to start from organisational scratch and as such invested a great deal in organisational change.

These organisational developments were reflected in the interviews with the former HV soldiers who indicate that group solidarity was successfully combined with the military discipline. Hence, most HV units linked micro-group level motivation with the organisational order: 'The discipline was good ... there was good communication between all of us' (Zoran HV); 'we all knew each other from before ... from the same

neighbourhood ... there was discipline that came from the friendship ...
we all carried out our tasks, and our fighting tasks' (Saša HV); 'there was
a military hierarchy ... we all respected mutual agreements' (Vlado HV);
'the commander was authority, there was no anarchy, alcohol, nothing'
(Boris HV); 'we followed their [commanders'] orders all the time as they
knew information that we did not have ... there was no difference
[between local and other commanders], a commander is a commander ...
you had to obey your commander' (Dražen HV).

In contrast, the VRS experienced little genuine structural transformation in this period. Moreover, it was inundated with organisational
problems including the poor operation of command and control, mobil-
ity, and integration of different forces. The HV's attack in 1995 generated
instant withdrawals of many VRS units. However, as the vice-president
of the Bosnian Serb entity (Republika Srpska) Nikola Koljević noted, this
was not ordered by the higher headquarters but 'by officers lower down
the chain of command, indicating a breakdown of command and control'
(Cigar 2001: 223).

Nevertheless, as Cigar (2001: 212) documents, the key problem was
the lack of internal cohesion: 'Instead of being a strength, it was the
human dimension (commitment, morale, leadership) which constituted
perhaps the VRS's greatest "critical vulnerability"'. The organisational
weaknesses contributed to further weakening of already poor social relations between the individual regiments, companies, and platoons on the
one hand and the military establishment on the other. For example, the
interviews with the former VRS soldiers indicate that this military force
was internally deeply divided with ordinary soldiers having little trust in
their officers: 'you see them [the VRS officers] on TV later depicted as
heroes but they treated us just as numbers' (Zoran 2 VRS); 'there was no
respect [for the officers] ... they would visit the troops every 10–15 days
from the command HQ which were about 10 km away... we had to pay
attention to their visits ... as the local commanders were pushing us to
show them some respect' (Dragan1 VRS). Furthermore, most VRS units
were characterised by pronounced lack of discipline and rampant drunkenness. In many instances ordinary soldiers came to the front without
any military training: 'I joined the volunteer unit ... they gave us uniforms, guns, munitions and put us on the bus to Jajce ... We came up
there in the evening ... and 90 to 95 per cent of soldiers were under the
influence of alcohol' (Dragan 1 VRS); '[the recruits] came to the front
without any training ... they took them from their homes, gave them guns
and told them to fight ... some were drunk... there was not much
discipline' (Dragan 1 VRS). The direct outcome of this mutual distrust
between ordinary soldiers and officers was reflected in two ways: (a) high

levels of desertion and draft dodging and (b) VRS's heavy dependence on officers for military actions. By 1995 VRS had up to 150,000 deserters and draft dodgers (Cigar 2001: 213). Furthermore, VRS's general staff's decision to rely heavily on professionals when conducting major military operations is well reflected in the casualty rates with officer deaths counting for 38 per cent of all VRS military deaths (Milovanović, 2011: 13). This staggering figure is in itself a good indicator of the low levels of trust between the professional officers and the ordinary recruits.

By early 1995 HV had substantially increased its organisational capacity and was able to integrate pockets of micro-solidarity that had developed within most squads, platoons, and companies. Furthermore, HV had also proved capable of extending cohesiveness throughout regiments, thus generating a highly motivated military organisation. In other words, as the armed forces developed, they gradually became more professionalised and in this process were able to move soldiers from unit to unit and still maintain robust social cohesion and pugnacity of its forces. In this context some former HV soldiers describe this transition as a move from units built around previously established friendships towards the units shaped around professional ethics. As one ex-soldier puts it: 'Initially we shared everything, we helped each other … just like family … as war advanced this changed … and everything became more like a job' (Vjeko HV). A former HV officer also emphasises this gradual shift from personal comradeships towards professional models of social cohesion:

[In 1995] there was no problem when somebody new joined in [the platoon or regiment] as everybody was now able to adapt … even if ten [new soldiers] arrive they all have to adapt … unit organisation, uniforms … and act as others … if they arrive in an orderly environment they will become orderly too regardless of their past … there was obvious difference between the early period when people did not know much about military organisation, obeying of orders and discipline and later when they realised that following the orders is to their own benefit and benefit of all the other soldiers … it was this [realisation] that saved their skins and that helped that the tasks are completed without much hussle … in this environment where there is no a mother, a father, a wife or the children people realise that they are dependent on each other … and then there is no rejection of the discipline … [there is] no … I don't do this, or I can't do this because if one does not do it or cannot do it then others have to do it for him … this is how people become levelled. (Davor HV)

This organisational shift was important and necessary. It allowed greater social integration of combatants without experiencing the detrimental effects of small group bonding. As some former soldiers emphasise, in the early years of war strong social bonds could act as an obstacle for military efficiency:

In the beginning I was with friends, and then they died in 1993 ... only a handful of them remained ... so we were moved to other regiments because a friend would die for a friend and more people then die ... for example once our friend died and we tried to pull him out and then two more people died and two got injured ... so that is why it was necessary to separate us ... you think more about your friendships ... when in other units you make fewer mistakes. (Vjeko HV)

This gradual shift from interpersonal bonding to professional bonding that developed within the HV indicates that the leading perspectives on social cohesion require serious rethinking. Neither King nor Siebold's approach can adequately explain this long-term transition where bonding remains central but its organisational character changes through time.

In contrast, VRS never achieved this transition from the unit-based comradeship towards social cohesion that combines emotional solidarity with professionalism. Although most soldiers retained their sense of small group attachment, the VRS military organisation proved incapable of successfully linking these pockets of micro-solidarity and utilising them for military purposes. For one thing, the organisation of VRS remained deeply polarised between the professional officers, most of whom were former JNA cadres, and ordinary conscripts who often distrusted their commanders. In the words of one highly experienced soldier who fought for three years in many theatres of war: 'there were some fools who were typical communist officers ... when we all had to go on the frontline this moron suddenly became ill and did not go with us to Olovo [a battlefield] but stayed the whole time in the barracks training recruits ... typical JNA [officer]' (Dejan 1 VRS). Others voiced similar concerns: 'I am really bitter about these officers and their attitude ... they were paid ... but their behaviour was terrible' (Jovo1 VRS). For another thing, most VRS units had little organisational support and had to fend for themselves: 'it is the sense of solidarity that kept us going ... that mutual leaning on each other ... the logistics of VRS was quite weak, we had poor food, had to eat from house to house ... so we always helped each other ... for cigarettes, food, medical supplies, services ... there was always a comrade at hand' (Milan VRS).

The ultimate outcome of these rather different patterns of organisational dynamics of social cohesion led to HV's overwhelming military dominance on the battlefield in the latter stages of war. The 1995 HV military operation Storm brought about quick defeat of both VRS and VSK. As HV soldiers comment, VRS and VSK forces largely disintegrated when faced with the HV attacks: 'We just chased them away ... there was not much fighting ... we came to their lines and could not catch them ... there was some fighting on a few spots, Karlovac and Petrinja where they fought but in other places as soon as we broke the line they run away' (Vjeko HV); 'we were well organised and had everything well prepared and developed before the Storm ... I thought it will take longer to break their lines, the spine, but they did not have force, resources or will [to fight] ... as we broke the line where there were some armed people the rest was an empty terrain ... we moved quickly and there was no resistance' (Davor HV).

Hence the inability of the VRS to maintain, enhance and institutional-ise the micro-level solidarities into the organisational capacity of its military contributed substantially to its ultimate downfall. In direct con-trast, the HV was much more successful in forging and utilising synergies between the micro-social bonds of its soldiers and the macro-organisational structures of its army. The consequence of these changing and contrasting experiences was a resounding military victory for the HV in the 1991–5 war.

8.5   Social Cohesion Beyond Interpersonal Affinities and Collective Performance

Military officers and scholars of war have always been aware that social cohesion plays a crucial role in soldiers' motivation to fight. There is now an abundance of literature indicating that group unity significantly con-tributes to the war effort. Although most military organisations invest substantially in military hardware such as new weaponry, better systems of logistics, and novel technological solutions for coordination of sol-diers, there is a degree of consensus that wars are often won and lost according to soldiers' willingness to fight (Biddle 2004). Hence much of the twentieth- and twenty-first-century military scholarship has focused on identifying the key social mechanisms that underpin social pugnacity. The classical studies of social cohesion in the military, mostly conducted in the wake of the Second World War, such as Shils and Janowitz (1948), Stouffer (1949), and Marshall (1947), have all focused on the role of the 'primary group' in maintaining cohesion within military forces and have also linked these group ties to the willingness of soldiers to fight even when facing extremely difficult conditions. This approach was later criticised as some scholars questioned this overemphasis on the micro-level factors while shifting the explanatory frameworks towards the macro-structural variables such as ideology, economics, or geopolitics (Bartov 1992, 2018; Collier 2000; Moskos 1975; Ross 2006). The new approaches in the study of military cohesion have rehabilitated the cen-trality of micro-social contexts and much of contemporary scholarship recognises that without social cohesion within small-scale military units the armies cannot be successful in war (Stewart 1991; Wong 2006). The two leading contemporary approaches in the study of social cohesion on the battlefield agree that micro-level social coherence and unity among the combatants play a crucial role in the efficiency of fighting. However, these two perspectives differ sharply in explaining how social cohesion is attained in the combat zone. While Siebold (2007, 2011, 2012) insists that the given psychological affinities of individual soldiers provide an essential social glue for military cohesion, King (2006, 2013, 2014) argues that group cohesion is generated through shared social action. In other words, whereas the former approach identifies effective fighting strategy with the enhanced bonds within military units the latter perspective associates increased group cohesion with successful collective performance on the battlefield.

In this chapter I have challenged both of these perspectives by shifting the analytical gaze from the micro towards the macro realities. This is not to say that the micro-group bonds are not important. On the contrary, as I have argued throughout this book, micro-level solidarities underpin much of human motivation including social pugnacity. Nevertheless, the point is that the micro-group dynamics is simply not enough to generate durable and sustainable social action. Instead in historical terms the key generators of social change are organisations such as states, militaries, private corporations, religious institutions, social movements, political parties, and so on. Hence the patterns of social cohesion remain dependent on the ebbs and flows of organisational power and the wider structural contexts. In this sense, cohesion and social pugnacity on the battlefield are a consequence of the fine-tuned interplay between the actions of micro-level agents and the organisational dynamics of macro-structural forces. Military cohesion does not stem simply from the inherent psychological propensities of soldiers, as argued by Siebold. It is not something that can be generated solely by shared collective performance, as argued by King. Instead, cohesion entails protracted organisational (and ideological) work. Although Siebold and King develop very different analytical frameworks to explain military cohesion they both remain hampered by the pronounced weaknesses of the Durkheimian perspective – its functionalist logic, its idealist epistemology, and its ahistorical understanding of social change.

While for Siebold social cohesion transpires simply and almost automatically from the psychological integration of soldiers, for King military unity is a consequence of functional interdependence. Reading this through the Durkheimian concepts it is clear that Siebold sees military units as a form of mechanical solidarity – the combatants feel attached to each other in a same way as members of an ancient tribal grouping. This is solidarity of resemblance as postulated by Durkheim (1986: 129):

'Solidarity which comes from likeness is at its maximum when the collective conscience completely envelops our whole conscience and coincides in all points with it'. As Durkheim (1986: 105) elaborates further 'not only are all the members of the group individually attracted to one another because they resemble one another, but also because they are joined to what is the condition of existence of this collective type ... they will as they will themselves, hold to it durably and for prosperity, because, without it, a great part of their psychic lives would function poorly'. In this understanding military cohesion is a by-product of psychological resemblance. The soldiers attain group solidarity through similarity – they display affinity to each other and as such fight in unison.

In contrast, in King's understanding military cohesion is the epitome of organic solidarity. The combatants do not fight because they resemble each other or have inherent psychological attachments. Rather military units are held together through the interdependence of their professional roles and responsibilities. Here again one can recognise Durkheim's (1986: 131) concept of solidarity at work. What defines organic solidarity is how it relates to the complex division of labour. Instead of unity through resemblance this form of solidarity presupposes difference:

The first [mechanical solidarity] is possible only in so far as the individual personality is absorbed into the collective personality; the second is possible only if each one has a sphere of action which is peculiar to him; that is, a personality. ... In effect, on the one hand, each one depends as much more strictly on society as labour is more divided; and, on the other, the activity of each is as much more personal as it is more specialized. ... Society becomes more capable of collective movement, at the same time that each of its elements has more freedom of movement ... the unity of the organism is as great as the individuation of the parts is more marked. (Durkheim 1986: 131)

Thus, social cohesion in the military is achieved through effective, transparent, and legitimate division of labour where soldiers perform their specific tasks and, in this way, indirectly make their military organisations more functional and more effective.

This neo-Durkheimian ideal type is useful to describe some aspects of military behaviour but it is far from being an adequate tool to explain the changing dynamics of social pugnacity. As argued in previous chapters, social pugnacity is a deeply contextual and variable phenomenon that cannot easily fit into this procrustean bed. The historical record indicates clearly that patterns of fighting differ across time and space and that the same individuals can act very differently in different social contexts. Both King and Siebold offer overly functionalist interpretations that pay little attention to this contextual, historical, and cultural variability. By focusing almost exclusively on the experience of contemporary American and

British military forces they are unable to recognise the sheer variety of combat motivation across time and space.

Furthermore, the epistemological idealism that underpins both of these perspectives leaves no analytical space for the study of political and organisational power dynamics that shapes the micro-level realities. Simply put, the micro-world of combatants remains disconnected from the macro-world of military organisations, governmental politics, administrative decision making, geopolitical changes, and many other variables that impact profoundly on the soldiers' behaviours on the ground. Both of these perspectives overemphasise the role of shared values, beliefs, and symbols while downplaying political, economic, and organisational factors.

Finally, the neo-Durkheimian perspective in both of its guises does not offer much in terms of understanding long-term social change. The psychological bonds and the shared collective action are both powerful mechanisms of group integration but if they are not sustained and enhanced by organisational structures, and if they are not continuously fused into the organisational shells of militaries they can also dissipate and evaporate. Making combatants fight is not an event produced by intrinsic psychological bonds or previous experiences of shared action but is an ongoing historical process that remains dependent on continuous structural input.

All of this indicates that the dominant neo-Durkheimian paradigm of social cohesion on the battlefield is inadequate to capture the complexity and the changing character of this phenomenon. Thus, to better understand the social processes underpinning group cohesion and the patterns of fighting it is necessary to zoom in on the long-term interaction between the micro-level solidarities and the macro and meso organisational power structures. In this chapter I have analysed two military organisations with very different experiences of social cohesion. By comparing and contrasting the war experience of the Bosnian Serb Army and the Croatian Army during the 1991–5 wars in the Balkans the chapter has attempted to show how the social dynamics of cohesion remains wedded to the organisational structures. Although the two militaries started the war with similar levels of unit cohesion, the Croatian Army's organisational investments fostered the expansion of micro-level solidarities throughout the wider military networks. In contrast, the Bosnian Serb Army remained beset by serious organisational problems, including the lack of trust between soldiers and their commanding officers which generated a weakening of unit cohesion that ultimately proved fatal for their war effort. This more processual analyses has indicated that social cohesion in the combat zone is shaped by variety of contextual influences. Hence to fully understand how and why social pugnacity is so variable, we must move away from the static functionalist and instrumentalist accounts with a view to developing more inter-dynamic perspectives that aim to link the organisational, ideological, and micro-interactional processes.

9   Emotions and Close-Range Fighting

9.1   Introduction

There is no doubt that close-range fighting entails distinct emotional dynamics. People who take part in violent encounters experience intense emotional responses ranging from fear, angst, anxiety, panic, and horror to anger, rage, boredom, and even elation. The acts of fighting are often preceded and followed by physiological changes such as increased heart rate, heavy breathing, dilation of the pupils, hormonal increases, and in some case the loss of urinary or bowel control. Since emotions have dominated battlefields for centuries there is a well-entrenched view that warfare generates very similar emotional reactions among soldiers. The conventional interpretations overemphasise a uniform response by humans who find themselves in similar extraordinary situations (Grossman 2004; Holmes 1985; Keegan 1994). This chapter challenges such established views and argues that the emotional dynamics of close-range fighting is historically variable and culturally flexible. The historical and sociological analysis of battlefield experiences indicates that there are substantial cultural and historical differences in the emotional reactions of individuals and groups who experience similar fighting situations.

The chapter is divided into three sections. The first section explores the range of emotional responses that have been documented on the battlefields throughout the world. The chapter briefly explores the emotional dynamics of close-range fighting and emphasises the contextual variations that appear in different conflicts. This section aims to highlight the central role that emotions play in the combat zone and to illustrate how military organisations have historically attempted to mould emotional reactions of soldiers on the battlefield. The last two sections of the chapter analyse the historical and cultural variables and aim to show how emotional responses and social pugnacity are shaped and changed by different cultural and historical contexts.

9.2   Emotions in the Combat Zone

Combatants who have experienced close-range fighting on the battlefield tend to describe it in vividly emotional terms. Frontline combat generates a unique emotional experience, ranging from fear, anxiety, anger, angst, and rage to panic, horror, boredom, and even elation and exhilaration. Throughout history, military organisations have attempted to shape the emotional responses of soldiers in order to increase their fighting capacity. In this sense nearly all emotions have been subjected to specific military regimes of control.

The two most common emotions that soldiers face in the combat zone are fear and boredom. As has often been stated by former combatants, 'wars consist of 5% horror and 95% boredom (or waiting)' (Maeland and Brunstad 2009: 2). Although boredom is more of an affect than an emotion,[1] it is a constant and shared experience of most soldiers in times of war. Soldiers spend much of their time waiting for the battle and even when they are on the battlefields boredom is the dominant experience. As one US Vietnam war veteran recollects: 'In Vietnam, three things seem to govern one's life. Work, boredom, and excitement. The latter lifted the men's morale while the former two fought each other to whittle away the spirits of everyone' (Laugesen 2016: 246). Both military organisations and the soldiers themselves see boredom as an obstacle. For militaries, the lack of activity can represent a threat to the readiness to fight – boredom is an enemy of morale. Many British and Australian officers identified boredom as a grave danger: 'demoralisation through idleness ... could not be overestimated' (Laugesen 2016: 156). For ordinary soldiers boredom can lead to negative emotions, as an abundance of free time enables them to think about their precarious situation and to reminiscence about their pre-war lives, their homes, and the loved ones whom they miss. In this sense boredom is an unpleasant affect that soldiers try to escape. Hence, to alleviate boredom soldiers develop hobbies, engage in humorous banter, or take up drinking, card playing, gambling, or in some cases visiting prostitutes. As Basham (2015: 134) shows, many of these activities developed to alleviate boredom are deeply gendered, as they frame excitement and move away from boredom in

---

[1] Most scholars differentiate between affect and emotion. An affect stands for a broader and basic form of feelings that range in terms of arousal (calm to agitated) and valence (pleasant to unpleasant). An emotion is usually conceptualised as a complex mental and physical phenomenon that is often directed towards a specific entity, and is defined by intense and subjectively experienced feelings. Emotional reactions also often involve behavioural and physiological changes in one's body (Collins 2008; Turner 2007). In this chapter the focus is primarily on emotions.

hyper-masculinist terms and activities: 'during the 95% of the time that soldiers spend waiting for war, emotional expressions are thus often regulated by gendered norms'. Military organisations have also devised a variety of techniques to ensure soldiers are kept busy on and off the battlefields (Maeland and Brunstad 2009: 2).

There is no doubt that fear is one of the most significant and most common emotional responses that is accompanied by many physiological changes. Fear is generally associated with heavy breathing, palpitations, excessive sweating, and body paralysis. In most combat situations soldiers experience fear, and in some instances intense fear can turn into panic, dread, and horror. In one of the earliest studies of combat experience, French colonel Ardant du Picq (2006 [1880]) found that fear was the principal emotion in the combat zone. In the 1860s he surveyed French officers and found that widespread fear paralysed military action, with many soldiers being incapable of fighting with or shooting at the enemy. Du Picq (2006 [1880]: 90) was very clear in his assessment and also recommended how to control such fear: 'man has a horror of death ... discipline is for the purpose of dominating that horror by a still greater horror, that of punishment or disgrace'.

The same emotional reactions were identified in many other wars. The largest study, conducted during the Second World War by Stouffer (1949), identified fear as the central emotion among US soldiers. Stouffer and his collaborators surveyed the US infantry regiments in France and found that over 65 per cent of soldiers had difficulty performing their military tasks because of constant feelings of fear. The same survey was undertaken among the US infantry soldiers in the Pacific theatre of war and the results were similar, with a very high percentage of soldiers identifying fear as the key obstacle for efficient military action: the soldiers confessed that they experienced violent pounding of the heart (76 per cent) and were sick to their stomachs (over 50 per cent); and many also broke out into cold sweats, or would tremble or faint (Stouffer 1949: 201). Very similar responses have been recorded in other wars and their soldiers (Bourke 2000; Collins 2008; Grossman 1996; Holmes 1985).

Many militaries have instituted rigorous punishments and courts martial for misbehaviour on the battlefield, with capital punishments regularly deployed as a measure for desertion or unwillingness to fight (see Chapter 6). Nevertheless, the intense feelings of fear were not the main cause of desertion, as many soldiers felt a strong sense of attachment and obligation towards their comrades and would not leave the battlefields even when experiencing a profound sense of dread, panic, or horror (Collins 2008; Malešević 2010). A more prevalent reaction to the fear and horror of the battlefield was soldiers' general unwillingness to target and shoot at the enemy soldiers. Thus, since S. L. A. Marshall's (1947) study on the behaviour of US soldiers in the Second World War, it has become evident that a large number of frontline combatants fail to fire their guns during combat or tend to deliberately miss or fire in the air. Marshall (1947: 50) argued that only between 15 and 25 per cent of soldiers would fire their weapons at the enemy while the majority would misfire or not fire at all. Although Marshall's work has been questioned and criticised for its methodological weaknesses (Mann 2019; Spiller 1988), other scholars have identified similar levels of non-firing in other theatres of war and other combat zones throughout the world (Bourke 2000; Collins 2008; King 2011).

Militaries have devised a variety of measures to counter the consequences of widespread fear. Some of these measures have centred on enhancing the coercive capacity of military units. Hence, most armies have introduced battle military police, which are responsible for preventing soldiers from escaping the battlefield but also for making sure that they shoot at the enemy (Collins 2008; Holmes 1985; Malešević 2010). In addition, officers have been specifically allocated to the combat zone so that they can observe the implementation of fighting commands. In the Second World War, many recruits were reluctant to shoot and would only do so when observed and pressured by their commander. As one frustrated US officer reflected on his experience during the invasion of Normandy in 1944: 'When I ordered the men who were right around me to fire, they did so. But the moment I passed on, they quit. I walked up and down the line yelling "God damn it! Start shooting!" But it did very little good. They fired only while I watched them or while some other soldier stood over them' (Bourke 2000: 74).

Other measures were centred on developing a more realistic combat training where soldiers would encounter environments that are similar to the one in the combat zone. This would include more physically and mentally demanding and exhausting training settings. For example, during the Second World War some officers would take new recruits to view defaced and damaged corpses before their first battle so that they could get used to the sight of death and destruction (Blake 1970: 340). These practices would also include learning 'instinctive shooting', that is, the ability to shoot under stress without seeing one's target. Many contemporary armies have focused on training soldiers in this practice of target focused shooting, which does not rely on the use of one's sight. Instead, a soldier repeats shooting movements focused on a target that have been practised in training and have become a habitual response. This style of shooting does not require visual confirmation but involves automatic reaction centred on a less visible target (Klein 2016). However, more recently some military organisations have had to develop effective countermeasures to prevent soldiers firing unconsciously at any potential threat. For example, between 2006 and 2007 Iraqi civilians were killed or injured at the coalition checkpoints every day. In most of these cases soldiers would shoot automatically, believing that they faced imminent threat. As Gregory (2019: 131) shows, many of these shootings were not based on rational calculations but on 'affective judgments' that are in part due to conditioning through the military training, that help inculcate responses which 'mark certain bodies as dangerous before they even have a chance to act'.

Another influential military practice devised to increase discipline but also manage fear and dread of the battlefield is drill. This age-old military tradition has played a crucial role in maintaining group cohesion in theatres of war as the coordinated rhythmic movement has proved influential in shifting the emotional dynamics from an individual sense of fear towards a collective experience of effervescence and bonding. As Holmes (1985: 42) explains: 'Part of the stress of battle stems from its puzzling and capricious nature: battle drills help to minimize the randomness of battle and give the soldier familiar points of contact in an uncertain environment, like lighthouses in a stormy sea.' McNeill (1997) has traced historically how drill played a decisive role in warfare throughout history. In his analysis, drill helped generate intuitive emotional ties of 'muscular bonding' that created capacity for collective action on the battlefield, thus preventing the soldiers from running away.

In addition to fear, dread, panic, and horror, soldiers can also experience a variety of other emotional reactions, ranging from anger, anxiety, and rage, over sadness, shame, guilt, and disgust, to pride, awe, elation, exhilaration, and even joy. Anger and rage are common emotions associated with violence. The first line of Homer's (2017) Iliad starts with the idea of rage and the poem itself depicts the anger and rage of Achilles and other warriors whose honour has been trampled upon. Nevertheless, anger and rage are usually interpreted through the reactive responses of soldiers. Soldiers who see their comrades killed or injured might be more inclined to express rage and anger: 'I did not hate the enemy [Viet Cong] for their politics, but for murdering Simpson [a friend] … revenge was one of the reasons I volunteered for a line company. I wanted a chance to kill somebody' (Caputo 1977: 231); 'real hatred of the enemy came to soldiers … when a buddy was killed. And this was often a total hatred: any German they encountered after that would be killed' (Beevor 2009: 260). These experiences of US soldiers losing close comrades during the Vietnam War and the Second World War have recently been mirrored by those fighting in the Afghanistan and Iraq. As Sebastian Junger (2010: 60) documents, anger and rage have motivated revenge attacks: 'I just wanted to kill everything that came up that was not American'. Feelings of anger have also been linked with a perception that the enemy is not fighting fair. Burleigh (2012: 379) depicts a situation from the Second World War in Tunisia when an imprisoned German soldier killed several British soldiers with a hidden gun: 'During the assault on Longstop Hill ... a captured German drew a concealed pistol and shot several of his Argyll and Sutherland Highlander captors'. The latter were 'roused to a state of berserk fury—We just had a hate—at the Germans, the hill, everything ... For a few days they accepted no surrenders.' Such anger was even more pronounced when encountering cases of cruelty, torture, or the slaughtering of innocent civilians (Bourke 2000; Collins 2008; Grossman 1996).

Shame and guilt also feature prominently in the emotional experiences of soldiers on the battlefield. Du Picq (2006 [1880]: 154) was already aware that most soldiers are concerned with how others see them and are eager to avoid any sense of shame: 'Self-esteem is unquestionably one of the most powerful motives which moves our men. They do not wish to pass for cowards in the eyes of their comrades.'

Shame could also be associated with inappropriate behaviour towards the enemy and especially civilians. In some instances, shame would trump the original enthusiasm or pride in shooting the enemy. The soldiers would experience the instant thrill of fulfilling the military aim, but this would soon transform into regret, shame, and guilt. For example, a US soldier who fought in the first Gulf War, Charles Sheehan Miles, recollects his experience of killing Iraqi soldiers who were escaping a burning truck: as one of the occupants ran ablaze from the truck, Miles fired his machine-gun and instantly killed him. His immediate response was, he said, 'a sense of exhilaration, of joy'. However, a moment later he experienced 'a tremendous feeling of guilt and remorse'. The image of the man on fire, running and dying, stayed with him 'for years and years and years', he said. His unit returned home amidst great celebration and he was awarded a medal, yet he felt, in his words, 'probably the worst person alive' (Skelly 2006).

A very similar emotional switch was experienced by other soldiers who took part in other wars. For instance, a US soldier who participated in the massacre of women and children in a Vietnamese village explains how he was struggling to reconcile his orders, peer pressure, and shame: 'I happened to look into somebody's eyes, a woman's eyes, and she – I do not know, I looked, I mean, just before we started firing, I mean, you know, I didn't want to. I wanted to turn around and walk away. It was something telling me not to do it. Something told me not to, you know, just turn around and not be part of it, but everybody else started firing, I started firing' (Bourke 2000: 191).

While some combatants felt ashamed of their actions, others were ashamed of not feeling guilty: 'The deep shame that I feel is my own lack of emotional reaction. I keep reacting as though I were simply watching a movie of the whole thing. I still don't feel that I have personally killed anyone ... Have I become so insensitive that I have to see torn limbs, the bloody ground, the stinking holes and guts in the mud, before I feel ashamed that I have destroyed numbers of my own kind?' (Bourke 2000: 221).

Hence, in some situations shame was linked with an instant sense of guilt while in other instances shame and guilt were completely disconnected. Many military organisations have attempted to mould these emotions by invoking a sense of shame and guilt to make surviving soldiers continue to fight 'for their fallen comrades'. By relying on feelings of guilt and shame, the militaries could shift the interpretative framework of war deaths: instead of locating responsibility for war in the policies of governments, the focus moves to the soldier's own responsibility to fight so that the previous casualties ('our fallen comrades') would not have died in vain (Malešević 2010, 2017).

The sense of guilt often appears in two principal forms: the feeling of being responsible for the deaths or injuries of others and the guilt of having survived the war while one's comrades have been killed. The killer's guilt is often rooted in a realisation that the enemy is just another human being like oneself: 'I had a tear myself, I thought to myself perhaps he has a Mother or Dad also a sweetheart and a lot of things like that, I was really sorry' (Moynihan 1980: 85). In his Vietnam War memoir, Caputo (1977: 117) describes how finding the personal photographs and letters of a dead Viet Cong soldier provoked a deep sense of empathy and guilt among the US soldiers: these personal items 'gave the enemy the humanity I wished to deny him', which led to the recognition that the enemy soldiers were also made of 'flesh and blood' instead of being 'mysterious wraiths'. This realisation caused 'an abiding sense of remorse' as the US soldiers recognised that Viet Cong are 'young men ... just like us. .In the Iraq War, the US military attempted to work through this universal sense of empathy by prompting soldiers to differentiate clearly between military targets and civilians. Hence, several US military commanders warned their soldiers: 'civilians should be treated as you would desire your family to be treated in similar circumstances', or 'Don't fucking waste a mother or some kid. Don't fire into a crowd. These people north of here have been oppressed for years. They're just like us' (Pettegrew 2015: 100). There is no doubt that the commanders' pleas were aimed at minimising civilian casualties, but they were also focused on averting the anticipated future guilt and remorse of young US soldiers.

Survivor's guilt is something that might appear during or immediately after a battle or can become much more prominent at the end of a violent conflict. For example, many soldiers have been deeply affected by the deaths of their friends and would blame themselves for this loss: 'Every time you lost a friend it seemed like a part of you was gone' (Shay 1994: 78); '[I experience] night sweats, nightmares, survivor's guilt, the feeling that you deserted your buddies by living' (Munson 2016). This sense of guilt is often symptomatic of the post-traumatic stress disorder (PTSD), which has shaped much of the post-war experience for soldiers who survived wars. Survivor's guilt is a mental condition characterised by strong feelings of having done something wrong by surviving a traumatic event when others have died. It is a feeling of responsibility for deaths of others that is expressed as taking somebody else's place among the living. This feeling of guilt has been present among soldiers who survived wars but also among Holocaust survivors and other individuals who survived major traumatic events such as epidemics, natural disasters, terrorism, airplane crashes, and so on. As Primo Levi (1995: 295), an Auschwitz survivor, describes it: 'It is the impression that the others died in your place; that you are alive gratis, thanks to a privilege you have not earned, a trick you played on the dead. Being alive isn't a crime but we feel it like a crime.'

Soldiers affected by PTSD often express this sense of guilt in their letters and memoirs. For example, a British soldier who survived the Battle of Arezzo in 1944 after most of his unit was killed reflected on his visit to their graves in 1971 in his memoir: 'Why hadn't I visited them? Because you didn't want to get too close to the dead, I thought. You wanted them buried alive in the book. They're rotting in their graves chum. You've got to face them there. You've been dodging the column, running away from the pain and guilt of being alive when the best are dead, their lives wasted. Thrown away. For what? A botched civilization. A bitch gone in the teeth' (Houghton 2019: 51).

In addition to survivor's guilt, soldiers also tend to experience another set of emotional responses that Shay (2014) and Litz et al. (2009) have called moral injury. This concept stands for a discrepancy between values and actions: an individual is obliged to follow the orders of legitimate authority, yet these orders can clash sharply with one's moral values. In this sense a moral injury is a condition that creates an emotional dissonance: by engaging in these actions individuals trample upon moral codes, an action which is likely to generate anxiety and feelings of shame and guilt. Although William Calley, US Army officer and convicted war criminal who was responsible for the My Lai massacre, is often presented as an individual who showed no emotion while in Vietnam or during his trial, it seems that, like many other Vietnam veterans, he also experienced a moral injury. In a recent 2009 public address he stated that 'There is not a day that goes by that I do not feel remorse for what happened that day in My Lai ... I feel remorse for the Vietnamese who were killed, for their families, for the American soldiers involved and their families. I am very sorry' (James 2009).

Although the battlefield experience is predominantly shaped by negative emotions, including fear, horror, panic, guilt, shame, anxiety, anger, rage, and sadness, the combat zone can also yield some positive emotional responses, including admiration, awe, pride, trust, elation, exhilaration, and joy. Furthermore, the shared experience of soldiers living and fighting together under extremely difficult circumstances generates a complex emotional dynamic that is often expressed in strong bonds of friendship and comradeship. Some of these bonds might develop into loving and lasting relationships with strong emotional attachments.

All military organisations rely on the soldier's sense of pride. In most instances individuals feel proud of belonging to a particular company, regiment, battalion, or a military branch. The leaders of military organisations are well aware that soldiers develop a strong sense of unit attachment and all military organisations foster these micro-identities as they enhance social cohesion within the military (see Chapter 8). Nevertheless, in a combat situation the sense of pride tends to be more localised and situational. Hence, there is more expression of pride in smaller units such as one's squad and platoon rather than battalion, brigade, or the army as a whole. In the traumatic environments of battlefields where individuals are exposed to continuous life-threatening situations and where they witness the daily deaths of their comrades, soldiers are more likely to identify strongly with these smaller, face-to-face, groups (Malešević 2017). In this context, pride emerges through the shared experience of hardship and ability to survive extraordinary conditions. Winning and surviving despite the odds also contribute to a sense of pride in one's squad or platoon. In two surveys conducted among US soldiers during the Second World War an overwhelming majority of respondents expressed a strong sense of pride in their company, platoon, and squad – 78 per cent were fairly proud or very proud and only 9 per cent said that they were not proud of their military units (McManus 2007: 321). One soldier described this sense of pride as stemming from the strong bonds of friendship that developed within the military unit:

The soldier feared separation from his squad more than he feared the enemy. He felt secure among men whose individual characters and capabilities he knew as well as he knew his own. They had been welded together by combat, and rightly or wrongly the infantryman was convinced that his chances of surviving the next firefight were much better with his own squad than they would be in any other. His first sergeant and platoon sergeant were like fathers ... and the other members of his squad were his brothers. (McManus 2007: 322)

In some cases, pride in one's squad or platoon was enhanced by the views other soldiers had about that particular squad or platoon. In other words, the valour and fearlessness of some platoons provoked a sense of awe and admiration among soldiers in other units. For example, in the Vietnam War the platoons that were willing to volunteer for difficult military operations or who had experienced excessive violence and had survived were admired for their 'crazy' behaviour: 'when [this] ... unit came in the bar, everybody else in the joint would shift out of the way ... They were all crazy, but I respected them ... I was fascinated with this group of men. They were all on their second or third tour of Nam ... Their kinship was even stronger than ours ... They didn't even think of anyone else around' (Baker 1982: 121).

There is no doubt that the combat zone is defined by a variety of negative emotions including fear, anger, contempt, disgust, or guilt. However, some soldiers also experience a number of positive emotions such as joy, happiness, contentment, elation, and exhilaration (Bourke, 2000). The memoirs and diaries of many combatants are full of descriptions where the battlefield is portrayed as an arena of infinite power and freedom. Some of the participants of the First World War who later became well-known writers depict their emotional reactions on the battlefield in terms of happiness and joy. Both Ernst Jünger, a conservative German nationalist, and Henri de Man, a Belgian socialist, describe their war experience through the prism of joy and elation. De Man (1920: 198–9) expresses no sense of guilt for killing enemy soldiers. In fact, he seems very happy about this: 'I secured a direct hit on an enemy encampment, saw bodies or parts of bodies go up in the air, and heard the desperate yelling of the wounded or the runaways. I had to confess to myself that it was one of the happiest moments of my life.' In a similar vein Jünger (2016 [1920]), who fought on the other side, writes about his own feelings: 'As we advanced, we were in the grip of berserk rage. The overwhelming desire to kill lent wings to my stride. Rage squeezed bitter tears from my eyes. The immense desire to destroy that overhung the battlefield precipitated a red mist in our brains. We called out sobbing and stammering fragments of sentences to one another, and an impartial observer might have concluded that we were all ecstatically happy.'

These emotional responses were also documented in the Vietnam War and the recent twenty-first-century Afghan war. A former US soldier who fought in Vietnam was very explicit about his feelings on the battlefield. He states how he fell in love 'with the power and thrill of destruction and death dealing ... there is a deep savage joy in destruction' (Marlantes 2011: 61–7, 160). Similar emotions were felt by US soldiers who fought in Afghanistan and Iraq (Junger 2010).

For some male soldiers, a battlefield is perceived as the ultimate test of their manhood – the opportunity to stretch one's physical, mental, and emotional capacities to the limits and see whether one can survive in this situation. In a patriarchal world where a sense of masculinity is often defined by physical prowess and capacity to endure external hardships, war is often viewed as a moral yardstick of manhood. Proving oneself on the battlefield and demonstrating that one can withstand pain and sacrifice means being a full man. This is a concept that many young recruits have been socialised with in their childhood and teenage years and have been brought up believing; they thus aspire to show to others that they are not boys but 'real men'. In this context, the popular depictions of previous wars which glorify military heroism and soldiers' willingness to fight and endure are often understood as moral exemplars of how young recruits should behave in the combat zone (Goldstein 2001). This is often referred to as the John Wayne syndrome – eagerness to get into action and became a hero. As another Vietnam veteran observes, many very young US soldiers were deeply influenced by the dominant cultural representations of war and particularly by films that romanticised war and fighting: 'The John Wayne flicks. We were invincible. So, when we were taken into ... war, everyone went in with the attitude, "Hey, we're going to wipe them out. Nothing's going to happen to us." Until they saw the realities and they couldn't deal with. "This isn't supposed to happen. It isn't in the script. What's going on? This guy is really bleeding all over me, he's screaming his head off"' (Bourke 2000: 28). Thus, initial elation and enthusiasm about the war regularly dissipates once young recruits experience the horrors of the battlefield environment.

This brief review indicates how central emotions are for warfare. Although wars are often conceptualised in instrumentalist and rationalist terms, the actual lived experience of the combat zone is principally defined by a variety of emotional reactions. There is no social pugnacity without emotions. All soldiers experience intense emotional reactions in the combat zone. Although fear is by far the most common emotion, the combatants tend to display a wide range of complex and changing emotional responses including both negative emotions such as anxiety, anger, rage, panic, horror, shame, guilt, and sadness as well as some positive emotions including happiness, joy, pride, elation, and exhilaration. Living in an exceptional situation of life and death, the individual actions and responses of soldiers are profoundly shaped by emotions. Military organisations have invested substantial resources and energy to shape these emotional responses in order to make ordinary soldiers into more efficient fighters. One of the defining features of modern warfare is the ever-increasing military reliance on science and academic research in general to devise new methods for moulding human emotions for battlefield purposes. The starting position of this endeavour is the assumption that human emotional responses are universal and, for the most part, identical. In this context much of contemporary military psychology of emotions has focused on the biological, and specifically physiological, foundations of emotional reactions.

9.3   Social Pugnacity and Emotional Variation in Time

The essentialist theories of emotions shed some light on the common patterns of behaviour on the battlefields. For example, there is no doubt that the overwhelming majority of soldiers have experienced fear in combat situations. Military organisations recognise that being fearful is a completely normal and expected reaction to the unprecedented violence and horror of battlefields. Contemporary military education devotes a great deal of attention to teaching soldiers how to manage their fear in combat. Most military organisations devise manuals and organise lessons on 'enhancing performance under stress', where the focus is on developing skills and techniques for 'fear inoculation' (Bausman 2016).

Nevertheless, this has not always been the case. In fact, for much of history the sense of fear was hidden, downplayed, denied, or only attributed to the enemy. As Kuijpers and van der Haven (2016) show, in Europe, until the eighteenth century, fear was almost uniformly depicted as a property of the other. Fear was something that only disgraced enemy soldiers were prone to feel whereas one's own comrades would regularly be praised for their bravery and heroism: 'The long tradition of soldiers' writing dictates the communication of fearlessness and other empowering masculine ideals that tend to suppress some emotions: fear, feelings of senselessness, disgust, personal grief, and underscore others such as the love of fatherland, courage and a fighting spirit' (Kuijpers and van der Haven 2016: 12).

For example, diaries of officers and clerks who recorded sixteenth- and early seventeenth-century battles throughout Europe tend as a rule to ascribe fear and horror to the enemy side: 'several thousand [enemy soldiers], induced by great anxiety and fear, had thrown themselves into the river Danube and drowned'. In direct contrast, one's own soldiers were depicted as heroic and fearless: 'though his Majesty died like a chevalier, the soldiers were not scared but attacked the enemy like lions, taking their pieces and beating the foe' (Bahr 2016: 53).

This attitude changes from the late seventeenth to the early nineteenth century when soldiers gradually start recording their own experiences of the battlefield. One of the first such documents is the memoir of Swiss mercenary Ulrich Bräker, in which he reflects on the horrors of war and his own dislike and fear of the battlefield (Füssel, 2016). During the nineteenth and twentieth centuries many ordinary soldiers and officers have produced diaries, letters, memoirs, and other written evidence of their personal struggles in the theatres of war throughout the world. In many of these records a personal sense of fear features prominently. However, this change in the depiction and understanding of fear was relatively gradual, and it was not irreversible as many militaries continued to conceal the realities of war from future recruits and from their own families. Even in the early twentieth century most military administrators avoided any references to the fear generated in combat situations or to the long-term emotional effects that the exposure to daily violence had on young soldiers. In this context, the concept of shell shock was introduced during the First World War to account for situations where soldiers were unable to function properly due to the traumatic experiences of war. The term was used in a vague sense and would include not only PTSD but also a sense of powerlessness, panic, fear, and inability to complete everyday tasks (Hochschild 2012). This change in attitude to, and depiction of, fear also went hand in hand with the diversity in the experiences of fear.

Although the great majority of combatants experienced fear through history, they did not experience it in the same way, did not show these feelings to others through identical physical expressions, and have managed their sense of fear in many different ways. Even soldiers who experienced tremendous fear on one day might act very differently next day. In the words of a German captain who fought in the First World War: 'Soldiers can be brave one day and afraid the next. Soldiers are not machines but human beings who must be led in war. Each one of them reacts differently, therefore each must be handled differently … to sense this and arrive at a correct psychological solution is part of the art of leadership' (von Schell 2013: 24).

Furthermore, the historical record indicates that fear is not only an individual reaction but is an emotional state that is shaped and managed differently by different military organisations. While historically some militaries discouraged, suppressed, and even punished any references to fear in the combat zone other militaries have been eager to recognise fear as normal, acknowledge its impact on the battlefield, and try to manage and channel such emotions. In other cases, fear was conceptualised as something that is not located in one's own body but as an external force that can strike unsuspecting individuals. For example, until the mid-nineteenth century the New Zealand's Māori warriors associated fear with the actions of spirits. Hence, if a soldier exhibits what we would often regard as the signs of fear (e.g., shaking, cold sweats, etc.) before the battle this was interpreted as an indication that the soldier was possessed by *atua* – spirits who react angrily to any breaches of social rules as defined in the Māori's canon of rules – *tapu*. This situation could be ameliorated through a specific ritual whereby a possessed warrior was required to crawl between the legs of a Māori woman of high social standing. The ritual cleansing would be judged as a success if there were no signs of fear in the warrior after the crawl: he would be free of *atua* and ready for the battle. If the signs of fear persisted the ritual would be deemed unsuccessful, and the warrior would not take part in the battle. At the same time there was no conceptual space for *atua* possessing somebody during the battle – this was thought to be impossible. Thus, in the pre-nineteenth-century Māori culture there was no room for fear on the battlefield and it seems that the Māori warriors did not experience a sense of fear in combat as fear was understood to be a property of an external force (Plamper 2015: 4).

The historical diversity of fear indicates that this is not a fixed biological given but an emotional reaction that is variable and situational. As Lutz (1988) rightly argues, the essentialist understandings of emotions that overemphasise the biological universals are too rigid to accommodate the complexity of human emotional reactions. It is thus necessary to 'deconstruct an overly naturalised and rigidly bounded concept of emotion, to treat emotion as an ideological practice rather than as a thing to be discovered or an essence to be distilled' (Lutz 1988: 4). Nevertheless, emotional reactions are not just a form of 'ideological practice' but also the product of specific historical changes. As Reddy (2001) argues convincingly, long-term social and political changes regularly coincide with changes in 'emotional regimes' and as such they establish new norms of emotional life. For example, the French Revolution unleashed an unprecedented social transformation that replaced the political, economic, and cultural hegemony of aristocracy with the dominance of the new bourgeois rulers. However, this change developed on the back of the changing emotional regimes that, by the late eighteenth century, had already affected many non-aristocratic elements of French society. This is well illustrated by the different emotional reactions to crying: 'while tears were frowned upon at Versailles, they were given full reign in the theaters and salons beyond the reach of the court' (Rosenwein 2010: 22).

Although human beings have some universal emotional traits, the emotional reactions on the battlefield are not uniform and static. Instead, the inner feelings and behaviours of soldiers are historically variable and highly diverse. In different time periods it is possible to witness very distinct ideas about emotions and also different emotional behaviours. This indicates that the biological foundations of emotional reactions are not transhistorical but have been shaped, moulded, and transformed by diverse structural contexts. For example, Scheer (2012) shows how combat motivation has changed historically through the use of different organisational measures ranging from coercive policing, remuneration, and compensation to military drill. All these measures have contributed to and have been shaped by the emotional responses of soldiers.

Van der Haven (2016) and McNeill (1997) identify drill as playing a decisive role in transforming emotions on the battlefield. While McNeill (1997) focuses on the dynamics of rhythmic movements of soldiers produced in the close-order drill which contributes to heightened emotional experiences of 'muscular bonding', van der Haven (2016) explores how the collective action of military organisations transforms fear into pride. In both cases the emphasis is on the changing historical dynamics of emotional responses on the battlefield. Analysing the seventeenth-century army manuals, van der Haven demonstrates how the military commanders were instructed to mould emotional reactions through drill and obedience. For example, in the army manuals used in the seventeenth-century French Army and the Dutch States Army, unquestioned obedience was seen as a precondition for effective social cohesion that would prevent expressions of fear: 'for we have seen a million times that soldiers who never broke their ranks – and were willing to maintain such order and unity together, never allowing the lines of their battalion be broken – never went into battle, nor moved without orders, always defeated their enemies sooner or later' (Billon 1617, quoted in van der Haven 2016: 28).

Thus, the introduction of drill contributed towards shifting battlefield behaviour from the traditional, aristocratic, focus on individual heroic deeds to successful collective action through hierarchical obedience. While the pre-modern aristocratic warriors were concerned with the individualised concepts of honour and shame resulting from their actions on the battlefield, early modern armies developed pride through coordinated collective military action. In addition, the practice of synchronised drilling allowed soldiers to refocus their attention on the details of

coordination of their behaviour with others, which proved highly beneficial on the battlefield: on the one hand, these new, almost automatic
skills, helped collective fighting and, on the other, by focusing their
attention on technical aspects of coordination the feelings of fear were
gradually transformed into other emotions.

For McNeill (1997), drill was also important as a mechanism of group
bonding that enhanced the emotional ties between soldiers. In the
seventeenth-century Dutch Netherlands military units were encouraged
to adopt a variety of collective practices, including a collective prayer
before the battle, sharing a meal with comrades, singing military songs
and religious psalms, and so on. The group character of daily close-order
drills impacts on emotional change in a similar way as these ritualistic
practices transform individual behaviour. The experience of regular participation in drills amplifies one's emotional response. As McNeill (1997:
2) reflects on his own experience as a soldier in the Second World War,
this prolonged everyday collective action of marching in unison with
others generates a strong 'muscular bond' where one experiences an
emotional change: 'A sense of pervasive well-being is what I recall; more
specifically, a strange sense of personal enlargement; a sort of swelling
out, becoming bigger than life, thanks to participation in collective
ritual.' This very Durkheimian experience of shared collective
excitement stands in opposition to the mostly individualised emotional
reactions of traditional aristocratic warfare and indicates clearly that
emotions are not fixed but highly diverse and historically changing
phenomena.

Nevertheless, drill was not the only social practice that transformed
emotional reactions. Another important ritual associated with the regulation of emotional dynamics was duelling. Whereas drill helped regulate
fear and anxiety, duelling was a practice that managed feelings of honour
and shame. Initially, duelling was a prerogative solely of the aristocracy.
This practice dates back to the Middle Ages and the code of chivalry and
was prevalent among the European nobility throughout the early modern
period. Although states tried to ban duelling it was still popular in the
nineteenth and early twentieth centuries. However, from the eighteenth
century onwards duels became 'democratised' in the sense that ordinary
soldiers would engage in duelling to restore their honour. Despite an
official ban and regulations that often stipulated the death penalty for
duelling, the practice was widely tolerated as many officers understood
that duelling was an effective mechanism of social and emotional control.
More specifically, duels helped regulate the dynamics of honour and
shame, thus maintaining a degree of cohesion and social pugnacity
within the military while also exalting the martial values of bravery, and

respect. As Berkovich (2016: 99) shows, ordinary soldiers often imitated their superiors and their duels were governed by similar informal yet highly influential codes: 'The social pressure to conduct duels was high … Jean Rossignol, who served eight years as a private in Louis XVI's army, describes fighting in no less than ten formal duels, as well as numerous brawls.' The widespread practice of duelling influenced the emotional dynamics on the battlefield. The soldiers who lost face and were unwilling to restore their honour through duels where shamed and deemed to be cowards. Thus, this historically specific ritual has played a significant role in shaping the emotions of ordinary soldiers, indicating yet again that emotions are not biological givens but highly contextual and dynamic social experiences.

9.4   Social Pugnacity and Emotional Variation in Space

Collective emotional experiences do not only change through time, they also exhibit significant cultural variation. Hence not all soldiers act in the same way on the battlefield. John Keegan (1994: 12) noted that specific cultural practices shape different trajectories of warfare. He questioned the dominant neo-Clausewitzian paradigm which interprets all wars as similar in terms of being an extension of politics by other means, and argued that war is 'an expression of culture, often a determinant of cultural forms, in some societies the culture itself'. In this context he found enormous differences between the military practices of different societies including Easter Islanders, Mamluks, Zulus, Japanese, and contemporary European armies. He also recognised the importance and cultural variability of emotions on the battlefield. In this context he differentiates between the three types of 'warrior traditions' – the primitive, the Oriental, and the modern 'Western way of war'. In his view the 'primitive war' is 'fed by passions and rancours that do not yield to rational measures of persuasion or control'. Hence, in his view, this kind of war is regulated by ritual practices: 'once defined rituals have been performed, the contestants shall recognise the fact of their satisfaction and have recourse to conciliation, arbitration and peace-making' (Keegan 1994: 58, 387). 'Oriental warfare' is associated with horse warriors and steppe nomads who rely on evasion, delay, and indirect fighting, which for Keegan was important in developing the tradition of military and emotional restraint. The third, modern Western type, developed through the face-to-face fighting of ancient Greeks and the Christian just war tradition, which, together with the technological military advancements since the 1700s, has centred on winning wars through decisive battles (Keegan 1994).

Keegan is right that battlefields are defined by different cultural practices and a variety of collective emotional experiences. However, his
cultural determinism, combined with crude Orientalism and essentialist
epistemology, have prevented him from articulating a subtle theoretical
framework for the analysis of emotional dynamics of battlefields
(Malešević 2010). Thus, rather than simply assuming that 'each culture'
has a singular and homogeneous emotional regime on the battlefield it is
important to recognise that cultural variations also exist within as well as
between and outside specific societies. In other words, there is no one
way of being a Zulu, Mamluk, or 'Westerner' on the battlefield.
Collective emotional dynamics are not determined by ethnic, national,
religious, or geographical categories. Such categories do influence group
dynamics on the battlefield, but they are far from being the only social
mechanism of emotional responses. Furthermore, the cultural influences
are not fixed in time and space, they also change and are shaped by
interaction with other groups. Taking all these important caveats into
account, one can focus on the social and cultural variation in theatres
of war.

The first problem that confronts the biological universalist approaches
is the fact that emotions are named and interpreted differently in different cultural settings. For example, what in a contemporary US context is
regularly described as sadness caused by depression, in a Buddhist social
environment is likely to be categorised as a form of suffering. While the
former emotional experience is deemed to be negative and as such would
call for an intervention and treatment by medical professionals, the latter
would be regarded as a positive emotional reaction that paves the way
towards the ultimate form of happiness – nirvana. These cultural values
are clearly reflected in the experiences of soldiers on the battlefield.
Although Buddhism teaches that it is better to die than kill in war,
soldiers can work towards reaching nirvana through suffering on the
battlefield (Demiéville 2010: 19). In contrast, suffering, depression,
and unhappiness are all seen as emotional problems that need to be
rectified when recognised among contemporary US soldiers.

There are many other examples where the emotional states of individuals are interpreted very differently depending on the cultural context.
For example, while in some societies solitude is perceived as normal or
even a sign of strength of an individual's character, other societies treat
loneliness as an emotional deficiency. Whereas self-sufficiency is prized
in highly individualised modern societies and reaching happiness within
oneself is valued in the Buddhist tradition, other cultural contexts treat
solitary action as an emotional impediment. As Fajans (1997) shows in
her ethnography of the Baining people of Papua New Guinea, solitary life

is understood in a highly negative sense where loneliness is associated with hunger. For most Bainings hunger is not a physiological state but an emotional condition, and not taking part in the common meal would automatically indicate a lack of sociability which in this worldview is the essence of human survival. In this context, fighting in war always entails a collective enterprise and leaving a soldier alone would mean starving him and thus deliberately causing pain.

Recognising that cultures are not homogeneous and static wholes does not mean that cultural differences do not play important roles in social action. For example, in some cultural contexts a strong emotional reaction can be regarded as a sign of severe illness while other social orders tend to tolerate such change in one's behaviour. In these situations, the naming of the emotional response plays a significant role in defining and understanding someone's actions. For example, running amok on the battlefield is likely to be interpreted very differently in Malayan cultural contexts than in European militaries. This behaviour usually involves an individual who without previous indication of anger suddenly becomes enraged and embarks on a rampage of violence or attempts to kill anyone she or he meets. The concept of running amok comes from the Malay word *meng-âmuk*, which can be translated as 'to make a furious and desperate charge'. In the traditional Malaysian interpretation such behaviour is a sign that the individual is possessed by an evil tiger spirit (*hantu belian*) and as such is not responsible for her or his actions (Hempel et al. 2000). In most contemporary societies this type of emotional frenzy is defined as a serious psychological disorder that requires medical treatment.

The second issue that the biological approaches cannot account for is the cultural variation in the expressions of emotions on the battlefield. While soldiers often encounter very similar conditions in the theatre of war, their emotional and physical responses can differ significantly. In some cultural contexts the horrific experience of the battlefield might provoke fear, anxiety, and panic while in other cultural settings the same experience is likely to generate a sense of excitement, anger, pride, honour, or a range of other very different emotional reactions. Furthermore, the same emotions can be expressed differently while similar physiological gestures could signpost very different emotional reactions. For example, in some societies a smile indicates happiness and serenity while in other cultural traditions a smile can be associated with shame or ignorance (Krys et al. 2016; Reddy 2001: 101). The same applies to war situations where some cultural settings are defined by stoic and aloof responses of soldiers to the brutalities of frontline fighting while in other cultural contexts soldiers show excessive emotional and physiological reactions. Hence many Italian infantry soldiers who fought on the various fronts during the First World War were often overwhelmed by fear and panic during the key battles. As reported by eyewitnesses, many of these young recruits, mostly illiterate peasants, would comply with the orders of their officers but their emotional reactions indicated their sense of horror. The Italian and British sources describe the behaviour of the soldiers during the Battle of the Isonzo in 1917 in the following terms: 'soldiers advanced crying. They did not rebel: when ordered out of the trenches they obeyed; but went crying"'; 'most of the men in the trenches were very young ... many of them were weeping and some had ice on their face [frozen tears]' (Wilcox 2012: 175). The few literate soldiers who wrote letters or kept diaries record the same emotional responses: 'long fits of crying' and 'shattered with hunger and sleep – tears fill our eyes, crying like babies' (Wilcox, 2012: 175). In direct contrast, when Fulani warriors fight, they exhibit no visible physiological reactions and their emotional responses are very different: 'They fight each other with sticks; when hit by opponents from other clans, they show no emotion in spite of the pain. They are proud of the scars they consequently receive' (Doob 1981: 35).

The third phenomenon that further challenges the simple biological universalist explanations of emotional dynamics is the cultural difference in emotional expression. In other words, the emotional reactions of soldiers tend to be culturally specific. For example, although most human beings express pain and grief when somebody close to them dies, the grieving process is culturally diverse. Whereas in many European societies grief and loss are associated with gloomy posture, sombre behaviour, or crying and weeping, in other cultural settings grieving involves other emotional and physical reactions. For instance, in some parts of Bali, laughter is a part of the grieving process. As Wikan's (1989: 297) ethnographic study indicates, losing a close family member is often associated with jokes and giggles. In one instance, following the funeral of someone's fiancé, the grieving friends and relatives, including the 'poised and bright' partner of the deceased, gathered around their shared photos, and started laughing. They all agreed with the comment from the one of the grievers: 'This was nothing to be sad about! The boy was dead, so what would be the use? Where one stick is broken, another grows ... No use grieving over one. Go on, be happy, let bygones be bygones! The world is bigger than a kelor leaf!'

These different cultural framings of emotional displays are just as visible on the battlefield. Some cultural contexts allow soldiers to express a full range of emotions while in other cultural settings the battlefield is firmly framed through limited and regulated emotional experiences. As

Barkawi (2017: 156) demonstrates in his analysis of Indian armies under British control during the First and Second World Wars, most Indian recruits had to be trained in an emotional regime that differed greatly to that which British officers associated with proper soldiering. Hence, 'instructors had to teach recruits forms of self-control and mastery of their emotions in these excruciating situations'. In many instances the British officers relied on shame to mould young and inexperienced recruits into a fully-fledged military force. In this context they utilised the caste divisions, gender, and age differences to demean those who resisted or were reluctant to fight for the British Empire: 'the instructors came out to harangue the trainees for being weak, childish, feminine, and unable to control themselves. Sometimes the trainees would be made to put on saris, i.e., women's clothes, to emphasise the point' (Barkawi 2017: 156).

There is no doubt that shaming soldiers through the use of rigid patriarchal categories of masculinity and femininity is something that is present throughout the world. This practice has been identified in different cultural settings. However, there is still a strong element of difference in how precisely battlefields are gendered and how soldiers' emotional reactions frame their sense of masculinity. For example, the actions of both British and Italian recruits during the First World War were strongly associated with typical twentieth-century notions of masculinity such as virility, courage, and determination. Nevertheless, as Wilcox (2012: 175) argues, the soldiers' emotional expressions were rather different: while many UK soldiers subscribed to 'the British working-class model of stoical endurance', including 'an assumption of confidence in the outcome of war, rather than indifference or doubt', the masculinity of many Italian soldiers was defined by 'peasant endurance and the capacity for silent suffering' regardless of the war outcome. Hence, while both the Italian and British soldiers would express similar emotional responses associated with a strong sense of manhood the social sources of these emotional displays would in fact be very different.

None of this is to say that the cultural framing of emotions is fixed and inflexible or that it does not change in time. On the contrary, cultural difference is influential precisely because it can change within different cultural contexts and also be changed by other cultural practices. Scholars of the French Revolution have demonstrated convincingly how the cult of sensibility inaugurated and promoted by the leaders of the revolution gradually permeated different social strata in France and also impacted on the emotional responses of French soldiers during the Revolutionary and Napoleonic Wars (Germani 2016; Reddy 2001). The cult of sentimentalism was in part built on the notion that 'nature was the well-spring of authentic, patriotic emotion' and the revolutionary leaders propagated the idea that one should differentiate between nature as 'a blind, natural force and nature as a moral imperative' (Germani 2016: 187). Drawing on Rousseau's view of the collective will, the revolutionaries rejected the traditional aristocratic concepts of fighting for one's family and king and in this process transformed the notion of filial attachments into a sense of moral obligation towards the community of equals: 'The heroism of revolutionary soldiers represented the triumph of the moral individual over natural man, a triumph made possible only because of a regenerative revolution' (Germani, 2016: 187–8). In a similar way, the nineteenth-century Russian military practice was significantly influenced by teachings of Mikhail Dragomirov, who was a general and a military writer responsible for the doctrine of what Plamper (2009) calls 'controlled berserkerdom'. This doctrine centred on the idea of channelling fear into a military virtue of self-sacrifice through denial. Dragomirov played a key role in the reorganisation of the military education system in Russia, which, under his influence, promoted this idea of self-denial as the ultimate military virtue. Relying on drill and the training of obedience, the Russian soldiers were taught to focus on self-denial as an 'effective antidote to fear'. These new military principles had some impact on changing the existing emotional regime within the Russian military, thus indicating the flexibility of cultural frames (Plamper, 2009).

9.5   Conclusion

Soldiers often emphasise that combat is profoundly emotional experience. Phil Klay, a US veteran of the Iraq War, writes in his memoir *Redeployment*:

Somebody said combat is 99 percent sheer boredom and 1 percent pure terror. They weren't an MP in Iraq. On the roads I was scared all the time. Maybe not pure terror ... But a kind of low-grade terror that mixes with the boredom. So, it's 50 percent boredom and 49 percent normal terror, which is a general feeling that you might die at any second and that everybody in this country wants to kill you. Then, of course, there's the 1 percent pure terror, when your heart rate skyrockets, and your vision closes in and your hands are white, and your body is humming. You can't think. You're just an animal, doing what you've been trained to do. And then you go back to normal terror, and you go back to being a human, and you go back to thinking. (Klay 2014: 42–3)

Fighting in war generates strong emotional reactions where fear and anxiety often mix with rage, anger, shame, honour, sadness, guilt, pride, elation, and joy. The conventional interpretations emphasise that human psychological and physiological reactions on the battlefield are universal in a sense that similar emotions are triggered by similar external stimuli and thus all soldiers are likely to experience the same emotional reactions in the combat zone. In this chapter I have questioned biological determinism, arguing that emotional reactions on the battlefield are highly diverse and situationally flexible. More specifically, the chapter advances an argument that although most human beings are regularly affected by the exceptional circumstances of the battlefield their emotional responses are rarely uniform. Taking part in theatres of war is likely to result in physiological and psychological changes in most soldiers. However, the cross-cultural and historical research indicates that almost identical situations of close-range violence can generate very different individual and collective emotional dynamics. Consequently, emotions cannot be reduced to physiology, and rather than bring 'triggered' by external stimuli emotional changes are largely shaped by historical and cultural forces. There are no emotional essences which are detached from their historical and cultural contexts. Instead, all emotional responses are embedded in specific social situations. Social pugnacity is variable precisely because human emotional (and cognitive) reactions are not uniform. This is not to say that biology does not matter but only that physiological responses are only part of the picture where they, together with the wider cultural and historical dynamics, shape the emotional reactions in the combat zone.

10 Killing in War

The Emotional Dynamics of Social Pugnacity

10.1 Introduction

Close-range killings in war are usually associated with two contrasting images. The more prevalent view depicts excessive violence as common, widespread, and easy to do. Popular films and TV programmes are saturated with the images of war where killing is the norm and an almost routine, everyday practice. For example, the recently featured and extremely popular *Game of Thrones* is full of such imagery where individuals show no moral qualms when getting involved in mass killings, torture, rape, and violent abuse. Moreover, such acts are encouraged and celebrated with the memorable lines such as 'Stick 'em with the pointy end' or 'There is only one god and his name is Death'. In direct contrast, the other common portrayal of war focuses on the traumatic experiences of soldiers who are unwilling to fight and when forced to take part in violent events where they kill other human beings, they express regret, remorse, and guilt. A plethora of critical war films and novels from *All Quiet on the Western Front* to *The Deer Hunter*, *Apocalypse Now*, and *The Hurt Locker* emphasise the sheer brutality of war and its deep traumatic impact on ordinary soldiers. In these narratives the act of killing is an extremely difficult experience which leaves lasting psychological damage on those who take part in it. As one protagonist in the film *Saving Private Ryan* states: 'I just know that every man I kill the further away from home I feel' (Hagelin 2008: 112). In this chapter my aim is to offer a sociological analysis of these phenomena with a focus on the role emotions play in the individual and social responses to killing in war. The chapter draws on the interviews conducted among the ex-combatants who fought in the wars in Croatia and Bosnia and Herzegovina (1991–5).[1] The first part of the chapter critically reviews the existing

---

[1] The information on methodology and data collection relating to this project is provided in the Appendix.

research on killing in war and articulates an alternative approach to understanding the emotional dynamics of killing in the context of social pugnacity. The second part explores different aspects of violent collective action on the battlefields through in-depth analysis of the interviews with the ex-combatants. The final part brings the theoretical arguments and the results of the empirical research together.

10.2   Killing Other Humans

Contemporary popular culture is saturated with violent images many of which suggest that killing another human being is easy. From bestselling war books and crime thrillers to the latest Hollywood blockbusters one can observe heroes and villains who kill thousands of faceless individuals without any moral qualms. Computer games and social media also perpetuate this perception – killing others is easy and it comes naturally. The traditional evolutionary accounts, involving the chart-topping books by Pinker (2011), Diamond (2012), Gat (2006), and many others, have also propagated this belief by insisting that humans, just like the rest of animal world, have no problem murdering other members of their species in order to survive and improve their genetic fitness. For example, anthropologist Chagnon (1988) has argued that some tribal societies such as the Yanomami of Amazonia have historically been exceptionally violent as this aggressive strategy has proved beneficial for their evolutionary adaptation with 'the killers having more children' than those who opted for the peaceful resolution of conflicts. Many neo-Darwinian scholars have argued that killing has been an optimal evolutionary tactic through which natural selection has privileged predatory and violent behaviour (Buss 2016; Gat 2017; Martin 2018; Pinker 2011; Potts and Hayden 2008).

However, much of recent research across various disciplines challenges these perceptions. Fry and Szala (2013: 453) show that mammals are very flexible in their responses to conflictual situations and although they engage often in agonistic behaviour much of it does not involve killing among the members of the same species: 'Intraspecific agonism, including physical aggression, tends to be much less bloody than predatory aggression, and is rarely lethal in mammals.' Kokko (2008) and Fry et al. (2010) document how restrained agonism rather than excessive violence has proved advantageous for the survival of many species. Hence many mammalian species avoid violent encounters through different practices: giraffes engage in ritualistic neck to neck contacts until one gives up, lions avoid interaction with other prides, chimpanzees tend not to venture into the peripheral areas of their ranges, and elephant seals rely on treats to avoid aggression against other seals (Fry and Szala 2013: 454). Even the species which have traditionally been regarded as quite violent such as gorillas and chimpanzees rarely engage in life threatening behaviour (Goodall 1986). Sussman and Garber (2007) have collected extensive data on the behaviour of monkeys and apes, and they show that apes experience less than one, mostly mild, agonistic act per month.

The findings from these biological studies are reflected in the psychological, anthropological, and sociological research on human behaviour. For example, many nomadic foragers have developed ritualistic practices that mitigate against actual violence. These include chest pounding, restrained verbal confrontations and threats, song and dance contests, sporting competitions, ritualised contests, and a variety of restrained physical interactions. The physical contacts that cause bodily injuries also tend to be regulated and limited to specific body parts. These include duels, wrestling contests, reciprocal blow striking to shoulders or head, club fighting, or firebrands fighting rituals (Fry and Szala 2013: 464). The psychological and micro-sociological research on the behaviour of soldiers, police and criminal gangs has demonstrated that even for the trained professionals violence does not come naturally, and they have to overcome severe ethical and psychological resistance to killing. Grossman (1996, 2004) and Bourke (2000, 2014) show that for most combatants close-range killings are extremely disturbing experiences and ordinary individuals who take part in these events become deeply traumatised. For example, American soldiers involved in face-to-face combat with Japanese and later Vietnamese soldiers described their experiences as sickening: 'I threw up all over myself ... I had urinated in my skivvies ... It was a betrayal of what I'd been taught since a child'; 'we started having a very personal contact with people we were killing ... I started to get really bad feelings ... just fucking bad feelings' (Barker 1982: 123; Grossman 1996: 88). In this context many studies on battlefield behaviour report that the majority of soldiers claim that they have never killed anybody during war or that they were shooting at the distance but have never seen an enemy soldier being killed by their fire (Bourke 2000, 2014; Grossman 1996; Malešević 2010: 229).

Collins (2004, 2008, 2015) has theorised these findings arguing that face-to-face violence is difficult for most humans as it interrupts the normal pattern of social interaction. Violent encounters must overcome the human physiological and social propensity to create interaction ritual chains which are rooted in complex emotional dynamics. Hence interpersonal violence must tear the emotional barriers in order to find pathways around normal social interactions. However, these processes are extremely demanding and regularly result in tension and fear for those involved. Collins argues that there is nothing automatic in violent encounters. They are difficult to enact and as such are mostly characterised by incompetence, bluster, and bluff. Consequently, most acts of violence entail the presence of social organisations which foster aggressive behaviour. Furthermore, as violence goes against the normal flows of human interaction it often transpires when there is a deep disconnect in social relations. Hence violent acts regularly involve profoundly asymmetrical relationships such as disproportional attacks and atrocities against weak opponents (e.g., domestic abuse, forward panic in wars, ethnic cleansing and genocide, gang attacks, etc.). Collins (2008, 2015) also shows that since violence is difficult it tends to be perpetrated by a small number of individuals who have attained a degree of competence at it: most killings in war are committed by a small number of soldiers, and the same offenders tend to be involved in multiple violent crimes including murders.

The micro-sociologists and psychologists who study human interactions have argued that violent encounters are more difficult in direct face-to-face interaction as human beings can read emotional responses from the facial expressions of others and as such are likely to empathise with the pain and fear of others. There is an abundance of research on the 'fingerprints' of emotions pointing that our facial expressions reflect biologically predetermined and thus universal human nature. This idea was initially formulated by Darwin in his 1872 book *The Expression of the Emotions in Man and Animals* where he advanced the thesis that emotions are an innate product of evolution and as such have universal facial expression. This idea was empirically tested by several experiments including the influential work of Tomkins and McCarter (1964), Izard (1994) and Ekman and his collaborators (Ekman 1992; Ekman and Cordaro 2011; Ekman and Friesen 1971). These experimental studies conducted among different groups throughout the world including the tribal population in Papua New Guinea seemed to indicate that facial expressions are universal across cultures. Using photographs of what they coded to be six basic emotions (fear, anger, disgust, surprise, sadness, and happiness) these scholars were adamant that they had proved that emotion recognition is universal and indicating that emotions are innate. Drawing on these findings Collins (2008) argues that since humans can read emotions of others they act on these emotional cues and this has implications for violent behaviour. For example, the conventional view is that hostages whose faces are covered are more likely to survive their ordeal because they have not seen their captors and as such would not be able to recognise them. Collins disputes this, insisting that the opposite is true as the captors who do not see the faces of their hostages are less likely to develop a degree of empathy as there has not been direct eye-to-eye contact and thus preventing the development of interaction ritual chains. Eye-to-eye contact is likely to create tension and fear thus mitigating against violence.

The argument I develop in this chapter challenges both the traditional, neo-Darwinian, accounts which see killing as easy and the more recent approaches that interpret taking a human life as an extremely difficult act. Drawing on the fieldwork and the interviews I conducted with the former combatants in the wars fought in Croatia and Bosnia and Herzegovina, I argue that the emotional dynamics of killing has less to do with biology and the alleged ingrained emotional fingerprints and much more with the social processes that precede, accompany, and follow the acts of violence. The psychological and micro-sociological arguments that criticise the conventional neo-Darwinian view of killing are on the right track. However, these approaches do not go far enough as they retain a degree of biological determinism that underpins the evolutionary theory of violence. These recent approaches question the premise that killing is automatic, natural, and genetically beneficial for survival. Nevertheless, they still maintain the key essentialist assumption centred on the idea that the ingrained emotional givens determine human response to violence. In this chapter my aim is to show that rather than being predetermined by fixed emotional states it is the violent experience itself that shapes the content of emotional responses. In other words, I argue that killing might be difficult not because of the ingrained and stable emotional responses that prevent the formation of successful interaction ritual chains. Instead, the pathways towards killing are shaped by the specific structural dynamics which influences the character of emotional reactions. Human emotions are not predetermined but are in fact created and framed by shared social action. In this context the acts of killing are not rooted in biological prerequisites but are structural products that themselves foster the content of emotional responses. Simply put, humans do not kill other humans because of anger, shame, fear, disgust, enjoyment, or sadness, rather these specific emotional responses are largely articulated in the very act of violence. This is not to say that biology does not matter at all. As I show in Chapter 1, there is no doubt that intense emotional reactions are often connected with pronounced physiological changes: increased heart rate, tightening of muscles, difficulties in respiration, the upsurge of adrenalin pumping by the hypothalamus, and other anatomical responses (Artwohl and Christensen 1997; Klinger 2004). The point is that physiology does not determine emotional dynamics.

Humans do not experience fear because their heart rate has increased, or their levels of adrenalin have jumped to the roof: instead, these biological responses are a consequence of structural changes which impact on individual and collective behaviour. Emotions are not simply triggered; they are spawned in action. This is why social pugnacity is not an inborn quality but a product of social environment.

This argument is not averse to recent research in neuroscience, cognitive psychology, and the sociology of emotions. On the contrary I draw on some strands of this scholarship to show that emotions are not biologically predetermined entities but phenomena that are highly dynamic, situational, and malleable (see also Chapter 1). The new studies in critical neuroscience challenge the notion of stable, ingrained, and clearly defined emotions. In contrast to the traditional views which were adamant that anger, fear, sadness, happiness, surprise, and other emotions have unambiguous physical fingerprints in the human brain or our facial muscles the wealth of experimental evidence shows that this is not the case (Barr 2007; Barrett 2006, 2012, 2017; Gross 2015; Lindquist et al. 2014, 2015). Instead of emotional uniformity one encounters enormous variation: some individuals express fear very differently from others and different cultural contexts shape very diverse facial and other responses to fear. Even the same people can show different types of emotional response to the same stimuli on different occasions. In a nutshell as Barrett (2017: xii) emphasises, summarising the abundance of recent experimental studies: 'your emotions are not built-in but [are] made from more basic parts. They are not universal but vary from culture to culture. They are not triggered: you create them.'

The new scholarship in critical neuroscience has emphasised that human brains and human facial muscles do not act uniformly when exposed to similar stimuli. Much of this research goes against the conventional psychological interpretations and especially challenges Paul Ekman's studies on universal facial expressions of emotions. As Barrett shows, the fact that Ekman's basic emotion method has been replicated on numerous occasions does not make it valid as all these studies make the same mistake of introducing the emotion words in their experiments and then reproduce the same conceptual apparatus in their findings: 'If humans actually had an inborn ability to recognise emotional expressions, then removing the emotion words from the method should not matter … but it did, every single time. There is very little doubt that emotion words have a powerful influence in experiments, instantly casting into doubt the conclusions of every study ever performed that used the basic emotion method' (Barrett 2017: 52).

The experiments that deploy facial electromyography (EMG)[2] to identify movements of electrical signals for facial muscle activation show that it is impossible to clearly separate and differentiate emotions. These experiments could only distinguish between rather vague pleasant and unpleasant feelings (Barrett 2017; Gross 2015; Lindquist et al. 2015). The same applies to the research on new-born babies who also do not show uniform facial responses that could be associated with specific emotions. Research on the bodily changes associated with specific feelings shows similar results: individuals exposed to the content likely to generate emotional response (e.g., horror film) do experience significant changes in respiration and heart rate but there are no uniform patterns of emotional responses. Furthermore, these new studies have not only been conducted in closed laboratory conditions and among European and North American respondents but have been replicated in natural settings throughout the world including hunter-gatherer populations ranging from Namibia and Tanzania to Papua New Guinea (Crivelli et al. 2016, 2017). All of these studies confirm that social context influences emotional reactions with human beings expressing a very high degree of emotional granularity: 'on different occasions, in different contexts, in different studies, within the same individual and across different individuals, the same emotion category involves different bodily responses' (Barrett 2017: 15).

None of this is to say that emotions are unimportant for human behaviour. On the contrary, humans are the most emotional creatures among mammals and much of our social action is shaped by emotional responses (Barbalet 1996, 2002; Turner 2007). The point is that these emotional responses are extremely diverse, plastic and context dependent and as such they do not have a clearly defined physical 'fingerprint' in our bodies. Hence, pre-given emotions do not determine our actions, instead it is our actions that create diverse emotional responses which are built from the emotionally undifferentiated material of our brains.

These recent findings in neuroscience, psychology, and microsociology can help us understand the social realities of war and especially the emotional dynamics of killing. Many studies on the behaviour of soldiers on the battlefield emphasise the crucial role emotions play in the context of violent action. However, the overwhelming majority of

---

[2] Facial electromyography is a measurement technique to assess muscle activity. It focuses on muscle contraction by identifying and amplifying electrical impulses that are created by muscle fibres as they contract. Much of the research focus has been on the two main facial muscle groups: (a) the corrugator supercilii group (involved in frowning) and (b) the zygomaticus major muscle group (involved in smiling) (Barrett 2017; Gross 2015).

these studies treat emotional responses as being biologically ingrained where the experience of violence allegedly triggers distinct emotions – fear, anger, sadness, shame, and so on. For example, one can read about the 'threat of violence triggering fear and the threat of contamination triggering disgust' (Norenzayan 2016: 858) or how 'the Life-or-Limb trigger provokes the ultimate and irresistible outrage of anger and commitment to war to punish or annihilate the attacker' (Fields 2016: 298). Even the more sophisticated micro-interactionist sociological studies are not immune to the assumption that violent acts only activate the already existing and clearly differentiated emotions: 'Symbols are loaded with meaning based on past experience, and trigger emotion' (Weininger and Lizardo 2018: 1). These and many other studies reinforce the view that violent acts just tap into already formed biological dispositions and help activate preformed emotional responses. Nevertheless, the emotional reactions that are ever present and often amplified in war environments are not triggered by violence but are often made in the context of shared violent experiences. More specifically, the acts of killing create the emotional responses and since such acts take place in different social contexts they can and do produce different social responses. Not all soldiers react in the same way to the experience of death: some find participation in the act of killing an emotionally extremely difficult experience while for others killing is perceived as a relatively routine practice with little emotional resonance. Nevertheless, in all instances the emotional responses to killing are context dependent so even the individuals that find some instances of killing unproblematic and unemotional tend to react very differently in other instances and might be emotionally deeply affected by deaths occurring in different contexts. Furthermore, there is a great variation of emotional responses to seeing the acts of killing and torture committed by other individuals as well as to situations where combatants anticipate the potential threats of death or torture. In all these instances violence does not automatically and uniformly trigger the same emotions. Instead, emotional responses are constructed through specific social contexts and interactions.

10.3   The Emotional Dynamics of Killing

The legal and moral systems of nearly all societies in the world deem the killing of another human being to be the worst form of transgression. Killers are often imprisoned for life or given lengthy prison sentences, sent to death row, or expelled and shunned from society. The religious teachings of all main denominations and major ethical codes have also characterised murder as the ultimate form of sin or ethical offence. The educational systems in most societies in the world also teach that human life is precious and that killing other humans is morally wrong. Nevertheless, in times of war these ethical principles are deeply challenged as soldiers are expected to kill enemy soldiers on the battlefield. Moreover, the killing of the enemy in wartime is not only accepted and encouraged but it is regularly glorified: while murder during peacetime is considered to be the worst possible crime, killing another human being ('the enemy') in wartime is often characterised as a heroic deed (Malešević 2010). The transition in the interpretation of how killings should be judged morally in times of peace and war is bound to affect young recruits who suddenly have to reframe and readjust their moral principles. The process of sudden ethical switching is very difficult, and many individuals find it extremely painful and deeply upsetting. This transition process is regularly shaped by complex emotional responses with soldiers perceiving killing, death, incapacitating wounds, and other battlefield experiences through the prism of fear, repugnance, anger, disgust, surprise, sadness, shame, and many other emotional reactions. However, some individuals seem to be able to adjust quicker and better than others and are capable of being involved in killing or torturing enemy soldiers and even civilians with few or no moral qualms (Mann 2019). Extreme violent acts are also characterised by intense emotional dynamics for some killers and torturers while others display very little emotion. To assess the complexity of the emotional dynamics of killing and other violent acts in times of war in Bosnia and Herzegovina and Croatia it is necessary to explore the wider social context. Hence my analysis zooms in on six key categories: (1) the direct experience of close-range killing; (2) seeing others kill or die; (3) the experience of torture and abuse of POWs; (4) fear of humiliation; (5) the emotional dynamics of sacrifice; and (6) the role of narcotics in close-range violence.

10.3.1   Face-to-Face Killing

With the technological transformation of warfare and the development of modern weaponry the direct interpersonal experience of killing has largely been replaced with mass destruction from distance (Bousquet 2018; Malešević 2010). Artillery caused most deaths in combat from the Napoleonic Wars of the early nineteenth century to the Second World War (Grossman 1996: 27). With the introduction of tanks and aerial bombardment in the twentieth century the experience of close-range killing became even rarer. For example, in the Second World War, 75 per cent of British military casualties were caused by long-range artillery shells, aerial bombs, mortars, and grenades; gun bullets were responsible for less than 10 per cent of deaths; and knives and bayonets accounted for a minuscule number of fatalities. During the Korean War, small arms caused only 3 per cent of American casualties (Holmes 1985). In recent wars such as Iraq and Afghanistan most deaths were inflicted through distance killing: high-altitude bombs, transcontinental missiles, and unmanned aerial vehicles (drones). Hence it is no surprise that since the Second World War most soldiers report that they had no direct experience of killing, and a substantial number of combatants say that they have never killed anybody during their time in war (Bourke 2000; Grossman 1996; Malešević 2010).

The militaries that fought in Bosnia and Croatia could not rely on the superior technology associated with more advanced military forces. However, even in these wars the casualty rates followed the pattern that characterises all modern violent conflicts. In other words, most soldiers (and civilians) were killed from a distance by artillery, mines, tank projectiles and other long-range weapons. Some interviewees described the chaotic scenes on the frontlines:

First night [on the battlefield] … I expected God knows what is going to happen … [the experienced soldiers] told me that the shootings happen in the evening and in the morning … I loaded my gun and was waiting for the shooting to start … Should I aim at somebody or do something? … I didn't know what to do … and when the night came the shooting started from their trenches which were far away … in some places you can see them and in other places the forest is so dense and there is no visual contact at all … you see a few trenches two hundred meters away. (Dragan, VRS)

Others point out that the main threat came from long-distance weapons such as grenades, missiles, and shells: 'You have to act as if there are no falling grenades and that is very difficult … they are not all aimed for you and that one that you can hear is not yours … the one that you do not hear will be yours' (Ivan 2, HV); 'the first time I was on the battlefield I was slightly injured … the mortar grenade hit me … it was not terrible … but you feel fear … it was not pleasant' (Saša, HV).

Many interviewees reported that they had no experience of killing somebody in a face-to-face encounter: 'I've never killed anybody in person, I don't know … there were some [enemy] soldiers in the woods and I've asked [the commander] how should I shoot at them … and then there was mass shooting … I've heard screams, but most have managed to escape … one soldier was injured, and we captured him' (Dragan, VRS); 'I have never fought in hand-to-hand combat [prsa u prsa]' (Nenad, HV); 'Luckily I have never had that experience' (Saša, HV); 'No, everything happened so quickly … I was responsible for the explosives, mines … mostly outside the combat zone' (Vlado, HV); 'I have never been in such a situation ... it was more gun fighting [over trenches]' (Milan, VRS); 'There was no such a thing, these are mostly stories ... people would usually die when grenade explodes ... or sniper ... a very few people would die in direct [hand-to-hand] combat ... this only happens in American movies' (Jovo, VRS). Thus, face-to-face killing was a rare event for most soldiers.

Even the soldiers who had experience of close-range fighting would state that they have not killed anybody in person: 'there was a fighting one on one, there was everything there but I have to say that even though I was in such situations I have never aimed at anybody and shot at him ... it was mostly running [and shooting] here and there but I've never seen that I've killed anybody, I did not kill ... and that makes me happy ... I had those experiences, but I cannot say that I've killed anybody, I don't know ... it was not my intention to go and kill somebody' (Ivan 1, HV). Many combatants emphasised this emotional distance from individualised experiences of killing.

When asked explicitly whether they aimed and shot at an individual most soldiers responded that they did not: 'I did not encounter a situation where I would look directly at somebody and would shoot at him ... I would shoot mostly in the air' (Dražen, HV); 'No I have never seen that I have killed anybody, but I had one [enemy soldier] in my target range ... I saw a man smoking a cigarette ... I could see him ... and my finger was on the trigger ... just press and he is gone ... but my finger was stuck, it would not move ... no chance' (Dejan, VRS). Other soldiers said that they are not sure: 'I don't know ... you shoot ... but cannot see what happened ... you might see him [the enemy soldier] lying down but you cannot be sure, and you are not really interested ... you just want to run away and save yourself' (Boris, HV).

A small number of soldiers reported having had experience of close-range killing. Some of these ex-combatants describe this experience as traumatic and painful while others emphasise how they gradually became hardened and insensitive to taking lives. For example, one soldier describes how he felt the first time he killed a man: 'When you shoot at somebody and he falls down, that is a real shock ... that is the worst, worst feeling that you could have. When you aim at the man and you shoot him ... not at that very moment but later ... that makes you change as a man, you age instantly and you remember that forever' (Vjeko, HV). Others reported: 'Yes, I fought hand-in-hand at Olovo [a village in Bosnia] ... strong emotions ... horrible, horrible ... you don't know where you are shooting ... kneeling, moving around ... I almost killed my own comrade ... aiming ... then moving your gun ... the worst thing

that could happen ... chaos' (Dejan, VRS): 'Yes, at Matuzići [a village in
Bosnia] ... but this is not like in the films ... you just look to save your
head ... literally you keep your head down like an ostrich and shoot ...
hoping that everything finishes quickly ... that it stops ... it goes through
your head ... run here, run there ... there is no Rambo ... and those who
were boasting the most would look to save their own skin' (Saša, VRS);
'Yes, a number of times, mostly in Bosnia ... you wake up in the morning
in a [somebody's] courtyard and Chetniks [Serbian paramilitaries] were
next door ... so who fires first he stays alive ... two yards next to each
other ... everything is mixed ... all kinds of things would happen' (Ivan 2,
HV); 'It is only then that I realised what is war. Until then it was just a
game, you have a gun, and you shoot at them ... and they shoot at you ...
until the first person dies. And then, it is hard to describe that feeling ... it
is a real death. That changes you, I've changed in one day ... everything
went through my head ... until then I've only seen this on TV' (Vjeko,
HV). Hence many soldiers describe face-to-face fighting as a traumatic
event, a deeply negative emotional experience that they wanted to get
away from as soon as possible.

Some soldiers emphasise that they felt bad and sad instantly after the
event, others indicate that sadness or remorse came later, while some
soldiers state that they did not feel anything during the whole process.
Hence one combatant was clear that he deeply regretted his actions:

Once I destroyed a tank, not once, but the first time, in Bosnia ... and when the
battle was over, I went to see [that tank] ... and when I looked inside, I saw the
cremated bodies. And this image haunts me all my life ... the worst ... I have
nightmares ... cannot sleep and suffer from PTSD ... this will follow me all my
life, even though I don't feel guilty ... only feel sorry ... I ask myself Why? What
for? I don't feel any more that this [war] was necessary. (Vjeko, HV)

A very similar attitude was shared by soldiers who emphasise that they
had 'bad feelings' after taking somebody's life: 'I did not want to hurt
anybody ... if it hurts me, it hurts the other ... I did not want to injure
others ... only when I had to defend myself and others' (Mile, VRS); 'I
felt bad. If a man is normal, has a limit, know what is right and what it
should be and what it should not be' (Nenad, VRS). Some soldiers
experienced profound trauma:

I saw the pigs eating people ... dead people on the streets ... injured ... everybody
reacts differently ... it hit me how old people urinate ... they cannot control [their
bladder] from fear ... these scenes ... catastrophe ... everything to see ... you have
people who just pass by [the dead] or kick them ... I could not sleep for
months ... and many older people had problems ... it is not all the same, it is
not something you can get used to. (Saša, VRS)

For most young recruits, the act of killing was difficult and morally disturbing. They were exposed to extreme violent situations that they have never encountered before.

In direct contrast other former combatants insist that they felt nothing when killing the enemy soldiers: 'There is no feeling, no feeling at all, just as if you were knocking down pins at bowling, that is how I felt ... they were just falling like the bowling pins' (Ivan, HV); 'I saw people sitting around the trenches and asked only how to shoot, in bursts or not ... and the shooting started ... I've heard screams' (Dragan, VRS); 'You get used to it' (Zdravko, VRS); 'You shoot ... but you don't go there to see is he [dead] or not ... you see he fell down ... I don't care if I hit [him]or not ... I did not care at all ... only that I have enough time to run away, to save myself' (Boris, HV); 'I was as cool as a cucumber [*mrtav ladan*] ... all dead people look the same, miserable ... once I was loading decapitated corpses onto the bread truck ... taking them to the pathology unit to identify them ... this become normal ... you just move the bread baskets a bit away and drive ... we had no ambulance trucks left' (Ivan 2, HV). For those soldiers killing was a routine, an ordinary military activity that they were expected to do, and in this process, they tried to remain as emotionless as possible.

A number of interviewees pointed out that they had no time to reflect on their actions during combat and it was only later that they experienced emotional backlash. For example: 'You don't have time, it is only later ... I did not think about it ... you cannot do this ... I was all bloody from [comrade's] injury ... his uniform ... everything ... you are aware that this happens ... but you pushed these things back into your memory' (Dejan, VRS); 'It did not affect me [on the battlefield] ... it starts affecting you later, when a man calms down and leaves that situation ... and regardless how strong one can be you feel it ... especially if you lose somebody who was close to you ... it leaves a deep scar' (Davor, HV). Here again one encounters another variation in the emotional responses: while many ordinary soldiers are shocked by the experience of fighting and killing, and some are indifferent towards these acts, these men disassociate themselves emotionally from the carnage of the battlefield but then later reflect on their shared experiences with death.

This diversity of responses indicates that the emotional dynamics of killing is complex and context dependent. Ex-combatants emphasise that their experience of killing was dynamic and protracted: it did not involve only the shooting on the battlefield but also individual and collective reflection after the battle. Some combatants singled out the emotional differences before, during, and after the battle. Here the emphasis is on the strong emotional reactions before and after the fighting while the actual fighting, including the acts of killing, is experienced differently. The emotional dynamics before the fight is largely shaped by fear, tension, and anticipation which are the collective and individual feelings shared by the majority of soldiers. The direct frontline experience leaves less room for emotional reaction as soldiers focus on their combat roles and survival on the battlefield. However, intense fighting is also sustained by shared, yet temporary, feelings of animosity towards the enemy. Once the fight is over the emotional dynamics change and soldiers are overwhelmed by other emotions – sadness, guilt, revulsion, or sorrow. The emotional responses resurface after the fighting when soldiers reflect on their experience. This complex emotional dynamic is well illustrated in the following description: 'There was a lot of panic and fear a few hours before the battle … then when we started the fight the fear was gone … when you fight up close then you start hating … Why? To survive … When everything is done [after killing] than you feel repugnance. Then you ask yourself: Why? Why is this for? That man has a mother, father, wife, children … I don't know … your emotions change … from the beginning to the end' (Vjeko, HV). Thus, the act of killing does not simply 'trigger' already existing and uniform emotions. Instead, it generates complex and contingent emotional dynamics ranging from fear, tension, and apprehension to animosity and even hate, to sadness, revulsion, and guilt.

Some soldiers indicated that their emotional state changed from one situation to another, with some individuals finding killing easier on some occasions and much harder at other times. For example, an interviewee who described his attitude to killing as a routine and without any feelings (just like 'knocking down bowling pins') also mentioned that at other times he found the experience of seeing people die very difficult. More specifically he identifies two situations where he experienced profound emotional reaction. On one occasion he became very emotional when witnessing an enemy soldier's corpse being dragged and humiliated: 'I see dead [enemy] soldiers laying on the ground and he [one of his own soldiers] just run over them, over dead people, that was so upsetting … I see one [enemy] soldier had his flask with water in his hand … he was trying to get some water before he was killed … that was one of the most upsetting scenes … when he run over this soldier with the car.' On another occasion he experienced an emotional breakdown when a fellow soldier was killed by a sniper: 'that was in 1991, in October, two of us were spending a lot of time together and would often walk a lot … on one of these long walks he was killed by the sniper and I could not come to terms with that at all, I was just crying … and nothing could help me' (Ivan, HV). Hence rather than operating as a biologically ingrained response, the experience of killing and witnessing death was shaped by specific social contexts and in turn the killing itself generated distinct emotional dynamics.

Although war adversaries are often perceived through a prism of deep mutual animosities, soldiers can also develop strong empathic feelings towards the enemy. This experience has been documented in many wars with soldiers often combining professional distance with a degree of empathy for individuals who find themselves in the same situation as they are (Bourke 2000; Holmes 1985; Malešević 2010). This attitude was shared by some respondents: 'I lost a couple of friends ... and for what ... so that we would be better off ... we are not better off ... Who do you shoot at? ... at some poor guy who was forced to be there ... and when we talked to each other [you hear] that they were forced [to fight] too ... you have to ... you could not come home to see your father and mother ... they force you like a prisoner ... you could only run away' (Saša, VRS); 'You get used to bullets during the war ... grenades are something quite different ... when I realised what is happening ... these are somebody's children [the enemy soldiers]' (Zdravko, VRS); 'Why? Why is this for? That man has a mother, father, wife, children (Vjeko, HV); 'I did not want to hurt anybody, if it hurts me, it hurts the other person too' (Mile, VRS).

What the experiences of Croatian and Bosnian Serb soldiers show is that the emotional reactions to killing are neither predetermined nor fixed but dynamic, context dependent, and contingent on wider social processes. The emotional reactions to killing are diverse and oscillate – the same individuals can feel fear and hatred for the enemy but also repugnance towards their own acts of killing and even empathy for the enemy. Moreover, these emotional reactions, just as the process of social pugnacity, are not fixed and biologically given waiting to be triggered by violence but are in fact created through shared collective and individual experience.

10.3.2 Seeing Others Die and Kill

Death is a defining feature of the battlefield. As the killings in modern wars are mostly undertaken at a distance, many ordinary soldiers do not have personal experience of taking somebody's life. However, a majority of soldiers who were involved in combat have seen others kill or die. In most instances these were deaths caused by mortar grenades, artillery shells, mines, and other weaponry fired from a distance. The experiences of the Bosnian Serb and Croatian ex-combatants were similar with many emphasising that most deaths were caused by long-range weapons:

'People were dying in different ways but mostly from grenades ... there were no precision hits, only an occasional sniper ... but mostly the unexpected grenades' (Dražen, HV). The studies focusing on combat zone behaviour indicate that for many soldiers the sight of death and carnage on the battlefield is profoundly distressing. Witnessing killing and dying is often shaped by intense feelings including fear, horror, rage, sadness, disgust, panic, or anger (Bourke 2000). However, some scholars emphasise that combatants often feel disdain for their involvement in violent acts while other researchers insist that prolonged exposure to violence anaesthetises emotional responses where killing and dying become routine activities. In contrast, Collins (2008: 50) reports that even experienced officers and soldiers have regular mental and emotional breakdowns after 'around a year of combat' indicating that 'the effect of combat experience is not just "hardening" but also "softening" through psychological and physical strain'. Holmes (1985: 222) finds that in the 1944 Normandy campaign the experienced British units performed worse than the new recruits. In contrast, Mann (2019: 27) reports that 'soldiers rarely do more than hesitate momentarily before their first killing. After that, killing eases, restricted only by the fears induced by prolonged battles.'

The majority of Croatian and Bosnian Serb interviewees describe their own experiences in traumatic terms. Encountering death was a shock for most combatants. For example, some soldiers depict their first combat situation where they observed killing and dying as deeply upsetting: 'We started shooting ... it was a traumatic experience ... shock' (Dragan, VRS); 'There was general panic ... people see things, shoot at anything ... any sound ... especially at night ... people break down ... through a bomb, shoot several rounds ... just in case ... it was easy to die ... you did not have to do anything wrong ... people died from the lack of knowledge, experience and ... from snipers' (Vlado, HV).

Some Croatian soldiers stress the suddenness of death caused by landmines and bombs: 'Somebody stepped on the mine and three of them were injured and that was really awful to see ... later I had worse experiences ... several times the bomb would fall close to the bunker and would destroy everything ... there were dead and wounded' (Ivan, HV); 'I worked with the mines ... and could see people wounded and dead ... and you feel it ... some boys experienced these situations and were in such a state that they could not perform their tasks and had to take compulsory leave or change their units' (Davor, HV). The same attitude was shared by Bosnian Serb soldiers: 'These war losses were very hard on us ... our comrades ... somebody who was sitting here with me five minutes ago dies or loses his leg ... that affects the entire unit, the morale

is down, nobody talks with anybody for a couple of days' (Milan, VRS);
'It was bad. A lot of fear ... the losses we experienced ... really bad, it
affects you badly ... especially when you knew somebody for years' (Saša,
VRS); 'I had an experience when we were retreating and were shelled ...
there was a unit commander with me and he died ... I also had to jump
over two dead young people ... ordinary recruits ... young people killed
by the grenade ... it was difficult ... when I realised what was
happening ... they are somebody's children' (Zdravko, VRS);
'Grenades from the mortar around the commanding trench ... two boys
died from the grenade ... some hundred metres from me ... normally
I was scared ... seeing them covered up and carried away'
(Dragan, VRS).

Most of these soldiers witnessed deaths that were caused by long-
distance weapons, and describe seeing somebody being killed as a traumatic and shocking experience. However, the focus here is less on the
immediate emotional responses and more on the unexpected and sudden
event which is later reframed and narrated using the discourse of specific
emotions: 'Horrible, the first time you see it, you can never get it out of
your head ... even today I cannot get it out of my head ... when
somebody dies who is your comrade, or when someone disappears ...
even worse as you don't know if he is a dead or alive' (Zoran, VRS); 'I've
only seen this on TV. And then when you see a man falling down,
bleeding ... that is horrific' (Vjeko, HV); 'We started shooting and ... it
was a traumatic experience ... shock ... a man, big, strong and it killed
him ... I did not expect this, I did not think that would kill him ... but he
died, strange ... you think it's just a wound ... that was a hard experience'
(Dragan, VRS); 'I've experienced this on the frontline, from time to
time ... snipers ... there was a colleague and I ... from his trench to mine
there was 10 metres ... we had just eaten ... and there was no sound of
shooting, you could only hear his scream and how he fell down ... he was
hit by the sniper' (Dragan, VRS).

Although losing a close comrade is likely to generate deep emotional
responses including profound sadness, grief, and pain these emotional
reactions usually take place after the event. In other words, the first
reaction usually involves the shock, surprise, and suddenness of the death
experience rather than clearly defined emotions such as sadness, sorrow,
or depression. These complex emotions tend to be articulated, framed,
and narrated later, after the battle. It is no coincidence that many soldiers
tend to connect their personal experiences to the war films they have seen
before they joined the military. These familiar images help individuals
make sense of their own personal traumas and violent realities of the
frontline. Furthermore, these individual traumatic episodes are usually

relived and discussed with comrades after the battle thus helping to foster shared emotional responses.

The intensity, speed, and tension of the fighting usually do not allow for reflective observations. The focus of most soldiers in combat situations is on the practical and technical issues that might help them overcome and defeat the enemy. Hence displaying emotions in such situations is discouraged and soldiers are aware that emotional reactions might get them killed. The perception of time on the battlefield is also very different with most soldiers having a feeling that the battles in which they took part were much shorter than they actually were. For example, one respondent commented on this: 'We were there in that hell for six hours [the battlefield] ... but I had a feeling it was only 15 minutes ... it happened so fast' (Dejan, VRS). A number of soldiers emphasised that one does not have much time to reflect during the fighting and the reactions are almost automatic: 'You don't have time to think, that was an open fight within the 50-metre radius' (Boris, HV). In such situations emotional reactions can prove an obstacle to tasks that are considered to be more important such as helping a wounded comrade. The interviewees emphasise that this was their priority: 'The first thing on my mind was to see if I can help ... you try ... I did not think about my safety at that moment ... only later when everything calmed down ... it was a stressful situation, a lot of pressure ... but the first reaction was to try to help' (Vlado, HV); 'He [my comrade] was hit in the knee and there were flies all over his wound in ten minutes ... in that moment you don't have time to think ... you have to take care of others, crawl to him, hide him behind the tree ...' (Boris, HV); 'I was in a situation where I had to carry a guy that was hit in the head ... his heart was still beating but he was gone ... and it was difficult to get him out under heavy fire, you cannot raise your head' (Dejan, VRS).

Witnessing a death of a close friend or a family member is likely to generate the greatest degree of shock. However, even in these situations soldiers would react differently and show a variety of emotional responses with some panicking, others being deeply upset, and some being completely numbed: 'I've seen a comrade getting killed by the mortar grenade in mid-1993 ... I was shocked but also numbed ... some soldiers were praying, and one man was shaking ... and you could not count on him any more' (Zoran, HV). Other interviewees share similar stories emphasising variety of emotional responses: 'from panic, fear to nothing ... no distinct feelings ... it depends ... people who had families and children and realised that they can die ... there was panic ... until you realise that this could happen to you don't worry much but when it starts around you and people are dying then you start thinking' (Dragan, VRS);

'People were dying from fear and the lack of knowledge ... there is nothing worse than the stench of human corpse when it starts disintegrating' (Ivan, HV); 'You feel the death in the air, your adrenalin starts working, it is not a nice feeling ... only those that are insane feel no fear' (Milan, VRS). Although many soldiers were initially horrified by the sight of death and carnage some developed a degree of emotional distance to such situations describing their reaction to the killing and death as 'numbed', 'hardened', or 'no feelings' (Zoran, HV; Ivan, HV).

A number of soldiers made the point that the fear and panic were more present among the young volunteers who initially were boasting about their eagerness to fight and once the fighting became reality they would experience complete shock: 'Kids, who were pumped up for war ... when they come [to the frontline] they just crapped themselves ... he would not know where to shoot at from utter fear ... they would annoy me ... they were panicking, injuring themselves ... he shoots, does not know from fear where he is supposed to shoot ... he would injure his own comrades' (Zoran, VRS); 'Some people did not know what they were doing from fear' (Boris, HV); 'There was a general panic ... people see things and shoot on anything that moves ... especially at night ... people go nuts' (Vlado, HV). The young recruits who expressed no enthusiasm about the war also shared some of these experiences: 'They scared the shit out of me ... a few months ago I was at the last rock concert of Azra [an ex-Yugoslav rock band] and suddenly I find myself in this situation ... I was not ready for this ... everything was destroyed ... people with no eyes, legs, hands ... I've only seen this in the movies ... it was horrifying' (Boris, HV). The intensity of the war situation affected some young soldiers to the point of completely losing their minds: 'There were people who had mental breakdowns ... a number of them ... one young guy who was completely normal, cultured, from the city, now he is like a zombie, you cannot have a two-sentence conversation with him ... very stressed' (Dejan, VRS).

Some interviewees also made clear that they suppressed their emotional reactions during the battle and in some cases for years after the war. When encountering close-range violence and deaths of comrades some soldiers responded in the following way: 'It really saved me that I did not think about this [the battlefield experience]' (Dejan VRS); 'You cannot forget ... [these memories] are always somewhere in you and can pop up from time to time ... when meeting friends and sharing [war] stories ... when you start remembering' (Vlado, HV); 'I would not go there ... that is buried somewhere in me' (Nenad, HV). Some soldiers used dark and sardonic humour to reflect on their wartime experience of death: 'You were lucky ... it did not kill you ... the end of the story ... our unit numbered 115 people in August 1993 only 14 of us survived ... some extensive pig slaughter [*malo jača svinjokolja*] as they would say' (Zoran, HV). Conscious blocking of intense emotional reactions has proved useful for some combatants during and immediately after the war but for some the emotional price was high resulting in constant nightmares, PTSD and the ever-present burden of 'moral injuries'.

Hence seeing other people getting killed or severely injured does not automatically and uniformly 'trigger' identical emotional responses. Instead, combatants display a variety of emotional reactions ranging from fear, panic, and anger, to sadness, numbness, and even utter calm. Moreover, the same individuals tend to experience and show diverse emotional responses when they see death and carnage on the battlefield and when they later collectively reflect on their shared experiences. The sight of death does not mechanically activate biologically wired emotions or pugnacity, rather emotional reactions are shaped and articulated by individual and collective action that takes place before, during, and after the battle.

10.3.3   Torture and Abuse of POWs

In addition to killing and injuring, warfare is also associated with the abuse and torture of POWs and civilians. The research indicates that torture, rapes, and other forms of non-lethal abuse of enemy soldiers and civilians are linked with the level of professionalisation. Formal military organisations with developed disciplinary rules and regulations are less likely to engage in these activities than irregular forces (Steffens 2017). The Yugoslav wars of succession follow this pattern in the sense that the paramilitary armed organisations were responsible for more torture, rapes, and abuse of prisoners than the regular militaries. There was also a difference between the more professional paramilitaries such as Serbian Volunteer Guards, Red Berets, and the Scorpions which targeted civilians systematically in order to ethnically cleanse specific territories and the irregular paramilitaries such as Yellow Wasps, Avengers, or Leva Supoderica which deployed extreme forms of torture without any clearly defined instrumental or strategic goals (Vukušić 2019).

Although none of the interviewed VRS and HV soldiers admitted having taken part in any such activities, a number of interviewees recognised that these practices took place occasionally. The scholarship on the ICTY for war crimes shows that although regular military and police forces were less involved in torture and rape than paramilitaries the political and military leaderships generally did not punish individuals and groups involved in such behaviour (Vukušić 2019). In this context one would expect similar patterns of torture and abuse of POWs but the interviews with the VRS and HV combatants indicate that these practices were highly context dependent and linked with the wider emotional group dynamics. In other words, while some military units were involved in torture others had no such experiences and those where the torture took place differed in terms of intensity and frequency of abuse.

Hence soldiers who acknowledged that torture took place showed a degree of shame and embarrassment about these practices and tended to attribute them more to the enemy. For example, the foreign volunteers were regularly blamed for torture and gruesome actions: 'There were massacres and torture … especially once these Arab warriors came, these mujahedeen … a guy from Tuzla [city in Bosnia] told me … he was a cop … and he was disgusted with what they did' (Novak, VRS). Consequently, the foreign volunteers often experienced more cruelty than the native population: 'I had a friend from Germany who came to Croatia and Bosnia and Herzegovina to fight, he was captured [by the Bosnian Serb Army] and was in Manjača [prison camp] for 15 months … he was beaten so much that he lost the sense of smell and taste, when he eats now, he feels nothing' (Boris, HV). When it was acknowledged that torture took place the tendency was to implicate the military units other than one's own: 'There were some on our side, the Scorpions … who they say, did some things from our side … but that did not happen in my unit' (Novak, VRS); 'Some people were imprisoned, in some village, two to three of them, Croats … I came to the local shop to buy something and could see the guards standing next to the barbed fence and the big wooden door … I hear shouting coming from the inside … a lot of soldiers, I ask them what is this … and I remember this well … those people … how could they … they have not done anything to me personally so I did not have that feeling … but there were people who were thinking like me, and looked at these acts with horror' (Dragan, VRS).

In other cases torture was reported as a personal experience: 'I was imprisoned in several camps, Vareš, Vareš Majdan, Tačin, Silos … 133 days and nights in imprisonment … they tortured me, were beating me regularly … I lost consciousness … they humiliated us, hurled insults, isolated us, put us into the dog's house, no hygiene, hard physical labour' (Milan, VRS): 'I was tortured by my own Croats, because I was in KOS [Yugoslav secret police] … they beat me up, 4 days in prison … they beat me with Serbs and what they did to them is impossible to describe … they [torturers] were bloodthirsty … so primitive … or just the worst people came to the fore' (Boris, HV). Thus, the patterns of torture were highly variable and context dependent within both military organisations.

The interviewees were also keen to stress that torture was more present in some theatres of war than in others. For example, some depicted the war in Bosnia as much crueller than what took place in Croatia. In the assessment of one soldier torture was a common practice among all three warring sides in Bosnia:

Everybody was persecuted by somebody else in Bosnia ... those who were the majority [ethnic] group would persecute those that were minority, they were excessively bloodthirsty ... Serbs by Muslims and Croats, Croats by Serbs and Muslims and Muslims by Serbs and Croats ... they all used terrible methods of torture ... in Croatia they were minority, maybe 10% in every unit with 1% in some units and 15% in others while in Bosnia there were 50% of those people ... that is horrible ... almost majority like that ... I was in Herzegovina, northern Bosnia, Tešanj ... they are all the same ... no difference ... the same mental profile ... Where did this hatred come from? (Boris, HV)

Other soldiers describe the dehumanising acts that took place in some combat zones but not in others: 'There were some inhumane individuals ... bloodthirsty men ... this [violent behaviour] was in their blood' (Mile, VRS).

Most interviewees condemned torture and attributed such behaviour to undisciplined and unprofessional individuals and 'sick people'. However, some were more cynical and were disgusted with the human race as such: 'I could see how the mind of people changes in the moment when you give them weapons ... it is horrifying how much the weapons change one's mind ... when you give a bit of power to a man, especially to a semi-literate man, he destroys others, he tortures, he kills' (Jovo, VRS).

The soldiers were particularly disturbed by the sexual abuse of POWs. Thus, one interviewee described a gruesome scene that he witnessed as a prisoner: 'There was an imprisoned Serb ... who was taken by the military police, who were drunk of course, and they took a sharp bottle opener and asked the prisoner: "What is this?" ... and then the policeman said "No" and took his tooth out ... he then said to the other prisoner "Take off your trousers and underwear" and then they forced the guy without the tooth to perform oral sex on the other guy ... while he was bleeding ... horrible' (Boris, HV). This extreme form of sexualised torture and abuse was often attributed to 'sick people'. However, as these events took place in front of other prisoners, soldiers, and military police it seems more likely that these were cases of performative violence deliberately displayed in order to mark the boundaries between the two groups: to differentiate the inferior 'feminine'/homosexual Serbs versus the 'hyper masculine'/heterosexual Croats and vice versa. These extremely violent performances were deployed to enhance the group bonds among members of the military. As Fujii (2011: 661) argues, these violent displays have a strong social dimension, they are intended 'to be seen and make people take notice'. The sexualised torture was not used here to extract strategic information or to trigger ingrained emotions among those who witnessed these violent acts. Instead, the violent act was performed deliberately in order to create new and shared emotional dynamics.

In other cases, the soldiers showed empathy towards the POWs who were recognised as being in a very similar situation to their own:

When you capture them you think I would do anything to him ... but once you see him, hungry, thirsty, scared, terrified and that he is here just as you are because somebody forced him to go, and he does not know where he is and what he is ... and what will be of him ... not a single hair from his head was missing ... we captured a prisoner and took him to our quarters ... I was not going to torture him and vent my spleen [for a killed comrade] ... we are not like that. (Zoran, VRS)

What the interviews show is that despite having similar, mostly lax, formal policies towards the treatment of POWs in the HV and the VRS there was no uniform behaviour regarding the deployment of torture and abuse. In most instances torture was not deployed by the ordinary soldiers and when the POWs were abused these acts were context dependent and shaped by specific emotional dynamics of different combat zones. This variability indicates that social pugnacity is never a matter of simple biological responses or universal ethical principles. Instead, the intensity and frequency of torture is often framed by the differences in emotional group dynamics.

10.3.4 Fear of Humiliation

Much of the existing scholarship on battlefield behaviour indicates that the combatants fear humiliation and loss of face in front of their comrades more than death (Bourke 2000; Collins 2008; Holmes 1985). This phenomenon is regularly gendered as humiliation is often understood through the prism of vulnerable masculinities (Chisholm and Tidy 2018). In some violent conflicts the adversary is also feared or resented for their cruelty due to the widespread rumours about the inhumane treatment of prisoners. Thus, the anticipation of possible death or torture also shapes the emotional dynamics on the battlefield. The outbreak of the wars in Croatia and Bosnia and Herzegovina was accompanied by dehumanising propagandistic portrayals of the enemy as regularly engaging in sadistic violence against the civilians and POWs (MacDonald 2003; Malešević 2002, 2006). These mass media representations amplified already widespread rumours about the cruelty of the enemy which in turn contributed to actual acts of cruelty and torture often being seen as justified retribution for the behaviour of the other side. Most of the interviewees have expressed strong views on this topic with many stating that they would prefer death to being captured as that might lead to torture and humiliation. In the words of the soldiers from the both sides: 'I will not be captured alive, even if I have to kill myself ... that was my biggest fear' (Zoran, VRS); 'When you see what happened to others and I've heard from people who were imprisoned ... I would rather kill myself [than get captured]' (Mile, VRS); 'My brother and I were together the whole time ... we had a pocket knife ... to cut our veins if we get captured ... that was in my head ... not to get captured alive ... and we agreed that ... if one falls that the other runs away ... so that one should be saved' (Dražen, HV).

Nevertheless, this fear of being captured was not the only emotional response among the combatants. Some rarely thought about this issue while others consciously repressed such thoughts: 'Whenever this thought [of being captured] came to my mind I tried to think of something else ... I did not want to think about what would happen to me if I were captured' (Vjeko, HV).

Furthermore, even the soldiers who expressed strong views about preferring suicide over capture did not show uniform emotional responses to this hypothetical situation. For some soldiers, the key motivation for this act was the avoidance of pain while for others it was a question of escaping the humiliation or maintaining their pride. Hence a number of soldiers emphasised that the enemy had no moral scruples and is likely to torture the prisoners: 'I've heard those stories from former POWs ... they experienced such horrible things' (Zoran, VRS). For other combatants, the key issue raised was the notion of being humiliated: 'At that time I thought if that happens, I would kill myself. Not because I could not withstand the pain of torture but because of some kind of pride and not wanting to be humiliated ... everybody thought like me'(Vjeko, HV); 'You hear various stories, what they are doing with the prisoners ... and then you think, that was the greatest fear, greater than getting killed ... humiliation, torture ... you get the picture ... you just pray to God that does not happen' (Dragan, VRS).

The anticipation of torture and humiliation was reinforced by the media representations and rumours where the enemy was often depicted as monstrous and therefore superhuman which enhanced the existing fears among some soldiers (MacDonald 2003). This was a challenge for the commanders as they had to reassure their soldiers that they were not fighting superhuman creatures. In the words of a Croatian officer: 'It was very difficult to convince the soldiers that Chetniks are also people made of flesh ... there was a lot of Serbian propaganda that Ustashas are slaughtering everybody, and our media were saying that Arkan is coming and that Šešelj is coming ... so I said guys those that are coming towards us are also made of flesh and blood and we have to defend ourselves' (Ivan, HV).[3]

The anticipation of possible torture or death had a strong emotional resonance among many combatants. Both VRS and HV soldiers reflected extensively on these issues and developed strong views underpinned by just as strong emotional reactions. Yet these shared emotional responses were not and could not be 'triggered' by actual events but were largely framed by the widespread rumours and media portrayals about the cruelty of the enemy. Here again it is possible to see how social context shapes the emotional dynamics. The hearsay, stories, and some actual acts of POW torture not only influenced soldiers' perceptions of war reality but in fact fostered distinct collective emotional responses with many soldiers expressing very similar emotions towards something that was not an actual event but just a hypothetical situation. Hence the emotional dynamics that developed around this issue shows clearly how rather than being ingrained, biological response emotions are created in collective action.

10.3.5 Emotions and Sacrifice

One of defining features of war is its sociality. Although human beings experience death, injury, and pain as individuals it is the social character of war that transforms these personalised events into socially and individually meaningful experiences. In other words, the intense social bonds forged in the theatres of war help individuals transcend painful realities whereby unique emotional and moral ties foster the belief that there is something bigger and more important than one's own life – the

---

[3] Ustashas and Chetniks were the extreme right-wing nationalist organisations that sided with Nazi Germany and fascist Italy respectively during the Second World War. Ustashas committed genocide against the Serbian, Jewish, and Roma civilians and also killed many anti-fascist Croats. Chetniks were involved in mass killings of Bosnian Muslim and Croat civilians. The labels 'Ustasha' and 'Chetnik' were also used in a derogatory sense for the Croats and Serbs respectively during the wars of 1991–5. Željko Ražnatović-Arkan was a convicted criminal and a leader of the paramilitary force Serbian Volunteer Guard. Vojislav Šešelj is a convicted war criminal, nationalist politician, and also the leader of the paramilitary force White Eagles. Both paramilitary organisations were involved in war crimes during the 1991–5 wars in Croatia and Bosnia and Herzegovina.

collective. These social experiences are particularly pronounced on the battlefields where combatants must respond quickly to life and death situations. Hence soldiers regularly describe their experiences of being wounded or helping the wounded in terms of emotional attachments and moral responsibility towards others: 'I was wounded twice ... and the second time, we were surrounded [by the enemy] ... many people died, my commander died ... I was wounded while carrying another wounded soldier ... there were 30 of us and 18 were wounded, 4 were uninjured and the rest were killed ... it hit me in the back ... a tank shell ... there was so much accidental deaths' (Boris, HV). Taking enormous risks and endangering one's one life on the battlefield in order to help a wounded comrade involves a distinct emotional dynamic. The conventional Durkheimian interpretations of this phenomenon tend to emphasise the centrality of social norms: soldiers are willing to sacrifice for each other because they have developed a shared moral universe (Smith 2003). As Durkheim (1986: 157, 203) puts it, 'morality begins where there begins an attachment to a group of any kind ... morals are what the society is'. The more recent, neo-Durkheimian approaches focus on the organisational functionality of military cohesion. For example, Anthony King (2013: 37) argues that the unity and solidarity of soldiers stems less from the strong interpersonal psychological bonds and more from the shared and 'successful collective performance' .

Nevertheless, the neo-Durkheimian perspective cannot properly account for the sheer diversity of emotional reactions on the battlefield. The willingness to sacrifice oneself for others is not a universal and uniform response in theatres of war: some soldiers do this while others are reluctant to endanger their own lives. Moreover, the combatants who try to save their comrades by risking their own lives do not all make such a decision for the same reasons. Some soldiers do this because they feel strongly attached to a specific individual, others do it to avoid anticipated shame or humiliation if they were to act differently, while some combatants do it on the expectation that the others would do the same for them. So, the motivations range from self-interest, moral commitment, and intense micro-group solidarity to shared social action and a variety of emotional reasons. Hence one combatant emphasises the combination of emotional and moral motivations: 'I was thinking instantly why the fuck I need this, only yesterday I was in Sibinje, my village, drinking beer with my friends, we had great time ... I want to live a minute or two ... but when he died, it would be dishonourable to leave him or any other wounded person [on the battlefield] ... it was a code of honour' (Boris, HV). Another soldier invokes the sense of strong group attachment forged in the shared experience of danger:

We were fighting for six hours in that hell ... you don't know any more who is who ... they thought they lost us all ... and in these situations you get to know people ... it was a simple reaction ... a man reacts the way he thinks he should react ... so you don't leave a man who is in danger so to save your own arse ... and [after the battle was over] I see these 20 guys real heroes all crying ... and unconsciously maybe I am crying too ... some feelings completely mixed up ... when I remember it feels hard ... you were lucky to survive that day ... and you are all like brothers ... a young boy, 19 years old from Gradiška, we called him Ćelo [Boldy], died, I am so sorry ... what have you achieved so young. (Dejan, VRS)

However, this willingness to sacrifice for others and the emotions that follow such life-threatening decisions were not generated on the battlefield on the spur of the moment. Such acts did not 'trigger' the emotions. Instead such reactions were largely a product of the long-term action and the social bonds which were developed over longer periods of time, through shared everyday life: 'Some units live on the frontline, people spend a lot of time together and they develop strong emotional bonds ... fighting does not take much time, most of the time is boredom, sitting in peace, so people have a lot of time, they talk, they get to know each other, so ... they develop emotional ties ... so when somebody dies that affects the whole unit' (Milan, VRS).

This willingness to sacrifice for others was mostly associated with fellow soldiers from the same unit but many combatants also felt a sense of moral responsibility and emotional attachment towards their families and friends at home: 'I felt fear when the military barracks in Osijek were captured [by the enemy] ... the bullets were flying over my head ... I was lost and I experienced fear ... not that I would die or be injured ... not that panicking fear, but ... the fear for my family much more than for myself' (Dražen, HV); 'When you see people dying ... I've changed ... the man changes a little and starts thinking ... if I had children then I probably would not fight anymore' (Vjeko, HV); 'You are full of fear and would run away from everything ... but your parents ... you are there ... your parents and everything' (Saša, VRS). In both of these cases, reflecting on the shared everyday life with comrades and the feelings towards family and friends at home, the emotional dynamics are complex and protracted: rather than being something activated on the frontline the emotional responses were created through sustained and shared life experiences.

10.3.6 Narcotics and Violence

There is a wealth of research demonstrating that killing and torture in war are often accompanied by an excessive use of narcotics (Collins

2008; Kamieński 2017; Malešević 2010, 2017). Theatres of war are extremely stressful environments, and the use of alcohol and drugs has often helped combatants to deal with everyday realities including the death of close friends and having to shoot and kill other human beings. Nevertheless, the use of narcotics has also generated violent excesses as drunken and drugged combatants have been involved in torture, rape, and abuse of civilians and POWs.

The use of narcotics on the battlefield usually appears in two forms: (1) the organised and controlled distribution of narcotic substances by the military organisations aimed at stimulating combatants to fight or to make it easier to operate in an exceptionally stressful and violent environment; and (2) the sporadic and spontaneous use of narcotics by combatants themselves in an environment where there is a pronounced lack of discipline and a poor organisational structure. The research indicates that while professional militaries are more likely to deploy narcotic use in the latter context, the paramilitaries and poorly organised groups dominate the former type of substance abuse. The interviews with the combatants from Croatia and Bosnia show that the use of alcohol and drugs was rampant during the war. In some, mostly rare, instances this was coordinated by the military organisation but in most other cases substance use was disorganised and initiated by the combatants themselves. As Vukušić (2018, 2019) demonstrates, many acts of extreme cruelty towards civilians and POWs during the Yugoslav wars of succession were undertaken by individuals who were excessively drunk or were high on drugs. This was particularly the case with the poorly organised paramilitary units such as Yellow Wasps, Avengers/White Eagles, or Leva Supoderica. A similar pattern of behaviour was also present among the regular military formations where the heavy use of narcotic substances was associated with excessive deployment of violence and torture.

Much of the research on the use of intoxicating substances among combatants overemphasises their chemical properties while downplaying or ignoring their social impact (Kamieński 2017). In this reading alcohol and drugs are deployed to numb the ingrained emotions and moral scruples that prevent many humans from engaging in killing or torture. Neo-Darwinians tend to explain the intoxication more in terms of loosening moral qualms and thus allowing biological proclivities to take over. In contrast many sociologists interpret the reliance on drugs and alcohol as a way to overcome the emotionally inbuilt reluctance to kill. Despite these pronounced differences both perspectives largely neglect to study the ways drugs and alcohol contribute towards the emotional dynamics of killing. Firstly, the use of these substances does not produce uniform outcomes. Thus, when drugs are distributed by the military to increase fighting efficiency, they tend to have very mixed results: some soldiers fight better while others experience hallucinations, paranoia, and fear and become ineffective fighters (Bergen-Cico 2015; Kamieński 2017). The same applies to the unsanctioned use of narcotics with some soldiers relying on the substances to fight more or better while others become too drunk or too high to fight at all.

Secondly, soldiers opt to use substances for different reasons. Rather than just focusing on suppressing their inbuilt emotional responses or moral values that prevent killing many combatants use narcotics for social purposes – to increase social pugnacity, to enhance micro-group solidarity, to forget that they are away from loved ones, to stop thinking about the past or future, to build a group mediated resistance to fear, and for many other non-fighting related reasons. Hence the relationship between killing and the use of narcotics is far from straightforward. Instead of having a purely chemical function the consumption of substances contributes to the development of complex emotional dynamics.

Judging from the responses of the interviewees it seems that only a small number of military units systematically received narcotics for combat related purposes. A member of the Croatian Defence Forces (HOS) who later joined the Croatian Army indicates that his unit was supplied with narcotics which they were instructed to use in case of injury or capture and that these tablets would allow soldiers to fight without pain: 'At the beginning of war they gave us some tablets that you need to take if you get wounded ... there were four tablets and if your wound was light you take one, and if it is a larger wound you take two ... and if you take all four you lose all feeling in a part of your leg, it becomes numb but you can still run ... I did not believe in this but we all took them' (Vjeko, HV).

In most other cases narcotics were used spontaneously and without official permission. However, the wide scale of use can also indicate that either the military authorities tolerated this practice or simply did not have organisational capacity to stop their soldiers using narcotic substances. Hence many soldiers were intoxicated during the fight or after the fight. Some combatants admit to relying on these substances on the battlefield: 'I was on the pills for nerves and was also regularly drinking *loza*, double dose of loza [a grape brandy] ... you lose all sense of reality ... and it took me two years to get off this' (Zoran, HV). In this context alcohol and drugs were used to navigate a sudden transition from a mundane and peaceful civilian life into a world of killing and dying.

The use of substances generated a variety of emotional responses. For example, heavy drinking contributed to conflicts between different groups of individuals with ordinary recruits often resenting volunteers and vice versa and with the non-drinking soldiers disliking their intoxicated colleagues: 'There was a lot of infighting between soldiers because there was a lot of alcohol' (Nenad, HV); 'He would do it even if he was sober ... that was simply in him ... only when you are drunk that comes out of you easily ... that negative energy ... [drinking] only erases the breaks' (Boris, HV).

In other instances, alcohol was used to build up social networks of volunteers who relied on substances to join the military, stay on the battlefield despite pronounced and shared feelings of fear, and to develop cohesive bonds with other volunteers. Such units of volunteers were recognised by other soldiers by their extreme nationalist rhetoric which was not reflected at all in their military skills. On the contrary a number of interviewees emphasise that many all-volunteer units were not very effective in military terms because they were ill-disciplined and constantly intoxicated: 'They were not warriors, there was not much use of them ... they were slow, they drunk a lot ... from fear ... I did not drink that much ... [they were] mostly volunteers' (Boris, HV); 'I've joined the all-volunteer unit where ... 90 to 95% people were under the influence of alcohol' (Dragan, VRS). The excessive reliance on alcohol in this case had little to do with biology and chemistry and much more with the enhancement of social ties. The substances were not used to supress or trigger emotions but to generate a distinct shared emotional dynamic where all volunteer units would feel a strong sense of group attachment. The use of alcohol did not stop the feelings of fear or military inadequacy; it actually increased those feelings. What alcohol did is to help foster a stronger sense of bonding among individuals who never met each other before.

10.4 Making Emotions through Violence

Human beings are decidedly emotional creatures. We experience a great variety of emotional experience daily. Some of our emotional responses are deep and intense while many others are mild and instantly forgettable. The most intense emotions are often associated with unexpected and traumatic events. Participation in war involves a plethora of such traumatic experiences that generate emotionally intense responses. The young recruits who find themselves in a situation where they have to kill other human beings or witness deaths and debilitating injuries of their comrades are likely to experience deep emotional reactions. Much of research on the battlefield behaviour has identified the strong commonalities across time and space in how soldiers and other combatants deal with the violent realities of war including killings, death, incapacitating injuries, and torture. These studies have been highly beneficial in detecting the patterns of violence and showing that killing other human beings does not come naturally and as such is not an easy act to undertake for most individuals. The neo-Darwinian perspectives which see violence as ubiquitous in the world of mammals and interpret killing as the natural mechanism of survival are deeply flawed. Much of the sociological research demonstrates convincingly that taking human lives is difficult for most individuals across time and space. The pinnacle of this research was Randall Collins's (2008, 2015) micro-sociology of violence which links violent experience to fear/tension generated in the context of failed interaction ritual chains. This research paradigm has significantly advanced our understanding of violent situations in general and acts of killing in particular. However, its overreliance on the traditional biological model of emotions has prevented this research perspective from identifying the complexities, contingencies, and contradictions that underpin acts of violence on the battlefield. Rather than simply assuming that violent events including killing, injuring, and torture trigger already ingrained emotions it is important to deconstruct the essentialist approach and show that emotional reactions are often made in the acts of violence themselves. Emotions are created, not triggered. This is not to say that human beings are a tabula rasa, and that the social environment can produce any emotional reaction. On the contrary, there are clear limits on how social context shapes the emotional dynamics. All human beings possess a set of emotional bundles which are indeed created through the evolutionary process. However, these emotional bundles are not fixed, stable, and uniform. Emotions such as fear, anger, sadness, or happiness do not have biological fingerprints. Despite the decades of comprehensive research in neuroscience, cognitive psychology, cytology, and developmental biology 'no one has found even a single reliable, broadly replicable, objectively measurable essence of emotion' (Barrett 2017: 173). Since emotional experiences are shaped by diverse social realities there are no uniform emotions, only a variety of context dependent emotional responses. Although most human beings experience fear, anger, sadness, happiness, and other emotions there is enormous variety in how, when, why, and where such emotions are experienced. Hence anger or happiness do not have a bodily pattern, they cannot be reduced to the same set of biological ingredients. Instead, they emerge from the interactions of different social processes and core systems of one's body. As Barrett (2017: 31) argues convincingly, on the basis of her life-long experimental work, 'emotions are not reactions to the world. You are not a passive receiver of sensory input but an active constructor of your emotions.' Not only are human emotions socially constructed but it is very difficult to clearly identify which emotions dominate a particular situation.

This is not to say that biology as such does not matter. On the contrary it is clear that the human emotional responses on the battlefield often involve physiological changes ranging from increased heart rate, dilation of the pupils, and sudden hormonal increases, to heavy breathing, focused attention to details, and losing bowel and urination control among many others (Grossman 1996, 2004). Researchers need to pay attention to such physiological transformations and especially how and when they follow diverse emotional reactions. Nevertheless, emotions are not biologically fixed properties that can simply be triggered but are highly complex and variable processes shaped and articulated through individual and collective action. There is no doubt that physiology is an important and constitutive element of emotional dynamics but as Mayr (1982: 87) rightly argued a long time ago, biology needs to be freed from 'the paralysing grip of essentialism'.

In this context it is possible to see that acts of killing do not automatically activate already existing emotions. Human beings do not mechanically experience fear, repugnance, shame, sadness, or anger after taking somebody's life or witnessing such an act. Instead, they exhibit a variety of emotional responses which are generated and articulated before, during, and after these violent acts. The experience of ex-combatants in the Croatian and Bosnian wars shows how the specific social contexts shape a diversity of emotional reactions. The soldiers who performed the act of killing did not react in the same way and their own emotional responses have been shaped by the changing individual and social environments. Hence the same individuals might feel hatred for the enemy but also display empathy, fear, and repugnance towards their own violent acts at other times. A similar process was detected among the soldiers who witnessed others kill or die. Their emotional responses exhibit enormous variability including sadness, fear, panic, and anger but also indifference and complete numbness. These reactions also change over time with the combatants' emotions oscillating substantially during the fighting and in its aftermath. This social construction of emotional responses is particularly pronounced in the context of anticipated death or torture. Although the majority of the interviewees had no experience of being POWs, their emotional reactions to the dominant narratives that alleged the prevalence of torture and slaughter among the enemy combatants tend to congregate around similar responses that ultimately reaffirm their emotional bonds to their units. Rather than triggering inbuilt emotions such shared narratives of anticipated violence were created, maintained, and reaffirmed through joint collective action.

The same applies to the willingness to sacrifice for others: these actions generally have multiple sources of motivation and are shaped by the collective action and shared everyday life with significant others. In all of these cases violence is shown to be a complex and contingent social process that is framed and articulated by specific social contexts. Hence killing is not difficult because it uniformly triggers unpleasant feelings or shatters the established moral universe. Rather the uneasiness stems from the similar social conditions under which emotions are created. Instead of activating already established emotions, violent acts create emotional responses.

10.5   Conclusion

There is no doubt that the participation in war changes most human beings for ever. War experience constitutes an extraordinary event that suddenly interrupts everyday life and transforms it profoundly. Even when the war ends and soldiers are demobilised, the legacy of violent experiences lives on and affects the lives of former combatants. Much of the research on these war legacies has focused on the traumatic consequences of violent experiences, including physical injuries, inability to adjust to living in a non-war environment, rampant PTSD and other mental problems that affect many war veterans. Nevertheless, every soldier has a different memory of war and their emotional responses to their war experience vary widely: while some soldiers centre their attention on the intense bonds of comradeship that were forged in war others decry the irrationality of violence and its painful lasting consequences. Some praise the heroism of their fellow soldiers while others feel cheated by their militaries and their governments and see their sacrifices as pointless or worthless. These highly diverse post-war responses just reaffirm the central argument of this chapter: violence does not trigger emotions but is a form of social action which forges emotional realities and consequently the human responses to killing and death are different and context dependent. The emotional dynamics of violence is not biologically predetermined, nor is it temporally and spatially fixed. Even the same individuals are capable of expressing a variety of mutually conflicting emotions. This is a social process that is highly variable and influenced by changing social environments. Human beings do not display simple and uniform emotional responses to killing and when killing is difficult it is the social contexts that make it so.

11   The Future of Close-Range Violence

11.1   Introduction

The overwhelming majority of popular science fiction TV shows, films, and novels depicting the world of the future do so in very similar, mostly post-apocalyptic, ways: with the collapse of governance structures human beings automatically turn to violence. The central assumption that underpins these depictions of the future is that the disintegration of law and order would inevitably lead to vicious and bloody struggle for survival. In many respects these fictional narratives draw upon and reproduce the ideas that have dominated political and military thought for centuries. From Machiavelli and Hobbes to the contemporary neorealists and cognitive evolutionary psychologists, violence and war are perceived to be the natural state of individuals, societies, and states. In this chapter I challenge these Hobbesian visions of violent futures and argue that the dynamics of social pugnacity is context dependent and highly variable. By focusing on the organisational, ideological, and - micro-interactional processes that make fighting possible I envisage different possibilities and trajectories of close-range violence in the future.

11.2   Hobbesianism and the Apocalypse

Two books with the same title, *The Last Man,* published at the beginning of the nineteenth century, Jean-Baptiste Cousin de Grainville's 1805 epic and Mary Shelley's 1826 novel, are often identified as the first modern publications depicting a post-apocalyptic world. These two works of fiction offer an extremely bleak outlook on the future where sterility and plague respectively wipe out the entire population of the planet. These early fictional accounts depict violence between human beings, but their focus is mostly elsewhere – de Grainville's morality tale invokes the images from the Book of Revelation and aims to reaffirm Christian teachings while Shelley offers a critique of the Enlightenment's failure to fulfil its humanist promises. Post-apocalyptic writing gained more

307

popularity in the twentieth century, but in the first two decades of the twenty-first century there has been a dramatic proliferation of this genre – from novels, films, and TV series to computer games, comics, and other media outlets. Yeung and Zhang (2014) note that while in the twentieth century only 110 apocalyptic-themed films were made, in the first thirteen years of this century there have already been hundreds of films and TV series centred on post-apocalyptic themes. Furthermore, violence seems to be a cornerstone of twenty-first-century dystopian thinking. While violent imagery was integral to much of the science fiction of the previous century, there seems to be much more emphasis on violent futures in the recent post-apocalyptic narratives. Whereas the earlier accounts tended to locate brutality in external causes such as asteroid strikes, deadly pandemics, nuclear wars, and environmental disasters the more recent storylines centre largely on the interpersonal violence between human beings where the external cause of the societal collapse is only a sideshow. Hence in films and programmes such as *Mad Max*, *I Am Legend*, *The Road*, *Children of Men*, *28 Days Later*, *After Earth*, *The World's End*, *This is the End*, and *The* Walking Dead the future is depicted through the prism of struggle for survival where the dominant theme is human-on-human cruelty. These representations of the post-apocalyptic world are very similar in the sense that they all portray a future where the sudden disintegration of governance structures leads to incessant violence. Similar themes are present in popular computer games such as *Fallout*, *Last of Us*, and *Stalker*. Despite some obvious narrative differences these films, TV programmes, and computer games promulgate a very similar vision of the future where the collapse of state organisation inevitably creates a new social reality where there is no trust and where the strong dominate the weak through violence.

These visions of the future are not only confined to the world of popular culture, they are also integral to many government plans on how to re-establish law and order after a future collapse. As recently released documents on the Carter presidency ('Federal Emergency Plan D') show, the US government's plans for the post-nuclear age have largely been centred on rebuilding the governance structures and preventing the violence and anarchy that might ensue in the wake of a nuclear war with the Soviet Union. The documents make a reference to 'the official survival items list, the stockpile of resources that would be needed to rebuild the government after nuclear war' in order to prevent 'civil disorder' (Ambinder 2017). One can only contemplate how far these plans have developed over the last twenty years.

These views of the post-apocalyptic world where violence reigns supreme have also been internalised by many ordinary individuals who often envisage the apocalypse through the prism of individual struggle for survival. For example, in a 2015 YouGov survey on the prospect of survival after the apocalypse, 74 per cent of Americans surveyed expressed the view that they would survive either longer than other individuals or the same as the people in their community. Interestingly there was a pronounced divide between conservatives and liberals. Hence 43 per cent of Republicans believe they would survive longer than most other individuals, compared to only 22 per cent of Democrats. In contrast, 47 per cent of Democrats think that they would live as long as other people in their community (Moore 2015).

The internet abounds with websites that provide advice and guidance on 'secrets of survival' after the collapse of state structures. These survival groups regurgitate the existing hegemonic images of never-ending violence in the near future. Such websites warn us that exceptional brutality is inevitable: 'Are you ready for a rise of outlaw gangs, sex traders, and supply raiders? This isn't the Old West. This is America or the UK, Canada, or Australia following a complete societal collapse. Better know how to survive – because outlaw gangs, murderous raiders and "highwaymen" are coming. They will hunt you and they will kill you' (Lawrence 2020). These self-proclaimed experts on survival are adamant that the collapse of governance will instantly bring about a world where nobody can be trusted and where murder, rape, and even cannibalism reign.

Nevertheless, these images of 'struggle for survival' are not confined to the extremist fringe. Indeed, they are reproduced in many ordinary outlets. For example, the UK based *Countryfile* magazine provides tips for survival where the collapse of civilisation is seen as an opportunity for the revival of countryside-based life: 'Cities will rapidly become death traps. Most food will quickly disappear from shelves, and fuel will run dry. Medicines will be snapped up. Law and order will collapse as desperate people wrest what supplies they can from each other' (Fairbairn 2019). Even though their focus is on practical advice to apocalypse survivors they also perpetuate the hegemonic image of the post-apocalyptic world where 'the greatest danger to you will be the millions of other survivors who will soon be combing the countryside for food, desperate enough to do anything to get it. For this reason, farms will, sadly, be a honeypot for hungry raiders looking for food and weapons' (Fairbairn 2019).

What is common to all these popular views of the future is the idea that once state structures collapse, violence is inescapable and is likely to affect everybody. The assumption is that in a world where there is no state or any other form of centralised authority individuals will return to the 'state of nature' where fear and distrust dominate, leading to a cruel and gory struggle for survival.

These highly popular understandings of violence largely draw upon and reproduce ideas that have dominated social, political, and military thought for centuries. Although Thucydides was probably the first known thinker who interpreted power relations through the social action between human beings rather than through the divine will or universal cosmologies it is with Machiavelli and Hobbes that the so-called realist view of political life was born. Not only did Hobbes and Machiavelli develop coherent theories of social order they also created an image of individual agency that is ontologically shaped by violence. For both thinkers violence is less a product of structural processes or organisational capacities and much more something that resides in individuals. Hence for Machiavelli (1985 [1532]) human beings are morally weak and self-interested creatures: 'it may be said of men in general that they are ungrateful and fickle, dissemblers, avoiders of danger, and greedy of gain'. When discussing violence Machiavelli focuses mostly on cruelty. For him cruelty is a political practice that uses the spectacle of fear to emphasise the asymmetry of power that one agent wields against others. By staging the periodic spectacles of cruelty rulers impress their subjects and through fear secure obedience. Nevertheless, cruelty can also be deployed by those who aspire to remove the rulers (Winer 2018). In this view violence is a means of control over others. It is something that is conceptualised as natural propensity that any human can and is likely to use at some point.

Similarly, Hobbes sees violence as a norm that permeated the original 'state of nature' – *Bellum omnium contra omnes* (the war of all against all). For Hobbes, the original humans had no social order and were at each other's throats: 'A man is a wolf to another man' and in the state of nature there are 'No arts; no letters; no society; and which is worst of all, continual fear, and danger of violent death: and the life of man, solitary, poor, nasty, brutish and short'. In his view morality cannot exist outside of state control and where is no external arbiter violence will always prevail: 'To this war of every man against every man, this also in consequent; that nothing can be unjust. The notions of right and wrong, justice and injustice have there no place. Where there is no common power, there is no law, where no law, no injustice. Force, and fraud, are in war the cardinal virtues' (Hobbes 2004 [1651]). Hence for both Machiavelli and Hobbes violence is intrinsic to human beings. Violence is prior to any form of social action and it is only through the social action of others that violence can be constrained.

This Hobbesian ontology of violence has influenced much of political and military thinking over the last four centuries and it still dominates the contemporary neo-realist views in political science, history, cognitive evolutionary psychology and biology, international relations, and many other fields of research. For example, highly influential scholars such as political scientists Kenneth Waltz and John Mearsheimer or cognitive evolutionary scholars such as Steven Pinker or Richard Dawkins and the essentialist military historians such as Azar Gat or John Keegan all espouse strong Hobbesian understanding of violence. For example, Pinker (2011: 483) argues that human beings are 'wired for violence' and that the collapse of law and order is bound to unleash violent conflicts. Similarly, Gat (2006) insists that violence is 'an innate but optional tactic' that humans, just like other animals, utilise in order to attain food, resources, and potential mates. Both scholars are explicit in their Hobbesian vision of the past, present and future. Gat (2012: 150) states explicitly: 'Hobbes was right, and Rousseau was wrong, about the great violence of the human state of nature' whereas Pinker (2018: 173) embraces the idea of the 'Hobbesian trap':

As Thomas Hobbes argued during the Age of Reason, zones of anarchy are always violent. It is not because everyone wants to prey on everyone else, but in the absence of government the threat of violence can be self-inflating. If even a few potential predators lurk in the region or could show up on short notice, people must adopt an aggressive posture to deter them. This deterrent is credible only if they advertise their resolve by retaliating against any affront and avenging any depredation, regardless of the cost. This "Hobbesian trap" ... can easily set off cycles of feuding and vendetta: you have to be at least as violent as your adversaries lest you become their doormat.

The neo-realist IR theorists such as Waltz and Mearsheimer see the struggle for survival as a driving force of individual and collective action. Hence for Waltz (1979: 92) what underpins the 'anarchy' of the international system is the universal struggle for survival: 'Survival is the prerequisite to achieving any goals that states may have, other than the goal of promoting their own disappearance as political entities. The survival motive is taken as a ground of action in a world where the security of states is not assured rather than as a realistic description of the impulse that lies behind every act of state.' In a similar vein Mearsheimer (2001: xi), a leading representative of the offensive realism approach in IR, argues that 'the cycle of violence will continue far into the new millennium. Hopes for peace will probably not be realized, because the great that shape the international system fear each other and compete for power as a result. Indeed, their ultimate aim is to gain a position of dominant power over others, because having dominant power is the best means to ensure one's own survival.' Although these scholars generally do not contemplate much or elaborate on the post-apocalyptic scenarios, they all share the Hobbesian ontology where human beings are understood to be intrinsically violent creatures. While some of these authors recognise that violent action is only a part of the individual repertoire (i.e., Gat's notion of optional tactic or Waltz's view that violence does not lie behind every act of state) they nonetheless insist that violent acts have 'innate' origins which determine the ever-present struggle for survival.

However, this hegemonic view where the sudden collapse of law and order is bound to trigger violence between human beings is historically inaccurate, epistemologically flawed, and sociologically unrealistic. Let us explore these issues in greater detail.

11.3   The Impossibility of *Bellum omnium contra omnes*

The dominant popular understandings of post-apocalyptic violence draw to a large extent from the long legacy of Hobbesianism. This view is grounded in the social contract tradition where the very existence of social order is premised on the establishment of a contractual bond between individuals that inhabit the social order. Nevertheless, all social contract approaches are sociologically unfounded as they depict an imaginary world that never existed (Gellner 1988). Despite their pro-nounced differences the classical social contract theorists including Hobbes, Locke, and Rousseau developed highly inaccurate accounts of the past. In these accounts 'the state of nature' was wrongly portrayed as a pre-social, apolitical, and ahistorical environment where human beings only exist as individuals. However, as anthropologists have observed on many occasions there was no such a thing as 'the state of nature'. The social order exists beyond, below, and outside of the state structures. The hunter-gatherers did not have states to police their social life and were still capable of developing and maintaining social order without violence. Fry (2007) shows that there are still over seventy hunter-gatherer com-munities who very successfully uphold social order without any resort to violence and without the presence of centralised organisational struc-tures. From Siriono in Bolivia and Palyan in India, to Cheq Wong and Semai in Malaysia and Mbuti in South Africa, societies have found the way to uphold order while avoiding violence and resolving conflicts through peaceful rituals. For instance, the Chew Wong language pos-sesses no words for war, violence, fighting, or aggression and their mythology has no reference to any violent events (Bonta 1996). This is not to romanticise non-state societies as there are also many complex hunter-gatherer societies that rely extensively on the use of violence to police their social orders. Instead, the point is to question the blanket statements that portray the complexity of human history as a homogeneous 'state of nature' where violence is an inevitable and constant presence.

Secondly, the Hobbesian image of war of all against all is historically completely unfounded on several counts. For one thing, as Collins (2008) convincingly shows, it is impossible to simultaneously fight with hundreds of other individuals. *Bellum omnium contra omnes* is a sociological impossibility. Any fight that involves a large number of individuals tends towards a degree of group formation whereby some individuals create alliances against other individuals thus generating clearly identifiable warring parties. The experience of continuous fighting often contributes to greater social cohesion within the newly created groups while simultaneously hardening the borders between the groups that fight each other (Banton 1983; Coser 1956). For another thing, ancient humans rarely acted as individuals and much more as members of their respective groups – clans, tribes, lineages, villages, and so on. Hence large-scale and prolonged fighting entails the presence of a group dynamics which requires organisation, coordination, and division of labour. If an individual is attacked, she would expect the support of other individuals from her group and the same principle applies to the attack on others which presumes a degree of group coordination and support.

Thirdly, the idea that the presence of the state apparatus is the only safeguard against reverting to a violent 'state of nature' is built on the flawed notion that our foraging predecessors were extremely violent creatures. As much of anthropological, archaeological, and palaeontological research demonstrates there is no evidence that the simple hunter-gatherers were prone to incessant violence. On the contrary the available evidence indicates that before the Neolithic era violent acts were rather rare and sporadic and mostly associated with interpersonal disputes. As Heuser (2010: 4) summarises the existing findings before the Neolithic and Holocene periods: 'all archaeological evidence of violent death ... is limited to finds of single bodies'. It is only in the last 10,000 years with the development of sedentary lifestyles including farming and state formation that violence proliferates substantially. As McCall (2009: 163) puts it succinctly: 'the prevalence of warfare among the foragers correlates strongly with sedentism, the storage of food, high population densities, perimeter defence territorial systems, social inequality, and relatively rich foraging environments'. In other words, the transition from hunter-gathering to farming was a pivotal moment in the increase of violence. The Hobbesian images of the 'state of nature' which have been reproduced for centuries and have become a part of popular culture and everyday doxa are based on profoundly inaccurate descriptions of the prehistoric world. As Cohen (1989: 116) concludes: 'the skeletal evidence provides little support for the Hobbesian notion that the hunter-gatherer life is particularly violent or for the assumption that hunting is particularly dangerous'. Moreover, he rightly questions the idea that the rise of state power has contained the supposedly pre-existing violent impulses: 'there is no evidence either from ethnographic accounts or archaeological excavations to suggest that the rates of accidental trauma or interpersonal violence declined substantially with the adoption of more civilised form of political organisation. In fact, some evidence from archaeological sites and from historical sources suggests the opposite' (Cohen 1989: 132).

Fourthly, which links up with the previous point, the assumption that violence is predominantly located in individuals is deeply problematic. The Hobbesians perceive human beings as self-interested creatures that in the state of nature are bound to fight each other over economic gain ('competition'), status ('glory'), and security ('diffidence'). In this view violence is a rational and expected response in the situation where no individual trusts other individuals. In this view attack is seen as the best form of self-defence. However, this radical individualist view of social order leaves no room for the structural, cultural, or political dynamics of social action. The non-existence of an external arbiter such as the state does not automatically render people into socially detached egoistic individuals who have no moral principles, ideological preferences, social ties, cultural values, institutional attachments, political allegiances, or social inclinations. This simplified and economistic cum biological view of human relations cannot account for the enormous historical variety in pre-state, non-state, and after-state societies. The anthropological research clearly indicates that living outside of state structures involves an enormous variety of social practices and attitudes to violence. While some complex hunter-gatherers such as Yanomami and Korubo of Amazonia, Nootka of British Columbia, or Mursi of Ethiopia have a history of extreme violence most other hunter-gatherers either avoid violent experience, as indicated above, or only fight when forced to do so (Fry 2007; Service 1978). Even when some tribes engage in periodic fights, they do this in very different ways. Some hunter-gatherers have developed elaborate ritualistic practices that might involve theatrical displays of strength without any human casualties. For example, many groups in Papua New Guinea such as Dani or Asmat engage in ritualistic wars where they focus on insulting or humiliating the enemy without killing them. These wars often end when one or two individuals are injured or killed rather than focusing on capturing land, resources, or people (Heider 1996). The same variation in experience has been identified in the context of collapsing structures of governance in times of war, natural disasters, or pandemic outbreaks. In all of these cases human response has varied from society to society, region to region, town to town, and village to village. While in some cases violence was present to a larger or lesser degree, in other instances humans demonstrated a high degree of solidarity with people who experienced similar calamity (Diamond 2005; Homer-Dixon 2006). The Hobbesian view makes no room for this variety of human responses to violence outside of state structures.

Furthermore, rather than locating violence within asocial individuals it is important to understand that social pugnacity is a product of collective action which when enacted regularly becomes a structural force. In other words, rather than looking at violence as a default position to which individuals revert when there are no structures of governance we should conceptualise violent action through the prism of structural processes. As both Mann (1986, 1993) and Tilly (1992) show, protracted violence entails a degree of organisational capacity that individuals could not generate by themselves. The ability to constrain violence resides in the increased coercive capacity of organisations. In this context violence does not vanish with the emergence of the state. It only transitions into the institutions of the state or other coercive organisations. The Leviathan does not eliminate violence, it only stores that violence within itself and is able to unleash that violent power at any point in time. This is the key point of Weber's well-known definition of the state. In this understanding the state possesses the monopoly on the legitimate use of violence over a particular territory. Nevertheless, this does not only imply that other actors inhabiting this territory cannot use violent force but also that through its monopoly the state acquires enormous capacity for violence. The legitimate monopolisation of coercive power provides the state with unprecedented organisational and ideological powers to use violence within and outside its borders, as in times of war.

The rise of state power through history indicates that organisations which were capable of increasing their coercive power and reach were more effective at expanding their control over people, territories, and resources. The last 10,000 years of human history have been shaped by the proliferation of warfare and other forms of organised violence. It is no coincidence that the emergence and development of statehood was paralleled with the expansion of warfare and the dramatic increase in the number of human casualties. Whereas most forms of pre-state violence were characterised by relatively low death rates the rise and expansion of imperial and other forms of statehood went hand in hand with mass scale violence. While the simple hunter-gatherers had no organisational means, technology, populations, ideological know-how or even interest to embark on mass killing sprees the rulers of the early empires were regularly involved in protracted wars over territory, resources, and slaves, and many of these wars generated enormous human losses. In contrast to the pre-state ritualistic wars such as those fought in Papua New Guinea or Amazon where a few casualties would signify the end of a violent conflict, imperial states just as the contemporary nation-states engage in prolonged wars that often result in hundreds of thousands if not millions of casualties. At the core of this process was the ever-increasing coercive organisational capacity, the ideological penetration of social order under state control and the ability of states and other social organisations to penetrate the networks of micro-level solidarity (Malešević 2010, 2017). Thus, instead of locating violence solely in human agency it is important to understand that violence develops and expands through the rise of structural mechanisms that allow rulers to control millions of individuals. In this context the collapse of state structures can create a situation where various organised groups attempt to regain a degree of monopoly on violence, and it is this organised struggle for monopolistic status that is more likely to generate violent acts than any spontaneous individual response. The disintegration of established social order together with the disappearance of police and criminal justice systems is unlikely to automatically lead to violence by itself. It is the previous experience of living in an environment of coercive dominance by a single authority that can generate violent situations. In other words, post-apocalyptic violence would not ensue because human beings are inherently violent creatures, but violence would be a by-product of sudden organisational transform-ation. The examples of simple hunter-gatherers who have never been part of an organised coercive system clearly indicate that the non-existence of police and criminal justice systems does not automatically lead to incessant violence. The collapse of state authority could lead to violent conflicts in some parts of the world, but this would be the legacy of existing coercive power, not a product of biology.

Finally, the notion that the collapse of state structure is something that is bound to happen suddenly, totally, and irreversibly is sociologically unrealistic. The overwhelming majority of post-apocalyptic narratives offer a very similar description where violence transpires in the wake of sudden and unexpected collapse of state structures. In these narratives entire civilisations are obliterated instantly and post-apocalyptic life starts from scratch – year zero. But the historical reality of known state collapse indicates that in most instances this is a protracted and slow process rather than a sudden and irreversible event (Diamond 2005; Middleton 2017). The collapse of world civilisations has happened in phases and was also characterised by periods of rise and fall and in many cases, it represented a situation of gradual contraction rather than abrupt, instant, and complete disintegration. For example, the collapse of Maya civilisation is often depicted through the prism of instant conquest by Spanish conquistadores in the early sixteenth century. In fact, as much of scholarship shows, the Mayan civilisation was gradually declining for generations before the arrival of the Spanish colonialists. As Hoggarth et al. (2016) show in their archaeological analysis, the Chichén Itzá civilisation declined in large part through the climatic changes including a century of drought. Although the most severe decline was experienced in a period of seventy-five years (between 850 and 925 CE), overall it was in many ways a slow process that took centuries.

The same process can be identified in the contemporary world. For example, the phenomenon of so-called 'failed states' refers to polities where central government has collapsed, and the state has lost the monopoly on the legitimate use of violence over its territory and is unable to provide basic services such as transport, communication, education, and so on. This concept has been in use since the early 1990s to describe a variety of states where the central government has lost control over its territory and population. However, the research on the 'failed states' conducted over the last thirty years indicates clearly that state collapse is neither instant nor irreversible. On the contrary many polities that have been described as failed or collapsed states in the 1990s largely recovered within the next two or three decades. For example, states such as Rwanda,[1] Sierra Leone, and Liberia all experienced collapse of central government and were sites of devastating civil wars in the 1990s. Although the state collapse was in part facilitated by the violent conflicts that ultimately expanded into fully fledged wars and in the Rwandan case also a genocide, the process of state collapse was gradual and can be traced to colonial and postcolonial politics. Nevertheless, once the peace accords were put in place the three nation-states experienced substantial development with the central authorities gaining full control over territory and the population living within their borders. Moreover, Rwanda has experienced unprecedented economic development and substantial increase in the organisational capacity of the state. From 1990 to 2018

---

[1] Although in the 1990s and early 2000s Rwanda was often described as 'a failed state' this was never the case. Pre-1994 genocide Rwanda was one of the most centralised states in Africa and after 1994 has become even more centralised (Malešević 2006: 204–26).

Rwanda's Human Development Index increased by 119.0 per cent while the life expectancy improved from 33.4 to 68.7 (Rwanda – HDR Report 2019). Drawing on these real-life experiences one can expect that collapse of state structure in the aftermath of climatic changes, deadly pandemics or world wars would not instantly create a Hobbesian environment of lawlessness and incessant violence of all against all. Instead, these cataclysmic events are likely to generate protracted but reversible decline in governance, characterised by diverse and uneven social conditions.

11.4   Organising Pugnacity: Beyond Hobbesianism

The dominance of the Hobbesian visions of post-apocalyptic violence has less to do with the future and much more with the present. In some respects, they reflect the popular fears of the contemporary world where competitive individualism frames access to resources, services, and state provisions as a zero-sum game where winners take all. In this understanding the Other is always a potential threat, and the presence of state authority is perceived as the only external arbiter capable of preserving security and violence of all against all. Literary scholars, such as Katherine Keller (1996) and Rowena Lee Quinby (1994), among others, have critically scrutinised the post-apocalyptic narratives in literature indicating that such portrayals tend to reinforce the status quo through their emphasis on the punishments for transgression and the salvation of the selected few. These narratives, often built around the idea that apocalypse brings about complete and permanent obliteration of existing reality, glorify the lone heroes who can survive in the new world that has no rules and as such privileges the strong. In many respects these narratives conjure up a survivalist utopia/dystopia that longs for a new beginning where there would be no room for the disliked Other. In this quasi-Darwinian post-apocalyptic reality, violence is perceived not only as inevitable but also as a great cleanser that would pave the way for a new, purer, and thus morally superior, world.

Leaving to one side the obvious far-right implications of these views it is important to show how sociologically unrealistic are such visions. For one thing since the collapse of social order is unlikely to be experienced as a sudden, intense, global, and symmetric event the violence that might accompany this collapse is also unlikely to be sudden, intense, global, and symmetric. Disintegration of institutions is often experienced as a gradual and an asymmetrical process that affects some people much more than others. In contrast to Ulrich Beck's (1992) notion of risk society as a global phenomenon that crosses all social cleavages and affects all individuals equally, it seems more plausible to understand potential future organisational collapses as asymmetric phenomena that are bound to affect individuals differently in terms of their geographical location and residence, their class and status position, their nationality, their wealth, their knowledge, their age group and so on. As Nixon (2013) rightly argues, this gradual and uneven exposure to harms is better conceptualised as 'slow violence' – something that expands steadily and, in many instances, also invisibly. Although the spectacular events of environmental destruction such as large-scale oil spills or nuclear disasters (e.g., Chernobyl, Bhopal, or the BP Gulf of Mexico oil spill) attract a great deal of attention, much environmental devastation happens gradually and affects underprivileged groups much more directly. As Nixon (2013: 4) points out, this slow violence 'exacerbates the vulnerability of ecosystems' and of people who are poor, disempowered, and often involuntarily displaced, while fuelling social conflicts that arise from desperation as life-sustaining conditions erode. Hence the disintegration of law and order is in most cases a gradual process that might not be directly linked with the origin, direction, and the dynamics of violence. Rather than simply assuming that the breakdown of social order will automatically and inevitably trigger violent responses it is important to understand that the slow violence might not actually be the effect but the cause of the structural disintegration.

For another thing, since protracted violence entails the presence of social organisations the complete dismantling of existing institutions and organisations is unlikely to lead to incessant aggression of all against all. As Collins (2008) shows convincingly, individual human beings left to their own devices are neither very good at nor willing to resort to violence if there are any other alternatives available. Everyday social relations entail development and maintenance of successful interaction ritual chains and violent acts break such interactions leading to tension and fear. Even when human beings experience violent encounters, they tend to overcome these experiences quickly by attempting to re-establish interaction ritual chains. Thus, successful and protracted use of violence requires a great deal of organisational (and ideological) work. As I have argued before, social organisations are the backbone of coercive power and as they have historically expanded so has the capacity for coercive action (Malešević 2017). In this context the collapse of existing institutions is unlikely to generate more violence than the world without social organisations. If one moves away from the sociologically unfounded views of violence as a spontaneous and natural reaction it becomes clear that sustained violence can proliferate only with the emergence and expansion of (new) social organisations. Social organisations such as the state, military, police, judicial system, and others can inhibit violent acts of individuals, but this is possible only because they possess much more coercive power than these individuals. Hence organisations do not just constrain violence, they also create, foster, store, and periodically release violence.

Since violence is always context dependent and situational its occurrence is contingent and variable. To track down this variability it is vital to explore the organisational, ideological, and micro-interactional processes that make protracted violence possible.

Firstly, if we conceptualise violence as a structural phenomenon then the focus is on the rise and decline of organisational capacity. Historically the waxing and waning of violence was linked with the rise and decline of organisational power. The first imperial polities in the world history proliferated and enslaved their neighbouring hunter-gatherers on the back of their coercive organisational might. Being in control of a complex division of labour, hierarchical chains of command, and disciplined and obedient soldiers the emperors could wage successful wars of conquest and in this process expand the territories and populations under their control. Modern nation-states have inherited much of this coercive organisational capacity. Moreover, as Mann (1993) and Tilly (1992) show, the contemporary state apparatuses have acquired historically unprecedented infrastructural powers that allow them to tax their citizens at source, to utilise sophisticated transport and communication networks to permeate everyday life, to collect and store enormous amount of information on their citizens and to monitor their activities, to recruit their population in times of war, to control the economy and welfare of their citizens, and so on.

The decline and collapse of specific nation-states has never resulted in mini-apocalypses or wars of all against all but in the expansion of existing (neighbouring) nation-states into these territories, the establishment of new states, or the creation of coercive social organisations that fight with other similar organisations to re-establish a monopoly on the legitimate use of violence over the particular territory. Even in the most extreme recent cases of state collapse such as Somalia or Yemen it was very clear that violence did not transpire in a disorganised and haphazard way but was initiated, pursued, and conducted in a very systematic fashion. The fact that many coercive organisations were involved has led some to view these civil wars as chaotic and profoundly irrational while in fact all the organisations involved have deployed violence in a very organised and strategic fashion (Kalyvas 2006; Keels et al. 2019). These examples indicate that social pugnacity remains dependent on organisational capacity not on the inherent biological impulses of human beings.

Since violence is created, managed, and unleashed by social organisations it can also be halted and terminated by these organisations. Hence
the disintegration of law and order does not automatically or inevitably
trigger violent struggle for survival, but violent acts can be generated, and
also curtailed, by the existing or newly emerging social organisations.
Nevertheless, since social conditions differ and vary substantially in time
and space so are the prospects for violent or non-violent action. In other
words, the presence and absence of violence in the context of state
collapse is dependent on the variety of situational factors and the dynamics of organisational power. As both Collins (2008) and Kalyvas (2006)
show, the existence of two or more coercive organisations that possess
relatively equal military capacity is likely to generate a less violent stand-
off while the profoundly asymmetrical power relations between the
adversary organisations are more likely to lead to violent attacks. The
scale and character of violence has very little to do with biological or
psychological 'impulses' and much more with the organisational
demands, strategic plans, or structural conditions. Precisely because
violence entails organisations, as organisational dynamics differ and
change so does the character of violence. The post-apocalyptic realities
are unlikely to engender a uniform response. Instead, the future of close-
range violence is more likely to be highly diverse.

Secondly, in addition to organisational capacity much of protracted
violent action requires a degree of ideological justification. While coercion is crucial for social control, prolonged domination is more effective
if perceived as legitimate. Hence historically the use of violence went
hand in hand with the creation and proliferation of normative codes
deployed to justify the existing systems of coercive power. Ideological
power has been articulated in a variety of guises including elaborate
mythological and religious doctrines, imperial creeds, dynastic traditions, civilising missions, and humanitarian codes. The expansion of
organisational capacity was often legitimised with specific ideological
principles while the presence of organisational structures allowed ideological power to permeate social orders under their control. Before
modernity, the focus was more on attaining a degree of ideological unity
among the aristocratic and other elite strata who themselves were capable
of controlling their, mostly peasant and illiterate, populations. With the
rise of mass politics, universal literacy, and notions of popular sover-
eignty legitimacy has become the cornerstone of organisational domination including the use of violence. In the world of nation-states, violence
is almost exclusively a privilege of governments and even the most
powerful rulers are cautious in deploying excessive violence without
elaborate justification. The proliferation of various normative discourses

has made ordinary people much more ideological, and the use of violence has become tied to ideological justification (Malešević 2017, 2019).

The collapse of state structures is unlikely to wipe out the ideological doctrines associated with the legitimacy of specific social orders. Individuals who have been socialised with particular belief systems or have lived most of their lives following certain doctrinal precepts will not suddenly abandon and change their beliefs simply because governance structures have collapsed. The image of a post-apocalyptic reality where everybody starts from scratch and the old value systems vanish overnight makes no sociological sense. The neo-Darwinian accounts are usually hostile to the idea of a human being as a tabula rasa, yet their own vision of the post-apocalyptic world is deeply wedded to an image of social order as a tabula rasa which has no past or can instantly be populated by novel normative frames. Nevertheless, neither individuals nor large collectives are blank slates and the historical record shows that the ideological codes remain influential for many years after the change of a social order. For example, after the collapse of the Austro-Hungarian Empire and more recently Yugoslavia many of their former citizens remained loyal to the old order and maintained a strong sense of attachment for years after these states had disintegrated. Moreover, these shared nostalgic values (i.e., Habsburg nostalgia and Yugo nostalgia) have experienced periodic revivals and in some instances have even strengthened with time. For instance, 'Over the 1980s and 1990s a whole series of monuments of Habsburg personalities, that had been systematically removed by Italian authorities after 1918, were restored to previous or newly determined public spaces in Trieste' (Baskar 2007: 3). The collapse of social order does not automatically obliterate existing cultural capital or shared memories of the previous order. In fact, such ideological ingredients are likely to serve as a social resource for building new social realities as well as regulating the use of violence in the post-apocalyptic environment.

Finally, although violence is a structural force that often entails ideological propping up, its activation requires the presence of human agency. Social organisations such as states, religious institutions, or social movements shape the social order under which most people live. However, the everyday life of most humans is centred on interactions with the specific individuals and small groups that constitute networks of personalised bonds. Since humans are a meaning-oriented and emotional species much of their everyday life is shaped by close-range interaction with the people they care about such as friends, family, and peers. It is through these interactions that most individuals achieve a degree of ontological security, emotional serenity, and moral fulfilment

(Malešević 2017, 2019). The strong bonds of micro-solidarity are defined by the prolonged emotional commitment that is often attained through regular face-to-face interactions and well-grounded networks of interdependence, reciprocity, and shared moral codes. Since most people derive their sense of self from these grids of micro-solidarity the social organisations have devised variety of techniques and mechanisms to tap into this micro-world in order to exploit the emotional and moral energies of these bonds. In many cases organisations couch their ideo-logical narratives in the language of close kinship and friendship. For example, all nationalist discourses utilise kinship terms such as mother, father, brother, or sister to emulate the emotional attachments of the micro-interactional world. Hence the bureaucratic entities such as nation-states become Motherland Russia or Fatherland Norway while political organisations incorporate kinship metaphors into their names and their political addresses to their supporters (e.g., Tamil Brotherhood Party, Fratelli d'Italia, Muslim Brotherhood, etc.). The sociology of violence shows clearly that mobilisation for violent acts including wars, insurgencies, terrorism, and revolutions all entail penetrating the micro-universe and appealing to individuals through the idioms of kinship and friendship. Thus, much of recent scholarship indicates that most indi-viduals opt for violent acts out of a sense of moral responsibility and emotional attachment to their micro-groups. While ideological calls can mobilise individuals, they have to be couched in the language of micro-solidarity to fully resonate (Malešević 2017).

While some narratives of post-apocalyptic violence recognise that indi-viduals are not social atoms that can be detached from their significant others, they tend to misinterpret the dynamics of social ties and to misunderstand social pugnacity. While the neo-Darwinian accounts view kinship through the prism of genetic reproduction in evolutionary terms, the economic and cultural approaches emphasise the self-interest for preservation or the lack of trust in a normless world. Nevertheless, the bonds of micro-solidarity are neither tied to a single source (e.g., biology, economics, culture) nor are they fixed in time and space. Instead, small group interaction is highly dynamic, process oriented, contextual, and contingent. Consequently, acts of violence are shaped by the changing emotional dynamics of group interaction. The collapse of social order does not lead to an automatic and uniform individual and social response. Rather since violence is a product of complex social relation-ships, organisational processes, and ideological framing, as these change so does the dynamics of violence. In some instances, human beings appear willing to sacrifice themselves for others while in other situations the same individuals might act very differently. The sociologists and historians of emotions show that collective action can generate and transform different emotional dynamics leading to a variety of behavioural responses. For example, in the Vietnam War the same individuals who took part in the merciless killings of Vietnamese civilians were also involved in saving other Vietnamese civilians, often risking their own lives in the process (Caputo 1977). This unprecedented change in behaviour was shaped by the changed emotional dynamics of the groups involved in these violent acts.

The micro-sociological research on violence indicates that for most people fighting and killing does not come naturally. Even the most professional, disciplined, and well-trained armed organisations face a problem of individual willingness to fight and kill the enemy. Since the Second World War, military sociologists have observed regularly that much of the fighting and killing is undertaken by a very small number of individuals while the majority of ordinary soldiers tend to deliberately misfire or shoot in the air (King 2013; Marshall 1947). Rather than being an automatic and instinctive response, face-to-face fighting is extremely difficult as it is often paralysed by fear, anxiety, angst, and horror. Hence to increase the fighting and killing ratios military organisations have devised a variety of techniques that keep soldiers on the battlefields: the presence of military police, the draconian punishments for desertion and non-fighting, the introduction of military drill to keep the soldiers in line, the established practices of shaming and emotional blackmail and so on. Other, non-state, armed organisations including terrorist groups, insurgencies and revolutionary groups and gangs all apply similar techniques to boost the fighting capacity of their membership.

Since well-established professional organisations have great difficulty in forcing individuals to fight and kill it seems that the post-apocalyptic environment would be even more averse to fostering face-to-face violence. With the lack of effective organisational pressure individuals would be more likely to avoid any dangerous encounters that might lead to violence. Even those individuals who in pre-apocalyptic times had extensive experience of brutality (gang members, police officers, etc.) may opt not to rely on violent action without any substantive organisational backing (the police force or criminal syndicates). Furthermore, as research on killing indicates, even those who might be willing to kill in some contexts might be fiercely opposed to killing in other situations (see Chapter 10). Thus, instead of Hobbesian war of all against all, the post-apocalyptic scenario is likely to generate very diverse situations of violence and non-violence. Since there is no uniform response to violence in face-to-face interaction today it seems unlikely that such uniformity would become a norm in the post-apocalyptic tomorrow.

11.5   Conclusion

In his book *Apocalypse* John R. Hall (2009) shows that the apocalyptic fiction has historically been a transformative force as it challenged the existing narratives of social order and invoked visions of different future. In this sense the apocalyptic images were often critiques of the status quo as they challenged the established hierarchies and power relationships. For example, for the early Christians the Book of Revelation with its promise of Jesus's return in the wake of the Apocalypse was a firm guide to resist the Roman Empire. In sharp contrast many of the recent post-apocalyptic narratives centre on interpersonal violence and reactionary dystopias where the Other is completely dominated or simply obliterated. In these popular visions of the post-apocalyptic world the cataclysmic disasters produce a new world where the chosen and fit few rely on incessant violence to subjugate the unfit Others. In this vision the collapse of law and order automatically bring about war of all against all. In this chapter I attempted to show that this Hobbesian image of violent futures is sociologically unfounded, and empirically unrealistic. Since social pugnacity is always context dependent and situational its future trajectories are unlikely to be uniform and predictable. The future of violence is not a blank slate but a phenomenon that is grounded in its past and present including the historical dynamics of the organisational, ideological, and micro-interactional processes which shape social life.

Conclusion
The Sociality of Fighting

In popular representations of violence, human-on-human attacks are depicted as historically pervasive, easy to do, and almost unavoidable. In such views, close-range fighting is regularly perceived to be very similar across time and space. These popular representations are often reinforced by some academics who argue that human violence has an immutable character: 'war has an essence that remains the same irrespective of time period or technology levels ... this essence stems from individual human psychology' (Martin 2018: 4). Hence if fighting is understood to be a biological and psychological given then this phenomenon does not require much explanation. If violence has a fixed essence and as such does not change much across history, geography, and micro-interactional contexts, there is no need to study its social mechanisms.

In this book I challenge such misconceptions. I show that violence does not have a biological, psychological, or economic essence but is a phenomenon defined by enormous historical, cultural, organisational, and interactional variability. By zooming in on the diverse experiences of close-range fighting I argue that violent action, just as any other form of social action, involves standard sociological processes and as such can be explained using the established sociological tools of analysis.

Other new sociological approaches to violence have also challenged these popular naturalist views. For example, Schinkel (2010), Wieviorka (2009), and Collins (2008) show that violent action is framed by complex interpersonal dynamics. For Wieviorka (2009) it is paramount to understand the subjective rationale of actors within the broader cycles of violence. Rather than assuming that there are inherently violent people it is crucial to understand that the victims can also be perpetrators of violence and that violence is linked more to one's identity and less to biology. Schinkel (2010) challenges the determinist explanations that centre on crime rate statistics and insists that violence can be a self-referential act not caused by other phenomena. Collins (2008) offers a radical micro-sociological approach which argues that face-to-face violence goes against normal patterns of human interaction and as such is extremely difficult for most individuals. In his view most attempts at violent action are aborted, fail, or are defined by incompetence. Hence the (rare) successful violent encounters must overcome the confrontational tension and fear that follows a break in the normal patterns of interaction between humans. As Collins shows, this is usually done through distant attacks to avoid close physical contact, through the presence of an audience that supports the perpetrator, or through attacking weaker, smaller, or outnumbered victims.

These new perspectives successfully challenge the dominant naturalist interpretations of violence. However, as they overemphasise the micro-level processes and are agency-centred they cannot adequately explain the historical, social, and cultural variation in human responses to violence. They pay scant attention to the structural contexts of violent action. Furthermore, while providing a potent critique of naturalism they, with the partial exception of Collins, inadvertently diminish the corporeal experience of violence. More significantly they tell us little about the relationship between the organisational, ideological, and micro-interactional processes that make close-range fighting possible.

Thus, to overcome the shortcomings of both naturalism and radical micro-sociology I argue that a coherent explanation of close-range fighting entails engagement with a variety of different processes. My starting point was the concept of social pugnacity which helps us account for the structural effects, spatial and temporal variability, and the contextual flexibility of close-range fighting. Rather than being a simple natural response in a situation of threat or an opportunity to establish domination over others, collective fighting involves a complex gamut of organisational, ideological, and micro-interactional processes. Social pugnacity is a relational phenomenon that emerges and is continuously shaped by different structural forces, agency, and contingent events. Instead of being a property of an individual or a group, social pugnacity is a situational product of historically situated configurations. This is an 'entity in motion' that is moulded by changing organisational capacities, the intensity of ideological framing, and the embeddedness of micro-level solidarities. Hence to understand why humans fight it is necessary to focus on the social environment that makes fighting possible. Since social pugnacity is a relational phenomenon that transpires in the confluence of different social processes, its workings cannot be explained by focusing on the motivations of individuals. Social fighting is not a tool of individual self-interest, unique personality traits, or uncompromising ideological commitments but a social and historical process that operates in part according to its own autonomous logic.

Using this relational concept allows a researcher to track down how the process of fighting starts, unfolds, and operates but also how the individual acts of violence are shaped by the wider structural forces. In this context one has to recognise the importance (and limits) of human physiology, anatomy, and nervous system. Although much of the con-. ventional research focusing on human bodies leans heavily towards biological determinism, some of the recent approaches including critical neuroscience, the sociology of emotions, and critical cognitive science show clearly that the human physical constitution influences but does not determine one's action. Human beings share common biological and psychological propensities but there is great variation in how these biological traits affect and effect individual and collective action. This variability in fighting experience is even more pronounced in relation to economic factors. Self-interested behaviour and social inequalities can shift disputes in the direction of violent fights, but utilitarian motives rarely determine the trajectories of social pugnacity. Ideology is also regularly identified as a principal cause of violence, but my analysis indicates that neither secular nor religious doctrines by themselves motivate combatants to fight. Instead of fixed and stable norms what matters more is the process of ideologisation through which violent actions are mobilised and justified. However, many instances of fighting are a consequence of coercive pressure: combatants are forced to fight other human beings. There is no doubt that coercive practices often underpin social pugnacity as social organisations that are involved in violent conflicts are created and exist through the expansion of their coercive capacity. However, coercion alone is rarely if ever enough to maintain the flow of social pugnacity. Both ideologisation and coercive power work most effectively when grounded in the existing networks of micro-level solidarities. As I show throughout this book, human beings are emotional creatures who operate most successfully when they are embedded in small groups of individuals who care about each other. In this sense many instances of close-range fighting involve fighting for significant others – one's family, friends, lovers, comrades, or peer group. Hence the coercive social organisations can make people fight only when they successfully penetrate this micro-world and couch their organisational goals in the language and practice of small group solidarity. The networks of solidarity are established, maintained, and reproduced through shared emotional experiences. The dynamics of social pugnacity is regularly determined by the confluence of all these factors and particularly the interplay between coercive organisational capacities, ideological diffusion, and the organisational envelopment of micro-level solidarities. Thus, the trajectory of close-range fighting is moulded by structural processes (organisational capacity, ideological penetration) and by agency (webs of emotionally tuned micro-interaction). Although emotions underpin human motivation, they do not trigger action. Instead, shared emotional dynamics is itself often created in social action. As I show in Chapter 10, killing in war is characterised by temporal, spatial, and situational diversity and this variability is a product of different emotional dynamics created in different types of social action. It is this complex set of social processes that frames the ebbs and flows of social pugnacity. Human beings do not fight for any specific individual reason such as economic self-interest, ideological fanaticism, fear of punishment, or strong political commitments. Instead, close-range fighting is a social consequence of several structural and agential processes that converge together and transform conflictual relations into violent action. Although fighting does not come naturally to human beings, as Mann (1986) shows, they have gradually become socially caged into the shells of the state structures.[1] This process started with the first imperial structures 10–12,000 years ago and has only intensified in the last 300 years. In this context fighting cannot be detached from the organisational apparatuses of states and other coercive entities. As long as such social organisations completely dominate our landscape human beings will find it difficult to evade fighting.

---

[1] I would just add that other social organisations are just as much involved in this process of social change.

Appendix   Methodology and Data Collection

Chapter 5 analyses the original letters written by frontline soldiers. These letters have been collected and published in Nelson and Hendricks (2013), Omissi (1999), Bartov (1992), Fritz (2010), and Shepherd (2016).

Chapters 7, 8, and 10 are based on the primary data collected over several years involving in-depth interviews with the former combatants in Northern Ireland Croatia and Bosnia and Herzegovina. Chapter 7 includes analysis of 32 interviews (18 former VRS soldiers and 14 ex-IRA volunteers). I conducted the interviews with the ex-VRS soldiers and Niall Ó Dochartaigh was responsible for interviews with the ex-IRA members. The interviews in Northern Ireland were conducted between June 2011 and August 2014 in Belfast and Derry. Since the focus here was on combatants who had direct experience of fighting all others who did not meet this criteria were excluded. Furthermore, since this type of respondent is very difficult to access this study relied on snowball (chain referral) non-probability sampling. However, the aim was still to select interviewees who broadly reflect the general population of these two military organisations. Hence the VRS sample consists of 16 conscripts and 2 volunteers (that were never part of JNA) which broadly reflects the VRS structure. Furthermore 17 out of 18 respondents were ordinary soldiers and only one was an officer, which also largely reflects the VRS structure where 98 per cent of its force were non-officers (Milovanović 2011). The IRA sample is slightly more weighted to the upper levels of the organisation with 3 commanders and 11 ordinary volunteers.

Chapters 8 and 10 also use primary data that I collected during several fieldtrips to Bosnia and Herzegovina and Croatia between June 2011 and September 2017 (in Banja Luka, Zagreb, Osijek, and Pula) – 35 in-depth interviews with ex-combatants. To avoid potential biases, the sample used broadly reflects the structure of the two military organisations with the overwhelming majority of respondents having been conscripted into VRS or HV, and only a small number of former combatants were volunteers. Hence, the sample used consists of 18 VRS soldiers (2 volunteers and 16 conscripts) and 17 HV soldiers (3 volunteers and 14 conscripts). The respondents also generally reflect the officer vs. private ratio with two officers in each military organisation being interviewed and the remaining 16 and 17 respondents respectively were ordinary soldiers. This is in line with the official data on the structure of these two organisations: in both VRS and HV, 98 per cent were ordinary soldiers and only 2 per cent were officers (Milovanović 2011; Špegelj 2001). Most soldiers interviewed here also broadly reflect the character of the two armies in terms of military training: the majority of ordinary soldiers did not have much military training and acquired many of their military skills during the three or four years of serving in the combat operations. In contrast, the officers were largely well-trained professionals: VRS inherited its officer corps from the Serb members of the Yugoslav People's Army officer cadre (JNA) while the HV officers represented a combination of former JNA Croat officers who defected before or during the war and the professional Croat soldiers who were trained in the French Foreign Legion and other military organisations abroad (Žunec et al. 2013).

Each interview lasted between 1 and 2.5 hours and was recorded with the permission of the interviewees. These recordings were later transcribed and in the Bosnian and Croatian case translated from Serbian/ Croatian to English. To ensure their anonymity, I identify the respondents only by pseudonyms (for the VRS and HV interviews) or letters (for the IRA interviews). The semi-structured interviews focused on four principal areas: mobilisation and motivation, experiences of armed action, attitudes to negotiation and compromise, and demobilisation. Asking questions on these topics presented significant methodological challenges which were quite different in the two cases. One of the main obstacles in gaining access to the respondents was the question of potential prosecution. In the case of former VRS and HV soldiers, interviewees were concerned that their statements might implicate them in the war crime court cases taking place at the International Criminal Tribunal for the former Yugoslavia (ICTY) in The Hague. The ex-IRA volunteers were equally worried that following the recent cases of the Boston college research interviews with ex-paramilitaries being used for prosecution that they might be liable for criminal prosecution (O'Donnell 2012, 2017). Hence some respondents were reluctant to discuss anything that might lead to legal challenges. See more about these issues in Malešević and Ó Dochartaigh (2018) and Malešević (2020). Nevertheless, most respondents were eager to share their war experiences and felt that they had not committed any crimes during the war.

References

2008. *The Holy Bible: Old and New Testaments.* Auckland: The Floating Press.
2008. *The Qur'an.* Oxford World's Classics. Oxford: Oxford University Press.
2010. *The Torah.* London: Kuperard Publishers.
Abbas, Y. and Trombly, D. 2014. Inside the Collapse of the Iraqi Army's 2nd Division. *War on The Rocks.* https://warontherocks.com/2014/07/inside-the-collapse-of-the-iraqi-armys-2nd-division/.
Abend, G. 2011. Thick Concepts and the Moral Brain. *European Journal of Sociology* 51(1): 143–72.
Adams-Graf, J. 2017. Desertion 'In Times of War'. *Military Trader.* www.militarytrader.com/jagfile/desertion-times-war.
Adorno, T., Frenkel-Brunswik, E., Levinson, D., and Sanford, N. 1950. *The Authoritarian Personality.* New York: Harper.
Ahmed, S. 2015. *The Cultural Politics of Emotion.* London: Routledge.
Aiello, L. C. and Dunbar, R. I. M. 1993. Neocortex Size, Group Size, and the Evolution of Language. *Current Anthropology* 34: 184–93.
Ainsworth, S. E. and Maner, J. K. 2012. Sex Begets Violence: Mating Motives, Social Dominance, and Physical Aggression in Men. *Journal of Personality and Social Psychology* 103(5): 819–29.
Al-Hammadi, K. 2005. The Inside Story of al-Qa'ida. *Al-Quds al-Arabi,* 22 March.
Allen, T., Atingo, J., Atim, D., Ocitti, J., Brown, C., Torre, C., Fergus, C. A., and Parker, M. 2020. What Happened to Children Who Returned from the Lord's Resistance Army in Uganda? *Journal of Refugee Studies* 33(4): 663–83.
Alonso, R. 2007. *The IRA and Armed Struggle.* London and New York: Routledge.
Althusser, L. 1971. Ideology and Ideological State Apparatuses. In *Lenin and Philosophy and Other Essays.* New York: Monthly Review Press, pp. 121–76.
Amarasingam, A. 2015. *Pain, Pride, and Politics: Social Movement Activism and the Sri Lankan Tamil Diaspora in Canada.* Athens: University of Georgia Press.
Ambinder, M. 2017. The American Government's Secret Plan for Surviving the End of the World. *Foreign Policy.* https://foreignpolicy.com/2017/04/14/the-american-governments-secret-plan-for-surviving-the-end-of-the-world/.
Angier, N. 1995. Does Testosterone Equal Aggression? Maybe Not. *The New York Times,* 20 June, p. 3.
Applebaum, A. 2003. *Gulag: A History.* New York: Doubleday.
Arciaga-Young, M. and Gonzalez, V. 2013. Getting Out of Gangs, Staying Out of Gangs: Gang Intervention and Desistence Strategies. *National Gang Center Bulletin* 8: 1–10.

Aristotle. 1988 [350 BCE]. *Politics*. Cambridge: Cambridge University Press.

Arlacchi, P. 1988. *Mafia Business: The Mafia Ethic and the Spirit of Capitalism*. Oxford: Oxford University Press.

Artwohl, A. and Christensen, L. W. 1997. *Deadly Force Encounters*. Boulder, CO: Paladin.

Asbridge, T. 2012. *The Crusades: The War for the Holy Land*. London: Simon & Schuster.

Asharq, Al-Awsat 2020. One-Third of Israeli Youth Avoid Military Service for 'Mental Health' Reasons. https://english.aawsat.com/home/article/2091011/one-third-israeli-youth-avoid-military-service-%E2%80%98mental-health-reasons#:~:text=To%20avoid%20the%20mandatory%20service,exempted%20from%20the%20military%20service.

Astroth, A. 2019. *Mass Suicides on Saipan and Tinian, 1944*. Jefferson, NC: McFarland & Co.

Attran, S. 2011. *Talking to the Enemy: Sacred Values, Violent Extremism, and What It Means to Be Human*. London: Penguin.

Avery, V. J. 2016. Whither Girard and Islam? Reflections on Text and Context. *Bulletin for the Study of Religion* 45(3–4): 29–34.

Bachman, D. 2006. *Bureaucracy, Economy, and Leadership in China: The Institutional Origins of the Great Leap Forward*. Cambridge: Cambridge University Press.

Backović, O., Vasić, M., and Vasović, A. 2001. Who Wants to be a Soldier? The Call-Up Crisis – an Analytical Overview of Media Reports. In B. Magaš and I. Žanić (eds.), *The War in Croatia and Bosnia-Herzegovina 1991–1995*. London: Frank Cass, pp. 329–45.

Baert, P. 1998. *Social Theory in the 20th Century*. Cambridge: Polity Press.

Bahr, A. 2016. Magical Swords and Heavenly Weapons: Battlefield Fear(less-ness) in the Seventeenth Century. In E. Kuijpers and C. van der Haven (eds.), *Battlefield Emotions 1500–1800: Practices, Experience, Imagination*. London: Palgrave Macmillan, pp. 49–70.

Baily, S. P. 2015. Obama: Fight Against Terrorism Is Not 'Between America and Islam'. *The Washington Post*, 7 December.

Baker, C. 2015. *The Yugoslav Wars of the 1990s*. Basingstoke: Palgrave Macmillan.

Baker, M. 1982. *Nam: The Vietnam War in the Words of the Men and Women Who Fought There*. New York: Morrow.

Banton, M. 1983. *Racial and Ethnic Competition*. Cambridge: Cambridge University Press.

Barbalet, J. 1996. Social Emotions: Confidence, Trust and Loyalty. *International Journal of Sociology and Social Policy* 16(8/9): 75–96.

2002. Introduction: Why Emotions Are Crucial. In J. Barbalet (ed.), *Emotions and Sociology*. Oxford: Blackwell, pp. 1–9.

Barkawi, T. 2017. *Soldiers of Empire: Indian and British Armies in World War II*. Cambridge: Cambridge University Press.

Barker, M. 1982. *Nam: The Vietnam War in the Words of the Men and Women Who Fought There*. New York: Abacus.

Barr, M. 2007. The Proactive Brain: Using Analogies and Associations to Generate Predictions. *Trends in Cognitive Sciences* 11(7): 280–9.

Barrett, L. F. 2006. Are Emotions Natural Kinds? *Perspectives on Psychological Science* 1(1): 28–58.

2012. Emotions Are Real. *Emotion* 12(3): 413–29.

2017. *How Emotions Are Made: The Secret Life of the Brain*. London: Palgrave Macmillan.

Bar-Tal, D. 1989. Delegitimization: The Extreme Case of Stereotyping and Prejudice. In D. Bar-Tal, C. F. Graumann, A. W. Kruglanski and W. Stroebe (eds.), *Stereotyping and Prejudice: Changing Conceptions*. New York: Springer, pp. 169–82.

2010. Causes and Consequences of Delegitimization: Models of Conflict and Ethnocentrism. *Journal of Social Issues* 46: 65–81.

Bartlett, M. N. 1874. *A Soldier's Story of War*. New Orleans: Clarke & Hofeline.

Bartov, O. 1992. *Hitler's Army: Soldiers, Nazis, and War in the Third Reich*. Oxford: Oxford University Press.

2001. *The Eastern Front, 1941–1945: German Troops and the Barbarization of Warfare*. Basingstoke: Palgrave Macmillan.

2018. *Anatomy of a Genocide: The Life and Death of a Town Called Buczacz*. New York: Simon & Schuster.

Barua, P. 2005. *The State at War in South Asia*. Lincoln: University of Nebraska Press.

Basham, V. 2015. Waiting for War: Soldiering, Temporality and the Gendered Politics of Boredom and Joy in Military Spaces. In L. Ahall and T. Gregory (eds.), *Emotions, Politics, and War*. Abingdon and New York: Routledge, pp. 128–40.

Baskar, B. 2007. Austro-Nostalgia and Yugo-Nostalgia in the Western Balkans. In B. Jezernik, R. Mursic, and A. Bartulovic (eds.), *Europe and Its Other: Notes on the Balkans*. Ljubljana: Oddelek EiKA, pp. 45–62.

Bauman, Z. 2002. *Society Under Siege*. Cambridge: Polity Press.

Bausman, C. 2016. *U.S. Military Methods for Fear Inoculation*. Jackson, WY: Mountain Tactical Institute. https://mtntactical.com/research/u-s-military-methods-fear-inoculation/.

Beal, D. J., Cohen, R. R., Burke, M. J., and McLendon, C. L. 2003. Cohesion and Performance in Groups: A Meta-Analytic Clarification of Construct Relations. *Journal of Applied Psychology* 88(1): 989–1004.

Bearman, P. S. 1991. Desertion as Localism: Army Unit Solidarity and Group Norms in the U.S. Civil War. *Social Forces* 70(2): 321–42.

Beck, U. 1992. *Risk Society*. London: Sage.

Beevor, A. 2009. *D-Day: The Battle for Normandy*. London: Penguin.

Bentrovato, D., Korostelina, K. V., and Schulze, M. (eds.). 2016. *History Can Bite: History Education in Divided and Postwar Societies*. Göttingen: V&R unipres.

Bergen-Cico, D. 2015. *War and Drugs: The Role of Military Conflict in the Development of Substance Abuse*. New York: Routledge.

Berkovich, I. 2016. Fear, Honour, and Emotional Control on the Eighteenth-Century Battlefield. In E. Kuijpers and C. van der Haven (eds.), *Battlefield Emotions 1500–1800: Practices, Experience, Imagination*. London: Palgrave Macmillan, pp. 93–110.

Bestock, L. 2018. *Violence and Power in Ancient Egypt: Image and Ideology before the New Kingdom*. London: Routledge.

Biddle, S. 2004. *Military Power*. Princeton: Princeton University Press.

Bishop, P. and Mallie, E. 1988. *The Provisional IRA*. London: Corgi.

Blake, J. 1970. The Organisation as Instrument of Violence: The Military Case. *Sociological Quarterly* 11: 331–50.

Blass, T. 1999. The Milgram Paradigm After 35 Years: Some Things We Now Know About Obedience to Authority. *Journal of Applied Social Psychology* 19 (5): 955–78.

Bloch, M. 2014 [1961]. *The Feudal Society*. London: Routledge.

Blok, A. 1974. *The Mafia of a Sicilian Village, 1860–1960. A Study of Violent Peasant Entrepreneurs*. Oxford: Basil Blackwell.

Bøås, M. and Hatløy, A. 2008. 'Getting In, Getting Out': Militia Membership and Prospects for Re-Integration in Post-War Liberia. *Journal of Modern African Studies* 46(1): 33–55.

Bodea, C. and Elbadawi, I. A. 2008. Political Violence and Underdevelopment. *Journal of African Economies* 17(2): 50–96.

Boehm, C. 2019. Gossip and Reputation in Small-Scale Societies: A View from Evolutionary Anthropology. In F. Giardini and R. Wittek (eds.), *The Oxford Handbook of Gossip and Reputation*. Oxford: Oxford University Press, pp. 253–74.

Bolten, C. 2012. *I Did It to Save My Life: Love and Survival in Sierra Leone*. Berkeley: University of California Press.

Bongars, G. 1905. The Speech of Urban II at the Council of Clermont, 1095. Fulcher of Chartres. In O. J. Thatcher and E. Holmes-McNeal (eds.), *A Source Book for Medieval History: Selected Documents*. New York: Scribner's.

Bonta, B. 1996. Conflict Resolution Among Peaceful Societies: The Culture of Peacefulness, *Journal of Peace Research* 33(4): 403–20.

Bougarel, X. 2006. The Shadow of Heroes: Former Combatants in Post-War Bosnia and Herzegovina. *International Social Science Journal* 58(189): 479–90.

Bou Nassif, H. 2015 'Second-Class': The Grievances of Sunni Officers in the Syrian Armed Forces. *Journal of Strategic Studies* 38(5): 626–49.

Bourdieu, P. 1990. *The Logic of Practice*. Cambridge: Polity Press.
    2014. *On the State*. Cambridge: Polity Press.

Bourgois, F. 2003. In Search of Respect: Selling Crack in El Barrio. Cambridge: Cambridge University Press.

Bourgois, P. Hart, L. K., Montero, F., and Karandinos, G. 2019. The Political and Emotional Economy of Violence in US Inner City Narcotics Markets. In E. B. Weininger, A. Lareau, and O. Lizardo (eds.), *Ritual, Emotion, Violence: Studies on the Micro-Sociology of Randall Collins*. London: Routledge, pp. 46–78.

Bourke, J. 2000. *An Intimate History of Killing*. London: Granta.
    2014. *Deep Violence*. Berkeley: Counterpoint.

Bousquet, A. 2018. *The Eye of War: Military Perception from the Telescope to the Drone*. Minneapolis: University of Minnesota Press.

Bowden, B. 2013. *Civilization and War*. Cheltenham, UK and Northampton, MA, USA: Edward Elgar Publishing.

Bowles, S. 2009. Did Warfare among Ancestral Hunter-Gatherers Affect the Evolution of Human Social Behaviors? *Science* 324(5932): 1293–8.

Bowyer Bell, J. 2000. *The IRA, 1968–2000: An Analysis of a Secret Army*. London: Routledge.

Box, S. 1987. *Recession, Crime and Punishment*. London: Macmillan.

Boyle, M. 2020. *The Drone Age: How Drone Technology Will Change War and Peace*. Oxford: Oxford University Press.

Bradley, G. and Feeney, B. 2012. *Insider: Gerry Bradley's Life in the IRA*. Dublin: O'Brien Press.

Briggs, J. 1970. *Never in Anger: Portrait of an Eskimo Family*. Cambridge, MA: Harvard University Press.

2009. *Innocents Lost: When Child Soldiers Go To War*. London: Hachette.

Brissot, J. P. 2007 [1791]. On the War. In S. Žižek (ed.), *J. J. Robespierre: Virtue and Terror*. London: Verso.

Brower, M. and Price, B. 2001. Neuropsychiatry of Frontal Lobe Dysfunction in Violent and Criminal Behaviour: A Critical Review. *Journal of Neurology, Neurosurgery & Psychiatry* 71(6): 720–6.

Brown, W. 2011. *Violence in Medieval Europe*. London: Routledge.

Browning, C. 1992. *Ordinary Men: Reserve Police Battalion 101 and the Final Solution in Poland*. New York: HarperCollins.

Brudholm, T. and Lang, J. (eds.). 2019. *Emotions and Mass Atrocity: Philosophical and Theoretical Explorations*. Cambridge: Cambridge University Press.

Buchanan, J. 1980. A Defense of Organized Crime? In S. Rottenberg (ed.), *Economics of Crime and Punishment*. Washington, DC: American Enterprise Institute, pp. 119–32.

Bufkin, J. L. and Lutterell, V. R. 2005. Neuroimaging Studies of Aggressive and Violent Behavior: Current Findings and Implications for Criminology and Criminal Justice. *Trauma, Violence, Abuse* 6(2): 176–91.

Buncombe, A. 2011. The Deserters: AWOL Crisis Hits the US Forces. *The Independent*. www.independent.co.uk/news/world/americas/the-deserters-awol-crisis-hits-the-us-forces-490897.html.

Burbank, J. and Cooper, F. 2010. *Empires in World History*. Princeton: Princeton University Press.

Burleigh, M. 2010. *Moral Combat: A History of World War II*. New York: HarperCollins.

Burnett, J. 2009. Mexican Drug Cartels Recruiting Young Men, Boys. *NPR*. www.npr.org/templates/story/story.php?storyId=102249839.

Bushman, B. J. 2017. *Aggression and Violence: A Social Psychological Perspective*. London: Routledge.

Buss, D. 2016. *The Evolution of Desire: Strategies of Human Mating*. New York: Basic Books.

Caddick-Adams, P. 2013. *Monte Cassino: Ten Armies in Hell*. Oxford: Oxford University Press.

Calvin, J. 2016. *Institutes of the Christian Religion*. Woodstock, ON: Devoted Publishing.

Canli, T. and Amin, Z. 2002. Neuroimaging of Emotion and Personality: Scientific Evidence and Ethical Considerations. *Brain and Cognition* 50(3): 414–31.

Caputo, P. 1977. *A Rumour of War*. New York: Ballantine.

Carneiro, R. L. 1970. A Theory of the Origin of the State. *Science* 169(3947): 733–8.

Carotenuto, F., Tsikaridze, N., Rook, L., Lordkipanidze, D., Longo, L., Condemi, S., and Raia, P. 2016. Venturing Out Safely: The Biogeography of Homo Erectus Dispersal Out of Africa. *Journal of Human Evolution* 95: 1–12.

Carrier, D. R. and Cunningham, C. 2017. The Effect of Foot Posture on Capacity to Apply Free Moments to the Ground: Implications for Fighting Performance in Great Apes. *Biology Open* 6: 269–77.

Casquete, J. 2008. Draft, Resistance and Evasion of. In L. Kurtz (ed.), *Encyclopedia of Violence, Peace, & Conflict*. New York: Academic Press.

Castro, J. 2015. Homo Erectus: Facts About the 'Upright Man'. *Live Science*. www.livescience.com/41048-facts-about-homo-erectus.html.

Catino, M. 2014. How Do Mafias Organize? Conflict and Violence in Three Mafia Organizations. *European Journal of Sociology* 55(2): 177–220.

Centeno, M. 2002. *Blood and Debt: War and the Nation-State in Latin America*. University Park: Penn State University Press.

Chagnon, N. 1988. Life Histories, Blood Revenge, and Warfare in a Tribal Population. *Science* 239(4843): 985–992.

Chakrabarty, B. 2006. *Social and Political Thought of Mahatma Gandhi*. London: Routledge.

Chambliss, W. J. 2001. *Power, Politics, and Crime*. Boulder, CO: Westview Press.

Chase-Dunn, C. and Podobnik, B. 1995. The Next World War: World-System Cycles and Trends. *Journal of World-Systems Research*, 1(1), 295–326.

Chenoweth, E. and Stephan, M. 2011. *Why Civil Resistance Works: The Strategic Logic of Nonviolent Conflict*. New York: Columbia University Press.

Chiocchio, F. and Essiembre, H. 2009. Cohesion and Performance: A Meta-Analytic Review of Disparities between Project Teams, Production Teams, and Service Teams. *Small Group Research* 40(4): 382–420.

Chisholm, A. and Tidy, J. 2018. *Masculinities at the Margins*. London: Routledge.

Choi, C. 2007. Why Time Seems to Slow Down in Emergencies. *Live Science* 11 December. www.livescience.com/2117-time-slow-emergencies.html.

Choudhury, S. 2009. Culturing the Adolescent Brain: What Can Neuroscience Learn from Anthropology? *Social Cognitive and Affective Neuroscience* 5(2–3): 159–67.

Choudhury, S. and Slaby, J. (eds.). 2016. *Critical Neuroscience: A Handbook of the Social and Cultural Contexts of Neuroscience*. London: Wiley.

Cigar, N. 2001. Serb War Effort and Termination of the War. In B. Magaš and I. Žanić (eds.), *The War in Croatia and Bosnia-Herzegovina 1991–1995*. London: Frank Cass, pp. 200–35.

Clagett, R. 2003. *After the Echo*. Prairie Village, KS: Varro Press.

Clark, C. 2013. *The Sleepwalkers: How Europe Went to War in 1914*. New York: HarperCollins.

Clarke, C. P. 2015. *Terrorism, Inc.: The Financing of Terrorism, Insurgency, and Irregular Warfare*. Santa Barbara: ABC Clio.

Classen, A. 2004. *Violence in Medieval Courtly Literature*. London: Routledge.

Clausewitz, C. 2008 [1832]. *On War*. Princeton: Princeton University Press.

CM (Combat Manual). 2003. *Force Protection Weapons Handling Standard Procedures and Guidelines (NTRP 3–07.2.2)*. Washington, DC: Department of the Navy Office.

Coccia, M. 2017. A Theory of General Causes of Violent Crime: Homicides, Income Inequality and Deficiencies of the Heat Hypothesis and of the Model of CLASH. *Aggression and Violent Behavior* 37: 190–200.

Cohen, M. N. 1989. *Health and the Rise of Civilization*. New Haven, CT: Yale University Press.

Coker, C. 2013. *Warrior Geeks: How 21st-Century Technology Is Changing the Way We Fight and Think about War*. London: Hurst.

Collier, P. 2000. Doing Well Out of War: An Economic Perspective. In M. Berdal and D. Malone (eds.), *Greed and Grievance: Economic Agendas in Civil Wars*. Boulder, CO: Lynne Rienner, pp. 91–112.

Collier, P. and Hoeffler, A. 2002. On the Incidence of Civil War in Africa. *Journal of Conflict Resolution* 46(1): 13–28.

2004. Greed and Grievance in Civil War. *Oxford Economic Papers* 56(4): 563–95.

Collins, E. and McGovern, M. 1997. *Killing Rage*. London: Granta Books.

Collins, R. 2004. *Interaction Ritual Chains*. Princeton: Princeton University Press.

2008. *Violence: A Micro-Sociological Theory*. Princeton: Princeton University Press.

2009. The Micro-Sociology of Violence. *British Journal of Sociology* 60(3): 566–76.

2011. Ritual Boundary Violence and Bureaucratic Callousness: Two Structural Causes of Cruelty. In T. von Trotha and J. Rösel (eds.), *On Cruelty*. Köln: Rüdiger Köppe.

2013. Does Nationalist Sentiment Increase Fighting Efficacy? A Sceptical View from the Sociology of Violence. In J. A. Hall and S. Malešević (eds.), *Nationalism and War*. Cambridge: Cambridge University Press, pp. 29–43.

2015. Emotional Dynamics of Violent Situations. In D. Ziegler, M. Gerster, and S. Krämer (eds.), *Framing Excessive Violence*. Basingstoke: Palgrave Macmillan, pp. 17–36.

2020. Social Distancing as a Critical Test of the Micro-Sociology of Solidarity. *American Journal of Cultural Sociology* 8: 477–97.

Contreras, R. 2019. Que Duro! Street Violence in the South Bronx. In E. B. Weininger, A. Lareau, and O. Lizardo (eds.), *Ritual, Emotion, Violence: Studies on the Micro-Sociology of Randall Collins*. London: Routledge, pp. 27–45.

Conversi, D. 2008. 'We Are All Equals!' Militarism, Homogenization, and 'Egalitarianism' in Nationalist State-Building (1789–1945). *Ethnic and Racial Studies* 31(7): 1286–1314.

Conway, K. 2014. *Southside Provisional: From Freedom Fighter to the Four Courts*. Dublin: Orpen Press.

Coogan, T. P. 1987. *The IRA*. Glasgow: Fontana.

Cooley, C. 1909. *Social Organization: A Study of the Larger Mind*. New York: Charles Scribner's Sons.

Cornish, D. and Clarke, R. (eds.). 1986. *The Reasoning Criminal: Rational Choice Perspectives on Offending*. New Brunswick: Transaction Publishers.

Cortright, D. 2005. *Soldiers in Revolt: GI Resistance During the Vietnam War*. New York: Haymarket Books.

Coser, L. A. 1956. *The Functions of Social Conflict*. New York: Free Press.

Crivelli, C., Jarillo, S., Russell, J. A., and Fernández-Dols, J.-M. 2016. Reading Emotions from Faces in Two Indigenous Societies. *Journal of Experimental Psychology: General* 145(7): 830–43.

Crivelli, C., Russell, J. A., Jarillo, S., and Fernández-Dols, J.-M. 2017. Recognizing Spontaneous Facial Expressions of Emotion in a Small-Scale Society of Papua New Guinea. *Emotion* 17(2): 337–47.

Crone, P. 1986. The Tribe and the State. In J. A. Hall (ed.), *States in History*. Oxford: Oxford University Press, pp. 48–77.

Curran, G. 2019. 'Waiting for Jardiwanpa': History and Mediation in Warlpiri Fire Ceremonies. *Oceania* 89(1): 20–35.

Dandeker, C. 1990. *Surveillance, Power and Modernity: Bureaucracy and Discipline from 1700 to the Present Day*. New York: St Martin's Press.

Daniel, J. 2011. *Sampling Essentials*. London: Sage.

Dart, R. 1953. *The Predatory Transition from Ape to Man*. Leiden: Brill.

DATAUNODC. 2020. Victims of Intentional Homicide 1990–2018. https://dataunodc.un.org/content/data/homicide/homicide-rate.

David, L. 2020. *The Past Can't Heal Us*. Cambridge: Cambridge University Press.

Dawkins, R. 1989. *The Selfish Gene*. Oxford: Oxford University Press.

Decker, S. and Lauritsen, J. 2002. Leaving the Gang. In C. R. Huff (ed.), *Gangs in America III*. London: Sage, pp. 51–68.

DeLisi, M. 2015. Low Self-Control Is a Brain-Based Disorder. In K. M. Beaver, J. C. Barnes, and B. B. Boutwell (eds.), *The Nurture Versus Biosocial Debate in Criminology*. London: Sage, pp. 172–82.

Della Porta, D. 2013. *Clandestine Political Violence*. Cambridge: Cambridge University Press.

De Man, H. 1920. *The Remaking of a Mind*. London: Allen & Unwin.

Demiéville, P. 2010. Buddhism and War. In M. K. Jerryson and M. Juergensmeyer (eds.), *Buddhist Warfare*. Oxford: Oxford University Press, pp. 17–58.

Demmers, J. 2006. Conflict Research: Lancunas, Mantras and Pitfalls. *ISYP Journal on Science and World Affairs* 2(2): 99–102.

Dentan, R. 1968. *The Semai: A Nonviolent People of Malaya*. New York: Holt, Rinehart & Winston.

De Soysa, I. 2002. Paradise Is a Bazaar? Greed, Creed, and Governance in Civil War, 1989–1999. *Journal of Peace Research* 39(4): 395–416.

D'Huys, V. 1987. How to Describe Violence in Historical Narrative: Reflections of the Ancient Greek Historians and their Ancient Critics. *Ancient Society* 18: 209–50.

Diamond, J. 2005. *Collapse: How Societies Choose to Fail or Succeed*. London: Penguin.

2012. *The World Until Yesterday*. New York: Viking Press.

DiMaggio, P., Bernier, C., Heckscher, C., and Mimno, D. 2019. Interaction Ritual Threads: Does IRC Theory Apply Online? In E. B. Weininger, A. Lareau, and O. Lizardo (eds.), *Ritual, Emotion, Violence: Studies on the Micro-Sociology of Randall Collins*. London: Routledge, pp. 81–124.

Dimitrijević, B. B. 2001. *Militarism and the Creation of Social Identities since 1945: A Comparative Study on Cases of Yugoslavia and Bulgaria*. Sofia: Centre for Advanced Studies.

Divjak, J. 2001. The First Phase, 1992–1993: Struggle for Survival and Genesis of the Army of Bosnia and Herzegovina. In B. Magaš and I. Žanić (eds.), *The War in Croatia and Bosnia-Herzegovina 1991–1995*. London: Frank Cass, pp. 152–77.

Dobkin, B. H. 2003. *The Clinical Science of Neurologic Rehabilitation*. Oxford: Oxford University Press.

Doel, M. 2017. *Geographies of Violence: Killing Space, Killing Time*. London: Sage.

Doob, L. W. 1981. *The Pursuit of Peace*. Westport, CT: Greenwood Press.

Dudley, S. 2015. Barrio 18 in El Salvador: A View from the Inside. *InSight Crime*. https://new.insightcrime.org/news/analysis/barrio-18-el-salvador-view-from-inside/.

Dunbar, R. 1992. Neocortex Size as a Constraint on Group Size in Primates. *Journal of Human Evolution* 22: 469–93.

2017. Group Size, Vocal Grooming, and the Origins of Language. *Psychonomic Bulletin & Review* 24: 209–12.

2021. *Friends: Understanding the Power of Our Most Important Relationships*. London: Little, Brown.

Dunbar, R. and Lehmann, J. 2013. Grooming and Social Cohesion in Primates: A Comment on Grueter et al. *Evolution and Human Behavior* 34: 453–5.

Du Picq, A. 2006 [1880]. *Battle Studies*. New York: Bibliobazar.

Durkheim, E. 1986. *Durkheim on Politics and the State*. Cambridge: Polity Press.

Eby, C. 2007. *Comrades and Commissars: The Lincoln Battalion in the Spanish Civil War*. Philadelphia: University of Pennsylvania Press.

Eisner, M. 2003. Long-Term Historical Trends in Violent Crime. *Crime and Justice* 30: 83–142

Ekman, P. 1992. An Argument for Basic Emotions. *Cognition and Emotion* 6: 169–200.

Ekman, P. and Cordaro, D. 2011. What Is Meant by Calling Emotions Basic? *Emotion Review* 3(4): 364–70.

Ekman, P. and Friesen, W. 1971. Constants Across Cultures in the Face and Emotion. *Journal of Personality and Social Psychology* 17(2): 124–9.

Ellman, M. 2002. Soviet Repression Statistics: Some Comments. *Europe-Asia Studies* 54(7): 1151–72.

Emlen, D. 2014. *Animal Weapons: The Evolution of Battle*. New York: Henry Holt and Company.

English, R. 2003. *Armed Struggle: The History of the IRA*. London: Pan.

Erdkamp, P. 2015. Manpower and Food Supply in the First and Second Punic Wars. In D. Hoyos (ed.), *A Companion to the Punic Wars*. London: Wiley Blackwell, pp. 58–76.

Fairbairn, H. 2019. UK Apocalypse Survival Guide: Where and How to Survive the End of the World. www.countryfile.com/how-to/uk-apocalypse-survival-guide-where-and-how-to-survive-the-end-of-the-world/.

Fajans, J. 1997. *They Make Themselves: Work and Play among the Baining of Papua New Guinea*. Chicago: University of Chicago Press.

Falkner, A. L., Grosenick, L., Davidson, T. J., Deisseroth, K., and Lin, D. 2016. Hypothalamic Control of Male Aggression-Seeking Behavior. *Nature Neuroscience* 19(4): 596–604.

Farb, P. 1991. *Man's Rise to Civilisation: The Cultural Ascent of the Indians of North America*. London: Penguin.

Fearon, J. D. 1994. Signalling versus the Balance of Power and Interests: An Empirical Test of a Crisis Bargaining Model. *Journal of Conflict Resolution* 38 (2): 236–69.

Fearon, J. D. and Laitin, D. D. 2003. Ethnicity, Insurgency, and Civil War. *American Political Science Review* 97(1): 75–90.

Ferguson, B. 1995. *Yanomami Warfare: A Political History*. Santa Fe: School for American Research Press.

2013. Pinker's List: Exaggerating Prehistoric War Mortality. In D. Fry (ed.), *War, Peace, and Human Nature: The Convergence of Evolutionary and Cultural Views*. Oxford: Oxford University Press, pp. 112–31.

Ferro, M. 2004. *The Use and Abuse of History: Or How the Past Is Taught to Children*. London: Routledge.

Fields, D. 2016. *Why We Snap: Understanding the Rage Circuit in Your Brain*. New York: Penguin.

Finegan, J. 2015. *Light from the Ancient Past*, Vol. 1. Princeton: Princeton University Press.

Finlan, A. 2004. *Collapse of Yugoslavia, 1991–1999*. Oxford: Osprey.

Fiske, A. and Rai, T. S. 2014. *Virtuous Violence: Hurting and Killing to Create, Sustain, End, and Honor Social Relationships*. Cambridge: Cambridge University Press.

Fong, R. S., Vogel, R. E., and Buentello, S. 1995. Blood-In, Blood-Out: The Rationale behind Defecting from Prison Gangs. *Journal of Gang Research* 2 (4): 45–51.

Forrest, A. 1989. *Conscripts and Deserters: The Army and French Society During the Revolution and Empire*. Oxford: Oxford University Press.

Foucault, M. 1975. *Discipline and Punish: The Birth of the Prison*. New York: Random House.

France, J. 1999. *Western Warfare in the Age of the Crusades, 1000–1300*. London: Routledge.

Frey, L. and Frey, M. 2004. *The French Revolution*. Westport, CT: Greenwood Press.

Friend, M. 1975. *The Notion of Tribe*. Menlo Park, CA: Cummings.

Fritz, S. 2010. *Frontsoldaten: The German Soldier in World War II*. Lawrence: University of Kentucky Press.

Fry, D. 2007. *Beyond War: The Human Potential for Peace*. Oxford: Oxford University Press.

2013. War, Peace, and Human Nature: The Challenge of Achieving Scientific Objectivity. In D. Fry (ed.), *War, Peace, and Human Nature: The Convergence of Evolutionary and Cultural Views*. Oxford: Oxford University Press, pp. 1–22.

Fry, D., Bonta, B. D., and Baszarkiewicz, K. 2009. Learning from Extant Cultures of Peace. In J. de Rivera (ed.), *Handbook on Building Cultures of Peace*. New York: Springer, pp. 11–26.

Fry, D., Schober, G., and Bjorkqvist, K. 2010. Nonkilling as an Evolutionary Adaptation. In J. Evans Pim (ed.), *Nonkilling Societies*. Honolulu: Centre for Global Nonkilling, pp. 101–28.

Fry, D. and Söderberg, P. 2013 Lethal Aggression in Mobile Forager Bands, and Implications for the Origins of War. *Science* 341: 270–3.

Fry, D. and Szala, A. 2013. The Evolution of Agonism: The Triumph of Restraint in Nonhumans and Human Primates. In D. P. Fry (ed.), *War, Peace and Human Nature: The Convergence of Evolutionary and Cultural Views*. Oxford: Oxford University Press, pp. 451–74.

Frydel, T. 2018. Judenjagd: Reassessing the Role of Ordinary Poles as Perpetrators in the Holocaust. In T. Williams and S. Buckley-Zistel (eds.), *Perpetrators and Perpetration of Mass Violence: Action, Motivations and Dynamics*. London: Routledge, pp. 187–203.

Fuentes, A. 2012. *Race, Monogamy and Other Lies They Told You: Busting Myths about Human Nature*. Berkeley: University of California Press.

Fujii, L. 2011. *Killing Neighbours: Webs of Violence in Rwanda*. Ithaca, NY: Cornell University Press.

Fuller, J. 1990. *Troop Morale and Popular Culture in the British and Dominion Armies 1914–1918*. Oxford: Clarendon Press.

Fulwiler, C. 2003. Discussion of "A Vicious Circle". *Modern Psychoanalysis* 28 (2): 247–257.

Fumaglli, M. and Priori, A. 2012. Functional and Clinical Neuroanatomy of Morality. *Brain* 135(7): 2006–21.

Füssel, M. 2016. Emotions in the Making: The Transformation of Battlefield Experiences during the Seven Years' War (1756–1763). In E. Kuijpers and C. van der Haven (eds.), *Battlefield Emotions 1500–1800: Practices, Experience, Imagination*. London: Palgrave Macmillan, pp. 149–72.

Gagnon, C. 2004. *The Myth of Ethnic War*. Ithaca, NY: Cornell University Press.

Galtung, J. and Ruge, M. H. 1965. The Structure of Foreign News: The Presentation of the Congo, Cuba and Cyprus Crises in Four Norwegian Newspapers. *Journal of Peace Research* 2(1): 64–91.

Gambetta, D. 1993. *The Sicilian Mafia: The Business of Private Protection*. Cambridge, MA: Harvard University Press.

  2009. *Codes of the Underworld: How Criminals Communicate*. Princeton: Princeton University Press.

Garnham, N. 2005. Military Desertion and Deserters in Eighteenth-Century Ireland. *Eighteenth-Century Ireland* 20: 91–103.

Gat, A. 2006. *War in Human Civilization*. Oxford: Oxford University Press.

  2012. Is War Declining and Why? *Journal of Peace Research* 50(2): 149–57.

  2017. *The Causes of War and the Spread of Peace: But Will War Rebound?* Oxford: Oxford University Press.

Gaub, F. 2011. *Military Integration after Civil Wars: Multiethnic Armies, Identity and Post Conflict Reconstruction*. London: Routledge.

Gellner, E. 1988. *Plough, Sword, and the Book: The Structure of Human History*. London: Collins Harvill.

Gerdes, F. 2013. *Civil War and State Formation: The Political Economy of War and Peace in Liberia*. Frankfurt: Campus Verlag.

Germani, I. 2016. Mediated Battlefields of the French Revolution and Emotives at Work. In E. Kuijpers and C. van der Haven (eds.), *Battlefield Emotions 1500–1800: Practices, Experience, Imagination*. London: Palgrave Macmillan, pp. 173–94.

Gerstle, G. 2017. *American Crucible: Race and Nation in the Twentieth Century*. Princeton: Princeton University Press.

Giddens, A. 1985. *The Nation-State and Violence*. Cambridge: Polity Press.

Girard, R. 2005 [1972]. *Violence and the Sacred*. London: Continuum.

Glenny, M. 2017. *The Balkans, 1804–2012: Nationalism, War, and the Great Powers*. London: Granta.

Gluckman, M. 1963. Gossip and Scandal. *Current Anthropology* 4: 307–16.

Go, J. 2020. The Imperial Origins of American Policing: Militarization and Imperial Feedback in the Early 20th Century. *American Journal of Sociology* 125(5): 1193–1254.

Go, J. and Lawson, G. 2017. Introduction: For a Global Historical Sociology. In J. Go and G. Lawson (eds.), *Global Historical Sociology*. Cambridge: Cambridge University Press, pp. 1–34.

Goldstein, J. H. (ed.). 1998. *Why We Watch: The Attractions of Violent Entertainment*. Oxford: Oxford University Press.

Goldstein, J. S. 2001. *War and Gender: How Gender Shapes the War System and Vice Versa*. Cambridge: Cambridge University Press.

Goodall, J. 1986. *The Chimpanzee of Gombe: Patterns of Behaviour*. Cambridge, MA: Harvard University Press.

Gordy, E. 2013. *Guilt, Responsibility, and Denial*. Philadelphia: University of Pennsylvania Press.

Gow, J. 1992. *Legitimacy and the Military: The Yugoslav Crisis*. London: Pinter.

Gowlett, J., Gamble, C., and Dunbar, R. 2012. Human Evolution and the Archaeology of the Social Brain. *Current Anthropology* 53(6): 693–722.

Gray, C. H. 1997. *Postmodern War: The New Politics of Conflict*. New York: Guilford Press.

Gregory, T. 2019. Dangerous Feelings: Checkpoints and the Perception of Hostile Intent. *Security Dialogue* 50(2): 131–47.

Griffith, J. 1988. Measurement of Group Cohesion in U.S. Army Units. *Basic and Applied Social Psychology* 9(2): 149–71.

Griffiths, J. G. 1991. *The Divine Verdict: A Study of Divine Judgement in the Ancient Religions*. Leiden: Brill.

Grillo, I. 2012. *El Narco: The Bloody Rise of Mexican Drug Cartels*. New York: Bloomsbury.

Grimes, T., Anderson, J., and Bergen, L. 2008. *Media Violence and Aggression: Science and Ideology*. London: Sage.

Gross, J. 2015. Emotion Regulation: Current Status and Future Prospects. *Psychological Inquiry* 26(1): 1–26.

Grossman, D. 1996. *On Killing: The Psychological Cost of Learning to Kill in War and Society*. Boston: Little, Brown.

2004. *On Combat: The Psychology and Physiology of Deadly Conflict in War and in Peace*. Millstadt, IL: Warrior Science Publications.

Gunaratna, R. and Oreg, A. 2010. Al Qaeda's Organizational Structure and Its Evolution. *Studies in Conflict and Terrorism* 33(12): 1043–78.

Guthrie, R. D. 2005. *The Nature of Paleolithic Art*. Chicago: University of Chicago Press.

Guyer, P. and Horstmann, R. 2019. Idealism. In *The Stanford Encyclopedia of Philosophy*, Edward N. Zalta (ed.), https://plato.stanford.edu/archives/win2019/entries/idealism/.

Hagelin, S. 2008. Bleeding Bodies and Post-Cold War Politics: *Saving Private Ryan* and the Gender of Vulnerability. In K. Randell and S. Redmond (eds.), *The War Body on Screen*. London: Continuum, pp. 102–19.

Haldén, P. 2018. Organized Armed Groups as Ruling Organizations. *Armed Forces & Society* 44(4): 606–25.

2020. *Family Power: Kinship, War and Political Orders in Eurasia, 500–2018*. Cambridge: Cambridge University Press.

Hall, J. A. 1986. *Powers and Liberties: The Causes and Consequences of the Rise of the West*. Oxford: Basil Blackwell.

Hall, J. R. 2009. *Apocalypse: From Antiquity to the Empire of Modernity*. Cambridge: Polity Press.

Hanley, B. and Millar, S. 2010. *The Lost Revolution: The Story of the Official IRA and the Workers' Party*. London: Penguin.

Hart, D. and Sussman, R. W. 2009. *Man the Hunted: Primates, Predators, and Human Evolution*. Boulder, CO: Westview Press.

Haslam, N. 2006. Dehumanization: An Integrative Review. *Personality and Social Psychology Review* 10(3): 252–264.

Hassan, R. 2011. *Suicide Bombings*. London: Routledge.

Hatala, K. G., Roach, N. T., Ostrofsky, K. R., et al. 2016. Footprints Reveal Direct Evidence of Group Behavior and Locomotion in Homo Erectus. *Scientific Reports* 6: 28766.

Heathcote, T. 1995. *The Military in British India: The Development of British Land Forces in South Asia, 1600–1947*. Manchester: Manchester University Press.

Heider, K. G. 1996. *Grand Valley Dani: Peaceful Warriors*. Belmont, CA: Wadsworth Publishing.

Hellmann-Rajanayagam, D. 1994. *The Tamil Tigers: Armed Struggle for Identity*. Stuttgart: Franz Steiner Verlag.

Hempel, A. A., Levine, R. D., Meloy, J. D., and Westermeyer, J. D. 2000. Cross-Cultural Review of Sudden Mass Assault by a Single Individual in the Oriental and Occidental Cultures. *Journal of Forensic Sciences* 45(3): 582–8.

Heuser, B. 2010. *The Evolution of Strategy: Thinking War from Antiquity to the Present*. Cambridge: Cambridge University Press.

Hiers, W. and Wimmer, A. 2013. Is Nationalism the Cause or Consequence of the End of Empire? In J. A. Hall and S. Malešević (eds.), *Nationalism and War*. Cambridge: Cambridge University Press, pp. 212–54.

Hillenbrand, C. 2000. *The Crusades: Islamic Perspectives*. London: Routledge.

Hintjens, H. 1999. Explaining the 1994 Genocide in Rwanda. *Modern African Studies* 37(2): 241–86.

Hitler, A. 2021 [1925]. *Mein Kampf*. New Delhi: Dimond Books.

Hobbes, T. 2004 [1651]. *Leviathan*. New York: Barnes & Noble.

Hochschild, A. 1999. *King Leopold's Ghost: A Story of Greed, Terror and Heroism in Colonial Africa*. New York: Mariner Books.
2012. *To End All Wars: A Story of Loyalty and Rebellion, 1914–1918*. New York: Mariner Books.
Hoebel, E. A. 1967. Anthropological Perspectives on National Character. *Annals of the American Academy of Political and Social Science* 370: 1–7.
Hoffman, D. 2011. *The War Machines: Young Men and Violence in Sierra Leone and Liberia*. Durham, NC: Duke University Press.
Hoggarth, J., Breitenbach, S. F. M., Culleton, B. J., Ebert, C. E., Masson, M. A., and Kennett, D. J. 2016. The Political Collapse of Chichén Itzá in Climatic and Cultural Context. *Global and Planetary Change* 138: 25–42.
Højbjerg, C. K. 2010. Victims and Heroes: Manding Historical Imagination in a Conflict-Ridden Border Region (Liberia-Guinea). In J. Knörr and W. Trajano Filho (eds.), *The Powerful Presence of the Past: Integration and Conflict along the Upper Guinea Coast*. Leiden: Brill, pp. 273–93.
Holbrook, D. 2010. Using the Qur'an to Justify Terrorist Violence: Analysing Selective Application of the Qur'an in English-Language Militant Islamist Discourse. *Perspectives on Terrorism* 4(3): 15–28.
Holmes, R. 1985. *Acts of War*. New York: Free Press.
Home Office. 2020. Homicide in England and Wales: Year Ending March 2020. www.ons.gov.uk/peoplepopulationandcommunity/crimeandjustice/datasets/appendixtableshomicideinenglandandwales.
Homer. 2017. *The Iliad*. London: Vintage Classics.
Homer-Dixon, T. 1999. *Environment, Scarcity, and Violence*. Princeton: Princeton University Press.
2006. *The Upside of Down: Catastrophe, Creativity, and the Renewal of Civilization*. Toronto: Knopf.
Houghton, F. 2019. *The Veterans' Tale: British Military Memoirs of the Second World War*. Cambridge: Cambridge University Press.
Humphries, M. 2005. Natural Resources, Conflict, and Conflict Resolution: Uncovering the Mechanisms. *Journal of Conflict Resolution* 49(4): 508–37.
Hunter, J. 2001. Death of the Englishman who Led the Provisionals. *The Observer*, 20 May.
Innes, M. 2006. *Bosnian Security After Dayton: New Perspectives*. London: Routledge.
InSight Crime. 2019. MS 13 El Salvador. https://insightcrime.org/el-salvador-organized-crime-news/mara-salvatrucha-ms-13-profile/.
IRA. 1977. Green Book I and II. https://cain.ulster.ac.uk/othelem/organ/ira/ira_green_book.htm.
Izard, C. 1994. Innate and Universal Facial Expressions: Evidence from Developmental and Cross-Cultural Research. *Psychological Bulletin* 115(2): 288–99.
Jablonka, E. and Lamb, M. J. 2005. *Evolution in Four Dimensions: Genetic, Epigenetic, Behavioral, and Symbolic Variation in the History of Life*. Cambridge, MA: MIT Press.
James, F. 2009. William Calley Makes First Public Apology for Vietnam War's My Lai Massacre. *NPR Newsletter*. www.npr.org/sections/thetwo-way/2009/08/william_calley_makes_first_pub.html?t=1635834622654.

Janis, I. L. 1985. *Group Think*. Boston: Houghton Mifflin.

Jayasundara-Smits, S. 2018. Lost in Transition: Linking War, War Economy and Post-War Crime in Sri Lanka. *Third World Thematic: A TWQ Journal* 3(1): 63–79.

Jović, D. 2001. The Disintegration of Yugoslavia: A Critical Review of Explanatory Approaches. *European Journal of Social Theory* 4(1): 101–20.

Judah, T. 1997. *The Serbs*. New Haven, CT: Yale University Press.

Juergensmeyer, M. 2000. *Terror in the Mind of God*. Berkeley: University of California Press.

Jünger, E. 2016 [1920]. *Storm of Steel*. London: Penguin.

Junger, S. 2010. *War*. New York: Grand Central Publishing.

Kadijević, V. 1993. *Moje vidjenje raspada: Vojska bez države*. Belgrade: Politika.

Käihkö, I. 2016. *Bush Generals and Small Boy Battalions: Military Cohesion in Liberia and Beyond*. Department of Peace and Conflict Research Report 109. Uppsala: University of Uppsala.

    2017. Liberia Incorporated: Military Contracting, Cohesion, and Inclusion in Charles Taylor's Liberia. *Conflict, Security & Development* 17(1): 53–72.

    2018. Broadening the Perspective on Military Cohesion. *Armed Forces & Society* 44(4): 571–86.

Kaldor, M. 2001. *Old and New Wars*. Cambridge. Polity Press.

Kalyvas, S. 2006. *The Logic of Violence in Civil War*. Cambridge: Cambridge University Press.

Kalyvas, S. and Kocher, M. 2007. How "Free" is Free Riding in Civil Wars? Violence, Insurgency, and the Collective Action Problem. *World Politics* 59 (2): 177–216.

Kamieński, L. 2017. *Shooting Up: A History of Drugs in Warfare*. London: Hurst.

Kaplan, J. 2009. The Lord's Resistance Army: Millennialism, Violence, and the Timeless Dream. *Religious Studies and Theology* 28(1): 95–127.

Kaposi, D. 2017. The Resistance Experiments: Morality, Authority, and Obedience in Stanley Milgram's Account. *Journal of the History of Social Behaviour* 47(4): 382–401.

Katunarić, V. 1991. Uoči novih etnopolitičkih raskola: Hrvatska i Bosna I Hercegovina. *Sociologija* 33(3): 373–85.

Keefer, P. 2012. *Why Follow the Leader? Collective Action, Credible Commitment and Conflict*. Policy Research Working Paper 6179. Washington, DC: World Bank.

Keegan, J. 1994. *A History of Warfare*. New York: Vintage.

Keeley, L. H. 1996. *War before Civilization: The Myth of the Peaceful Savage*. Oxford: Oxford University Press.

Keels E., Benson, J., Filitz, J., and Lambert, J. 2019. *Reassessing Rebellion: Exploring Recent Trends in Civil War Dynamics*. Broomfield, CO: OEF Research.

Keen, D. 2012. Greed and Grievance in Civil War. *International Affairs* 88(4): 757–77.

Keene, J. 2007. *Fighting for Franco: International Volunteers in Nationalist Spain during the Spanish Civil War*. London: Bloomsbury.

Keller, K. 1996. *Apocalypse Now and Then: A Feminist Guide to the End of the World*. Boston: Beacon Press.

Kellett, A. 2013. *Combat Motivation: The Behaviour of Soldiers in Battle*. New York: Springer.

Kemeroff, A. 2018. War for Money: Leading Private Military Companies of the World. *Medium*. https://medium.com/smartaim-tech/war-for-money-leading-private-military-companies-of-the-world-eab9f9fe2de8.

King, A. 2006. The Word of Command: Communication and Cohesion in the Military. *Armed Forces & Society* 32(4): 493–512.

 2007. The Existence of Group Cohesion in the Armed Forces: A Response to Guy Siebold, *Armed Forces & Society* 33(4): 638–45.

 2013. *The Combat Soldier: Infantry Tactics and Cohesion in the Twentieth and Twenty-First Centuries*. Oxford: Oxford University Press.

 2014. Cohesion: Heroic and Post-Heroic Combat. In S. Scheipers (ed.), *Heroism and the Changing Character of War*. Basingstoke: Palgrave Macmillan, pp. 221–36.

 2015. Discipline and Punish: Encouraging Combat Performance in the Citizen and Professional Army. In A. King (ed.), *Frontline: Combat and Cohesion in 21st Century*. Oxford: Oxford University Press, pp. 93–116.

King, M. L. Jr. 2011 [1964]. *Why We Can't Wait*. Boston: Beacon Press.

Kirschenbaum, L. 2015. *International Communism and the Spanish Civil War: Solidarity and Suspicion*. Cambridge: Cambridge University Press.

Klay, P. 2014. *Redeployment*. London: Penguin.

Klein, C. 2016. *Instinct Combat Shooting: Defensive Handgunning for Police*. Boca Raton, FL: CRC Press.

Klinger, D. 2004. *Into the Kill Zone: A Cop's Eye View of Deadly Force*. San Francisco: Jossey-Bass.

Knickerbocker, B. 1982. Army's COHORT Plan Keeps Units Together, Builds Morale. *Christian Science Monitor*. www.csmonitor.com/1982/1222/122243.html.

Koehler, K., Ohl, D., and Albrecht, H. 2016. From Disaffection to Desertion: How Networks Facilitate Military Insubordination in Civil Conflict. *Comparative Politics* 48(4): 439–57.

Kohn, S. 1987. *Jailed for Peace: The History of American Draft Law Violators, 1658–1985*. Westport, CT: Greenwood Press.

Kokko, H. 2008. Animal Behaviour Studies: Non-Primates. In L. Kurtz (ed.), *Encyclopaedia of Violence, Peace and Conflict*. New York: Elsevier.

Kort, M. G. 2015. *The Soviet Colossus: History and Aftermath*. New York: M. E. Sharpe.

Krys, K., Vauclair, C. M., Capaldi, C. A., et al. 2016. Be Careful Where You Smile: Culture Shapes Judgments of Intelligence and Honesty of Smiling Individuals. *Journal of Nonverbal Behaviour* 40: 101–16.

Kuijpers, E. and van der Haven, C. 2016. Battlefield Emotions 1500–1800: Practices, Experience, Imagination. In E. Kuijpers and C. van der Haven (eds.), *Battlefield Emotions 1500–1800: Practices, Experience, Imagination*. London: Palgrave Macmillan, pp. 3–22.

Kumar, K. 2017. *Visions of Empire*. Princeton: Princeton University Press.

2021. *Empires: A Historical and Political Sociology.* Cambridge: Polity Press.

Kuzawa, C. W. and Sweet, E. 2009. Epigenetics and the Embodiment of Race: Developmental Origins of US Racial Disparities in Cardiovascular Health. *American Journal of Human Biology* 21(1): 2–15.

Ladd, J. 1986. *SAS Operations.* London: Leisure Circle Book Club.

Laitin, D. D. 2007. *Nations, States and Violence.* Oxford: Oxford University Press.

Lande, B. 2007. Breathing Like a Soldier: Culture Incarnate. *The Sociological Review* 55(1): 95–108.

Laugesen, A. 2016. *'Boredom is the Enemy': The Intellectual and Imaginative Lives of Australian Soldiers in the Great War and Beyond.* London: Routledge.

Lawrence, M. 2020. How to Survive in a Violent Post Apocalypse. *Secrets of Survival.* https://secretsofsurvival.com/how-to-survive-violent-post-apoca lypse/.

Lawson, G. 2019. *The Anatomies of Revolution.* Cambridge: Cambridge University Press.

Lea, J. 2002. *Crime and Modernity: Continuities in Left Realist Criminology.* London: Sage.

Leader Maynard, J. 2014. Rethinking the Role of Ideology in Mass Atrocities. *Terrorism and Political Violence* 26(5): 821–841.

2019. Ideology and Armed Conflict. *Journal of Peace Research* 56(5): 635–49.

LeBlanc, S. A. 2007. Why Warfare? Lessons from the Past. *Daedalus* 136(1): 13–21.

LeBlanc, S. A. and Register, K. E. 2013. *Constant Battles: Why We Fight.* New York: St. Martin's Press.

Le Bohec, Y. 2013. *The Imperial Roman Army.* London: Routledge.

Lehmann, J., Korstjens, A., and Dunbar, R. 2007. Group Size, Grooming and Social Cohesion in Primates. *Animal Behavior* 74: 1617–1629.

Lenin, V. I. 1919. Letter to the Workers of Europe and America. *Lenin Internet Archive.* www.marxists.org/archive/lenin/works/1919/jan/21.htm#fw01.

Le Texier, T. 2019. Debunking the Stanford Prison Experiment. *American Psychologist* 74(7): 823–39.

Levi, M. 1997. *Consent, Dissent, and Patriotism.* Cambridge: Cambridge University Press.

Levi, P. 1995. *If Not Now, When?* London: Penguin.

Levy, R. I. 1975. *Tahitians: Mind and Experience in the Society Islands.* Chicago: University of Chicago Press.

Liebau, H. 2017. Martial Races: Theory of. *International Encyclopedia of the First World War.* https://encyclopedia.1914-1918-online.net/article/martial_ races_theory_of.

Lilja, J. 2009. Trapping Constituents or Winning Hearts and Minds? Rebel Strategies to Attain Constituent Support in Sri Lanka. *Terrorism and Political Violence* 21(2): 306–26.

Lim, N. 2016. Cultural Differences in Emotion: Differences in Emotional Arousal Level between the East and the West. *Integrative Medicine Research* 5(2): 105–9.

Lindquist, K., Gendron, M., Feldman Barrett, L., and Dickerson, D. C. 2014. Emotion Perception, but Not Affect Perception, Is Impaired with Semantic Memory Loss. *Emotion* 14(2): 375–87.

Lindquist, K., Satpute, A. B., Wager, T. D., Weber, J., and Feldman Barrett, L. 2015. The Brain Basis of Positive and Negative Affects: Evidence from a Meta-Analysis of the Human Neuroimaging Literature. *Cerebral Cortex* 26 (5): 1910–22.

Ling, R. 2008. *New Tech, New Ties: How Mobile Communication Is Reshaping Social Cohesion.* Cambridge, MA: MIT Press.

Lippard, C., Osinsky, P., and Strauss, L. 2018. *War: Contemporary Perspectives on Armed Conflicts around the World.* London: Routledge.

Litz, B., Stein, N., Delaney, E., Lebowitz, L., Nash, W. P., Silva, C., and Maguen, S. 2009. Moral Injury and Moral Repair in War Veterans: A Preliminary Model and Intervention Strategy. *Clinical Psychology Review* 29(8): 695–706.

Lizot, J. 1985. *Tales of the Yanomami: Daily Life in the Venezuelan Forest.* Cambridge: Cambridge University Press.

Lodge, T. 1983. *Black Politics in South Africa since 1945.* London: Longman.

Lorenz, K. 1966. *On Aggression.* New York: Harcourt Brace Jovanovich.

Lowenthal, D. 1985. *The Past is a Foreign Country.* Cambridge: Cambridge University Press.

Loyal, S. and Malešević, S. 2021. *Classical Sociological Theory.* London: Sage.

Lu, L. and Gilmour, R. 2004. Culture and Conceptions of Happiness: Individual Oriented and Social Oriented SWB. *Journal of Happiness Studies* 5(3): 269–91.

Luft, A. 2019. Dehumanization and the Normalization of Violence: It's Not What You Think. *Items.* https://items.ssrc.org/insights/dehumanization-and-the-normalization-of-violence-its-not-what-you-think/.

Lutz, C. 1988. *Unnatural Emotions: Everyday Sentiments on a Micronesian Atoll and Their Challenge to Western Theory.* Chicago: University of Chicago Press.

Lyall, J. 2020. *Divided Armies: Inequality and Battlefield Performance in Modern War.* Princeton: Princeton University Press.

Lynch, K. 2013. *A Plagued Mind: The Justification of Violence within the Principles of Maximilien Robespierre.* History Student Papers 9. Providence College: Digital Commons.

MacCoun, R. J. and Hix, W. M. 2010. Unit Cohesion and Military Performance. In B. D. Rostker et al. (eds.), *Sexual Orientation and U.S. Military Personnel Policy.* Santa Monica, CA: RAND.

MacDonald, D. 2003. *Balkan Holocausts? Serbian and Croatian Victim-Centred Propaganda and the War in Yugoslavia.* Manchester: Manchester University Press.

Machiavelli, N. 1985 [1532]. *The Prince.* Chicago: University of Chicago Press.

Madej, V. 1978. Effectiveness and Cohesion of the German Ground Forces in World War II. *Journal of Political and Military Sociology* 6: 233–48.

Maeland, B. and Brunstad, P. 2009. *Enduring Military Boredom: From 1750 to the Present.* New York: Palgrave Macmillan.

Magaš, B. and Žanić, I. (eds.). 2001. *The War in Croatia and Bosnia-Herzegovina 1991–1995.* London: Frank Cass.

Malabou, C. 2011. *What Should We Do with Our Brain?* New York: Fordham University Press.

Malatesta, E. 1921. The Revolutionary 'Haste'. *Errico Malatesta Archive*. www
.marxists.org/archive/malatesta/1921/09/haste.htm.
Malešević, S. 2002. *Ideology, Legitimacy, and the New State*. London: Routledge.
    2006. *Identity as Ideology: Understanding Ethnicity and Nationalism*. New York:
    Palgrave Macmillan.
    2010. *The Sociology of War and Violence*. Cambridge: Cambridge University
    Press.
    2013. *Nation-States and Nationalisms: Organization, Ideology and Solidarity*.
    Cambridge: Polity Press.
    2017. *The Rise of Organised Brutality: A Historical Sociology of Violence*.
    Cambridge: Cambridge University Press.
    2018. The Structural Origins of Social Cohesion: The Dynamics of Micro-
    Solidarity in 1991–1995 Wars of Yugoslav Succession. *Small Wars and
    Insurgencies* 29(4): 735–53.
    2019. *Grounded Nationalisms: A Sociological Analysis*. Cambridge: Cambridge
    University Press.
    2020. Is It Easy to Kill in War? Emotions and Violence in the Combat Zones of
    Croatia and Bosnia and Herzegovina (1991–1995). *European Journal of
    Sociology* 62: 1–31.
    2021. The Act of Killing: Understanding the Emotional Dynamics of Violence
    on the Battlefield. *Critical Military Studies* 7(3): 313–34.
Malešević, S. and Ó Dochartaigh, N. 2018. Why Combatants Fight: The Irish
    Republican Army and the Bosnian Serb Army Compared. *Theory and Society*
    47(3): 293–326.
Mann, M. 1986. *The Sources of Social Power, Vol. 1: A History of Power from the
    Beginning to A.D. 1760*. Cambridge: Cambridge University Press.
    1993. *The Sources of Social Power, Vol. 2: The Rise of Classes and Nation-States,
    1760–1914*. Cambridge: Cambridge University Press.
    2012. *The Sources of Social Power, Vol. 3: Global Empires and Revolution,
    1890–1945*. Cambridge: Cambridge University Press.
    2013. *The Sources of Social Power, Vol. 4: Globalizations, 1945–2011*.
    Cambridge: Cambridge University Press.
    2019. Fear, Loathing, and Moral Qualms on the Battlefield. *Thesis Eleven* 154
    (1): 11–27.
Manning, A. 2016. How Violent Street Gang MS-13 Operates in Massachusetts.
    Boston.com. www.boston.com/news/local-news/2016/01/29/how-violent-street-
    gang-ms-13-operates-in-massachusetts.
Marks, J. 2015. *Tales of the Ex-Apes: How We Think about Human Evolution*.
    Oakland: University of California Press.
Marlantes, K. 2011. *What It Is Like to Go to War*. New York: Atlantic Monthly
    Press.
Marshall, S. L. A. 1947. *Men against Fire: The Problem of Battle Command*. New
    York: Morrow.
Martin, M. 2018. *Why We Fight*. London: Hurst.
Marx, K. and Engels, F. 2005. *The Communist Manifesto*. New York: Haymarket
    Books.
Mayr, E. 1982. *The Growth of Biological Thought: Diversity, Evolution, and
    Inheritance*. Cambridge, MA: Harvard University Press.

McCall, G. S. 2009. Exploring the Origins of Human Warfare through Cross-Cultural Research on Modern and Prehistoric Foragers. *International Journal of Contemporary Sociology* 46(2), 163–83.

McCleery, M. 2016. Randall Collins' Forward Panic Pathway to Violence and the 1972 Bloody Sunday Killings in Northern Ireland. *British Journal of Politics and International Relations* 18(4): 966–80.

McClelland, K. 1985. On the Social Significance of Interactional Synchrony. Unpublished paper. Grinnell College, Department of Sociology.

2014. Cycles of Conflict: A Computational Modeling Alternative to Collins's Theory of Conflict Escalation. *Sociological Theory* 32(2): 100–27.

McDougall, W. 2015 [1908]. *An Introduction to Social Psychology*. London: Psychology Press.

McLauchlin, T. 2015. Desertion and Collective Action in Civil Wars. *International Studies Quarterly* 59(4): 669–79.

2020. *Desertion: Trust and Mistrust in Civil War*. Ithaca, NY: Cornell University Press.

McManus, J. 2007. *The Deadly Brotherhood: The American Combat Soldier in World War II*. New York: Random House.

McNab, C. 2009. *Armies of the Napoleonic Wars*. Oxford: Osprey Publishing.

McNeill, W. 1984. *The Pursuit of Power*. Chicago: University of Chicago Press.

1997. *Keeping Together in Time: Dance and Drill in Human History*. Cambridge, MA: Harvard University Press.

Mearsheimer, J. J. 2001. *The Tragedy of Great Power Politics*. New York: W. W. Norton.

Mehta, P. and Beer, J. S. 2010. Neural Mechanisms of the Testosterone–Aggression Relation: The Role of Orbitofrontal Cortex. *Journal of Cognitive Neuroscience* 22: 2357–68.

Melson, R. 1992. *Revolution and Genocide*. Chicago: University of Chicago Press.

2003. Modern Genocide in Rwanda: Ideology, Revolution, War, and Mass Nurder in an African State. In R. Gellately and B. Kiernan (eds.), *The Specter of Genocide: Mass Murder in Historical Perspective*. Cambridge: Cambridge University Press, pp. 325–38.

Middleton, G. 2017. *Understanding Collapse: Ancient History and Modern Myths*. Cambridge: Cambridge University Press.

Milanović, B. 2019. *Capitalism, Alone: The Future of the System That Rules the World*. Cambridge, MA: Harvard University Press.

Milgram, S. 1974. *Obedience to Authority: An Experimental View*. New York: HarperCollins.

Miller, J. 2002. *One of the Guys: Girls, Gangs, and Gender*. Oxford: Oxford University Press.

Miller, W. I. 2000. *The Mystery of Courage*. Cambridge, MA: Harvard University Press.

Milovanović, M. 2011. Stvaranje i razvoj Vojske Republike Srpske u toku Odbrambeno-Otažbinskog rata u BiH 1992 do 1995 godine. In *Vojska Republike Srpske u Odbrambeno- Otadžbinskom ratu: Aspekti, Organizacija, Operacije*. Banja Luka: Republički centar za istraživanje ratnih zločina.

Mitchell, P. D. 2004. *Medicine in the Crusades: Warfare, Wounds, and the Medieval Surgeon*. Cambridge: Cambridge University Press.

2013. Violence and the Crusades: Warfare, Injuries, and Torture in the Medieval Middle East. In C. Knüsel and M. Smith (eds.), *A History of Human Conflict: Osteology and Traumatised Bodies from Earliest Prehistory to the Present*. New York: Routledge, pp. 251–62.

Mkandawire, T. 2002. The Terrible Toll of Post-Colonial 'Rebel Movements' in Africa: Towards an Explanation of the Violence against the Peasantry. *Journal of Modern African Studies* 40(2): 181–215.

Moloney, E. 2002. *A Secret History of the IRA*. London: Penguin.

Moloney M., MacKenzie, A., Hunt, G., and Joe-Laidler, K. 2009. The Path and Promise of Fatherhood for Gang Members. *British Journal of Criminology* 49 (3): 305–25.

Moorad, J., Promislow, D., Smith, K., and Wade, M. 2011. Mating System Change Reduces the Strength of Sexual Selection in an American Frontier Population of the 19th Century. *Evolution and Human Behavior* 32(2): 147–55.

Moore, P. 2015. How Would You Fare During the Apocalypse? *YouGov*. https://today.yougov.com/topics/lifestyle/articles-reports/2015/03/03/how-would-you-fare-apocalypse.

Morgan, M. H. and Carrier, D. R. 2013. Protective Buttressing of the Human Fist and the Evolution of Hominin Hands. *Journal of Experimental Biology* 216: 236–44.

Morgenthau, H. J. 1978. *Politics Among Nations: The Struggle for Power and Peace*. New York: Alfred A. Knopf.

Morillo, S. 2006. A General Typology of Transcultural Wars: The Early Middle Ages and Beyond. In H. Henning Kortüm (ed.), *Transcultural Wars: From the Middle Ages to the 21st Century*. Berlin: Akademie Verlag, pp. 29–42.

Morris, J. S., Cunningham, C. B., and Carrier, D. R. 2019. Sexual Dimorphism in Postcranial Skeletal Shape Suggests Male-Biased Specialization for Physical Competition in Anthropoid Primates. *Journal of Morphology* 280 (5): 731–8.

Morton, N. 2016. *Encountering Islam on the First Crusade*. Cambridge: Cambridge University Press.

Morton-Jack, G. 2018. *The Indian Empire at War: From Jihad to Victory – The Untold Story of the Indian Army in the First World War*. London: Little, Brown.

Moskos, C. 1975. The American Combat Soldier in Vietnam. *Journal of Social Issues* 31(4): 25–37.

Moynihan, M. 1980. *Greater Love: Letters Home 1914–1918*. London: W. H. Allen.

Müller, R. 2016. *Hitler's Wehrmacht, 1935–1945*. Lexington: University Press of Kentucky.

Muñoz-Reyes, J. A., Gil-Burmann, C., Fink, B., and Turiegano, E. 2012. Physical Strength, Fighting Ability, and Aggressiveness in Adolescents. *American Journal of Human Biology* 24(5): 611–617.

Munson, C. 2016. *Battlefield Commission*. Bloomington, IN: Author House.

Mussolini, B. 2006 [1932]. *My Autobiography: With 'The Political and Social Doctrine of Fascism'*. Mineola, NY: Dover Publications.

Nathanson, D. L. 1998. From Empathy to Community. *The Annual of Psychoanalysis* 25: 125–43.

Nelson, C. and Hendricks, J. (eds.). 2013. *Madrid 1937: Letters of the Abraham Lincoln Brigade from the Spanish Civil War*. London: Routledge.

Niebergall-Lackner, H. 2016. *Status and Treatment of Deserters in International Armed Conflicts*. Leiden: Brill.

Nietzel, S. and Welzer, H. 2012. *Soldaten: On Fighting, Killing and Dying – The Secret Second World War Tapes of German POWs*. London: Simon & Schuster.

Nixon, R. 2013. *Slow Violence and the Environmentalism of the Poor*. Cambridge, MA: Harvard University Press.

Norenzayan, A. 2016. The Origins of Religion. In D. Buss (ed.), *The Handbook of Evolutionary Psychology, Vol. 2: Integrations*. Hoboken, NJ: Wiley, pp. 848–66.

O'Ballance, E. 1995. *Civil War in Bosnia 1992–94*. London: Macmillan.

Oberschall, A. 2000. The Manipulation of Ethnicity: From Ethnic Cooperation to Violence and War in Yugoslavia. *Ethnic and Racial Studies* 23(6): 982–1001.

O'Brien, B. 1999. *The Long War: The IRA and Sinn Féin*. Dublin: O'Brien Press.

O'Byrne, D. 2018. Perpetrators? Political Civil Servants in the Third Reich. In T. Williams and S. Buckley-Zistel (eds.), *Perpetrators and Perpetration of Mass Violence: Action, Motivations and Dynamics*. London: Routledge, pp. 83–98.

Ó Dochartaigh, N. 2010. Nation and Neighbourhood: Nationalist Mobilisation and Local Solidarities in the North of Ireland. In A. Guelke (ed.), *The Challenges of Ethno-Nationalism*. Basingstoke: Palgrave Macmillan, pp. 161–76.

O'Donnell, R. 2012. The Boston College Tapes. *History Ireland* (April): 12–16.

2017. The Provisional IRA: History, Politics, and Remembrance. In J. Smyth (ed.), *Remembering the Troubles: Contesting the Recent Past in Northern Ireland*. Notre Dame, IN: University of Notre Dame Press.

O'Leary, B. 2007. Analysing Partition: Definition, Classification and Explanation. *Political Geography* 26(8): 886–908.

2019. *A Treatise on Northern Ireland, Volume I: Colonialism*. Oxford: Oxford University Press.

Oloya, O. 2013. *Child to Soldier: Stories from Joseph Kony's Lord's Resistance Army*. Toronto: University of Toronto Press.

Olsson, C. and Malešević, S. 2017. War. In W. Outhwaite and S. P. Turner (eds.), *The Sage Handbook of Political Sociology*, Vol. 2. London: Sage, pp. 715–33.

Omissi, D. 1999. *Indian Voices of the Great War: Soldiers' Letters, 1914–18*. London: Palgrave Macmillan.

Operation Banner: An Analysis of Military Operations in Northern Ireland. 2006. www.vilaweb.cat/media/attach/vwedts/docs/op_banner_analysis_released.pdf.

Orr, C. 2016. Functional Morphology of the Primate Hand: Recent Approaches Using Biomedical Imaging, Computer Modeling, and Engineering Methods. In T. L. Kivell, P. Lemelin, B. G. Richmond, and D. Schmitt (eds.), *The Evolution of the Primate Hand*. New York: Springer, pp. 227–58.

Othen, C. 2008. *Franco's International Brigades: Foreign Volunteers and Fascist Dictators in the Spanish Civil War*. London: Reportage Press.

Overmans, R. 2004. *Deutsche militärische Verluste im Zweiten Weltkrieg*. Munich: Oldenbourg.

Palumbo, S., Mariotti, V., Iofrida, C., and Pellegrini, S. 2018. Genes and Aggressive Behavior: Epigenetic Mechanisms Underlying Individual Susceptibility to Aversive Environments. *Frontiers in Behavioural Neuroscience* 12: 117.

Papendorf, K. 2006. 'The Unfinished': Reflections on the Norwegian Prison Movement. *Acta Sociologica* 49(2): 127–37.

Parker, G. 2002. *Empire, War and Faith in Early Modern Europe*. London: Allen Lane.

Pettegrew, J. 2015. *Light It Up: The Marine Eye for Battle in the War for Iraq*. Baltimore: Johns Hopkins University Press.

Piketty, T. 2020. *Capital and Ideology*. Cambridge, MA: Harvard University Press.

Pinker, S. 2003. *The Blank Slate*. London: Penguin.

2011. *The Better Angels of Our Nature: Why Violence Has Declined*. New York: Viking Books.

2018. *Enlightenment Now*. New York: Viking.

Pipes, R. 2001. *Communism: A History*. New York: Random House.

Plamper, J. 2009. Emotional Turn? Feelings in Russian History and Culture. *Slavic Review* 68(2): 229–37.

2015. *History of Emotions: An Introduction*. Oxford: Oxford University Press.

Plamper, J. and Lazier, B. (eds.). 2012. *Fear: Across the Disciplines*. Pittsburgh: University of Pittsburgh Press.

Poldrack, R. A., Monahan, J., Imrey, P. B., Reyna, V., Raichle, M. E., Faigman, D., and Buckholtz, J. W. 2018. Predicting Violent Behavior: What Can Neuroscience Add? *Trends in Cognitive Sciences* 22(2): 111–23.

Polk, K. 1994. *When Men Kill: Scenarios of Masculine Violence*. Cambridge: Cambridge University Press.

Potts, M. and Hayden, T. 2008. *Sex and War: How Biology Explains Warfare and Terrorism and Offers a Path to a Safer World*. Dallas, TX: BenBella Books.

Powers, R. 2016. Navy Buddy Enlistment Program. *The Balance*. http://usmilitary.about.com/cs/navyjoin/a/navybuddy.htm.

Prabhakaran, V. 2016. Tamil National Leader Hon. V. Pirapaharan's Interview. https://web.archive.org/web/20160803164100/http://www.eelamweb.com/leader/interview/in_1986/.

Pratt, T. C. and Lowenkamp, C. T. 2002. Conflict Theory, Economic Conditions, and Homicide: A Time-Series Analysis. *Homicide Studies* 6(1): 61–83.

Pravilo službe VRS. 1993. *Banja Luka: Vojska Republike Srpske*.

Prunier, G. 1999. *The Rwanda Crisis: History of a Genocide*. New York: Columbia University Press.

Pulley, J. G. and Tatum, T. C. 1988. *The Cohort System: Is It Meeting the Army's Needs?* USAWC Military Studies Program Paper. Carlisle Barracks, PA: U.S. Army War College.

Pustilnik, A. C. 2009. Violence on the Brian: A Critique of Neuroscience in Criminal Law. *Wake Forest Law Review* 44(1): 183–237.

Quinby, R. L. 1994. *Anti-Apocalypse Exercises in Genealogical Criticism*. Minneapolis: University of Minnesota Press.

Rainsford, S. 2006. Hijack highlights Turkish refuseniks. *BBC News*. http://news .bbc.co.uk/2/hi/europe/5407040.stm.

Ramet, S. 2006. *Thinking About Yugoslavia*. Cambridge: Cambridge University Press.

Ray, L. 2016. Explaining Violence: Towards a Critical Friendship with Neuroscience? *Journal for the Theory of Social Behaviour* 46(3): 335–56.
    2018. *Violence and Society*. London: Sage.

Redding, R. 2006. The Brian-Disordered Defendant: Neuroscience and Legal Insanity in the 21st Century. *American University Law Review* 56(1): 51–127.

Reddy, E. S. 1987. *Struggle for Freedom in Southern Africa: Its International Significance*. New Delhi: Mainstream.

Reddy, W. 2001. *The Navigation of Feeling*. Cambridge: Cambridge University Press.

Renan, E. 2018. *What Is a Nation and Other Political Writings*. New York: Columbia University Press.

Richards, J. 2014. *An Institutional History of the Liberation Tigers of Tamil Eelam (LTTE)*. CCDP Working Paper Series, No. 10. Geneva.

Ripley, T. 1999. *Operation Deliberate Force: The UN and NATO Campaign in Bosnia 1995*. Lancaster: CDISS.

Robarchek, C. A. and Robarchek, C. J. 1998. Reciprocities and Realities: World Views, Peacefulness, and Violence among Semai and Waorani. *Aggressive Behaviour* 24: 123–33.

Roberts, G. 2006. *Stalin's Wars: From World War to Cold War, 1939–1953*. New Haven, CT: Yale University Press.

Ron, J. 2003. *Frontiers and Ghettos: State Violence in Serbia and Israel*. Berkeley: University of California Press.

Rosaldo, M. Z. 1980. *Knowledge and Passion: Ilongot Notions of Self and Social Life*. Cambridge: Cambridge University Press.

Rose, A. M. 1951. The Social Psychology of Desertion from Combat. *American Sociological Review* 16(5): 614–29.

Rosenberg, S., Templeton, A. R., Feigin, P. D., Lancet, D., Beckmann, J. S., Selig, S., Hamer, D. H., and Skorecki, K. 2006. The Association of DNA Sequence Variation at the MAOA Genetic Locus with Quantitative Behavioural Traits in Normal Males. *Human Genetics* 120(4): 447–59.

Rosenwein, B. 2010. Problems and Methods in the History of Emotions. *Passions in Context* 1. www.passionsincontext.de/uploads/media/01_Rosenwein.pdf.
    2016. *Generations of Feeling: A History of Emotions, 600–1700*. Cambridge: Cambridge University Press.

Roser, M. and Ritchie, H. 2019. Homicides. *Our World in Data*. https:// ourworldindata.org/homicides.

Ross, M. 2006. A Closer Look at Oil, Diamonds, and Civil War. *Annual Review of Political Science* 9: 265–300.

Rossino, A. 2003. *Hitler Strikes Poland: Blitzkrieg, Ideology, and Atrocity*. Lawrence: University Press of Kansas.

Rummel, R. J. 1997. *Death by Government: Genocide and Mass Murder since 1900.* New York: Transaction Publishers.

Runciman, S. 1987. *A History of the Crusades.* Cambridge: Cambridge University Press.

Rush, R. 1999. A Different Perspective: Cohesion, Morale, and Operational Effectiveness in the German Army, Fall 1944. *Armed Forces & Society* 25 (3): 477–508.

Ruta, C. 2013. Forced to Fight, Children Suffer All Their Lives. *Deutsche Welle.* www.dw.com/en/forced-to-fight-children-suffer-all-their-lives/a-16590697.

Rwanda – HDR Report. 2019. United Nations Development Programme. http://hdr.undp.org/en/countries/profiles/RWA.

Ryan, J. 2015. The Sacralization of Violence: Bolshevik Justifications for Violence and Terror during the Civil War. *Slavic Review* 74(4): 808–31.

Sait, B. 2019. *The Indoctrination of the Wehrmacht: Nazi Ideology and the War Crimes of the German Military.* New York: Berghahn Books.

Sanchez-Jankowski, M. 1991. *Islands in the Street: Gangs and American Urban Society.* Berkeley: University of California Press.

Santos, M. R., Testa, A., Porter, L. C., and Lynch, J. P. 2019. The Contribution of Age Structure to the International Homicide Decline. *PLoS ONE* 14(10): 1–12.

Sapolsky, R. M. 2004. Stress and Cognition. In M. S. Gazzaniga (ed.), *The Cognitive Neurosciences.* Cambridge, MA: MIT Press, pp. 1031–42.

Sawyer, W. and Wagner, P. 2019. Mass Incarceration: The Whole Pie 2019. www.prisonpolicy.org/reports/pie2019.html.

Scheer, M. 2012. Are Emotions a Kind of Practice (and Is That What Makes Them Have a History)? A Bourdieuan Approach to Understanding Emotion. *History and Theory* 51(2): 193–220.

Schinkel, W. 2010. *Aspects of Violence: A Critical Theory.* New York: Palgrave Macmillan.

Schleim, S. 2014. Critical Neuroscience – or Critical Science? A Perspective on the Perceived Normative Significance of Neuroscience. *Frontiers in Human Neuroscience* 8: 336.

Schneider, J, and Schneider, P. 2011. The Mafia and Capitalism: An Emerging Paradigm. *Sociologica* 2(1): 1–23.

Schulte, T. 1989. *The German Army and Nazi Policies in Occupied Russia.* Oxford: Berg.

Schulte-Bockholt, A. 2001. A Neo-Marxist Explanation of Organized Crime. *Critical Criminology* 10: 225–42.

Scott, J. S. 1998. *Seeing Like a State: How Certain Schemes to Improve the Human Condition Have Failed.* New Haven, CT: Yale University Press.

Scott, J. P. 1966. Agonistic Behavior of Mice and Rats: A Review. *American Zoologist* 6(4): 683–701.

Scurr, R. 2006. *Fatal Purity: Robespierre and the French Revolution.* New York: Henry Holt and Company.

Segal, D. R. and Segal, M. W. 1983. Change in Military Organization. *Annual Review of Sociology* 9: 151–70.

Segal, M. and Kestnbaum, M. 2002. Professional Closure in the Military Labor Market: A Critique of Pure Cohesion, In D. M. Snider and G. L. Watkins (eds.), *The Future of the Army Profession*. New York: McGraw-Hill, pp. 441–58.

Sell, A., Hone, L. S. E., and Pound, N. 2012. The Importance of Physical Strength to Human Males. *Human Nature* 23(1): 30–44.

Serrano, A. 2020. Eighteenth Street: The Origins of 'Barrio 18'. *Small Wars Journal*. https://smallwarsjournal.com/jrnl/art/eighteenth-street-origins-barrio-18.

Service, E. 1978. *Profiles in Ethnology*. New York: Harper & Row.

Shay, J. 1994. *Achilles in Vietnam: Combat Trauma and the Undoing of Character*. New York: Scribner.

2014. Moral Injury. *Psychoanalytic Psychology* 31(2): 182–91.

Shepherd, B. 2016. *Hitler's Soldiers: The German Army in the Third Reich*. New Haven, CT: Yale University Press.

Shils, E. and Janowitz, M. 1948. Cohesion and Disintegration in the Wehrmacht in World War II. *Public Opinion Quarterly* 12: 280–315.

Siebold, G. 1999. The Evolution of the Measurement of Cohesion. *Military Psychology* 11(1): 5–26.

2007. The Essence of Military Cohesion. *Armed Forces & Society* 33(2): 286–95.

2011. Key Questions and Challenges to the Standard Model of Military Group Cohesion. *Armed Forces & Society* 37(3): 448–68.

Simmel, G. 1971 [1908]. *Conflict and the Web of Group Affiliations*. New York: Free Press.

Simpson, D. P. 2000. *Cassell's Latin and English Dictionary*. London: Wiley.

Simpson, S. W., Quade, J., Levin, N. E., Butler, R., Dupont-Nivet, G., Everett, M., and Semaw, S. 2008. A Female *Homo erectus* Pelvis from Gona, Ethiopia. *Science* 322: 1089–92.

Singer, P. W. 2004. *Corporate Warriors: The Rise of the Privatized Military Industry*. Ithaca, NY: Cornell University Press.

2006. *Children at War*. Berkeley: University of California Press.

2008. *Corporate Warriors: The Rise of the Privatised Military Industry* (Updated edition). Ithaca, NY: Cornell University Press.

Singh Bhasin, A. 2001. *India–Sri Lanka Relations and Sri Lanka's Ethnic Conflict Documents, 1947–2000*. New Delhi: Indian Research Press.

Skelly, J. 2006. Iraq, Vietnam, and the Dilemmas of United States Soldiers. *Open Democracy*, 24 May. www.opendemocracy.net/en/iraq_vietnam_3588jsp/.

Slaby, J. 2010. Steps Towards a Critical Neuroscience. *Phenomenology and the Cognitive Sciences* 9(3): 397–416.

Smith, A. 2003. *Chosen Peoples: The Sacred Sources of National Identity*. Oxford: Oxford University Press.

Smith, K. A. 2017. The Crusader Conquest of Jerusalem and Christ's Cleansing of the Temple. In E. Lapina and N. Morton (eds.), *The Uses of the Bible in Crusader Sources*. Leiden: Brill, pp. 19–41.

Smith, M. L. R. 1995. *Fighting for Ireland? The Military Strategy of the Irish Republican Movement*. London: Routledge.

Smith, P. 2005. *Why War? The Cultural Logic of Iraq, the Gulf War, and Suez*. Chicago: University of Chicago Press.

Snyder, L. L. 1968. *The New Nationalism*. Ithaca, NY: Cornell University Press.

Sofsky, W. 1997. *The Order of Terror: The Concentration Camp*. Princeton: Princeton University Press.

Špegelj, M. 2001. The First Phase, 1990–1992: JNA Prepares for Aggression and Croatia for Defence. In B. Magaš and I. Žanić (eds.), *The War in Croatia and Bosnia-Herzegovina 1991–1995*. London: Frank Cass, pp. 14–40.

Spierenburg, P. 2008. *A History of Murder: Personal Violence in Europe from the Middle Ages to the Present*. Cambridge: Polity Press.

Spiller, R. 1988. S. L. A. Marshall and the Ratio of Fire. *RUSI Journal* 133(4): 63–71.

Stark, R. and Corcoran, K. 2014. *Religious Hostility: A Global Assessment of Hatred and Terror*. New York: IRS Books.

Steffens, B. 2017. *Human Rights in Focus: Torture*. San Diego: ReferencePoint Press.

Stephen, L. 2005. *Zapotec Women: Gender, Class, and Ethnicity in Globalized Oaxaca*. Durham, NC: Duke University Press.

Stephen, M. 2009. *Civilian Jihad: Nonviolent Struggle, Democratization, and Governance in the Middle East*. New York: Springer.

Steimer, T. 2002. The Biology of Fear- and Anxiety-Related Behaviors. *Dialogues in Clinical Neuroscience* 4(3): 231–49.

Stern, J. 2003. *Terror in the Name of God: Why Religious Militants Kill*. New York: HarperCollins.

Stewart, N. K. 1991. *Mates and Muchachos: Unit Cohesion in the Falklands/Malvinas War*. New York: Brassey's.

Stokke, K. 2006. Building the Tamil Eelam State: Emerging State Institutions and Forms of Governance in LTTE-Controlled Areas in Sri Lanka. *Third World Quarterly* 27(6): 1021–40.

Stouffer, S. 1949. *The American Soldier: Combat and Its Aftermath*. Princeton: Princeton University Press.

Sun Tzu. 2017 [500 BCE]. *The Art of War*. New York: Quatro Publishing Group.

Sussman, R. 1999. The Myth of Man the Hunter, Man the Killer and the Evolution of Human Morality. *Zygon* 34(3): 453–471.

Sussman, R. and Garber, P. 2007. Cooperation and Competition in Primate Social Interactions. In C. J. Campbell, A. Fuentes, K. C. MacKinnon, M. Panger, and S. K. Bearder (eds.), *Primates in Perspective*. Oxford: Oxford University Press, pp. 636–51.

Sussman, R. and Marschak, J. 2010. *Are Humans Inherently Killers?* Honolulu: Centre for Global Nonkilling.

Suvilehto, J., Glerean, E., Dunbar, R. I. M., Hari, R., and Nummenmaa, L. 2015. Topography of Social Touching Depends on Emotional Bonds between Humans. *Proceedings of the National Academy of Sciences* 112: 13811–16.

Symons, D. 1979. *The Evolution of Human Sexuality*. Oxford: Oxford University Press.

Takano, M. and Ichinose, G. 2018. Evolution of Human-Like Social Grooming Strategies Regarding Richness and Group Size. *Frontiers in Ecology and Evolution* 6: 8.

Tarrow, S. 2012. *Strangers at the Gates: Movements and States in Contentious Politics*. Cambridge: Cambridge University Press.

Taylor, I. 1999. *Crime in Context: A Critical Criminology of Market Societies*. Cambridge: Polity Press.

Taylor, M., Roach, J., and Pease, K. (eds.). 2015. *Evolutionary Psychology and Terrorism*. London: Routledge.

Taylor, P. 1997. *Provos: The IRA and Sinn Féin*. London: Bloomsbury.

Terpstra, N. and Frerks, G. 2017. Rebel Governance and Legitimacy: Understanding the Impact of Rebel Legitimation on Civilian Compliance with the LTTE Rule. *Civil Wars* 19(3): 279–307.

Thomas, H. 2003. *The Spanish Civil War*. London: Penguin.

Thucydides. 2019 [400 BCE]. *The History of the Peloponnesian War*. New York: Independent Publishers.

Tilly, C. 1964. *The Vendée*. Cambridge, MA: Harvard University Press.

1985. War Making and State Making as Organized Crime. In P. Evans. D. Rueschemeyer, and T. Skocpol (eds.), *Bringing the State Back In*. Cambridge: Cambridge University Press, pp. 169–91.

1992. *Coercion, Capital, and European States*. Oxford: Blackwell.

2003. *The Politics of Collective Violence*. Cambridge: Cambridge University Press.

2008. *Contentious Performances*. Cambridge: Cambridge University Press.

Tomkins, S. 1962. *Affect, Imagery, Consciousness, Vol. 1: The Positive Affects*. London: Tavistock.

1991. *Affect, Imagery, Consciousness, Vol. 3: The Negative Affects –Anger and Fear*. New York: Springer.

Tomkins, S. and McCarter, R. 1964. What and Where Are the Primary Affects? Some Evidence for a Theory. *Perceptual and Motor Skills* 18(1): 119–58.

Toolis, K. 2015. *Rebel Hearts: Journeys Within the IRA's Soul*. New York: St. Martin's Press.

Trotsky, L. 2012. *My Life: An Attempt at an Autobiography*. Mineola, NY: Dover Publications.

Tsai, J. L. 2007. Ideal Affect: Cultural Causes and Behavioral Consequences. *Perspectives on Psychological Science* 2(3): 242–59.

Turner, J. 2007. *Human Emotions: A Sociological Theory*. London: Routledge.

Turner, J. and Maryanski, A. 2008. *On the Origins of Human Society by Natural Selection*. Boulder, CO: Paradigm Press.

Turner, J. and Stets, J. 2005. *The Sociology of Emotions*. Cambridge: Cambridge University Press.

Tus, A. 2001. The War in Slovenia and Croatia up to the Sarajevo Ceasefire. In B. Magaš and I. Žanić (eds.), *The War in Croatia and Bosnia-Herzegovina 1991–1995*. London: Frank Cass, pp. 41–66.

Tyerman, C. 2004. *The Crusades: A Very Short Introduction*. Oxford: Oxford University Press.

2005. Interview: Christopher Tyerman Discusses His Book on the Crusades. *NPR*. www.npr.org/programs/wesun/transcripts/2005/feb/050227.tyerman .html.

Uhalley, S. 1985. *Mao Tse-Tung: A Critical Biography*. New York: New Viewpoints.

UN Commission on Human Rights. 1998. Conscientious Objection to Military Service. www.refworld.org/docid/3b00f0be10.html.

Üngör, U. U. 2020. *Paramilitarism*. Oxford: Oxford University Press.

van Creveld, M. 1982. *Fighting Power: German and US Army Performance, 1939–1945*. Westport, CT: Greenwood Press.

van der Haven, C. 2016. Drill and Allocution as Emotional Practices in Seventeenth-Century Dutch Poetry, Plays and Military Treatises. In E. Kuijpers and C. van der Haven (eds.), *Battlefield Emotions 1500–1800: Practices, Experience, Imagination*. London: Palgrave Macmillan, pp. 25–47.

van Evera, S. 1994. Hypotheses on Nationalism and War. *International Security* 8 (4): 5–39.

van Voris, W. 1975. *Violence in Ulster: An Oral Documentary*. Amherst: University of Massachusetts Press.

Varese, F. 2011. *Mafias on the Move: How Organized Crime Conquers New Territories*. Princeton: Princeton University Press.

Vastapuu, L. 2018. *Liberia's Women Veterans: War, Roles and Reintegration*. London: Zed Books.

Venugopal, R. 2003. *The Global Dimensions of Conflict in Sri Lanka*. QEH Working Paper Series, QEHWPS 99. Oxford: University of Oxford.

Vertigans, S. 2011. *The Sociology of Terrorism*. London: Routledge.

Vickers, A. 2005. *A History of Modern Indonesia*. Cambridge: Cambridge University Press.

von Schell, A. 2013. *Battle Leadership*. Brattleboro, VT: Echo Point Books.

Vukušić, I. 2018. Nineteen Minutes of Horror: Insights from the Scorpions Execution Video. *Genocide Studies and Prevention* 12(2): 35–53.

2019. Paramilitarism, Organised Crime and the State. PhD thesis, Utrecht University.

Wallerstein, I. 1995. *Historical Capitalism, with Capitalist Civilization*. London: Verso.

Waltz, K. 1979. *Theory of International Politics*. New York: McGraw-Hill.

Wang, P. 2017. *The Chinese Mafia: Organized Crime, Corruption, and Extra-Legal Protection*. Oxford: Oxford University Press.

Weber, M. 1968. *Economy and Society*. New York: Bedminster Press.

Weber, T. 1998. *On the Salt March: The Historiography of Gandhi's March to Dandi, India*. New York: HarperCollins.

Weininger, E. and Lizardo, O. 2018. Introduction. In E. B. Weininger, A. Lareau, and O. Lizardo (eds.), *Ritual, Emotion, Violence: Studies on the Micro-Sociology of Randall Collins*. London: Routledge, pp. 1–24.

Wendorf, F. 1968. Site 117: A Nubian Final Paleolithic Graveyard near Jebel Sahaba, Sudan. In F. Wendorf (ed.), *The Prehistory of Nubia*. Dallas: Southern Methodist University, pp. 954–87.

Werner, J. J. 2012. Mating Behavior in Australopithecus and Early Homo: A Review of the Diagnostic Potential of Dental Dimorphism. *University of Western Ontario Journal of Anthropology* 22(1): 11–19.

Whiteley, L. E. 2012. Resisting the Revelatory Scanner: Critical Engagements with fMRI in Popular Media. *BioSocieties* 7(3): 245–72.

Wiessner, P. and Pupu, N. 2012. Toward Peace: Foreign Arms and Indigenous Institutions in a Papua New Guinea Society. *Science* 337(6102): 1651–4.

Wieviorka, M. 2009. *Violence: A New Approach*. London: Sage.

Wikan, U. 1989. Managing the Heart to Brighten Face and Soul: Emotions in Balinese Morality and Health Care. *American Ethnologist* 16(2): 294–312.

Wilcox, V. 2012. "Weeping Tears of Blood": Exploring Italian Soldiers' Emotions in the First World War. *Modern Italy* 17(2): 171–84.
  2016. *Morale and the Italian Army during the First World War*. Cambridge: Cambridge University Press.

Willems, E. and van Shaik, C. 2017. The Social Organization of *Homo ergaster*: Inferences from Anti-Predator Responses in Extant Primates. *Journal of Human Evolution* 109: 11–21.

Williams, J. 1997. Casualties of Violence in Northern Ireland. *International Journal of Trauma Nursing* 3(3): 78–82.

Wilson, E. O. 1975. *Socio-Biology: The New Synthesis*. Cambridge, MA: The Belknap Press.

Wilson, M. L., Boesch, C., Fruth, B., et al. 2014. Lethal Aggression in Pan Is Better Explained by Adaptive Strategies than Human Impact. *Nature* 18:513 (7518): 414–17.

Wilson, T. 2020. *Killing Strangers*. Oxford: Oxford University Press.

Wimmer, A. 2012. *The Waves of War: Nationalism, State Formation and Ethnic Exclusion in the Modern World*. Cambridge: Cambridge University Press.

Winer, Y. 2018. *Machiavelli and the Orders of Violence*. Cambridge: Cambridge University Press.

Winslow, D. 1997. *The Canadian Airborne Regiment in Somalia: A Socio-Cultural Inquiry*. Ottawa: Canadian Government Publishing.

Wintrobe, R. 2006. *Rational Extremism*. Cambridge: Cambridge University Press.

Wittekind, E. 2012. *Violence as Entertainment: Why Aggression Sells*. Mankato: Capstone Publishers.

Wohlstein, R. and McPhail, C. 1983. Individual and Collective Behaviors within Gatherings, Demonstrations, and Riots. *Annual Review of Sociology* 9: 579–600.

Wong, K. 2013. Case for (Very) Early Cooking Heats Up. *Scientific American*. www.scientificamerican.com/article/case-for-very-early-cooking-heats-up/.

Wong, L. 2006. Combat Motivation in Today's Soldiers: US Army War College Strategic Studies Institute. *Armed Forces & Society* 32(4): 659–63.

Wood, E. J. 2003. *Insurgent Collective Action and Civil War in El Salvador*. Cambridge: Cambridge University Press.

Wrangham, R. and Peterson, D. 1996. *Demonic Males: Apes and the Origins of Human Violence*. Boston: Mariner Books.

Wright, V. 2010. *Deterrence in Criminal Justice: Evaluating Certainty vs. Severity of Punishment*. Washington, DC: Sentencing Project.

Yanagizawa-Drott, D. 2014. Propaganda and Conflict: Evidence from the Rwandan Genocide. *Quarterly Journal of Economics* 129(4): 1947–94.

Yeung, K. and Zhang, Z. 2014. The Never-Ending Apocalypse. *The Princeton Buffer*. https://princetonbuffer.princeton.edu/2014/01/23/the-neverending-apocalypse/.

Žanić, I. 2007. *Flag on the Mountain: A Political Anthropology of War in Croatia and Bosnia*. London: Saqi.

Zhao, D. 2015. *The Confucian-Legalist State: A New Theory of Chinese History.* Oxford: Oxford University Press.

Zimbardo, P. G. 1972. *Stanford Prison Experiment: A Simulation Study of the Psychology of Imprisonment.* Stanford: Philip G. Zimbardo, Inc.

Zukerman Daly, S. 2012. Organizational Legacies of Violence: Conditions Favoring Insurgency Onset in Colombia, 1964–1984. *Journal of Peace Research* 49(3): 473–91.

Žunec, O. 2001. Operations Flash and Storm. In B. Magaš and I. Žanić (eds.), *The War in Croatia and Bosnia-Herzegovina 1991–1995.* London: Frank Cass, pp. 67–83.

Žunec, O., Petrović, N., Lucić, D., and Golubović, S. 2013. *Oficir i časnik.* Zagreb: Hrvatska Sveučilišna Naklada.

Zwierzchowski, J. and Tabeau, E. 2010. War in Bosnia and Herzegovina: Census-Based Multiple System of Estimation of Casualties' Undercount. Global Costs of Conflict conference. The Households in Conflict Network (HiCN) and The German Institute for Economic Research (DIW Berlin), 1–2 February, Berlin.

Index

abuse, 53, 100, 117, 124, 172, 181, 274, 277, 282, 293–6, 301
Adorno, Theodor, 99–101
Afghanistan, 49, 54, 75, 98, 117, 163, 192, 256, 261, 283
Africa, 20, 48, 54, 111, 113–14, 118, 148, 175, 180, 184–5, 188, 227, 312, 317
African National Congress (ANC), 184
aggression, 17–18, 20, 22, 24–6, 29, 35–6, 38–41, 43, 173, 187, 275, 312, 319
ahimsa, 179
Albania, 53
Algeria, 113
Almighty Latin Kings, 118
Al-Qaeda, 71, 76, 117, 228
American Civil War, 163
Amish, 166, 179
anarchism, 69, 74, 76, 127
anatomy, 12, 16–17, 23, 25, 27, 34, 328
Angola, 49, 173
anthropology, 12, 16, 21, 34, 42, 134, 229
apocalypse, 309, 318, 320, 325
archaeology, 21
Argentina, 54
Armenian genocide, 75
Armenians, 88
Ashurnasirpal II, 1, 3
Australia, 55, 92, 113, 173, 309
Austro-Hungarian Empire, 322

Bahai, 166
Barkawi, Tarak, 52, 112–14, 148–9, 151, 271
Barrett, Lisa Feldman, 34, 279–80, 304
Barrio 18, 120–1, 127
Bartlett, Myron Napier, 2
Bartov, Omer, 73, 108, 152–6, 158, 191, 193, 224, 246, 330
battlefield, 2, 14, 30–1, 34, 97–8, 112, 137, 139, 141, 144–7, 149–50, 154–5, 157, 163, 192–3, 199, 208, 212, 219–20, 222, 224–5, 233, 242, 245, 247, 249, 251, 253–6, 259–65, 267–70, 273, 276, 280, 282–3, 286, 288, 291–3, 296, 299–303, 305
Bauman, Zygmunt, 48
Belgium, 53, 58
Benin, 54
Bevel, James, 179
Bible, 2, 78, 140
biology, 6, 8–9, 12, 16–17, 23, 26, 34, 42, 129, 273, 278, 303–5, 311, 316, 323, 326
biomechanics, 23, 27, 29, 42, 44
Boko Haram, 71, 76
Bolivia, 173, 312
Bolsheviks, 78
boredom, 251–2, 272, 300
Bosnia and Herzegovina, ix, 14, 189, 194–6, 205–6, 234–6, 238, 241, 274, 278, 282, 294, 296, 298, 330
Botswana, 173
Bourdieu, Pierre, 11
Bourke, Joanna, 4, 98, 253–4, 257, 260–1, 276, 289
brain, 25, 27, 29, 31–2, 39–41, 43, 131–3, 279
Brazil, 54, 111
breathing rhythm, 31
British, Britain, UK, 4, 52, 54, 70, 77, 98, 113–14, 135, 140, 142–3, 148–9, 167, 175, 183, 194–6, 201–2, 212, 214–15, 218, 220, 227, 232, 249, 252, 256, 258, 270–1, 282, 289, 314
Buddhists, Buddhism, 72, 166
Burma, 113

Cambodian genocide, 74–5
Canada, 35, 54–5, 113, 173, 309
caste, 91, 113, 148–9, 152, 160, 199, 271
Catholic Church, 88
Central African Republic, 58, 123
centrifugal ideologisation, 11, 82–4
Chenoweth, Erica, 181, 185, 188

363

CPSIA information can be obtained
at www.ICGtesting.com
Printed in the USA
LVHW081352141222
735209LV00009B/624